ME, ME, ME?

Jon Lawrence works on modern British social, cultural, and political history, and is now based at the University of Exeter, having taught previously at University College London, the University of Liverpool, Harvard University, and the University of Cambridge. He has published extensively on British social and political history, including *Speaking for the People: Party, Language and Popular Politics in England, 1867–1914* (1998) and *Electing Our Masters: The Hustings in British Politics from Hogarth to Blair* (2009), and has written for the *London Review of Books, History Today, Renewal,* and *BBC History Magazine.* He has also contributed to television history programmes on BBC2, Channel 4, and the Parliament Channel.

Praise for *Me, Me, Me?*

'In this lively and generous study of postwar English life Lawrence makes a powerful case for the flexibility and intrinsic optimism of working-class people in their efforts to balance the demands of family, place and wider society'

Lynsey Hanley, *The Financial Times*

'Remember when everyone left doors unlocked and borrowed cups of sugar? No? Then this richly researched history of community may well appeal. Jon Lawrence uncovers the reality behind romantic cliches of our postwar past.'

Selina Todd, *The Guardian*

'smart, forensic, geographically situated ... [Lawrence's] book is a lesson in listening.'

Susan Pedersen, *London Review of Books*

'reads with the colour and interest of a novel.'

Gordon Parsons, *The Morning Star*

'*Me Me Me?* is a compelling, incisive, and, above all, humane and empathetic exploration of the changing, but not dying bonds among individuals, families, and community in post-war Britain.'

Stephen Brooke, *Contemporary British History*

'Elegantly written and based on patient and admirably empathetic engagement with a vast body of sources, Lawrence's analysis yields rich results that urge us to rethink the relationship between individualism and community.'

Bernhard Rieger, *English Historical Review*

'With his careful, sympathetic re-reading ... Lawrence is able to capture the complexity of social relations and individual identity that has always made generalizations about class in Britain so challenging.'

Christopher Lawson, *Twentieth-Century British History*

'a must-read for anybody interested in learning about the complexities of British cultural heritage and society.'

Colour PR Blog

ME ME ME?

the search for community in post-war england

JON LAWRENCE

OXFORD
UNIVERSITY PRESS

OXFORD
UNIVERSITY PRESS

Great Clarendon Street, Oxford, OX2 6DP,
United Kingdom

Oxford University Press is a department of the University of Oxford.
It furthers the University's objective of excellence in research, scholarship,
and education by publishing worldwide. Oxford is a registered trade mark of
Oxford University Press in the UK and in certain other countries

First published 2019
First published in paperback 2023

Impression: 1

Published in the United States of America by Oxford University Press
198 Madison Avenue, New York, NY 10016, United States of America

British Library Cataloguing in Publication Data
Data available

Library of Congress Cataloging in Publication Data
Data available

ISBN 978–0–19–877953–7 (Hbk.)
ISBN 978–0–19–877954–4 (Pbk.)

Printed and bound by
CPI Group (UK) Ltd, Croydon, CR0 4YY

To Jane

ACKNOWLEDGEMENTS

This book could not have been written without the generous support of the Leverhulme Trust's Major Research Fellowship scheme. I am also grateful to my former employers, the University of Cambridge and Emmanuel College, for granting me sabbatical leave to complete the bulk of the writing, and to the University of Exeter for providing a congenial intellectual home since September 2017. In addition, I would like to thank the British Academy, the University of Cambridge, and Monash University for research grants that helped facilitate my research at various points. The book itself draws heavily on archived social-science research data, and I am very grateful to the respective archives and copyright holders for permission to consult and quote from this material. In particular, I would like to acknowledge the following institutions and individuals: the LSE Library for permission to quote from the Sir Raymond Firth papers; Churchill Archive Centre and Mr Toby Young for permission to quote from the Michael Young papers; the Bishopsgate Institute for permission to quote from the papers of Raph Samuel; the National Social Policy and Social Change Archive, Albert Sloman Library Special Collections, University of Essex for permission to quote from the Affluent Worker collection; the Modern Records Centre, University of Warwick, and Qualidata for permission to quote from Professor Richard K. Brown's project 'Shipbuilding Workers on Tyneside'; and the UK Data Service for facilitating access to many valuable social-science datasets including John Goldthorpe and David Lockwood's 'Affluent Worker' study, Ray Pahl and Claire Wallace's Sheppey study of 'Household Work Strategies', Hartley Dean and Margaret Melrose's study 'Poverty, Wealth and Citizenship', and Yvette Taylor's project 'From the Coalface to the Car Park?'. In all cases, any names and other identifying information about individual respondents involved in these studies have been omitted or changed; in addition, I am obliged to state that those who carried out the original work and analysis bear no responsibility for the further analysis or interpretation in the present study. I am very grateful to Peter Brannen, Jim Cousins, and Claire Wallace for making the time to discuss aspects of their research experience with me. I would also like to thank Carrie Hickman for her help sourcing picture credits and Rowena Anketell and Neil Morris for their meticulous copy-editing and proofreading.

Over the years, many friends and colleagues have helped me think through the issues at the heart of this book, and some have kindly agreed to read and comment on individual chapters. I would particularly like to thank Lynn Abrams, Stephen Brooke, Lise Butler, Alex Campsie, Mark Clapson, Deborah Cohen, Clare Corbould, Stefan Couperus, David Cowan, Graham Crow, Andrew Davies, Lucy Delap, Charlotte Greenhalgh, Simon Gunn, Mark Hailwood, Chris Hilliard, Ben Jones, Harm Kaal, Nev Kirk, Claire Langhamer, Dawn Lyon, Helen McCarthy, Peter Mandler, Ben Mercer, Stuart Middleton, Melanie Nolan, Guy Ortolano, Stefan Ramsden, Mike Savage, Camilla Schofield, Julie-Marie Strange, Florence Sutcliffe-Braithwaite, Pat Thane, Selina Todd, Natalie Tomlinson, James Vernon, Chris Wallace, Rob Waters, and Andy Wood. I am also grateful for having had the chance to discuss these questions with many brilliant Special Subject students at both Cambridge and Exeter over the past decade. In addition, I would like to extend special thanks to Andrew Gordon, of David Higham Associates, who offered invaluable help shaping the project in its early stages, and Matthew Cotton, at Oxford University Press, who has been tirelessly supportive and helpful throughout. But as ever, my greatest intellectual and personal debt is to Jane Elliott. This book is dedicated to her with love and ceaseless admiration.

JON LAWRENCE
Murchington, 2018

CONTENTS

LIST OF FIGURES

LIST OF MAPS AND TABLES

Maps

Tables

LIST OF ABBREVIATIONS

CCC   County Cricket Club

DIY   Do-it-yourself (home decorating)

ESRC   Economic and Social Research Council

GPO   General Post Office

IPPR   Institute of Public Policy Research

IS   International Socialists (later the SWP)

LCC   London County Council

LSE   London School of Economics

MTF   Margaret Thatcher Foundation

NEC   National Executive Committee (Labour Party)

OCR   Optical Character Recognition (computer scanning)

SWP   Socialist Workers Party

T&G   Transport and General Workers' Union

UKDA   United Kingdom Data Archive (University of Essex)

Source material

Coalface to Car Park Collection	UKDA, Y. Taylor (2012), *From the Coalface to the Car Park? The Intersection of Class and Gender in Women's Lives in the North East, 2007–2009* [data collection], UK Data Service, SN: 7053 (http://doi.org/10.5255/UKDA-SN-7053-1)
CPI	Cambridge Pilot Interview, in UKDA, J. Lawrence (2016), *Affluent Worker Study 1962–1964: Questionnaire Files* [data collection], ReShare 10.5255/UKDA-SN-852166

Dean and Melrose Study | UKDA, H. Dean and M. Melrose (1999), *Poverty, Wealth and Citizenship: A Discursive Interview Study and Newspaper Monitoring Exercise, 1996* [computer file], UK Data Service, SN: 3995 (http://dx.doi.org/10.5255/UKDA-SN-3995-1)

Firth Papers | LSE Library, London, Sir Raymond Firth Papers

Goldthorpe and Lockwood, SN 6512 | UKDA, J. H. Goldthorpe and D. Lockwood (2010), *Affluent Worker in the Class Structure, 1961–1962* [data collection], UK Data Service, SN: 6512 (http://dx.doi.org/10.5255/UKDA-SN-6512-1)

LHI | Luton Home Interview, in UKDA, J. Lawrence (2016), *Affluent Worker Study 1962–1964: Questionnaire Files* [data collection], ReShare 10.5255/UKDA-SN-852166

LNMHI | Luton Non-Manual Home Interview, in UKDA, J. Lawrence (2016). *Affluent Worker Study 1962–1964: Questionnaire Files* [data collection], ReShare 10.5255/UKDA-SN-852166.

Sheppey Collection | UKDA, C. D. Wallace and R. E. Pahl (2004), *Social and Political Implications of Household Work Strategies, 1978–1983* [data collection], UK Data Service, SN: 4876, http://doi.Org/10.5255/UKDA-SN-4876-1 [Pahl Papers, Isle of Sheppey Collection]

Shipbuilding Workers | Modern Records Centre, University of Warwick, Shipbuilding Workers on Tyneside: Research Papers of Professor Richard K. Brown 'Qualidata: Shipbuilding workers' (MSS.371/shipbuilding workers)

Stevenage Survey	Bishopsgate Institute, London, Ruskin Papers, RS1/301–6, 'Survey on Social and Political Attitudes in Stevenage and Clapham, 1959–1960'
Young Papers	Churchill Archive Centre, Cambridge, Michael Young Papers

PREFACE TO PAPERBACK EDITION

When I finished writing *Me, Me, Me?*, in late 2018, Britain was already gripped by the polarizing fall-out from the 2016 referendum on EU membership, but Brexit was not yet 'done' and the pain and dislocations associated with the COVID-19 pandemic remained the stuff of dystopian fiction and (at least to some extent) government scenario planners. In many ways we are all still living through the overlapping and deeply entangled consequences of both the pandemic and Brexit. For years to come, both will have profound consequences for our lives and hence also for this book's central concern: how we understand (and nurture) the yearning for social connection and community that continues to pulse in our highly individualistic and privatized society.

Before considering the implications of COVID-19 for community life, I first want to re-emphasize one of this book's key political messages: the need to challenge overly simplistic, dichotomizing accounts of society today. Yes, inequality has grown massively in western societies, and especially in Britain, since the 1970s, and this has had major consequences for social cohesion, public health, and social mobility,[1] but the wounds that this has inflicted on society are not reducible to simple oppositions such as metropolitan versus provincial, cosmopolitan versus nativist or rich versus poor. Both society as a social system, and the people who make up society, are more complicated than that. Recognising this complexity is imperative, but it is not enough. We also need to map the common ground that unites people across apparently unbridgeable divisions of class, ethnicity, and culture. This is what Grayson Perry did in 2017 when he got rival groups of 'Leave' and 'Remain' supporters to design large pottery vases that symbolized what they loved about Britain. With good reason, Perry called the resulting work 'Matching Pair'. Personalities aside, both groups turned to a common stock of ideas and images to encapsulate their (shared) country.[2] As their name suggests, finding common ground is also the driving force behind the work of 'More in Common,' the research and policy organization founded in the aftermath of the murder of Jo

---

[1] Tony Judt, *Ill Fares the Land* (Penguin, London, 2011), 14–21.
[2] *The Guardian*, 30 May 2017.

Cox MP in 2016. More in Common describes its mission as being 'to understand the forces driving us apart, to find common ground and help to bring people together to tackle our shared challenges. Our vision is to build a more united, inclusive, and resilient society where people believe that what they have in common is stronger than what divides them.'[3] When so many in politics and the media continue to see stoking division and hate as the surest way to gain attention, we need to redouble our efforts to highlight the distortions and injuries their activities inflict on our shared social life.

But how has Covid impacted on our sense of community? Historians are always wary of declaring their hand prematurely. I recall that, in the late 1970s, our school history teacher encouraged us to take the long view of history by saying that Chinese communist leader Zhou Enlai had recently declared it to be 'too early to tell' what the historical effects of the French Revolution had been (in fact, we now know, Zhou thought he had been asked to assess effects of the Parisian revolutionary *evènèments* of May '68). Certainly, much remains unknown about the effects of the COVID-19 pandemic, including whether it has even run its course, but organizations such as the British Academy, NatCen, the Nuffield Foundation and the Institute for Community Studies have already compiled lengthy reports synthesizing social-scientific research into the impact of the pandemic on social cohesion and community resilience.[4] In broad terms, their picture of the cross-cutting pull of self and society through the pandemic is consistent with the story set out in the pages that follow. First the positive story. Across the country, people responded to the initial public health crisis by improvising ways to support friends and neighbours in need, especially those who had been advised to self-isolate. Much of this activity took place off the radar, through informal, micro-level acts of kindness such as food-shopping and sourcing prescriptions and other medical supplies, but many front-line voluntary organisations also reported increased levels of help and support, while hundreds of thousands became NHS Volunteer Responders helping with the vaccination programme and generally supporting the health services. Places that already boasted residents' groups and community-building initiatives reported

---

[3] https://www.moreincommon.org.uk/ (last visited 1 August 2022). The Belong Network has a similar vision, see https://www.belongnetwork.co.uk/ (last visited 2 August 2022).

[4] The British Academy, *The Covid Decade: Understanding the Long-term Societal Impacts of COVID-19* (British Academy, London, 2021); National Centre for Social Research, *They Think It's All Over: The Social Legacy of the COVID-19 Pandemic, Society Watch 2022* (NatCen, London, 2022); Dominic Abrams, Jo Broadwood, Fanny Lalot, Kaya Davies Hayon, and Andrew Dixon, *Beyond Us and Them: Societal Cohesion in Britain Through Eighteen Months of COVID-19* (Nuffield Foundation, University of Kent, Belong Network, Nov. 2021); Institute for Community Studies, *The Social Implications of Covid-19 on Communities* (Institute for Community Studies, London, Dec. 2020). These reports are drawn on extensively in the following paragraphs.

the most systematic and wide-ranging social support programmes, but everywhere people rallied to offer help in a crisis. Social scientists have long recognized that crises can stimulate altruistic, communitarian behaviour. Indeed, Michael Young's positive model of close-knit, working-class community, including the vital role of extended family networks (which is critically explored in Chapter 2), was strongly influenced by his study of the aftermath of the terrible floods of January 1953 (when a massive tidal surge claimed over three hundred lives along the English east coast and many more in the Netherlands).[5]

More broadly, studies conducted during 2020-21 point to people's widespread urge to connect with neighbours, especially during periods of enforced lockdown when, ironically, the call for strict social isolation was combined with the spare time necessary for casual socializing. This was also the time when video conferencing platforms broke into the mainstream; when to 'zoom' became a commonplace verb. Technology helped people maintain contact with friends and family whom they could no longer visit in person (especially if they were abroad). People held innovative virtual quizzes and drinks parties, reading groups and community choirs moved online, as did parties. I zoomed into a virtual disco to celebrate the birthday of an old friend and former neighbour. She was in Liverpool, her son, the DJ, was in London and the party revellers were scattered far and wide. But virtual socializing could not wholly supplant people's need for face-to-face, personal connection. Testimony collected by researchers suggests that this was one of the driving forces behind the 'clap for carers' during the first lockdown in spring 2020. Yes, people wanted to show their appreciation for the NHS and other 'key workers', but they also cherished the chance to connect with neighbours and show solidarity *together*.[6] It wasn't quite Italy's collective communal singing from apartment balconies, but it probably served the same fundamental purpose: the need to connect.

But as *Me, Me, Me?* demonstrates, face-to-face community can also have its darker, more coercive side. This also played its part in the COVID-19 pandemic. People might report an increased sense of neighbourliness and local community, but across the country local councils recorded increased levels of complaint about noisy and anti-social neighbours.[7] In part, this probably reflected the simple fact that lockdowns meant there was no escape from disruptive neighbours, and nowhere else for disruptive neighbours to be noisy. But it probably also reflected how the national emergency legitimized many people's reflex urge to police community norms. In short, people were often shopping their neighbours for breaking lockdown rules as

---

[5] Michael Young, 'The role of the extended family in a disaster', *Human Relations*, 7:3 (1954), 383–91.
[6] Abrams, *Beyond Us and Them*, 111–12.
[7] Institute for Community Studies, *Social Implications of Covid-19*, 3, 48–49.

much as, or more than, for being a nuisance. This urge to enforce conformity by policing the behaviour of others is arguably hard-wired into face-to-face community, and it appears to have come to the fore in the extraordinary context of the national lockdowns. Of course, it didn't help that there was widespread uncertainty about the difference between legal requirements and official guidance: what exactly constituted permitted 'exercise'; were there legal limits on the time one could spend exercising; how far could one travel from home etc.? There was also the added ingredient of fear. Even in normal times, fear easily attaches to young people congregating in groups, but now it was heightened by anxiety that their behaviour could undermine community efforts to protect vulnerable adults.[8]

There is also evidence that community support networks could be patchy and inadvertently exclusionary during the pandemic, especially when they were ad hoc and hyper-local. Groups relying largely on social media platforms such as WhatsApp and Facebook to organize volunteering necessarily placed the digitally-excluded into a passive, cliental relationship and could easily overlook them altogether if local intelligence was imperfect.[9] Me, Me, Me? makes much of the distinction between 'lived community', the sum of people someone knows and interacts with, and community as demographic fact—all the people who live in a given place. Here, the gap between the two could represent the difference between receiving support and being left to fend for oneself even in the absence of a deliberate intention to exclude (which may, of course, also have happened).

Finally, we also need to reckon with the plethora of media stories about selfish panic buying and lockdown rule-breaking. After all, shortages of loo roll did happen nationwide in the early days of the emergency. It would be easy to portray such behaviour as the epitome of twenty-first century 'me-first' individualism, but we should be wary of leaping to condemn ourselves (or rather condemn others; 'we' never stockpile, at most we buy prudently). Certainly, there is nothing new about panic buying in a crisis. It is arguably as natural as the impulse to rally round in support of those in need—and doubtless sometimes the same people did both. Hoarding has a long history. During the First World War, the stockpiling of scarce commodities was rife and there were high-profile prosecutions of people accused of hoarding foodstuffs such as sugar, flour, and tea, some widely publicized as a warning to others (the Unionist MP for West Down was fined £400 in 1918).[10] Nothing comparable was seen during the COVID-19 pandemic. In fact, most of the

---

[8] British Academy, *Covid Decade*, 81.

[9] Institute for Community Studies, *Social Implications of Covid-19*, 16–18.

[10] See Adrian Gregory, *The Last Great War: British Society and the First World War* (Cambridge University Press, Cambridge, 2008), 28–9, and *The Times*, 5 Feb. 1918, 3.

shortages experienced during 2020 could be attributed to the combined impact of disrupted 'just-in-time' supply chains and modest (one might even say prudential) shifts in consumer purchasing patterns due to the necessity to eat in, the understandable renewed interest in home baking etc.. This was not selfish individualism red in tooth and claw.[11]

So far, only a fraction of the research conducted on the social effects of the pandemic has reached the public domain. By summer 2022, the UKRI, the British government's principal agency supporting scientific research, listed 936 projects it had funded to explore different aspects of the COVID-19 pandemic. More than half of these (445) have been funded by the UKRI's social-science and humanities research councils (the ESRC and AHRC) and can therefore be assumed to focus predominantly on the pandemic's social and cultural consequences.[12] Topics include studies of Covid's impact on inequality, the elderly, disabled people, children's play, the prevalence of conspiracy theories and much else besides. Probably only a handful of these studies will seek to generate the sort of rich, well-contextualized personal testimony that was so valuable to me as I wrote the chapters that follow. It will also take some years for the testimonies collected by the current generation of social science researchers to be archived and made available for re-analysis. But when that happens, I hope historians and others will find *Me, Me, Me?* a useful model for how to work constructively and respectfully with people's archived testimony. In short, I hope they will ignore the sceptics who question the value of using archived interviews to write history, and use the testimonies collected during and after the pandemic to help us understand how ordinary people sought to navigate and make sense of the extraordinary times they lived through. That, in a nutshell, is what *Me, Me, Me?* is about.[13]

---

[11] For a general critique of our tendency to believe the worst about human behaviour see Rutger Bregman, *Humankind: a Hopeful History*, trans. Elizabeth Manton and Erica Moore (Bloomsbury, London, 2020).

[12] UKRI Gateway to Research https://gtr.ukri.org/ (last visited 2 August 2022). Approximately three hundred of these ESRC and AHRC-funded projects had Covid in their title.

[13] For a useful discussion of the pros and cons of conducting 'secondary analysis' of the testimony collected by social scientists see the roundtable discussion 'Historians' Uses of Archived Material from Sociological Research', *Twentieth-Century British History*, 33, 3 (2022), 392–459, including my essay 'On Historians' Re-Use of Social-Science Archives'.

INTRODUCTION

Decline of community?

Many commentators tell us that everyday life has become selfish and atomized in recent decades; that individuals now live only to consume. They are wrong. Friendship, family, and place remain central to everyday life. Community hasn't died, but it has changed.[1] This book maps that change and explores its political implications. It shows how, in the years after the Second World War, people came increasingly to question the idea that their lives should be determined by custom and tradition. The social pressure to conform to externally defined standards became both more resented, and more widely resisted. At the same time, informal local mechanisms for enforcing social conformity became less effective, partly because many parents chose to break with the dictum that what had been good enough for them was also good enough for their children. Post-war social change was not the simple generational conflict that contemporary media accounts often suggest.[2]

Even in the tightly packed, face-to-face urban communities thrown up by Victorian industrialism, people had always sought to protect the privacy of family life from neighbours and 'outsiders'.[3] From the 1920s, when urban housing densities began to fall precipitately through the growth of new suburbs, many jumped at the chance to live in spacious surroundings where privacy could be more easily maintained. But escaping from a social world in which everyone tended to know everyone else's business did not mean throwing off society as a whole. Rather, people came to embrace new ways of living. Community became more voluntary; increasingly what mattered were relationships based on genuine affection, not just proximity and need. New technologies such as the car, the telephone, and most recently the Internet have facilitated the flourishing of these more personalized forms of community. By the late twentieth century people had never been better connected; never better placed to sustain the relationships that mattered to them. Since the start of the new millennium, the rise of social media has simply accelerated these trends towards greater social connectivity. We need to value and nurture these new forms of personal, chosen community, rather than simply lament the loss of

1

supposedly better, more 'real', forms of community in the past. The visceral sense of loss that drives stories about the decline of community needs to be understood, not least because it represents a powerful critique of the forces that threaten to atomize social life today. However, we should not mistake this sense of loss for an accurate description of how things used to be. It is all too easy to hold on to an overly nostalgic view of community in the past.

This book challenges many of the preconceptions about community and individualism in recent English history. Focusing on how ordinary men and women from a broad range of social backgrounds and geographical locations made sense of social change in their own words, it seeks to overturn simplistic assumptions about the 'decline of community' since the Second World War. In doing so, it explores how people have sought to reconcile the deep-rooted individualism of English popular culture with the urge for social connection through family and community. Crucially, by taking the long view of post-war social change, it suggests ways in which individualism and community can be reconciled, today, in everyday life and in politics. Only by understanding the ambivalences and tensions between self and community in people's everyday lives can we hope to forge a successful democratic political project.

Illuminating the ways in which ordinary people made sense of, and helped to shape, the changes transforming everyday life in England since the Second World War reminds us that people do not live their lives according to the dictates of social and political theory. Everyday life is rich, messy, and riven with ambivalence. Unlike philosophers, most people happily live with contradictions; individualism and community may be polar opposites in social theory, but not in lives as they are actually lived. On the contrary, for many they are the twin pillars of what we might call the vernacular 'Good Life'. This book aims to tune into this vernacular strain of common-sense philosophy, weaving the voices of men and women from across six decades and eight different communities to challenge the doom-laden accounts of contemporary society which currently prevail throughout the Western world.

Social theorists such as Zygmunt Bauman argue that we have entered a new age of 'Liquid Modernity' in which we have all been reduced to isolated individuals obsessed by our 'solitary individual fears'.[4] Most influentially, in the 2000s the American political scientist Robert Putnam captured the attention of politicians and policymakers worldwide with his stark assessment of social fragmentation in a world where everyone supposedly goes 'Bowling Alone'.[5] In Britain, we are surrounded by talk of the 'collapse of community' and the 'broken society', and by think-tanks and government departments constantly hatching new ways to rebuild what, following the lead of the social scientists, they have come to call our 'social capital'.

There is a danger that we pay too much attention to these powerful narratives of decline and too little attention to what ordinary people have to say about their own lives. By contrast, in this book I have attempted to listen carefully to the testimony emerging in everyday speech. From the 1940s, social scientists in Britain began, for the first time, systematically to treat ordinary people as informed observers of their own lives, rather than just as subjects for study by experts. Two decades after its emergence in America, the age of the community study was born;[6] where the original field-notes and interview transcripts survive, these studies allow us to hear people making sense of their life and times *in their own words* and, crucially, without the potentially distorting lens of retrospection. The results are striking and challenge many of our dominant assumptions about both past and present. This book draws on the surviving field-notes, interview transcripts, and recordings of ten major social-science studies conducted across six decades (between 1947–9 and 2007–8). They include two studies from London, two from the North East, three from the South East, and three from the East of England (see Map 1). The earliest study is Raymond Firth's anthropological investigation of kinship and community in Bermondsey undertaken between 1947 and 1949, the last is Yvette Taylor's study of women's experience of deindustrialization and urban regeneration in the North East conducted during 2007–8.

It is undeniable that in the early twenty-first century most people are living lives that are socially much *more* connected than their ancestors seventy years ago. They have more leisure, more money, more mobility, more ways to communicate, and more space (and inclination) to entertain each other at home. Community doesn't just survive, it flourishes, but because it often takes new forms—less constrained by geography, less formal—it is too swiftly dismissed by social commentators fixated on the old ways of living. For sure, we need to be careful not to overstate the parallels between virtual and face-to-face communities, but what really matters is how a range of innovations in communication have actually made it easier to sustain real-world social relationships.[7] The sociologists Liz Spencer and Ray Pahl argue that vibrant friendship networks provide the social glue of modern life—what they call its 'hidden solidarities'.[8] Spencer and Pahl specifically stress the importance of *personal* communities, and insist that just because modern technologies allow them to be more dispersed than in previous generations, we should not conclude that these communities are less meaningful to people, or less potent as bulwarks against social atomization.

So why are we wedded to the idea of social fragmentation and the collapse of society? Perhaps at a personal level we all find it hard not to conflate our view of the past with nostalgic feelings towards our own younger selves. For at least two

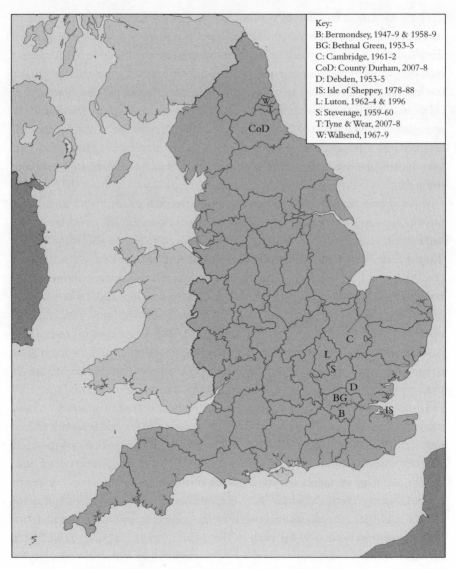

Key:
B: Bermondsey, 1947-9 & 1958-9
BG: Bethnal Green, 1953-5
C: Cambridge, 1961-2
CoD: County Durham, 2007-8
D: Debden, 1953-5
IS: Isle of Sheppey, 1978-88
L: Luton, 1962-4 & 1996
S: Stevenage, 1959-60
T: Tyne & Wear, 2007-8
W: Wallsend, 1967-9

Map 1. Location of the social-science case studies (with dates)

centuries, cultural critics like Coleridge, Ruskin, and Eliot have been comparing their own fragmented, hedonistic, and selfish times with an earlier age of social harmony and community. In romanticizing local, face-to-face community at the expense of other types of social relationship we forget that there was always a dark side to non-voluntary forms of community. Up until the Second World War most English people may have been obliged by economic necessity and overcrowding to live on intimate terms with their neighbours, but privacy was always jealously guarded. People feared the prying eyes and malicious tongues of neighbours. In consequence, relations with neighbours were often wary, and many lived by the maxim 'we keep ourselves to ourselves and then you can't get into trouble', as one Bermondsey resident put it to anthropologist Raymond Firth in 1947.[9] Even those who socialized more freely tended to do so in the street, over the garden fence, or down the pub, and not just for practical reasons of space. There were strong taboos around allowing anyone but family and one's closest friends into the home to 'know your business'.[10]

Physical proximity did mean that kinship ties were generally closer in intimate, face-to-face communities, but again it is easy to romanticize the extended family. In practice, people regularly fell out with close blood relations, and many felt the downside of living under the watchful eye of disapproving relatives.[11] It is all too easy to forget that our forebears often had good reason to want to escape the constraints of close-knit community in the decades after the Second World War. They were not simply hoodwinked by planners and advertisers peddling false dreams of suburban domesticity. Yes, they wanted better homes, with more space and modern facilities, but many also wanted the chance to withdraw from *forced* sociability—to socialize instead on their own terms, with the family and friends of their choosing.

Significantly, as prosperity increased and overcrowding diminished, so taboos around socializing within the home began to weaken. People had less need to hide their poverty, or their domestic sleeping arrangements (always one of the most sensitive issues for those fearful of malicious gossip). But this apparently small-scale shift in popular custom was driven by much more fundamental social changes. In her book *Family Secrets*, Deborah Cohen explores how, during the second half of the twentieth century, the determination to protect domestic privacy mutated into a more powerful assertion of the right to live as one wished, in public as well as in private.[12] By this reading, what defeated the tyranny of gossip was not atomization and the retreat into private life, but rather people's growing refusal to accept that there was only one right way to live, either for themselves or for others. And as the pressure to conform diminished, so the space for a more relaxed sociability within and without the home increased. At the same time it was becoming more common for couples to socialize together, rather than apart, and for the home to seem a natural place to do this.[13] Here, the great symbolic shift was the demise of the 'best' room (or front parlour) as a domestic space off limits to family except on special occasions. (Into the 1970s both my widowed grandmothers maintained best front rooms in their small terraced houses. These were used only at Christmas, if at all; the rest of the year they were left unused, save for brief forays to dust the china ornaments and the upright piano.) But during the 1960s and 1970s more and more families decided to dispense with this traditional marker of respectability, knocking through their downstairs rooms in order to create a large *living* room more suited to modern lifestyles, including socializing at home. It was social revolution on the micro-scale, and a perfect example of how, at the level of the everyday, the assertion of self and the urge for community could go hand in hand.

Lost voices

By revisiting personal testimony collected over many decades we can begin to understand the different ways in which ordinary people have sought to reconcile individualism and community, self and others, in their own lives. These rich and still under-used sources can give us unparalleled access to the world-view of men and women who would otherwise have left little or no written record. Using them makes it possible to write a new type of social history: one in which ordinary people's thoughts and feelings *at the time* take centre stage—where they become the experts on their own lives.[14]

We are not here talking about trying to distil some supposedly 'pure' vernacular voice, uninfluenced by either the original social-science research process or the wider culture in which both researcher and subject were enmeshed. Indeed, there is no reason to believe that any such pure, vernacular culture existed in twentieth-century Britain. This was a highly mediated, pluralist society. Eric Hobsbawm may be right to argue that many urban districts possessed their own distinctive subculture, and right to call this 'working-class culture', if one allows a very broad definition of 'working class' to include publicans, shopkeepers, and anyone else who lived in these districts and shared their customs (this was really a culture of place more than of class), but this urban subculture was not hermetically sealed from the wider culture; print, cinema, and radio all reinforced the deep-rooted interconnections that characterized British culture—interconnections which long predated the new mass communication technologies.[15] It is in this sense that, at least by the 1930s, Britain possessed what Dan LeMahieu has termed a common culture—not a single culture, but rather a richly diverse cultural life with important elements of commonality and connection.[16]

We do not, therefore, need to worry unduly that social-science field-notes may have been 'contaminated' by the social interaction inherent in the research process. Yes, we have to read for this influence, but illuminating how people from different subcultures navigated each other in this way is itself of historical interest.[17] It is also important to know what was considered socially acceptable to say in different contexts at different times. But what I have been most struck by in post-war social-science encounters is the way in which the actual process of research often encouraged respondents to think and speak as historians and sociologists *of their own lives*. Doubtless there is something artificial about this process—being asked to offer an account of oneself to power (or at least to a constituted expert sitting across the living room) probably does encourage a particular type of formalized, rational discourse. But, contrary to Mike Savage's arguments in his important book *Identities and Social Change*, I have found that what people say in such situations is rarely a direct echo of the tropes and idioms of sociology.[18]

Rather, the social-science encounter often acts as a catalyst for the exercise of that deep-seated human urge to impose meaning and pattern on life. Time and again, confronted by the official expert, people appear to feel empowered to present themselves as the representatives of a popular counter-expertise. There is much to be learned from interrogating these exercises in the making of vernacular sociology (which has, of course, now become vernacular history). Certainly, we should take people's claims to be experts about their own lives more seriously than many social scientists were inclined to do at the time.[19]

Both historians and social scientists have become increasingly interested in the reanalysis of interview transcripts and other raw social-research data in recent years. Among others, Mike Savage, Selina Todd, and Florence Sutcliffe-Braithwaite have all demonstrated the enormous potential of such material as historical evidence.[20] Conventional social histories tend to rely either on the views (or data) of outside experts from the time, or on retrospective accounts based on people's memories. There is nothing wrong with either approach, but they cannot take us into the contemporary thought-world of ordinary people. This is the terrain that the great literary critic Raymond Williams famously called the 'structure of feeling': the deep, underlying ethos and values of an age.[21] He felt that it could best be accessed through literature, but, with careful reading, more commonplace, everyday language can be used to recover the '*structures* of feeling' of ordinary people.

Note the plural usage here; I am not claiming that there is some single, unified popular thought-world that can somehow be revealed by the application of close-reading techniques. We must expect to find heterogeneity and complexity. We need to remember, as Stuart Middleton has observed, that Williams's original conception of the 'structure of feeling' was heavily influenced by the holisitc gestalt movement in social psychology.[22] But there is nonetheless much to be gained from focusing on ordinary people's meaning-generating activities. Indeed, historical interpretations influenced by the modern hermeneutic tradition, with its emphasis on the recovery of subjective meaning, are arguably generating some of the most intellectually satisfying, context-sensitive, and humanistic interpretations in social and cultural history.[23]

Ten studies

Only studies focused on a specific locality have been used in this book because context is all-important when trying to interpret personal testimony (see Table 1). Focusing exclusively on place-based studies makes it easier to grasp the social and economic context of people's utterances and actions. However, it does not require us to take on board the preconceptions about 'community' which sometimes shaped the social scientists' original projects.[24] In fact, none of the ten studies

Table 1. Details of reanalysed social-science studies

Place	Project Leads	Years covered	Chapter	Source type
Bermondsey	Raymond Firth	1947–9 & 1958–9	2	Field-notes; research notes
Bethnal Green	Michael Young Peter Willmott	1953 & 1955	2	Interview notes & reports, some transcriptions
Debden, Essex	Michael Young Peter Willmott	1953 & 1955	3	Interview notes & reports, some transcriptions
Stevenage	Raph Samuel	1959–60	3	Completed questionnaires
Cambridge	John Goldthorpe David Lockwood	1961–2	4	Completed questionnaires
Luton	John Goldthorpe David Lockwood	1962–4	4	Completed questionnaires
Wallsend/ Tyneside	Richard Brown	1967–9	5	Field-notes; transcriptions & completed questionnaires
Isle of Sheppey Kent	Ray Pahl	1978–88	6	Interview transcripts, field-notes, questionnaires, &c.
Luton	Hartley Dean Margaret Melrose	1996	7	Interview transcripts
Tyneside/Co. Durham	Yvette Taylor	2007–8	7	Interview transcripts

See the Appendix for further details of the studies in this table chosen can be considered a full-blown community study in the tradition of the Lynds' famous interwar studies of 'Middletown' (Muncie, Indiana), where the emphasis was on offering a total picture of social and cultural life in a single place.[25] Almost every study had at its heart a substantive sociological question which the researchers believed was best explored through an intensive study of a specific locality. Only Michael Young and Peter Willmott appear to have been directly influenced by the community-studies tradition, and hence by its tendency to exaggerate both the cohesiveness and the insularity of local social systems. We need to read for this influence when reanalysing their field-notes from 1950s Bethnal Green and Debden, but in practice there are few signs that respondents felt the need to tailor their responses to mirror Young and Willmott's idealized model of the supposedly traditional, working-class community.[26]

Even in the 1940s, many social scientists had been sceptical about the concept of community, but by the late 1960s the whole idea of undertaking community studies was starting to go out of fashion.[27] One consequence is that it is much harder to locate local social-science studies from the 1970s and 1980s, although fortunately sociologist Ray Pahl, himself a stern critic of 'community' as a sociological concept, continued to believe in the intensive, place-based social survey.[28] Indeed his work on the Isle of Sheppey, off the north Kent coast, between 1978 and 1988 represents one of the most sustained and wide-ranging attempts to study everyday life at the micro-level in British sociology.[29] Fortunately, it is also one of the best preserved twentieth-century social-science projects.[30]

The earliest of our ten local studies is Raymond Firth's pioneering anthropological study of Bermondsey, south-east London, conducted immediately after the Second World War. Firth was primarily interested in exploring the extent and nature of kinship ties in an old, established working-class district, including the role kinship played in community cohesion. A few years later, similar motives took the sociologist Michael Young to nearby Bethnal Green. In contrast to Firth, Young and his subsequent collaborator Peter Willmott had a strong political agenda. They questioned the post-war planning and housing policies which required hundreds of thousands of Londoners to leave the city in order to relieve the capital's acute overcrowding problem.[31] Young and Willmott therefore also undertook a parallel study of Bethnal Green families who had moved out to one of the new London County Council (LCC) out-of-town estates (Debden in suburban Essex). Surviving testimony from this study is examined alongside more than 140 questionnaires generated by a late 1950s study of families who had moved to the post-war Hertfordshire 'new town' of Stevenage. This project was also funded by the Institute of Community Studies, the organization that Young had established in 1953 to promote his vision of organic, community-based socialism.[32]

Moving into the 1960s, we stay in the booming post-war South to look at social change in two very different towns, the ancient university city of Cambridge and the rapidly expanding industrial town of Luton (home of Vauxhall Motors). Both surveys were conducted by sociologists John Goldthorpe and David Lockwood and were aimed primarily at dispelling the then influential argument that affluent manual workers were somehow becoming middle class through the growth of post-war prosperity and consumerism.[33] Although men were the principal focus of these two studies, the Luton project included home interviews designed explicitly to involve wives (all the men interviewed were married and aged between 21 and 46). The final study from the sixties shifts the focus to the industrial North, re-examining the extensive field-notes and interview transcripts that survive from industrial sociologist Richard Brown's massive study of Tyneside shipbuilding workers conducted between 1967 and 1970.[34] This is the only study to focus exclusively on men, and the only study to offer extensive fieldwork observations of the workplace.

In many ways the iconic cultural changes associated with the 'Swinging Sixties' barely register in any of these studies, but there are nonetheless clear signs of a radical change in social and cultural attitudes when they are compared with the testimony from earlier studies. The next major project to have left good records is Ray Pahl's massive study of the Isle of Sheppey begun in 1978. These were hard times for this remote Kentish community, and Pahl's study offers important insights into the ways in which a broad range of people experienced and responded to the opportunities and threats associated with the rapid economic and social restructuring of the 1980s. Finally, we look at two social-science projects which revisited places first studied in the 1960s: Hartley Dean and Margaret Melrose's research into social attitudes among Luton workers in the mid-1990s and Yvette Taylor's detailed life-course interviews with Tyneside women from 2007 to 2008.[35] Counterbalancing Brown's study of shipbuilding workers, Taylor's project is the only collection to focus exclusively on women. Taylor's principal interest was to explore the social and cultural effects of deindustrialization on the region through the eyes of women rather than men, but by its nature her life-course approach generated rich, wide-ranging testimony touching on many of the themes central to this book.[36]

But why England rather than Britain? Well, partly this is because I did not find good surviving field-notes from Welsh or Scottish studies when planning the project. But more fundamentally, it is because many of the issues at the heart of Me, Me, Me? played out differently across the four nations of the United Kingdom. Although I have deliberately not framed the wider project through the language of class, preferring class to emerge from my sources rather than be imposed upon them, I *am* clear that class resonated differently in England compared with the other home nations. As in the settler societies of the Anglo-world, in Scotland, Wales, and Ireland one frequently finds people portraying class as a foreign, specifically English, importation. It is also evident from the English community-based studies I have used that non-English respondents often struggled to grasp what their interviewers meant by 'class', or understood the term differently from their English counterparts. For instance, at Luton in the early 1960s, researchers observed that Irish migrants tended to discuss class less emotionally than their English counterparts, seeing it as just a matter of money differences with no broader implications about a person's supposed status or social worth.[37] I don't want to suggest that class lacked a psychological dimension for anyone but the English—a brief engagement with Sennett and Cobb's famous study of blue-collar America, *The Hidden Injuries of Class*, would soon dispel that theory—but I would argue that ingrained hierarchical and status-based models of social difference placed an especially heavy burden on cross-class social encounters conducted in England.[38]

Community and class seen from below

In terms of the big picture of post-war historical change, turning to contemporary personal testimony gives us insights into how ordinary people understood the major turning points of national history. From the 1940s we get a sense of what it meant to people to 'win the peace', and how they viewed the social reforms of the post-war Labour Government that were often presented as the fruits of victory. Similarly, we gain insights into how people felt about the material gains of the late 1950s and 1960s, and in particular what meanings they attached to the consumer items widely hailed as harbingers of a new mass affluence. By the late 1960s we find people trying to relate permissiveness and the wider cultural revolution associated with London's avant-garde counterculture, to what often seemed like the humdrum continuities of their own lives. Crucially, we also get a sense of the inherent contingency of the post-war social democratic settlement—the compact between State and people forged in the war years and cemented by Labour's post-war reforms. Not only was it the product of a specific moment, but it was always a dynamic settlement rooted in ideas about shared progress and 'betterment'. The only question was about *how* it would change, not whether. By the 1970s and 1980s, a combination of cultural and economic change was beginning to weaken the more collectivist aspects of the post-war settlement. Many of the hallmarks of sixties counterculture became embedded, albeit often in mutated form, in the fabric and the language of everyday life. We find working-class women happy to proclaim their independence from men, sometimes explicitly in the name of 'women's lib', and widespread articulation of radical sixties doctrines about personal autonomy and self-realization. On the other hand, testimony from the 1980s and 1990s suggests that many people recoiled from the ascendancy of unbridled economic individualism during these decades, and continued to seek ways in which they could reconcile the claims of self and society in their own lives. The great epochal shift from social democratic to neo-liberal politics looks a lot messier when seen from below.

These insights into how people made sense of, and placed themselves within, large-scale processes of historical change are valuable, but it is in illuminating change on the micro-scale—at the level of home, family, and neighbourhood—that social-science testimony really comes into its own. Like the quiet revolution that saw the overthrow of the respectable but little-used front parlour, small decisions about lifestyle, multiplied millions of times across the country, could have a major impact on patterns of social interaction. But by no means all micro-level change was cumulative in this way. Often social change, seen from below, was more personal and parochial: adapting to the social expectations of new neighbours after moving house, of new work colleagues after changing jobs, or, for the socially mobile, of new taste tribes (Grayson Perry's 2012 series of tapestries *The Vanity of Small Differences*, and the accompanying Channel 4 television series, is essentially an extended artistic-cum-anthropological exploration of this social pressure to adopt the distinctive lifestyle markers of our peers[39]). Humans are social animals and at some level adaptation to the perceived norms of one's immediate neighbours is probably close to instinctual (this is the central insight of Pierre Bourdieu's influential concept of 'habitus'[40])—though, crucially, not so instinctual that people proved incapable of articulating how it felt to have to adapt to new ways of living on moving into a new neighbourhood, or, worse, how it felt moving to a place where everyone was a newcomer and local social norms had to be worked out from scratch.

Not only do social norms vary from place to place, but over time there has also been a perceptible diminution in the claims that custom is allowed to make on personal conduct. It is important to recognize that many people had always refused to accept the writ of neighbourhood opinion, but such defiance counted for little while social reputation remained the key to securing credit at the local shop or to getting a job.[41] But by the later 1950s, with full employment and a general rise in living standards, these coercive aspects of community had begun to lose much of their force. In Karel Reisz's film *Saturday Night and Sunday Morning* (1960), the central character, factory worker Arthur Seaton, is repeatedly shown defying the self-appointed

Figure 1. Mr Seaton complaining that his son Arthur (centre) and nephew Bert have let the Bulls into his house [*Saturday Night and Sunday Morning*, 1960; Snap Stills/REX/Shutterstock]

guardians of local morality and standards. The impotency of the old order is underscored when Seaton shoots Mrs Bull, the street's chief matriarch, in the backside with an air rifle. Significantly, Seaton's father is angrier to learn that the Bulls have forced their way into his house than he is to discover that his son's rebellious behaviour may have reached a violent new level (see Figure 1).[42]

This clash between the Seatons and the Bulls reminds us, not just that community norms could be contested, but that in any locality there could be multiple, overlapping 'lived communities' existing side by side. For Seaton senior, violating his domestic privacy apparently represented a more serious breach of established custom than assaulting a neighbour. In turn, Mrs Bull would doubtless have seen herself as an established member of the local community, deeply embedded in reciprocal social networks that others decried as gossip circles, and therefore wholly within her rights to pass judgement on neighbours bringing shame on the street (as Arthur Seaton was, in her eyes, by conducting an illicit affair with a workmate's wife).[43]

Social surveys generally throw up less dramatic scenarios than fiction, but it is evident that respondents often saw their own personal social networks as proof of the vibrancy of local community, apparently unaware that many neighbours might feel actively excluded from the same networks. In testimony from the 1950s and 1960s we see this most often among women with young children, where non-working mothers are recorded celebrating strong communal support networks, while working mothers complain of being actively excluded by their neighbours because the activities of such groups were generally organized during the working day. Non-working women may not have intended their networks to be exclusionary, but that was how working mothers often perceived things.[44] In turn, such feelings of social exclusion could breed a powerful rejection of any pretence at conforming to externally determined social norms, and the assertion of a powerful credo of personal autonomy and the sovereignty of the self.

Although lived community is often presented, by its very nature, as habitual and unthinking, it is striking how often interviewees showed themselves perfectly capable of articulating the contours of community in their own neighbourhood. Nor was this true only of those who felt themselves to be excluded from local social networks. Regardless of age, class, or gender, many respondents showed themselves able to stand back and explain who belonged to tightly defined social networks, and who did not. Indeed, some especially reflexive respondents recognized that the experience of lived community was closely tied to the life-course: community was something that children, the parents of young children, and the elderly felt most strongly because their social networks were more tightly bound to place.

Perhaps understandably, people who had made an active choice to live in a particular place often proved especially thoughtful about the nature of 'community'. Sociologists talk about the phenomenon of 'elective belonging' and see it as a hallmark of contemporary affluent consumerism, and especially of wealthy elites accustomed to seeing all aspects of their lives as an extension of, and statement about, themselves.[45] It is therefore striking to find Luton factory workers in the early 1960s deploying broadly the same language of choice and personal taste to explain their decision to live in rural commuter villages.[46]

But if there is one thing that shines through in the raw testimony collected by the ten studies considered here, it is the rich diversity of working-class life and culture. Writing in 1958, Raymond Williams famously declared, 'There are in fact no masses; there are only ways of seeing people as masses.'[47] It is certainly a lesson we need to heed if we want to draw useful conclusions about the politics of everyday life and their implications for formal, organized politics.

That said, workers themselves were not necessarily averse to 'self-massification' if it served a tactical purpose (such as obscuring class differences in an interview). As Mike Savage has observed, when British workers were quizzed about social class they typically sought to deflect the classificatory power of the question by proclaiming themselves to be just 'ordinary'; refusing to recognize social distinctions between themselves and those nominally above and below them in the class hierarchy that they rightly suspected to be in the minds of their interrogators.[48] We see this most clearly in manual workers' refusal to acknowledge the significance of the customary distinction between shop-floor work and office work—that is, between manual and non-manual labour. Crucially, this refusal of class was a two-way process. Even in the 1950s and 1960s, when the social and cultural distinction between manual and non-manual labour remained sharp, many office workers also claimed to be 'ordinary' and insisted on the basic equality of workers by hand and by brain (as Clause IV of the Labour Party's Constitution famously put it 1918).[49]

This is not to deny that there were real differences in the experiences of manual and non-manual workers, especially in the workplace itself. It is merely to acknowledge that a good deal of psychic and emotional energy was invested by both sides in denying the salience of these distinctions *outside* the workplace. One reason for this was arguably the deep-rooted traditions of individualism within English culture. Not the assertive, economic individualism of the marketplace, which was widely seen as a corrosive force eroding more personal forms of social relationship, but a quieter individualism rooted in ideas about personal independence and the moral autonomy of the self (traditions that likely had their origin in the social and cultural fallout from the Protestant Reformation). Savage has written about the paradox of post-war working-class culture in which trade-union collectivism was seen as the best strategy for preserving workers' historic right to a measure of autonomy and independence in the workplace. By contrast, non-unionized office workers were seen as less independent, and in a sense less free and 'individual', because firms demanded a much higher degree of loyalty from 'staff' than from 'workers'.[50]

On the shop floor, individualism and collectivism went hand in hand, something worker-writer Jack Common had commented on in the mid-1930s when discussing the paradoxical circumstances (and world-view) of secure, well-paid trade unionists in sheltered trades like the railways and public transport. Common observed that in his native North East they were known as 'pease-pudding men' because things were 'dolloped out to them soft'.[51] Throughout the chapters that follow, we repeatedly find individualism and communalism intertwined in people's complex everyday lives. Indeed, a central aim of the book is to reconstruct how the interconnections between these two fundamental strands of popular culture have changed over time. This is not a neutral, purely academic exercise. On the contrary, it has profound implications for how we conceptualize political practice today, especially for anyone who, like me, wants to see a fundamental recalibration of the balance between the market and the public good in British politics.

In understandable reaction against the ascendancy of liberal economics and competitive individualism in recent decades, many on the Left have set themselves firmly against liberal individualism as a whole. This is true both of the socially conservative Left, where there has been a revival of what can probably best be described as nativist communitarianism, and of the socialist Left, which has redis-covered the language of class. The 'Blue Labour' response to the economic crash of 2007–8, with its argument that liberal elites had hijacked the Labour Party and betrayed its socially conservative, mutualist working-class base, was an early example of right-wing communitarianism.[52] The Brexit vote of 2016 added cred-ibility to this analysis, intensifying fears of an irrevocable social and cultural schism on the Left that could cripple progressive politics for a generation.[53] According to political scientist David Runciman, the Brexit vote highlighted a fundamental division between the highly educated and the less educated, which was mirrored among Labour supporters in a split between educated libertarians and less educated authoritarians.[54] David Goodhart, the founder of *Prospect* magazine and former director of centre-left think-tank Demos, has a similarly polarized, Manichaean perspective, but chooses a different, more explicitly spatial language. Early twenty-first century Britain, he argues, is divided between the 'somewheres' and the 'nowheres'; between less mobile, less educated people with a strong commitment to place, family, and community, and a privileged minority who are more mobile, more highly educated, and who have weaker social commitments with little geo-graphic specificity.[55] It is a compelling argument, even though political scientists have already largely dispelled the claim that the Brexit voters of 2016 were predom-inantly working-class, uneducated 'left behinds'.[56]

But psephological details are not the only problem with bold, black-and-white accounts of social and cultural difference in modern Britain. Such accounts ignore the importance of place and family to many people who would nominally appear to be classic members of the rootless, mobile 'liberal elite' (hence the phenomenon sociologists call 'elective belonging'). More fundamentally, they risk offering a caricatured picture of the less mobile, less educated majority which falls squarely into Raymond Williams's trap of flattening social discourse which reduces people to homogeneous 'masses'.

It seems likely that part of Jeremy Corbyn's appeal as Labour leader since 2015 has been the hope that his radical economic policies can bridge the schism perceived to run through Labour's electoral base between the liberal, middle-class progressives and long-term working-class Labour supporters who tend to be socially conservative, but economically radical.[57] Labour's unexpected gains at the 2017 election offered hope to many, although it is important to remember that the party actually *lost* another clutch of classic industrial, working-class seats including Mansfield, Walsall North, Stoke-on-Trent South, Derbyshire North-East, and Copeland in Cumbria. However, the chapters that follow may offer Labour grounds for optimism precisely because tracing popular attitudes over the long term highlights the strong hold of a quiet, non-assertive liberal individualism over English popular culture. This is good news for Labour because it suggests that the schism running through its electoral base may be less deep-seated and insuperable than many imagine. Working-class Labour voters may, on average, offer less liberal responses than middle-class Labour voters to pollsters' trigger questions on crime, LGBT rights, and immigration, but it does not follow that they are instinctively illiberal in their world-view. These attitudinal differences spring largely from people's different life situations and experiences, hence the rapid shifts in popular attitudes to sexuality and racial difference over the past half-century as people's awareness of such issues has changed.[58]

Ironically, the greater danger for Labour lies in turning its back on liberal individualism as part of its reaction against the free market excesses since the 1980s, and the broader malaise of social democratic politics since the economic crisis of 2007–8. This is where it becomes important to map the contours of popular individualism more precisely than tends to be possible through the question and response mode of conventional opinion polling. Even when we turn to the much richer testimony to be found in the field-notes of large-scale community studies, this exercise is still fraught with difficulties. What people say about the balance they strike between self and society needs to be read through the filter of perceived social expectations. This means probing the space between performance and practice, something that is only possible when one has access to a rich set of observations—more than a brief questionnaire can provide. For instance, Ray Pahl's Sheppey interviews from the early 1980s throw up a number of examples of people performing independent self-reliance within the interview, despite elsewhere acknowledging strong reciprocal support networks with friends and relatives.

On the other hand, we also need to be wary about taking frequent popular disavowals of materialism and selfish individualism at face value. Again, this is partly about recognizing the performative aspects of the interview, especially the cross-class interview, and how this may shape what it is socially acceptable to say. But even if people were often more materialist than they liked to acknowledge, it still matters that throughout the decades of post-war affluence popular attitudes towards material objects consistently affirmed the distinction between use value and

17

status value. Similarly, even if people often lived more reciprocal, interconnected lives than they cared to acknowledge, it matters if they chose to espouse a credo of personal autonomy and self-reliance.

Indeed, it is this powerful ideology of independent selfhood that politicians of any stripe need to understand and respect if they are to enjoy sustained electoral success. It may not correspond to the model of profit-maximizing individualism encoded in classical economic theory, but it is deeply individualist for all that. So when people disparage crass materialism and claim only to value things that are useful, we need to remember that implicit in their claim is an absolute conviction that only they may judge what is, and is not, 'useful'. In many ways Arthur Seaton, the rebellious anti-hero at the centre of Sillitoe's *Saturday Night and Sunday Morning*, can be seen as the epitome of this strain of cussed individualism. Obliged to attend an army summer camp, Seaton's confrontation with a sergeant major leads him to ask 'What am I?' His answer is simple, and justly famous: 'I'm me and nobody else; and whatever people think I am or say I am, that's what I'm not, because they don't know a bloody thing about me.'[59] Sillitoe penned these words in the late 1950s, but half a century later they still resonated strongly enough in British popular culture for the Sheffield-based rock band Arctic Monkeys to call their record-breaking first album 'Whatever people say I am, that's what I'm not' (adopting the slightly punchier wording of Sillitoe's screenplay).[60] As we will see, rugged individualism can run in tandem with a strong commitment to family and friends, and even a strong belief in community and shared values, but that should not lead us to underestimate the underlying rock-like commitment to personal autonomy and self-realization. Rather, the task for politicians is to imagine the conditions which will enable people most fully to reconcile self *and* society in their daily lives.

CHAPTER 1

FAMILY AND PLACE

Most of this book is woven from the stories, and the wisdom, of people I will never meet; people who shared their thoughts, and sometimes their hopes and fears, with interviewers trying to capture how society was changing around them. Indeed, as a condition of using such material one has to agree not to make any attempt to contact the people involved. But the book is also informed by stories told to me by my own family, and especially by my late parents, Doreen and Ron. These quintessentially small, personal stories about births, marriages, and deaths, about dreams crushed or hopes realized, help us to humanize the big narratives of history—stories about war and peace, prosperity and poverty at the societal level—which shape our understanding of Britain's past. In recent years academic historians have begun to champion the value of family history as a way to enrich our understanding of the past, allowing individuals who left few if any written records to take their place on the historical stage.[1]

It has also become increasingly popular to mine one's own family history to offer an intimate, personal perspective on the large-scale social and economic changes that have transformed Britain over the past two centuries.[2] Turning to family history allows us to capture change, not just across the life-course—from birth to death—but also across generations. In the case of my own family, the picture one gleans by combining family stories passed down across the generations alongside the techniques of modern genealogy underscores the great diversity of personal experience within working-class families, and the very different relationships people could have with place and community. In one branch of my family, the Straw-bridges (my paternal grandmother's family in the male line), generation after generation of men had the same job—artisan gilder—and from at least the mid-eighteenth century also lived in broadly the same districts of East Bristol (a gilder was someone who applied gold leaf to fine objects such as picture frames, books, and jewellery—the fact that many were recorded as 'carver and gilder' suggests that picture frame-making may have been their main trade).

The Strawbridges epitomized that section of the classic urban, artisan elite fortunate enough to possess craft skills left largely unaffected by the Industrial

Revolution of the nineteenth century.[3] But the geographical and occupational stability of their lives was unusual. The Lawrence branch of my family is perhaps more typical. For generations my ancestors in the male line can be found trading as butchers in the small north Somerset village of Worle (now effectively incorporated into the seaside town of Weston-super-Mare, probably most famous for its Grand Pier and as the birthplace of John Cleese, Jill Dando, and Jeffrey Archer). But in each generation only the oldest male could hope to inherit the family business; all his siblings had to make their way in the world. Some migrated to the big city (Bristol), to find work in its expanding trades and industries, while others went further afield. Joseph Lawrence, my great-grandfather, became a marine based at Devonport in south Devon, where he married a Cornish woman called Emma and had two sons before being killed in service in 1900. The sons were adopted by two aunts who had moved from Worle to Bristol as young women. Both aunts had subsequently married and started families of their own in the big city. My grandfather, also Joseph (born 1891), was adopted by Mary Ann Kent and her bricklayer husband Benjamin who lived in a newly built terraced house in working-class Lower Easton (though perhaps significantly the couple had met and married 150 miles away in the small Sussex town of Steyning where Mary Ann had originally found work as a domestic servant). In the mid-1900s Joseph secured an apprenticeship with a local tinsmiths' company (see Figure 2). By 1916 he was a machine gunner on the western front. Unlike many of his generation he returned home fit enough in body and soul to resume his trade, marry a local girl (my grandmother Emily Strawbridge), and raise a family. But gas attacks and shrapnel wounds had left him with chronic health conditions that would later play their part in his sudden and premature death aged just 50.

When I was young I believed my mother to have been born into a Welsh family that had only recently migrated to Bristol. Not just because her maiden name was Lewis, but because her mother had been born in South Wales, her paternal grandfather had been a Welsh miner, and in the 1930s she herself had won a reading prize at a local eisteddfod. But the truth proved to be both more complicated and more revealing about the mobility of many working-class lives before the First World War. Florence Fowler, my maternal grandmother, had been born in Pontypridd in 1897 only because her father, Joseph Fowler, had just moved to South Wales in the hope of finding well-paid work in the region's booming coal industry (thousands of Englishmen made the same journey in the years before the First World War).[4] Both he and his wife Lizzie had been born and raised in Bristol, and within a few years they would be living there again. By the time of the 1901 census Joseph, still only 25, is recorded as working as a sawyer in his father's trade of stone cutting, and the whole family were again living in East Bristol.

Figure 2. Studio photograph of Joseph Lawrence in Sunday best, *c.*1914 [private collection]

My maternal grandfather, George Henry Lewis (born 1900), also had strong connections with South Wales. His father, George, spent much of his life living and working on the Welsh coalfield, although he had been born and brought up in Bristol, the son of a small-time local haulier (who, by chance, had himself been born in Worle, the north Somerset village where the Lawrences had been butchers since at least the 1780s). George senior only became a miner after his family was broken up by the death of his wife. It seems likely that initially the extended family in Bristol looked after George's two children: the infant George and his sister Lizzie, twelve years his senior. Within a few years George senior had established a new home near Abertillery, Monmouthshire. He and his new partner, whose name has sadly not been passed down, appear never to have married, but around 1910 his son, George Henry, came to live with them, only to return to Bristol again in search of work during the First World War (this time lodging with his sister, who was now in her late twenties). George Henry was conscripted into the newly formed RAF and chose to stay on after demobilization. Stationed in Iraq in the early 1920s, he was part of the ground support for the RAF's controversial bombing campaign against Kurdish rebels. By 1925 he was back in Bristol, working as a driver for the Bristol Omnibus Company, but he remained a reservist with the RAF throughout the interwar years, being called up again in 1938 during the Munich Crisis. In moving back to Bristol, George Henry was anticipating the large-scale reversal in cross-Bristol Channel migration brought on by the Welsh coal industry's serious post-war slump, but his own movements probably had more to do with affective kinship ties than economics.[5] Nonetheless, the story of the Fowlers and the Lewises reminds us that even within families with strong local roots—the two families had been living in Bristol from the 1850s and the 1860s respectively—economic necessity often generated significant geographical upheaval in apparently settled working-class communities.

Until the 1920s the lives of my ancestors (the Strawbridges apart) were characterized by dramatic patterns of mobility and change. As elsewhere in the UK, most migration took place on a regional scale—over distances of between 20 and 50 miles, but sometimes people travelled much further in search of a better life.[6] In my family the most dramatic example comes from the 1850s when a great-great-grandfather on my father's side, George Gilvear (born 1836), moved 370 miles from his Edinburgh birthplace to Bristol to find work as a bellows maker. It reminds us that the mobility of recent decades is not as new as one might imagine. What makes it *feel* new is that between 1914 and 1950 families in Britain were less mobile than they had been for generations, despite the upheaval of two world wars and the interwar expansion of the suburbs appearing to suggest the opposite. The reason is simple: rent control. In 1915, as rents soared and strikes by key workers threatened to interrupt war production, the Government brought in legislation pegging working-class rents to their August 1914 level for the duration of the war. Crucially, after the war rent controls remained in place, but *only* on unbroken tenancies. Overnight the Government created a premium on immobility. In a context where something like nine in ten households rented their accommodation it had long been normal to move house on an almost annual basis, even if it was only round the corner; now it became normal to put down roots. As late as 1931 only 11.2 per cent of pre-war working-class houses had been decontrolled (that is, returned to a market rent).[7] A survey conducted in the middle of the Second World War found that more than a third of those living in older, pre-1914 houses had lived at the same address for more than twenty years, and in one pre-war industrial district in the Midlands half the population had lived in the same house for more than twenty years.[8] The increase in home ownership levels in the 1920s and 1930s, rising from 10 to 32 per cent of households, also served to consolidate the shift to more settled, stable patterns of residence.[9]

In the 1960s, when I was a young child, my surviving grandparents, and many of their siblings, all lived within a few streets of each other in Redfield, East Bristol. They lived in houses they had occupied continuously since the interwar years (in many cases first as tenants and later as owners). The relatively stable, face-to-face community of the middle decades of the twentieth century, which came to be hailed by post-war sociologists as 'traditional', was therefore in many respects a new and fleeting phenomenon with no parallel either before or since. Certainly my parents and their siblings, who were all born in the 1920s and 1930s, lived more mobile, changing lives, though it is perhaps striking that only one, the youngest (Patricia, born 1938), ended up moving away from the greater Bristol area. This was still geographical mobility on the local scale—sometimes accompanied by social mobility, sometimes not.

Doreen and Ron

No one's life is 'typical' of anything but themselves. But, for all that, my parents' lives do encapsulate many of the shifts in the texture of everyday life that took hold in the decades immediately after the Second World War—changes that we will see running through the personal testimonies that dominate the chapters that follow. Born near Lawrence Hill, East Bristol, in November 1926, just as the miners' lockout that prompted the General Strike was coming to an end, my father was the second of three brothers. Christened Ronald, he joined Kenneth, born five years earlier at the height of the post-war slump, and was followed two years later by Raymond. Even their names tell us a great deal about social change. For generations, the Lawrences, like most English plebeian families, had been intensely conservative in their choice of given names. Naming was a way of honouring kinsfolk and asserting family traditions. Firstborn children were generally named after the mother or father, and a small number of names recur across generations of Lawrences: Joseph, John, Thomas, and Edward for boys; Ellen, Ann, Elizabeth, and Mary for girls. No one broke from this tradition in five generations. But suddenly, immediately after the First World War, new names came into vogue both within my family and more widely.

It is impossible now to know why names like Kenneth, Ronald, and Raymond appealed to a tinsmith and his wife in 1920s Bristol, but it's hard to avoid the conclusion that much of the appeal lay precisely in the fact that such names signalled a break with custom and tradition (though not a complete break—each boy was given a traditional middle name: hence my father was named Ronald *John* Lawrence).

It may seem trivial, but in choosing modern names from other cultures (Kenneth and Ronald are Scottish names, Raymond is Norman French in origin), Joseph and his wife Emily were quietly asserting their individuality and personal taste against the dictates of 'tradition'. As cultural historian Matt Houlbrook has argued, there are signs that the First World War helped to shape a new relationship with mass culture, especially popular fiction and film, which placed a premium on personal self-fashioning and the expression of individuality.[10] In turn this recalibration of subjectivity encouraged an increasing number of parents to hope that their children might lead lives that were different from, and better than, their own.[11] In many ways, the mid-twentieth century break in working-class naming practices was a product of these deeper cultural shifts. For generations, my mother's family in the paternal line, the Lewises, had consisted of multiple generations with recurring names like George, Henry, and William for boys and Alice, Mary, Edith, and especially Elizabeth for girls. But between the wars, George and Florence, my mother's parents, had four children, all of whom were given non-traditional, modern names not previously seen in either family: Doreen, Desmond, Jean, and Patricia. The oldest, my mother Doreen, was given the middle name of May in honour of her mother's only sister (although it probably helped that she had been born in May 1927).

Elsewhere the same change seems to have happened a little later. In inner London districts such as Bermondsey and Bethnal Green traditional naming practices held out until the Second World War. Between the wars classic London names familiar from the novels of Dickens or Gissing, such as Ada, Albert, Fred, and Lizzie remained dominant, but the fashion for novelty took hold in the 1940s, and observers noted that the new generation were christened with more modern names like Brian, Jonathan, Carol, and Marilyn.[12] It was a small change, but one which nicely captured the opening up of working-class life to new cultural influences such as popular fiction, film, and radio.[13]

Naming apart, in other respects my father's life was all too typical of generations of his working-class forebears. A gifted artist who, in his teens, developed a lucrative sideline drawing 'glamorous' pictures of movie stars, he had expected to take up a place at the West of England College of Art at 16. But tragedy intervened. In late May 1942 he came home to find his father choking to death in the family kitchen after an old shrapnel wound had suddenly ruptured, causing a severe haemorrhage. My dad was 15, his father Joseph just 50. Art school now had to be forgotten in favour of finding a well-paid job (this also meant that my father had no chance to follow in the footsteps of his father, his older brother, or generations of Strawbridges, by becoming apprenticed to a skilled trade). There was nothing unique about his story—thousands of families faced similar tragedies every year.

24

Like almost everyone he knew, my father left school with no formal qualifications, only a 'certificate of character' from his elementary school which he kept all his life (he was said to be 'lively, keen, reliable and trustworthy'). Perhaps crucially, he also had a character reference from Mervyn Stockwood, the local parish priest, Labour Party stalwart, and future 'Red' Bishop of Southwark (see Figure 3). When tragedy struck it was probably this reference, combined with Stockwood's socialist connections, which helped my father to find a secure and reasonably well-paid job with the local Co-operative Society. When he died, in 2002, I found Stockwood's 'character' folded neatly inside the Bible that the priest had presented to my father at his Anglican confirmation in 1940. After a short paragraph establishing my father's connections with the Church, all it said was: 'I know Lawrence personally and I have no hesitation in saying that he is thoroughly reliable and trustworthy and that he will put his back into his job. He is well above the average and I can thoroughly recommend him in every way.' We may hear the lofty patrician tones of mid-century English socialism; my dad heard the ticket to a decent job.

My father was also an accomplished sportsman. He became a southern army boxing champion during his National Service, played local league football into his thirties, and league cricket on Clifton Downs well into his forties. It was only at his funeral in September 2002 that I discovered that, on demobilization in 1948, he had turned down the offer of a contract with the team we both supported, Bristol Rovers, in favour of going back to his job with the Co-op. A 'job for life' was still highly prized in the years immediately after the Second World War. No one was sure that full employment would last, and in any case lower-league football was even worse paid then than it is today. It was a pragmatic choice, the first of many he would make over the next half-century.

Probably the main reason for choosing the Co-op over life in League Division Three (South) was that my father wanted to marry and settle down. He had got to know my mother during the war, when they were both teenagers, and sustained the relationship by post throughout his four years overseas with the army between 1944 and 1948 (initially in Burma, then partition India, and finally northern Nigeria (see Figures 4 and 5)). Against considerable resistance from his widowed mother, supposedly based on my mother being from a 'lower class' family because her father was 'only' a bus driver, my parents finally married in April 1951, seven years after they began courting. But the acute post-war housing shortage meant that, like thousands of couples, they could not find anywhere to live. Perhaps if relations had been less frosty between mother and daughter-in-law they would have moved into my father's childhood home (my mother's parental home was too crowded, with two teenage sisters still living at home). Instead, they took furnished lodgings on

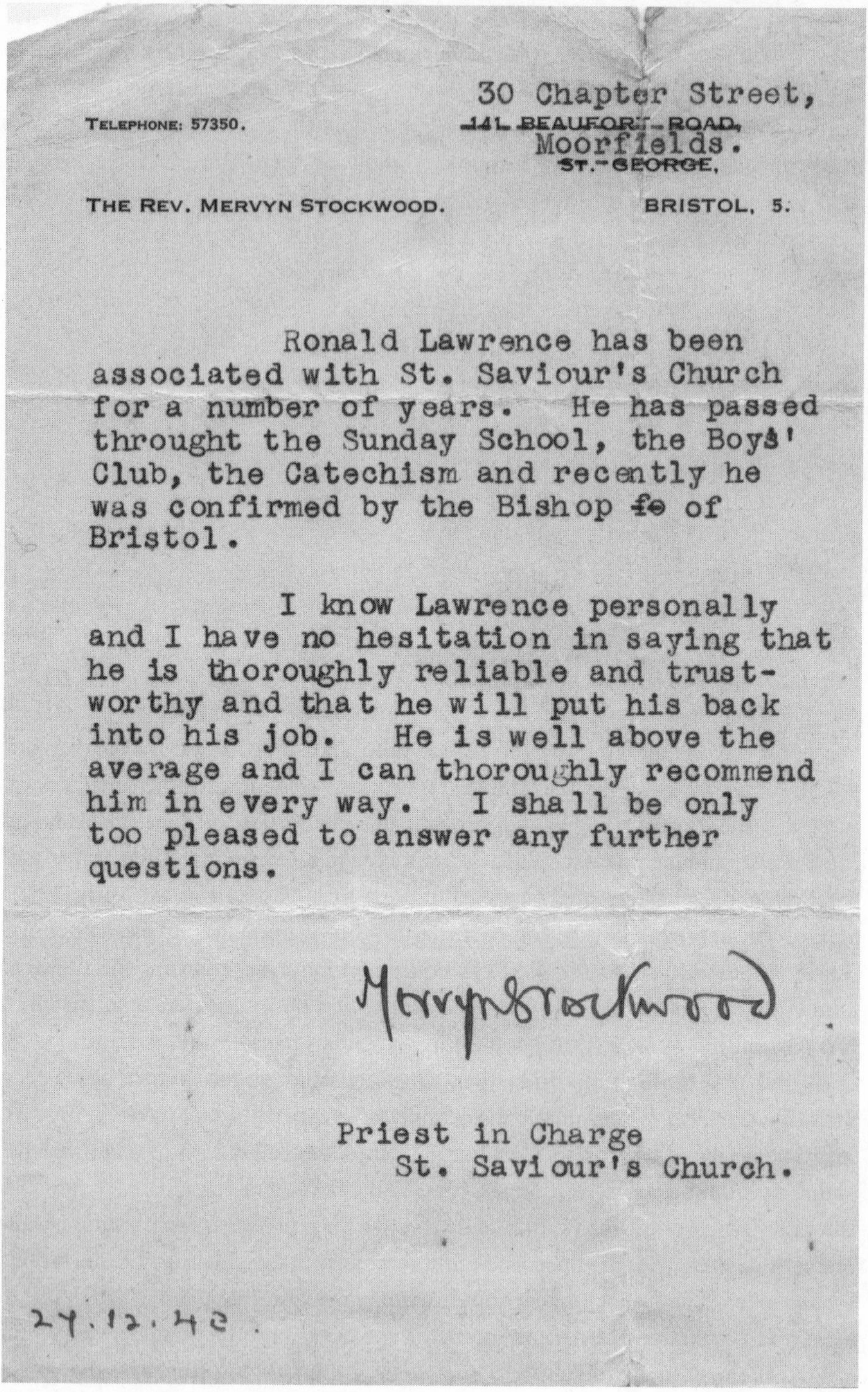

TELEPHONE: 57350.

THE REV. MERVYN STOCKWOOD.

30 Chapter Street,
141 BEAUFORT ROAD,
Moorfields.
ST.-GEORGE,
BRISTOL, 5.

Ronald Lawrence has been associated with St. Saviour's Church for a number of years. He has passed throught the Sunday School, the Boys' Club, the Catechism and recently he was confirmed by the Bishop fe of Bristol.

I know Lawrence personally and I have no hesitation in saying that he is thoroughly reliable and trustworthy and that he will put his back into his job. He is well above the average and I can thoroughly recommend him in every way. I shall be only too pleased to answer any further questions.

Mervyn Stockwood

Priest in Charge
St. Saviour's Church.

24.12.42.

Figure 3. Mervyn Stockwood's testimonial for Ron Lawrence, dated 27 December 1940 [private collection]

Figure 4. Ron Lawrence, May 1948; sent from Nigeria to celebrate my mother's twenty-first birthday [private collection]

the other side of the city and joined the thousands of young post-war couples searching for a more permanent home. With none to be had on the open market (either to rent or buy) this meant joining the waiting lists run by the council and by local private builders. Desperate for somewhere to set up home, my parents saw little difference between the two options. All that mattered in the early 1950s was to get a house, any house (when the Tories famously promised to build 300,000 houses a year at the 1951 election they too made no distinction between council and private provision—for the first few years at least, all that mattered was to build).[14]

It's a sobering thought that, had their name come up with the council, they would probably have started a family immediately and I might never have been born. Instead they got the offer of a new-build semi-detached house in Hanham (see Figure 6), a semi-rural suburb on the edge of Bristol's newly designated green belt. Having a mortgage to service made it impossible for my mother to give up her well-paid job as a telephonist (she earned more than my father for most of the 1950s), and so, like other couples caught by the same dilemma, they had no children for the first ten years of married life despite the baby boom that was happening all around them.[15]

Figure 5. Doreen Lawrence, July 1945; signed and posted to my father in India to be kept in his wallet 'for the duration' [private collection]

Figure 6. The house on Memorial Road, Hanham, after my father had built his own garage (*c.*1955); the first car, a second-hand Austin A30, would come later [private collection]

With two full-time jobs they were able to take regular holidays, pay down their mortgage, and even run a small car by the late 1950s. Commentators began to talk of Britain enjoying a new 'age of affluence', which was certainly stretching things for them and millions like them, but by the late 1950s they enjoyed a level of comfort and security unimaginable to most of their forebears, and still unobtainable for many of their contemporaries.[16]

By chance, my father had trained as a butcher after rejoining the Co-op, never knowing that this had been the trade of his ancestors for at least 200 years. In fact, he knew nothing about the main branch of the family at Worle beyond the vague fact that Mary Ann Kent, the aunt who had adopted his orphaned father, had had relatives 'that way' (until recently the bonds of working-class kinship often struggled with distance, even when, as in this case, we are talking barely 20 miles).[17] In the late 1950s he was promoted to be the manager of a new Co-op supermarket at Keynsham, a small town 3.5 miles from Hanham. I've long assumed that it was this that finally made having children possible—first me in 1961, then my brother Adrian two and a bit years later. My mother was 34 when she had her first child. This was definitely not typical in 1961, when the average age of first-time mothers was barely 24 (in the mid-2010s it was still less than 29).[18]

It's intriguing to think that, for my parents, Dad becoming a store manager meant only one thing: finally being able to live out the dream of post-war suburban life by starting a family. But to a sociologist it would have signalled that they had crossed the great invisible barrier between the working class and the middle class. The class of a household was still determined entirely by male occupation in the 1960s, so it's ironic to think that they would have become 'middle class' just as they hit hard times by having to forgo my mother's white-collar salary while at the same time having to meet the considerable costs associated with having kids (the smart new pram was still mandatory in early 1960s suburban England). Over the next two decades my father would cross and recross the sociologists' invisible boundary between the working class and the middle class. I am sure he never noticed. In 1965, just after my brother was born, my parents took the one big gamble of their lives. After twenty-three years, my dad chucked in his job with the Co-op, and they sold their suburban house to plough everything into a run-down drapers shop on Two Mile Hill Road, Kingswood. It sounds faintly bucolic, but trust me, it wasn't (this is the A420, the main road that runs east from the city centre). Many people had this fantasy in the 1960s—as we will see, it was especially common among Luton car-workers keen to get off the production-line treadmill—but not many tried to make it come true.

The nation's high streets had not yet succumbed to the chain-store juggernaut, and at first the gamble paid off. Business was good for 'Doreens'. For a few years my dad even managed to buy a new car as a business expense (always a Luton-built Vauxhall Viva). But it didn't last. By the early 1970s, as inflation gathered pace, he began supplementing the shop's income by selling insurance door to door. He then tried his hand selling office paper, before taking a job on the night shift of Fry's chocolate factory back in Keynsham. My mum kept the shop ticking over, but things were tight. Finally, they closed the shop and my mum went back to work as a telephonist with the GPO (General Post Office, forerunner of British Telecom). The gamble had failed—they were back where they'd started, except they'd swapped their quiet suburban semi for an empty shop on a busy main road in East Bristol. Finally, my dad took a job he hated—night shift in a cold store loading lorries with frozen food—because it paid enough money for them to be able to sell up, get a new mortgage, and move to a 1960s suburban semi—this time in the pleasant commuter village of Frampton Cotterell on Bristol's northern fringe (see Figure 7).

It was the ultimate pragmatic decision. He could only live the life he wanted by doing a job that made him so physically exhausted and sleep-deprived that he couldn't fully enjoy it. Millions make the same bargain every day. He was 48. He

Figure 7. My father planting out the garden after moving to Frampton Cotterell (*c.*1977) [private collection]

did this job until he was too old to withstand the intense pace any longer, retiring due to ill health in 1991, aged 64. Unlike in the 1950s, this time he was unambiguously the family's main breadwinner, but my mother continued to work part-time until the late 1980s. She enjoyed the camaraderie of working on a big switchboard, first at the Bristol Royal Infirmary and later at Bristol University, but she also derived satisfaction from knowing that her efforts made it a little easier to pay the household bills.

Mobility, place, and the sense of 'belonging'

It would be easy to overplay the contrast between my parents' life of mobility and change, and their own parents' apparently fixed, unchanging lives. Yes, my grandfathers both had the same job for the great bulk of their adult lives, while their wives did not go back to work after marriage. It is also true that Emily Lawrence lived in the same terraced house in Gerrish Avenue, Redfield, for forty-two years (from 1935 until her death in 1977), while Florence Lewis lived a block away, at 1 Cooksley Road, for exactly the same length of time (from 1929 until her death in 1971).

But these terraced streets of modest six-roomed, turn-of-the-century houses were socially a world away from the Dean Lane area, where my grandparents had grown up, courted, and begun their married lives. Though barely a hundred yards from the Redfield streets where they would live out the bulk of their adult lives, the dense network of nineteenth-century courts and alleys east of Lawrence Hill station had already been labelled a slum by the time my parents, Ron and Doreen, were born there, a street apart, in the mid-1920s (on Bishop Street and Deacon Street respectively, see Map 2).

As newly-weds, their parents would have been unlikely to enjoy the benefit of controlled rents, and hence had less reason to stay put than many. Initially, my father's family moved out to a new suburban council estate being built a few miles away, but like many families they failed to settle.[19] They complained that family and work were too far away, and that the new houses had been built before any shops or pubs. Disillusioned, they returned to live in the same slum district they had recently left, living there until they had saved enough money to secure a mortgage on a pre-war terraced house on Gerrish Avenue. Joseph Lawrence's promotion to foreman tinsmith at around the same time (1935) doubtless helped smooth the process.

That George Lewis, the 'lower class' bus driver, had been able to buy a superior, bay-windowed house on Cooksley Road six years earlier probably added to my paternal grandmother's sense of petty jealousy.[20] Apart from Methodist sobriety, the key to George's good fortune had been Ernie Bevin, the tough-minded leader

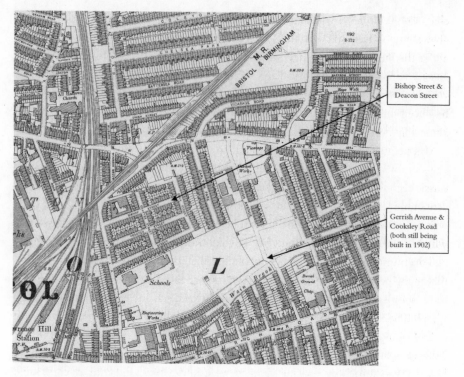

Bishop Street &
Deacon Street

Gerrish Avenue &
Cooksley Road
(both still being
built in 1902)

Map 2. Annotated 1902 Ordnance Survey map of East Bristol (detail) [reproduced by permission of the National Library of Scotland Ordnance Survey 25 inch Gloucestershire LXXII.13 (published: 1903) rDoD: 109729816. National Library of Scotland

(and architect) of the Transport and General Workers' Union. Before his meteoric rise to national prominence during the war, Bevin had been the driving force behind the unionization of dock and transport workers in the Bristol area.[21] It was largely thanks to the 'T&G' that George's employer, the Bristol Omnibus Company, offered its drivers good wages and secure employment—the key ingredients for obtaining a mortgage, then as now.[22] George would have been one of Jack Common's 'pease-pudding men', able to enjoy a 'soft' life thanks to the union.[23] Certainly, it is easy to imagine that that is how Emily Lawrence saw things as she struggled with the unfamiliar pain of bereavement and poverty in the years immediately after the Second World War.

But how, one might ask, can stories gleaned from family history speak to larger historical questions, such as the central issue at the heart of this book: how ordinary people struck the balance between self and community across the twentieth century? As Alison Light has brilliantly demonstrated, the small stories of family history can be used not just to deepen but also to recast our understanding of broader social change.[24] Personally, I gained much from listening to my parents' stories about growing up in East Bristol in the 1930s and 1940s. In particular, the way they talked about the different streets they had lived on made me come to doubt some of the central assumptions of historical and sociological writing about so-called traditional working-class communities. I also came to doubt the idea that working-class people had been unreflexive about the communities they lived in: that community had in some way been lived 'instinctively' rather than consciously acknowledged.

My parents' testimony appeared to stand in stark contrast to social historian Robert Colls's moving account of first reading *The Uses of Literacy* (1957), Richard Hoggart's classic reconstruction of mid-twentieth-century working-class culture, as an adolescent grammar school boy in South Shields, County Durham, in the mid-1960s. Colls writes, 'In the beginning, I didn't know I belonged to a "culture", but at the moment when I realized I did, I felt estranged.'[25] By contrast, both my parents' reminiscences and the transcripts of social-science encounters that inform this book strongly suggest that many people did not need to go to grammar school, or read Hoggart, to be able to recognize (and talk about) the distinction between self and community.

Certainly, growing up in East Bristol I never shared the simple, unreflexive sense of 'belonging' that Colls recalls from South Shields. From an early age—even before I started school—I was inculcated with a sense that we lived in an area, Two Mile Hill, that was somehow 'rougher' than we were. Lurid stories of Saturday-night knife fights outside the local pub—at least one of which ended in a fatality—seemed to underscore the reality of this family narrative. So too did the routinized violence acted out in the playground once I started at primary school the following year. It probably didn't help that classmates claimed to think I was American because my Bristolian accent was a little less broad than theirs (presumably the influence of my GPO-trained mother), but I certainly never experienced the unreflexive immersion in place that Colls recalls from his childhood in South Shields.

When I first read Hoggart, aged 17, I did so knowingly—my goal was to find affirmation (and an authentic language) for an inchoate sense of class identity I had developed as a grammar-school 'scholarship boy' from the 'wrong' (i.e. the east) side of town. But it was only later, studying class in a more impersonal, detached way at university, that I began to quiz my parents about their own sense of class, and particularly about their memories of growing up in working-class East Bristol between the wars. One story that seemed to illuminate both reflexivity and the diversity of working-class cultures concerned the apparently innocuous topic of children's street games. My father frequently told me stories about how his childhood had been dominated by impromptu street games of football and cricket. On one occasion he explained how local parents would club together if a child

33

accidentally broke a neighbour's window while playing. It was a type of informal insurance system, though he explained it more prosaically by saying that no one could have afforded to replace a window on their own. But then one day he told me about an occasion when he got into trouble for a misdirected shot that broke a neighbour's window, landing his father with a hefty glazier's bill. As the young do, I leapt on this apparent contradiction, only to be told: 'Oh, we'd moved by then—things were different on Gerrish Avenue; *teachers* lived on that street.'

To my eyes this 'Avenue' seemed unambiguously 'working class'—the name was misleading, there can *never* have been any trees (though it did perhaps point towards social pretensions wholly absent from the nearby 'slum' streets where my father had been born). Long rows of small Edwardian terraces on one side faced an ugly factory on the other. But though it was only a few hundred yards from his birthplace on Bishop Street, where everyone had 'chipped in' in a crisis, this was indeed another social world. The household returns from the 1911 census (the most recent available) don't record any schoolteachers living on Gerrish Avenue, but there were shopkeepers, clerks, a music tutor, lots of warehousemen, and even an estate agent. It was still an overwhelmingly working-class street: only one in four heads of household had a non-manual job (less than one in five if one excludes warehousemen; see Table 2). The big difference was that compared with Bishop Street there were ten times fewer labourers and other unskilled workers living on Gerrish Avenue (less than 4 per cent of workers, compared with 40 per cent on Bishop

Table 2. Percentage of workers in different occupational class categories on two East Bristol streets, 1911 (heads of household *only* in parentheses)

	Bishop Street	Gerrish Avenue
Non-manual	0 (0)	22.5 (26.0)
Skilled manual	39.7 (48.1)	38.7 (48.0)
Semi-skilled manual	20.6 (11.1)	32.4 (22.0)
Unskilled manual	39.7 (40.7)	6.3 (4.0)
TOTAL	100 (99.9)	99.9 (100)

Note: Based on a modified version of 1921 Registrar General occupational classification in W. A. Armstrong, 'The uses of information about occupation', pt. 1, app. A; warehousemen classified as non-manual following the practice in Board of Trade, *Enquiry into the Cost of Living of the Working Classes*, PP1908 Cd.3864, vol. cvii; also miners as skilled manual; gardeners, machinists, packers, and various 'assistants' as semi-skilled; charwomen, general domestic service as unskilled.

Source: 1911 Population Census Enumerators' returns, St George, Bristol.

Street). In turn, there were *no* shopkeepers, warehousemen, or clerks living on Bishop Street in 1911. People also had smaller families on Gerrish Avenue: an average of 1.8 children against 4.4 on Bishop Street. Since the houses here were also a little larger (with six rather than five rooms), and less likely to be subdivided, there was also considerably less overcrowding.[26] It is not difficult to imagine that my father was right about the contrasting social character of the two streets despite their proximity and the heavy predominance of manual workers on both. But what is striking about the story is less the suggestion that micro-environments matter when it comes to understanding the dynamics of popular culture than the suggestion that a 10-year-old boy living in the mid-1930s could apparently be fully conscious of these micro-differences in communal expectations and mores.

My mother also told stories that offered insights into how people negotiated the social pressures of living in face-to-face communities. For instance, she recalled from a young age being asked to take a flagon to the beer shop at the end of the road so that her nominally teetotal, Methodist father could enjoy the quiet pleasure of a hard-earned pint without being seen to cross the threshold of a public house. Since he was not, by nature, a lazy man it must be assumed that this was his way of reconciling communal ideas about 'respectability' with his personal sense of how life should be lived. Both she and my father also recalled the various small ways in which people upheld local social norms which allowed neighbours to affirm each other's 'respectability', and perhaps more importantly their shared sense of belonging. In both Cooksley Road and Gerrish Avenue, women regularly swept the pavement in front of their houses, as well as keeping their own doorstep and paintwork spotless (see Figure 8). They also hung clean nets (net curtains) in their front windows, in part to maintain privacy in houses that sat close by the pavement, but also to signal that they were on top of life and dirt, rather than the other way around.[27] Similarly, into the 1970s, it remained conventional in these streets to signal a death in the household by leaving the front curtains drawn until the deceased family member had been buried.

My mother told such stories with pride for the place and the values that had made her. But, again, we should not assume that she had an unproblematic relationship with the community that gave these social practices their powerful symbolic meaning. She was also happy to recall how, during the heavy aerial bombardment of East Bristol in 1940–1, she refused to use the communal street shelter because many of the families that did so were dirty and uncouth. She much preferred to take her chances hiding under the stairs at 1 Cooksley Road. Although she knew whole families who had been killed by direct hits on their houses, she was adamant that she would rather die alone in her own house than be cooped up all night in the local

Figure 8. Woman cleaning the pavement outside her house with bleach and a donkey stone, Bolton, 1938 [Humphrey Spender, Copyright Bolton Council]

shelter. Or at least that was the family story passed down to the next generation and rehearsed by her younger siblings at her funeral in 2015. It was a way of signalling a particular type of belonging, one framed very much on *her* terms rather than those of the wider community.

Like their five siblings, my parents moved away from the terraced streets of East Bristol once they were old enough to marry and set up home. Two of the six new couples formed from the Lawrence and Lewis households stayed in the services and were stationed far from Bristol; one took a council house on the large Hartcliffe estate on the city's southern edge, but the three who bought houses in the 1950s all chose to move out to the same rapidly expanding eastern suburb: Hanham. Until they started having children at the end of the decade the three couples saw a great deal of each other, even taking summer holidays together. Nor had the move to the suburbs cut them off from parents (the siblings' spouses had also all grown up in Redfield). Though technically in Gloucestershire, rather than the city proper, Hanham was only 2.5 miles from Redfield, with good direct bus links. In fact, my mother regularly walked to and from her parents' house in the 1950s and early 1960s, claiming she enjoyed the exercise, but also underscoring the strong pull that family still asserted despite her flight to the suburbs. As social historian Selina Todd has argued, it is too easy to accept the sociologists' framing of working-class life as fixed and unchanging, bounded by the tight confines of a few well-known streets.[28] In practice, identities were more mutable, and connections more easily sustained through social upheaval, than many supposed at the time.[29]

Historically, geography and sport are strongly intertwined in Bristol. In football, the working-class south supports City, the working-class east Rovers (for the middle-class west, at least historically, 'football' meant rugby union). In cricket, which always had greater cross-class appeal thanks in part to the improbable feats of local doctor W. G. Grace (Gloucestershire CCC 1870–99), loyalties were split along a north–south axis, with the meandering River Avon marking the frontier between the rival county sides. Though a county in its own right since the fourteenth century, the districts lying north of the river retained their historical identification with Gloucestershire, while those lying to the south looked more towards Somerset. Certainly my Redfield-born ancestors all identified strongly with Rovers, and rather more loosely with the Gloucestershire county cricket sides of Wally Hammond (1903–65), Tom Graveney (1927–2015), and more recently South African Mike Procter (born 1946). I always assumed that it was these place-based loyalties that led my parents to live almost the whole of their married lives in different parts of what one might call Bristolian Gloucestershire (Hanham, Kingswood, Frampton Cotterell, Yate, and finally—for my mother alone— W. G. Grace's Downend). But now that family history has demonstrated that the Lawrences, Fowlers, and Lewises all had their roots in Somerset (and the Strawbridges most likely hailed originally from Devon judging by maps of surname frequency),[30] it seems likely that personal and practical ties always mattered more than geographical identities: being close not just to siblings but also to bus routes offering speedy journeys to see family members back in Redfield. By the time car ownership had freed my parents and their siblings from many of these practical concerns 'Bristolian' Gloucestershire had become their 'manor'—this was the world they knew and understood. Concrete as much as sentimental attachments bound them to place.

But bounded they still were. My parents moved more often than most, but they still never lived more than 11 miles from Redfield, and all the houses they lived in could be encompassed by a circle with a radius of less than 6 miles. The siblings that joined them in Hanham in the 1950s stayed there for the rest of their lives. Their four children, my first cousins and my brother, now all in their fifties and sixties, also still live and work locally (including the only one to go to university, who studied at Bath and settled in Hanham).[31] In David Goodhart's terms these families represent the 'somewheres', people with strong local roots and tight family networks (although, predictably, their values and attitudes are much more personal and diverse than Goodhart's schematic, polarizing model would suggest).[32] I, on the other hand, am undoubtedly one of Goodhart's classic 'anywheres'. Education took me away from Bristol in 1980 and I have not lived there since. But whether mobility corresponds to rootlessness, as Goodhart suggests, is more debatable. In the thirty-seven years since I went to university I have spent twenty-six years living in Cambridge, eleven years in Liverpool, and a little over a year abroad (true, I have just made the one big gamble of my own life by relocating to Dartmoor, but I intend that to be a final move taking me back to my native West Country). In my wider family, the cousins who have been mobile have not been particularly nomadic—they too have spent the bulk of their lives in one or two places.

Goodhart's somewhere–anywhere dichotomy undoubtedly speaks to some deep truths about the divisions running through twenty-first-century Britain, but it does so at the expense of flattening the complexity of people's everyday lives. Goodhart himself acknowledges that perhaps a quarter of the population are 'in-betweeners', displaying characteristics of both 'somewhere' and 'anywhere' lifestyles and outlooks.[33] But he is less inclined to acknowledge the diversity of attitudes and aspirations among both the mobile 'anywheres' and the supposedly fixed 'somewheres'. The fixity of 'somewhere' lives is boldly mythologized, with little recognition of the churn beneath the surface revealed when we engage with people's life stories, or with family history. At the same time, the rootless mobility of 'anywhere' lives is also exaggerated. As we will see time and again over the chapters that follow, those uprooted in the search for better homes and jobs often proved especially committed to building community ties in their newly adopted homes. People with considerable social and economic resources often develop a highly conscious, personal identification with the places in which they choose to settle[34]—'choose' being the operative word here. This 'elective belonging' is in many ways the epitome of the interplay of individualism and communalism we find in post-war Britain. Here belonging is reworked as part of a new personal politics of self-realization, rather than being rooted in mythologies about what it means to be 'born and bred' somewhere. Crucially, this sense of personal choice and self-making is not confined to privileged fractions of the middle class, which is not to suggest that it has been (or is) available to everyone.[35]

This interplay between individualism and community, between self and society, runs through the contemporary testimonies from which the following chapters are woven. But to end this discussion of everyday life seen through the lens of family history I want briefly to return to the story of Ron and Doreen in their last years. Building on the pioneering work of figures such as Joseph Sheldon and Peter Townsend, sociologists have written extensively on the community life of older people in recent years; on the strength of people's social networks and their ability to adapt to rapid social and demographic change.[36] For a decade after my father left the cold store my parents enjoyed a good old age together. Living in the same house for over twenty years, they had built good relations with their neighbours and played an active part in the social life of their local church (they were both devout Catholic converts by this time). But money was always short, and in 2000, when my father realized he could not afford to replace his clapped-out Ford Sierra, they decided to cash in their equity by moving from the desirable commuter village of Frampton Cotterell to Yate, a small town just over 3 miles away. They bought a 1960s end-terrace house a few hundred yards south of the town centre, in a neighbourhood built under the Government's post-war 'expanded towns' initiative (a housing programme designed to relieve overcrowding in Britain's larger cities by decamping populations beyond the newly designated green belt).[37]

My parents having lived in Frampton Cotterell for a quarter of a century and grown old with many of their neighbours, the move represented a major disruption of their social networks. It didn't help that Yate was in a different Catholic parish, or that their area was dominated by couples with young families, but the house was modern and comfortable. My mother struggled with the fact that south Yate lacked the social prestige of their former address, but took solace in the working-class creed of taking people as she found them, which turned out to be friendly and generous-spirited. In addition the Church quickly helped my parents to make friends in both north and south Yate. It was a good example of how community, in this case rooted in faith, can transcend physical place.[38]

My father was now 74 and was beginning to struggle with health problems, including Type-2 diabetes and psoriasis. Barely a year after they had moved to Yate he was diagnosed with late-stage lung cancer. Four months later, in September 2002, he died. My mother continued to live in the house they had chosen together for another ten years, till she was 85. During that time she benefited from many small kindnesses from her neighbours. Both her brother Desmond and her younger son Adrian visited weekly. Friends from church were also frequent visitors, and there was usually someone to take her to Mass or prayer group. By sustaining these connections of blood and friendship, painstakingly accrued over a lifetime, she was able to affirm her personal independence well into her eighties despite failing powers of sight and mobility. It was another powerful example of self and society being mutually interdependent rather than antagonistic.

Eventually, however, her increasing frailty prompted a final move to sheltered accommodation in Downend. Here, my mother sometimes struggled to adapt to the enforced communalism of life. She never wholly abandoned the world-view of the adolescent girl who had refused to use Cooksley Road's communal air-raid shelter in 1940–1. But she nonetheless made many friends. Newly built and well equipped, the complex accommodated people with a wide range of care needs and from a diverse range of social backgrounds. There cannot be many places in twenty-first-century Britain where people from such different class backgrounds mix freely together— opera and bingo clubs flourished side by side, and even managed to have some overlapping membership. Instinctively, my mother knew who was 'rougher' than her and who was 'posher' (her terms). At times she found interacting with both a social strain. Navigating this unfamiliar social environment cannot have been easy in her late eighties.

For the first time, at least in my hearing, she came to express these status tensions by making explicit statements about her own class identity. For her, the language of class proved to be a valuable cultural resource to bolster her sense of personal dignity and integrity, and to help navigate unfamiliar and sometimes fraught social relationships. What surprised me was that in doing so she chose to declare herself proud to be a 'working-class woman' with strong roots and strong values. For her at least, class and belonging were deeply intertwined; together they gave her a sense of self-identity that in turn made her feel more comfortable making new social connections. It was a perfect example of the indivisibility of selfhood and community in an individualist society like modern Britain.

CHAPTER 2

COMMUNITY AND PRIVATE LIFE IN POST-WAR ENGLAND

S ocial scientists had studied working-class lives, and especially working-class living standards, for generations, but in the years after the Second World War they were animated by a new spirit shaped in large part by two interrelated phenomena: the wartime celebration of working people as the backbone of the nation in arms, and Labour's dramatic, landslide election victory of July 1945 (Labour's first outright victory which was secured with the greatest swing of opinion in British election history).[1] The social scientists who chose to study urban working-class districts in the 1940s and 1950s went in search of 'community'—or, to be more specific, in search of the community spirit they believed had animated people's defiant response to the Blitz and then underwritten Labour's decisive electoral breakthrough.[2] Wartime propaganda had done much to celebrate the 'cockney' spirit,[3] but many social scientists also had direct personal experience of war on the home front. This was true for both Raymond Firth and Michael Young, the key figures behind the major post-war investigations of Bermondsey and Bethnal Green which provide the personal testimony that runs through this chapter. In 1941, Young spent time volunteering with the Friends' Ambulance Unit in London's East End while he worked on the pamphlet 'London under Bombing'.[4] Firth, a renowned anthropologist, had been in the field in Malaya at the outbreak of war, but returned to London in late 1940, after a tortuous Atlantic convoy crossing. Speaking in his late nineties, he still had vivid memories of sleeping in his father-in-law's sandbagged cellar in Highgate as bombs fell on less fortunate parts of the capital.[5]

Firth was first in the field. In 1947, three years after being appointed to the chair of anthropology at the London School of Economics, he assembled a large team of LSE graduates, postdoctoral students, and staff members to investigate the relationship between kinship ties and community in the working-class riverside district of Bermondsey (see Map 3). Altogether twenty-two LSE anthropologists from seven countries took part in the project, with Firth (himself a New Zealander) carrying out detailed work on three families and their extended kin.[6] Firth's team initially hypothesized that existing studies of working-class life, such as Margery Spring Rice's 1939

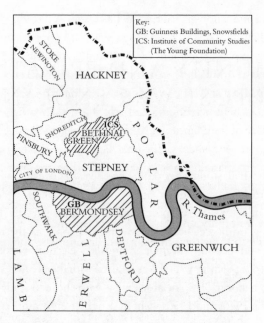

Map 3. East and south-east London showing Bermondsey, Bethnal Green, and the location of Guinness Buildings and the Institute of Community Studies

Penguin paperback *Working-Class Wives*, had played down the importance of the wider family as a source of social support and as a bulwark of community feeling.[7] They also argued that anthropologists still possessed only the shakiest understanding of how kinship systems worked in advanced urban societies like Britain. But from the outset some members of the team were sceptical about idealized conceptions of 'community', while others played down the importance of kinship to social solidarity.[8] This diversity of opinion, coupled with the fact that, unlike most British social scientists, Firth's colleagues did not see research as a handmaiden of Labour's post-war project of socialist reconstruction, made it easy for them to drop their original hypotheses about kinship and community when supporting evidence proved elusive.[9]

By contrast, Michael Young was much more strongly committed both to Labour politics and to an idealized model of working-class community (he had played a major role in the drafting of Labour's 1945 election manifesto as director of the Labour Research Department). Perhaps predictably his ideas proved much less mutable faced by the messy reality of people's everyday lives.[10] After stepping down from his position in the Labour Party in 1951, Young started a PhD at the LSE and simultaneously founded an Institute of Community Studies in Bethnal

Green with friend and fellow libertarian socialist Peter Willmott. They seem to have been drawn to Bethnal Green, in London's East End, by reading Ruth Glass and Maureen Frenkel's powerful account of its vibrant community life published at the end of the Second World War.[11] In a study designed to influence post-war reconstruction in the badly war-torn borough, Glass and Frenkel had celebrated Bethnal Green as 'a place where neighbours can rely upon each other, where there is a general atmosphere of friendliness, of strength and independence'. They argued that 'however aged, poor and shabby, [Bethnal Green] has solved one of the urgent problems of modern planning: how to create an urban community'.[12] In addition, Young and Willmott had also read P. J. O. Self's 1945 study of voluntary services in the borough, which was only slightly less glowing in its praise for Bethnal Green's strong 'sense of community' and its 'village' atmosphere.[13]

Young and Willmott saw their mission as delineating the contours of this 'urban community', not just to understand it, but also, crucially, to underscore Glass and Frenkel's original political argument that everything possible should be done to ensure its preservation. Their fieldwork was conducted in two sweeps in 1953 and 1955 and focused on Bethnal Green families waiting to be rehoused. The research would inform probably the single most influential account of Britain's post-war urban, working-class communities, the 1957 classic *Family and Kinship in East London* (Penguin paperback, 1962). This book is estimated to have sold over half a million copies and for many years was a staple text on British social work training courses.[14] In it, Young and Willmott stressed the continued importance of the extended family in sustaining tight-knit, face-to-face local communities in old working-class districts like Bethnal Green. In many ways their work became the definitive statement about working-class life as place-bound, homogeneous, and communal.

By contrast, Raymond Firth came to stress the relative *isolation* of the nuclear family, and the powerful tension between community feeling and the strong impulse towards privacy and individual self-expression.[15] But if the two published studies differed sharply in their conclusions, the same cannot be said about the original personal testimony surviving in their respective field-notes. Not that the field-notes offer decisive support to either interpretation. On the contrary, what they show us is the remarkable diversity of lifestyles and attitudes to be found among the people of both districts. This diversity exposes the absurdity of imagining that there was ever such a thing as a single 'working-class culture' or 'working-class community'—despite the ubiquity of such terms in both contemporary and retrospective accounts. At the same time, the testimony from Bermondsey and Bethnal Green is difficult to reconcile with the claim that the idea of 'community' is entirely a romantic, retrospective myth. Place mattered to people, and much of that importance was bound up in often emotionally charged social relationships with family and friends. Lived community was much messier and much less inclusive than myths of close-knit community might suggest, but it still played a vital part in people's everyday lives.

Although we cannot hope to distil the outlines of a unified, homogeneous culture from the testimony collected in post-war Bermondsey and Bethnal Green, we can identify meaningful patterns in the ways in which people talked about key aspects of their lives, including community, place, and family. It is striking that people did generally recognize what the sociologists would call normative—that is generally upheld—codes of behaviour, but they saw these as operating at a micro-level—in their street or block of flats, rather than on a broader scale. Like my father in his recollections about life in 1930s Redfield, people who had moved were especially likely to discuss the need to adapt to unfamiliar local customs, but even long-term residents could be reflexive about the need to conform to the expectations of neighbours, especially if they chose to live by different codes at home. Returning to the surviving testimony from these projects conducted on the streets of cockney London in the first decade after the 'People's War' can help us to understand how ordinary people sought to reconcile the competing claims of community and individualism in districts conventionally held up as the epitome of close-knit, face-to-face sociability.

Legacies of war

When Firth began his Bermondsey project, the Second World War was still fresh in people's memory. His team concentrated their research on a small estate of 'model dwellings' owned and managed by the Guinness Trust, a philanthropic housing charity (see Figure 9). The Snowsfields estate had been built in 1898 as six blocks providing 355 tenement flats, but two blocks had been completely destroyed by wartime bombing, including a V-1 raid in August 1944 which had left fourteen dead and fifty-two injured.[16] Across the borough, it is estimated that more than 900 people died in wartime bombing raids, with more than 3,000 injured. Nearly a quarter of Bermondsey's housing stock had been destroyed or rendered unusable, along with half the schools and at least 300 factories and warehouses.[17] In 1947, the scars of war would have been visible all along Snowsfields, including the rubble-strewn site where Blocks A and B of the Guinness Buildings had once stood. One of Firth's early informants had seen her teenage daughter killed in the V-1 raid, and had herself been severely injured. Other residents had only moved into the Buildings because their former homes had been destroyed in the war.[18]

Figure 9. Guinness Buildings on Snowsfields, Bermondsey, 2014 [private collection]

As one might imagine, war brought considerable flux to Bermondsey. People talked of losing touch with relatives who had enlisted or moved away for work. Mrs Buckland, a widow in her late fifties, had lost contact with her brother and his family in 1940 and now knew only that they were somewhere 'up north'.[19] But the war loomed large in other ways. There were signs that the wartime celebration of the cockney spirit fed locals' pride, not just in their resilience, but also in their new-found centrality to the national story. Wars rarely radicalize the victors, and Britain in 1945 was no exception, bar one vital aspect: for the first time the vast majority of working people believed that it was their birthright to enjoy a decent standard of life 'from cradle to grave'. The war radically raised popular expectations about what the State could and should do to ensure that the people—*all* the people—lived lives free from the scourge of poverty and disease.

When Raymond Firth visited Bermondsey in 1947–8 this social democratic narrative of progress was newly minted. Told early on that 'You can always start an argument on politics, even though they are mostly Labour', his team explicitly sought to avoid raising political issues, but even so they captured traces of this post-war mood.[20] When two brothers who had grown up in the Buildings quizzed Firth

45

about welfare provision in his native New Zealand, Firth's answers prompted the older of the two to complain about the inadequacy of British pensions. His sense of entitlement was clear: 'pensions of 26 shillings per week [were] not enough to live on decently', he declared, not after a man had worked 'for his country' for more than fifty years.[21] The war wasn't mentioned, but the idea that men worked for the country, not for themselves or their families, drew directly on government propaganda justifying conscription in the two world wars. That this was an argument about *men's* entitlements also sprang from this logic.[22] But Firth also found a more general sense of post-war optimism in Bermondsey. People frequently emphasized the dramatic improvements that had been secured since the war, including 'good wages' and 'no unemployment', and in doing so stressed the contrast with pre-war hardships. On a number of occasions members of the team were told about a woman from the Buildings who had 'died of starvation' in the 1930s rather than submit to the hated means test. On one occasion the story was linked directly to post-war rationing, which was said to be 'very fair'.[23]

There were also strong indications that people expected a better life for their children than they had known themselves; and that many were determined to make this happen.[24] Ken Gorman, a fitter from South Wales, said he had moved to London to give his young son Robbie 'better chances and education'. Later Gorman talked about the possibility of sending Robbie to boarding school, declaring 'I want him to have what I never had the chance of'.[25] The Ingles, the Bermondsey couple Firth got to know best, displayed a similar attitude towards their only son Bernard. In his notebook Firth records that Sarah Ingles's earnings as a school dinner lady 'go into clothes for Bernard &c. [She] likes to keep him looking nice. She wants him to have better chance than she had.'[26] As we will see, the Ingles were fierce defenders of their privacy and 'respectability': Firth writes that they would not let Bernard play with most children in the Buildings, including blood relations such as the children of Mrs Ingles's cousins.[27] But they were not cravenly deferential and insisted on being treated as equals by those in authority. Showing Firth the small, damp attic room above their flat which the Guinness Trust suggested they should use as Bernard's bedroom, Sarah Ingles declared: 'Would you put your child there? I won't.'[28] Not everyone took the same view of children—Stanley Ingles explicitly objected to the harsh attitude of neighbours who said 'let 'em come up the hard way'—but the belief that a better life was within reach, at least for the young, was strong in post-war Bermondsey.[29]

Michael Young found similar cases while studying poorly housed families in Bethnal Green in the mid-1950s. Ron Jefferys, a garage mechanic who bitterly regretted never having learned a trade because it meant having to do what he called a 'semi-skilful' job, attacked the poor education provided for local children.

According to Jefferys, 'Elementary education is 100 per cent of working-class education. We don't have no other unless you can pay for anything more.' The comment is striking for the man's ready identification of himself as 'working-class' when in conversation with the privately educated Young, but it also suggests that the 1944 Education Act, which had introduced universal secondary education to age 15, had not necessarily changed the *experience* of education on the ground. Jefferys described his youngest son as 'the brains of the family' and told Young, 'If I had my way I'd send him to the best schools there are, [but] I haven't the financial means.'[30] But as social historian Selina Todd has argued, parents keen to give their children a better life were not necessarily focused on education and social advancement. Many just wanted their children to have more fun than they had had, even if this meant making financial sacrifices themselves.[31] A particularly striking example was Mrs Sartain, a mother of eight aged between 5 and 21, who explained that she would rather go out to work as an office cleaner than take more money from her four oldest children, all of whom had jobs. She told Young,

> I wouldn't be happy if I had to take more from them. That's how children go wrong. They all like to be tidy and have new clothes like their friends. They do their own saving for their clothes. They don't have any to spare. I'd rather go out myself, earn my few shillings, than take from them and make them feel unhappy and disagreeable about things.[32]

It was a comment elicited by Young's questions about the economics of moving to a new house on an outer London satellite estate. A little later Mrs Sartain returned to the issue, apparently spontaneously, with a comment which nicely captured not just her views about adolescent children's right to enjoy themselves, but also how this should form part of a happy home life for a family:

> The children were brought up in Bethnal Green and they all have their own clubs at Oxford House and the Webbe. There are no clubs out there [Debden in Essex], and they'd have to stay up here after they finished work. There are boys and girls out there on the estates who won't stop with their mothers because there aren't any clubs. My daughter's girl-friend lives at Hainault. She comes here after she finishes work and they go out to the club together four nights a week. She doesn't get back home till 10 o'clock. At the weekend she sleeps with my daughter or a married sister. What sort of home life is there for that girl?[33]

Lived community

It is striking that Firth drew very heavily on the Ingles' testimony in the published account of his 'South Borough' (Bermondsey) project. Most of the examples of what he saw as the qualified communalism of life in the Guinness Trust Buildings came directly from the Ingles, including what Firth described as the 'frequent comment' that 'we keep ourselves to ourselves, and then we can't get into trouble'.[34] Though active members of the local Parent–Teacher Association, the Ingles shunned other communal activities including the tenant-run Social Club and the organized summer excursions to popular seaside resorts such as Margate and Southend (known locally as 'Beanos').[35] Stanley Ingles was well aware that others lived by a different code. He told Firth that the Buildings were 'like a country village—anything happens everyone knows it—news travels', adding 'they all seem to help one another' before recounting how people regularly organized collections if someone in the Buildings died. His use of 'they' is revealing—this was not *his* custom, though he knew better than to refuse to contribute should someone come knocking at his door. Mr Ingles claimed to have donated to at least six collections without knowing anything of the deceased in question.[36]

Others spoke very differently about such collections. Firth's colleague Richard Scobie, another New Zealander, did much of his fieldwork in local pubs like the Rose and the Wheatsheaf (places the Ingles claimed never to visit). Jack Green, barman at the Rose, proved a particularly willing informant. Green took pride in telling Scobie: 'It's the poor that looks after the poor.' His first example was the generosity everyone had shown to the 'boys' home on leave during the war, but he then offered a detailed account of the 'whip-rounds' local people organized in cases of 'misfortune' such as illness, death, or unemployment. Green explained:

> The Londoners look after each other. When there is a death, a list is opened, maybe at the pub or at work and people put 2 bob [10p] in or, if they can't manage that, they give what they can. This is given to the person and may help him over a bad period or may help to pay for the funeral. As soon as the list closes, the money & the donations are checked & the list is hung in the pub.[37]

Posting the list was a defence against the danger of fraud, but it was also a way to advertise who belonged, and who did not. Green explained that collections were made without the beneficiary's knowledge, and presented without 'fuss'. This was to be seen as social solidarity, not charity, which may explain why Green added: 'if he didn't take it he wouldn't belong. Sometimes some people don't contribute in which case nobody worries about them.'[38] It was possible to opt out of the performance of 'community', but only at the price of social exclusion. The Ingles knew this well— that was why they donated when asked; they knew not to keep themselves *totally* to themselves. Even if they viewed the culture of Snowsfields almost as much from the outside as Scobie and Firth, they, unlike the researchers, also had to live there.

Intriguingly, given that *Family and Kinship* would make so much of working-class communalism in Bethnal Green, Young and Willmott's surviving field-notes offer few comparable examples of community in action. There are many cases where people proudly celebrate their deep roots in the locality, and explain why they would never want to leave, but we learn much less about community as lived experience. This probably tells us more about the questions asked (and not asked) than it does about local social relations (Young and Willmott's field-notes from Bethnal Green and Debden are less rich than most field-notes I have reanalysed and generally include only brief snippets of recorded speech). However, we can get a strong sense of informal social networks from the diary that Judith Henderson kept while living on Bethnal Green's Chisenhale Road in the late 1940s. A sister-in-law of Virginia Woolf, Henderson was an anthropologist by training and had been hired by the local University House settlement to help train professional social workers to better understand the people they worked with in Bethnal Green. Initially Henderson comes across as irritated by a neighbouring family's persistent requests to borrow things, but gradually the Hendersons and the Samuels appear to draw closer and the exchanges become genuinely reciprocal.[39] In a sense we observe Henderson gradually bending towards local customs, adapting to her environment almost in a mirror image of how my father's family must have adapted to life on the uber-respectable Gerrish Avenue in the 1930s. Peter Willmott's wife Phyllis also kept a diary while living in Bethnal Green. During 1954–5, while the fieldwork for *Family and Kinship* was in progress, the Willmotts and their two young children lived in the attic flat above the Institute of Community Studies (see Figure 10). (Young, by contrast, lived in Hampstead, north London.) Willmott's diary offers glimpses of neighbourly reciprocity in action, most involving a young mother called Daisy whom Phyllis Willmott befriended at the local school gates (the Willmotts had no immediate neighbours). Willmott also records seeing a 'hand-written notice' stuck in the window of a house near Victoria Park with a message thanking 'my dear neighbours' for 'the lovely flowers you sent to my husband'.[40] A note that speaks both to community in action and in some ways to its limits: this was not face-to-face interaction after all.

The surviving field-notes from Young and Willmott's project mainly shed light on the tensions thrown up by the perceived obligation to be a 'good' neighbour when families were forced to live cheek-by-jowl. Local housewife Mrs Porter is a classic example. She occupied the top half of an old Victorian workers' cottage. Much to her embarrassment her family was so overcrowded that Mrs Porter's 12-year-old daughter was forced to share a bedroom with her 14-year-old son, and this room was itself only separated from the parents' bedroom by a folding door; she

Figure 10. The Young Foundation, Victoria Park Square, Bethnal Green (formerly the Institute of Community Studies); the Willmotts lived in the attic flat [Paulmiller/Wikimedia Commons/Public Domain]

plaintively observed, 'It's not decent is it?' The Porters had been waiting thirteen years to be rehoused, perhaps partly because she was dead against flats: 'having people underneath, overhead and sideways—you're never on your own. Children need a garden too.' It was this comment which led her to explain that although their current house did have a small garden, concern for her neighbour's privacy made her bar the children from using it: 'they would have to play right outside the window of the woman downstairs and she wouldn't have any privacy at all'.[41]

Not everyone was as hostile to living in flats as Mrs Porter, but most recognized that they posed special challenges when trying to strike a balance between sociability and the preservation of domestic privacy. People often reacted sharply against the organized communalism found in blocks of flats. Explaining her preference for a house, Mrs Heal, a mother of four from Bethnal Green, commented that 'with flats, you have to sweep the stairs and the balcony which other people use too, and some of them don't do their turn or leave a lot of muck on them'.[42] Regulations were particularly strict in the Guinness Trust's Bermondsey flats. Here the supervisor inspected communal areas on a daily basis. Mrs Buckland explained that if he found a landing had not been cleaned he would 'knock on a door and ask whose turn it was, if you did not tell he made you sweep it up until you remembered!'[43] Indeed the Ingles told Firth that on nearly every landing there was 'someone who never does it... someone who spoils it'.[44] Some also complained about the need to share sinks and laundry facilities with their neighbours. Mrs Nicholson, a widow in her sixties, insisted that 'you have to keep yourself to yourself in a place like [Guinness Buildings]. There would be quarrelling over sharing the sinks otherwise. As it is people wash up in their flats and carry out the dirty water.'[45] But in 1959, Mrs Buckland, also an elderly widow, was lamenting that there was 'less friendship on the landings' precisely because all the flats now had their own sinks and hot water heaters.[46] The two claims appear to be contradictory—especially as they are presented as general truths about 'the community'—but we should not assume that Mrs Buckland would have felt as positively about the benefits of queuing for a sink when she still had no choice in the matter. As likely as not it would have depended on with whom she had to queue.

The difficulty of maintaining domestic privacy was often cited as a reason to avoid living in flats. Mr Jefferys, who was renting a large house scheduled for early demolition by Bethnal Green council, was adamant that he would refuse any offer of a flat: 'We was in Hackney and when we moved into flats it was like a palace really. It was very nice and clean but I didn't like it really. It was like being in a Home. You could hear people getting up at night. It was like the Army—being so close to one another.'[47] Mrs Heal said she worried about 'the noise of children—yours annoying other people & theirs annoying you. At night too you hear noises from the flats on either side of you.'[48] Perhaps predictably, Young and Willmott found even greater hostility to flats when interviewing former Bethnal Green residents who had moved out to suburban Debden in order to get a council house. Mr Maggs missed Bethnal Green more than most, but he was adamant that he would never live in a flat: 'They're alright if you believe in Communism & Socialism—you only want to have communal feeding & it's all in. You don't get the privacy in flats. Everyone knows all your business.'[49]

Phyllis Willmott registered similar concerns in her Bethnal Green journal. In February 1955 she got into conversation with a woman pushing a pram in Victoria Park. The woman was anxious because her house of twenty-three years was scheduled for early demolition. Like Mrs Porter she mentioned unease about having people 'on top, underneath and all around you', but most of all she feared having bad neighbours. She complained that 'they [the ubiquitous term for those in authority] ought to come and look at your home and see what sort you are. But

51

they don't. They mix you up with all sorts.'[50] Willmott also recorded a story about a local woman who was 'indignant' on moving into a new flat because 'a neighbour came in and borrowed custard powder from her almost at once'.[51] Probably it was the 'coming in' as much as the borrowing that was at issue here—this was a classic example of the clash of expectations about what it meant to be a good neighbour that could arise when everyone was new, and no local customary norms had been established.[52]

There was nothing new about this fear of intrusive neighbours—this was not a case of post-war prosperity beginning to erode more solidaristic social codes. During the war a major survey of popular attitudes towards housing by the Mass-Observation organization concluded that 'one of the main objects of having a home of one's own was to keep other people out of it, unless they were specifically invited in'.[53] The American sociologist E. Wight Bakke had found similar attitudes among working-class residents of Greenwich in the early 1930s. Bakke incurred the wrath of his landlord, a skilled engineer, by inviting workmen back to his lodgings to help with his research into the social effects of unemployment benefits. Perhaps prompted by his tenant's nationality, the man explained that 'An Englishman's home is his castle. I wouldn't want my next-door neighbour in here. No one but my very closest friends. This is where I live, and my family lives .... we don't want people in here whom we don't know. They'll go away and talk about what we had in our home and it's none of their business.'[54]

This fierce culture of domestic privacy and the isolated family did not preclude wider social connections within the neighbourhood, but it did pose greater challenges to smooth relations between neighbours than commentators like Michael Young generally cared to acknowledge. In *Family and Kinship*, Young and Willmott argued that 'exclusiveness in the home runs alongside an attitude of friendliness to other people living in the street'.[55] It was a typically bold general-ization, and one which ignored the extent to which neighbours (and strangers) could be perceived as a threat not just to privacy, but also to people's powerful sense of their right to live as they chose. When Firth began his work in Bermond-sey he was repeatedly warned that residents would not take kindly to researchers cold-calling at their door. Much better, he was told, to get to know people through the Social Club, and through personal introductions.[56] Eight months into the project, Sarah Ingles told Firth about some of the things local people had said once they knew she was cooperating with his research into kinship and family trees. One had simply declared: '[I] don't want anyone prying into my past life', while another had asked 'How do you know they're not coming to your place to find out all your business?'[57]

Sociologist Mike Savage has written about the 'rugged individualism' at the core of British working-class culture. He was writing specifically about male workplace culture, but the same spirit can also be seen burning brightly in the home.[58] In Bethnal Green, Young interviewed a mother of two in her late thirties who took special pride in declaring herself 'independent' and a 'rebel' like her late father, adding that when she left school 'I broke away; I was never one for great friends.' She claimed to take the same approach with her neighbours, saying hello to them, but otherwise having nothing to do with them.[59] Others struck a similar attitude. Mrs Kimber, a widow with seven children, said she could not afford to move to the suburbs, but insisted that it had nothing to do with being 'afraid of being cut off from people, as one was "better off if you keep yourself to yourself"'. Interestingly, Young wrote 'Again!' after her comment—this was clearly a recurrent saying in Bethnal Green as much as Bermondsey, even though *Family and Kinship* would suggest otherwise.[60] Mrs Quail, a young mother of two, offered a different version of the same homily, telling Young that her motto was 'Don't mix up with the neighbours. Just pass the time of day, that's all,' before adding: 'I don't like to borrow off of anyone'.[61] Similarly, the elderly Mrs Wood told Firth that she had refused to borrow coal from neighbours when fuel had run short during the big freeze of 1947 (temperatures barely rose above freezing for seven weeks between late January and March). Instead she turned to relatives living some distance away, explaining that 'she preferred to turn always "to her own"' rather than to 'strangers'.[62]

That said, we need to recognize that there may have been a performative aspect to this rejection of intimacy with 'strangers'. Historians have rightly suggested that one rarely finds working people self-defining as 'respectable', but this does not mean that they were indifferent about appearing 'respectable' to others—especially to well-to-do outsiders like Firth and Young.[63] Certainly, people regularly talked about some streets, and neighbours, being 'rough' to signal social difference from themselves, and no one claimed to *be* 'rough'. It was as unlikely as anyone imitating George Bernard Shaw's Alfred Doolittle by proudly declaring themselves one of the 'undeservin' poor', but we do find people self-defining as 'rough and ready', a more homely term which, in 1940s Bermondsey, seems to have functioned as a grittier version of the claim to 'ordinariness' that Mike Savage identifies with affluent workers of the 1960s.[64] In practice, although most people maintained friendly relations with neighbours, they sought to distinguish this from the overly familiar behaviour associated with neighbours who were always dropping in *uninvited*.[65] Mrs Silverman rented the upper floor of a dilapidated workman's cottage with her mother and four children, having been deserted by her husband in the war. Like many Bethnal Greeners she adamantly told Young that 'none of the neighbours

53

comes in', but acknowledged that she sometimes borrowed tea or sugar from the woman who lived below, and also that they routinely made tea for one another: 'She sends me up a cup of tea and I send her down one whenever I make it.' She had also just told Young that they had had a party till midnight on Christmas Day, inviting close family and 'some neighbours', all of whom put in 10 shillings [50p] to help buy the drink.[66] Neighbours clearly did 'come in', but it was important to Mrs Silverman that Young should not think that they came in *all the time*.[67]

Pride of place

It is striking that many of the people who stressed their indifference to neighbours nonetheless insisted that they would never leave the neighbour*hood*. Mrs Kimber declared that on 'no account' would she leave Bethnal Green, and Mrs Silverman boasted proudly of being 'bred and born' in the borough, just like her mum.[68] Attachment to place *as place* mattered—as one man put it to Firth: 'Bermondsey gets you.'[69] Mr and Mrs Corbett told Firth that they had both been born in Bermondsey and 'they would like to die and be buried there'.[70] But the sense of place was at its most powerful, not at the level of the municipal borough, important though that was, but at the level of the individual street, court, or block. Firth's team were quick to notice how local people spoke of 'our block' as readily, and warmly, as they spoke of 'our mum', and that non-residents would spontaneously be labelled as someone who 'doesn't live in the Buildings'.[71] Conversely, Mrs Keogh, who ran the local non-denominational Arthur's Mission on Snowsfields, was described as 'a resident *and product* of the Buildings'.[72]

When the Guinness Trust surveyed the Snowsfields Buildings in 1957 they found that forty-seven tenancies (15.9 per cent) had been held by the same family, sometimes the same person, for over forty years; twelve tenancies had been held continuously for more than fifty years; and one dated from the development's completion in 1898 (Table 3). On the other hand, 149 tenancies (50.5 per cent) had begun *after* Firth's original 1947 fieldwork (although forty-one of these had been passed on to relatives by former tenants).[73] The Buildings, like London as a whole, encompassed remarkable stability over generations alongside the relentless churn of metropolitan life. However, while we should not doubt people's intense sense of 'belonging', neither should we imagine that this was universal. Interviewed in 1959, Mrs Peters spoke with joy about having moved back to her birthplace, the 'Down-town' district of Rotherhithe on Bermondsey's eastern, riverside perimeter. She explained how people now stopped her in the street to pass the time of day, and how one woman declared 'we have not lost your mother so long as you are with

Table 3. Length of tenancies at Guinness Trust Buildings, Bermondsey, in December 1957 (years)

Tenancy length	Number	Percentage of tenancies
>40	47	15.9
31–40	17	5.8
21–30	26	8.8
11–20	42	14.2
6–10	41	13.9
2–5	66	22.4
<2	42	14.2
No Data	14	4.7
TOTAL	295	99.9

Note: 'No Data' includes 10 flats double-let with other flats, two left blank, one empty flat, and one illegible, damaged entry.

Source: LSE Library, Firth Papers, 3/2/8, 'Census Dec. 1957'.

us'.[74] But for the previous eleven years, from when she had been bombed out in the war, Mrs Peters had being living on the other side of the borough, cut off from her old neighbours by the vast complex of the Surrey Commercial Docks. Claims that the idea of 'community' was largely a retrospective myth, or that social solidarity was purely contractual, cannot do justice to Mrs Peters's experience.[75] On the other hand, the fact that she had spent eleven years 'in exile' reminds us that such a sense of belonging could never be all-encompassing.

It is striking that Mrs Peters had no difficulty reflecting on what community meant to her. In this she was typical of many respondents in both Bermondsey and Bethnal Green, who frequently displayed an acute awareness of the myths of cockney communalism by which they might be judged. For the most part they seem to have valued these myths at least as much as their academic visitors. Whatever the situation may have been in Robert Colls's South Shields, community here was not just a question of unthinking habit.[76] A woman who had recently returned to Bermondsey from Yorkshire implored Firth to 'say we're real cockneys', while barman Jack Green told researchers to go down to Kent during the hop-picking season if they wanted 'to see the Londoner' having a good 'knees up'.[77] It was as though locals assumed that the researchers were looking for specimens of a type—the 'genuine cockney'—perhaps reinforced by a fear that Bermondsey's everyday street life would somehow fall short of expectations. Similarly, a man from Bethnal Green described his grandmother as 'one of the real old Bethnal Green Cockney Cockneys. She could drink like a fish. She was not afraid of any man, however tough. They carried her home many times.'[78] This desire to meet expectations may also explain why transport worker and Guinness Social Club official Dick Sexton encouraged Firth's team to come down to Bermondsey for the royal wedding of Princess Elizabeth and Philip Mountbatten on 20 November 1947, an event which he predicted would involve a real 'pub party... like the Jubilee'. But when Audrey Richards went to investigate she found absolutely no celebrations whatsoever, in strong contrast to the scenes she had encountered en route walking through the West End.[79] On another occasion Kenneth Little, a pioneer of the sociological study of black Britons, commented on the 'evident pride in being community conscious' in the Buildings, although he suspected that sometimes it was being 'over-accentuated' for his benefit. An astute social observer, Little recognized the performative aspect of claims that everyone in the Buildings had 'lived here all our lives' or that 'any stranger would be spotted at once'.[80]

Although a few people took a different approach, making it clear that they could not wait to get away from the 'bricks, smoke and dirt' of Bethnal Green, or the 'slum' conditions of Snowsfields, most displayed a strong sense of local pride.[81] Like some of the claims about 'community', this may have been accentuated for visitors' benefit, but if so this merely reinforces the sense that place mattered to people; they wanted outsiders to leave with a positive impression of where they lived.

The family way

By contrast, in both Bermondsey and Bethnal Green people often spoke openly about family feuds and the general failings of their relatives. This was not because family was unimportant. Like the woman who would only borrow coal from her 'people', there was widespread recognition of the moral importance of blood ties. However, as Firth quickly realized, this ran alongside a general belief that one should also like one's relatives; duty held sway only between parent and child, and even that could sometimes break down. A specialist on Polynesia, Firth was used to societies where custom, rather than personal preference, governed relations between kin, and recognized that many of the disputes between relatives stemmed from the social pressures created by the freer, more personal system that operated in Bermondsey, and (he assumed) more generally across urban Britain.[82]

But how did people explain the significance of family in their own words? Many certainly subscribed to an idealized view of the family as an indissoluble unit. Mrs Buckland's teenage daughter May told Firth 'I don't think the family works as individuals; we work as a combined unit. We don't do anything without consulting one another.'[83] But a few minutes later, Mrs Buckland was explaining that she had had no contact with her brother since the war because he had moved 'up North'.[84] It seems clear that May Buckland was thinking of the family as the household unit: her parents and her three siblings still at home. Although Young would make much of the extended family as the backbone of social cohesion in post-war Bethnal Green, one struggles to find supporting evidence either in his own field-notes or in Firth's.[85] When people talked about families 'sticking together', it was often in the context of explaining why their own did not.[86] Again people regularly displayed a sophisticated ability to reflect on such issues. John Corbett, a labourer from Bermondsey, described himself as the 'lone wolf' of his family, because he chose to see nothing of his brothers despite the fact that they lived nearby.[87] Other people underscored the role of choice in family relations by describing themselves as 'not one for the family'.[88] After discovering that Corbett did maintain close ties with a brother in Birmingham whose son had lodged with them from time to time, Firth concluded that in 'modern cultures' instrumental reciprocity governed kinship relations; it was a question of 'what advantages the individual can take or can offer to his kin and relatives'.[89]

It was a typically 'functionalist' response (Firth had been taught by Bronisław Malinowski, the great interwar pioneer of social anthropology who argued that all cultural traits formed part of an interconnected and functional social system).[90] For Firth, the loose, unstructured nature of kinship bonds encouraged people to make rational choices about who was (and was not) 'close family' based partly on utility and partly on personal taste (he noted the tendency for people to make a special effort to maintain contacts with relations who lived near the sea in Kent or Essex).[91] But this is to underestimate the emotional undertow of family life. Sometimes relatives did just drift apart, but there were also many dramatic accounts of family breaches which were shot through with pain and anger. This reflected tension between the idealization of 'family' and the belief that one should *like* rather than simply honour one's relatives. Often relatives were disowned for some perceived failure to 'do right' by the wider family. In Bermondsey, Mrs Woodcock explained that two of her sons had not spoken to her sister since she had sold up her late husband's business without giving them a chance to buy it.[92] Martha Weald explained that both she and her mother had broken off contact with her older brother because they disliked his wife: 'She's not up to our standard' (the breach presumably resulting from the brother taking his wife's side rather than theirs).[93] More pettily, Mrs Buckley explained that she and her sister Lizzie had fallen out over 2 shillings (10p—a few pounds in today's money). Convinced that Mrs Buckley's refusal to lend the money reflected a lack of trust, Lizzie never spoke to her sister again (she had died without breaking the silence).[94]

Breaches within the nuclear family could be especially traumatic. Mr Rushton, a postman from Bethnal Green, claimed that he would walk past his own father if he saw him in the street; apparently they had not spoken since the son's marriage to a divorced woman with children. Rushton's siblings also disapproved of the marriage. He took particular exception to his sister calling his wife a 'prostitute'; as he put it, 'now I couldn't have any of that could I?' However, the siblings did still speak. As he explained: 'At Christmas time we forget the feuds we have all year, and they bring presents up for the children.'[95] Mrs Nulli had also broken with her father, declaring boldly, 'He's dead to me because I never see him.' She blamed her father's new wife for preventing contact, but later acknowledged that her 'people' had been 'against' her husband from the day they married (Young wondered if this reflected hostility to his Italian ancestry).[96]

Relations could be fraught even when families remained nominally close. Mrs Whiteside saw her married daughters every day, but she took no pleasure from the role of matriarch, proclaiming herself 'not one for the family'. She told Young that she wanted to leave Bethnal Green to escape them, complaining that they 'come to me with all their troubles—makes me ill—about having no money— or baby-minding, or something of the sort. I say when they're married they've got to look after themselves. They've made their bed and they've got to lie in it.'[97] Firth's team came across a similar case in Bermondsey. Mrs Henderson, described by the researcher as 'a small, clean, toothless, bad tempered, abrupt & filthily spoken little woman', complained bitterly about the way her flat was used by her married daughter and her four 'badly behaved boys'. The grandmother claimed to be 'very angry' that they came down to her flat every evening so that her son-in-law could have some peace and quiet when he came in from work.[98]

Again we need to be alert to the performative aspects of such exchanges. Mrs Henderson may well have felt put upon, but it's quite possible that when she 'rose in wrath with a large carving knife' (swearing profusely as she did so), she was trying to shock her interviewer as much as her grandchildren.[99] Family, including dysfunctional family, could also be *performed*. And if Whiteside and Henderson chose to subvert the role of caring family matriarch, most took the opposite course. Mrs Sartain, the mother of eight who went out to work rather than deprive her adult children of spending money, took great pride in the fact that since her mother's death she, rather than her older sister, had come to be recognized as the de facto head of the family in times of crisis. By contrast, she was dismissive of her husband's family for failing to 'cling together'.[100]

Perhaps inevitably, the performance of family could sometimes fray at the edges. When Firth's team made a return visit to Mrs Buckland in 1958 her daughter Maggie, now in her early forties, insisted that though she had moved out to the Hither Green estate, she still visited Bermondsey three or four times a week and always popped in to see her elderly, frail mother. Subsequent visits painted a less rosy picture. Firstly, it became clear that, in practice, most weeks Maggie only managed to visit her mother once (this came out when the researchers tried to schedule a return visit). More worryingly, it was also clear that Mrs Buckland's youngest child, Ray, was about to marry and move out of London leaving her alone in Bermondsey. Her five daughters, all of whom had already left the borough, had met up to try and find a solution but their efforts failed because they all agreed that 'their husbands must come first'. Perhaps significantly, it was assumed that Mrs Buckland's sons (and their wives) could not be expected to help.[101]

Mrs Shipway, a skilled engineer's wife from Bethnal Green, proudly told Young that her family gathered together regularly every Saturday afternoon: 'We sit jawing, get amused with the children when all of them get together, play cards and listen to the wireless. [We] don't do much drinking unless there's a wedding or something like that.' It was a cosy picture of family harmony—Mrs Shipway stressed that no one would leave till about 10.[102] But a few minutes later she was bitterly denouncing her eldest sister, Margaret, who had married a farmer during the war while working as a land girl in Devon. Mrs Shipway complained that Margaret rarely bothered to get in touch with the family because 'money had gone to her head', adding 'we have only seen her three children by photo'. Arguably, the fact that Margaret sent photos of her children suggests she was keen *not* to break off contact despite the problem of distance, but for Mrs Shipway what mattered was that she had chosen to place herself outside the family network. To underscore the point Mrs Shipway stressed that if she decided to move away from Bethnal Green she would still return to her mother's every Saturday for the family get-together.[103]

But perhaps the most poignant case of the gulf between family performed and family lived concerned Mrs Woodcock, a Bermondsey widow who had played an active role in organizing social events at Snowsfields in the 1930s and 1940s. When Firth's researchers visited her in 1947 she was still working, alongside her married daughter, at a local bottling factory, and boasted that her five sons all had good jobs in the printing and transport trades. Pictures of the five sons adorned 'almost every wall' of her small flat, and she was said to 'talk about them incessantly', calling their wives 'my Maggie', 'my Dora', etc.[104] But when researchers returned to Bermondsey in 1958 Mrs Woodcock, now in her late seventies, presented a sad picture of physical and mental decline. They learned that only three of the five sons made financial contributions to help their sister, with whom Mrs Woodcock now lived. Mother and daughter complained that none offered practical help, not even lifts in their cars. None visited more than once every three or four weeks; two had not been seen for months, while their wives, once spoken of so fondly, visited even less often. When interviewed separately, the son, who still lived in Snowsfields, openly acknowledged that he 'did not go to see his mother "much"'.[105]

As Young and Willmott emphasized, the mother–daughter bond was at the heart of the post-war working-class family. Men's primary role was as provider for their own immediate family; they might be expected to play an increasingly active role as fathers within that family, but their wider caring responsibilities remained limited.[106] Mrs Woodcock's sons may have done less than was expected of them, but as with Mrs Buckland, there was no suggestion that sons, rather than daughters, might take primary responsibility for care. Unlike their subsequent feminist critics, Young and Willmott played down the enormous pressure family life placed on the mother–daughter relationship.[107] We have already seen how some mothers found the expectations of their daughters intolerable, and, what's more, said so openly. But as feminists predicted, most daughters found it harder to say the 'unsayable' about their mother, at least to middle-class male outsiders. However, in her conversations with mothers at the local school gates, Phyllis Willmott did pick up some of the resentments that daughters could feel towards demanding or critical mothers. In October 1954 she noted how two women who had often spoken 'in warm terms about their extended families' began rehearsing their anger and frustration at mothers who would never accept they could do anything right, with one confessing 'Ooh! I used to think, "I'll do you one of these days".'[108] We also need to remember that many young women willingly moved away from inner London after the war, even if this meant leaving their mothers behind. We have seen how the Buckland daughters ultimately placed their husbands' needs above those of their elderly mother in Bermondsey. Similarly, Mrs Threader declared herself 'not much of a one' for relatives, and told Young that both she and her husband wanted to get out of Bethnal Green even though it would mean leaving their mothers behind. Strongly influenced by psychologist John Bowlby's then fashionable theories about maternal attachment, Young was convinced that only psychological maladjustment could explain an only child willingly leaving her mother behind (he mused that it might be because Mrs Threader's mother had always worked).[109] But given that the population of Bethnal Green (like Bermondsey) had already halved since the 1910s, and would continue to fall, Young was pathologizing life choices that were being made on a daily basis across London, and most other large English cities, in the 1950s as the country sought to build its way out of the acute post-war housing shortage.[110]

The outsiders

As families moved out, so the churn of population increased, and established social networks weakened. This was not a new phenomenon—the capital's population had always been mobile and shifting, but it does seem likely that the pace of change increased across the 1950s.[111] Even in 1953, Young interviewed one family, the Sarsons, who complained that all their relatives had long since moved out to suburban council estates. They themselves had moved to the LCC's Mottingham estate, near Bromley, in the 1930s, but had ended up back in Bethnal Green through the upheavals of war. The family felt deeply isolated. Mr Sarson's parents had been killed in the V-1 raids, and they had lost contact with most of their other relatives through their frequent moves. With their six children, aged between 1 and 20, they now lived in a requisitioned house in an unfamiliar part of the borough and were desperate to move away. Mrs Sarson mentioned that her children were always 'getting into mischief in the street', and this may help to explain the open hostility which led them to boycott their local Coronation street party in 1953; they complained that neighbours would throw things in their faces in the street.[112]

The Sarsons may have been an extreme case, but they were not the only people to be spurned as 'outsiders'. It was not uncommon, as we have seen, for families to reject someone 'marrying in', and even to break off contact with their own blood relative in the process. As Young suspected in the case of Mrs Nulli, this may sometimes have been about ethnic exclusivity, but *any* outsider was likely to be viewed with suspicion, at least at first. The Wealds were not the only people to reject a close relative's spouse for not being 'up to our class'. Mrs Smith, the wife of a pest control worker from Bermondsey's Neckinger estate, explained that her family would have nothing to do with an aunt who had 'married a docker and let herself go', describing this woman (who had more than a dozen children), as 'not our class'.[113]

Nor were the Sarsons the only white working-class family to feel themselves 'outsiders' unable to tap into local social networks. Ken Gorman, the Welsh fitter who had moved to Bermondsey after the war, complained that when his wife left him and their young son Robbie neighbours initially proved sympathetic, but within a few weeks help had dried up and they were on their own.[114] Ken wanted to move back to Wales, where his sisters would help look after Robbie, but felt this would be unfair on his son (the 1957 survey of the Buildings shows them still living there, but sadly they were not reinterviewed). John Buckden, one of the organizers of the Snowsfields Social Club, was particularly conscious of his outsider status. Buckden had moved to Bermondsey from Yorkshire under mysterious circumstances which made him wary of Firth's project. Unusually, he challenged them directly about this, pointing out that their social ease and 'complete self-assurance' marked them out as 'not one of us' (itself a fascinating insight into popular understandings of the social psychology of class). But Buckden also played up his own outsider status within the Buildings, making frequent observations about what 'they'—the other tenants—were like.[115] He talked about them being 'almost "illiterate"' and having 'queer ways', and on one occasion declared, 'The people here have three religions: babies, boozing and gambling.'[116]

When Firth's researchers returned to the Snowsfields Buildings in the late 1950s, they met with frequent complaints that there were 'hardly any of the old families left'; or as Mrs Warden put it, just lots of 'strangers [and] the best part of them are Irish'.[117] With more than half the tenancies having changed hands since 1947, this was indeed a community in flux. Mrs Warden was not the only person to mention the increased Irish presence in the Buildings, and the Guinness Trust census for 1957 does highlight a significant cluster of newcomers from London districts traditionally associated with Irish migration such as Kilburn, east Finchley, and north Kensington, though only one family had come direct from Ireland itself (Table 4).[118] Since many of the original tenants had also been of Irish descent (including the Mission's Mrs Keogh), we should be wary of seeing this solely in ethnic terms. Some residents *were* hostile to foreigners, Irish or otherwise, but for most this was just a convenient way of complaining about rapid and unwelcome change.[119] By 1957, less than half the Snowsfields residents (47.1 per cent) had been born there or came from elsewhere in Bermondsey; more than a third had been living in the Buildings for five years or less.[120] We don't have comparable information for Bethnal Green, but some of Young's witnesses certainly experienced similar levels of upheaval. Speaking in 1953 Mr Banks, a bootmaker, complained that 'War split everything up; there is only one tenant in this block that I remember from early days, they've all moved out, or died, and new ones come in.'[121] Young and Willmott conducted a random survey with 933 individuals for *Family and Kinship* which suggested that just over half the population of Bethnal Green (53 per cent) had been born there.[122] This was high by London standards, but still suggested a greater degree of churn than one might expect given their powerful argument about stable, organic urban communities standing on the brink of destruction by planners.

Table 4. Previous place of residence of Guinness Trust Bermondsey tenants, 1957

Previous address	Number of tenancies	Percentage
GTB Buildings	44	14.9
Bermondsey	95	32.2
Adjacent south-east boroughs	17	5.8
Other inner south London	30	10.2
East London	13	4.4
West London	13	4.4
North & north-west London	31	10.5
Other London	26	8.8
South East (not LCC)	7	2.4
Rest of UK	3	1.0
Ireland	1	0.3
Overseas	1	0.3
No Data	14	4.7
	295	99.9

Note: 'No Data' includes ten flats double-let with other flats, two left blank, one empty flat, and one illegible, damaged entry.

Source: LSE Library, Firth Papers, 3/2/8, 'Census Dec. 1957'.

As Young began his fieldwork for *Family and Kinship* social psychologist James Robb was just finishing a major study of popular anti-Semitism in Bethnal Green. He had chosen Bethnal Green mainly because of its notoriety as a centre of Oswald Mosley's fascist Blackshirts in the 1930s.[123] Robb, like Young, had close links both to the London School of Economics and to the Tavistock Institute, probably the leading centre for applied social psychiatry in post-war Britain. But though Young and Willmott were aware of Robb's work, they did little to integrate his arguments about the sectarian, ethnically exclusive connotations that could become attached to popular ideas of 'community' into their own study (something Young came to regret in later life).[124] Young recognized that identification with place was intensely local, but he did not dwell on the implications of this for 'outsiders'. Once again Phyllis Willmott's Bethnal Green diary is illuminating here. In February 1955 she records that her friend Daisy is 'indignant' to discover that the new flats put up at the end of her mum's turning were being let to outsiders: 'They are from Shoreditch; lots of them.' In an addendum Willmott notes that she has discovered that the new tenants were indeed coming from Shoreditch, 'but from the part of it that was within the Borough of Bethnal Green'. One suspects that this technicality would have been of little comfort to Daisy: they were still 'outsiders' to *her* Bethnal Green.[125] It certainly mattered little that they were fellow white British East Enders.[126]

The surviving Bethnal Green field-notes themselves throw up few hints of exclusivity (ethnic or otherwise). The only clear example is an elderly woman telling Young, 'You have to be a foreigner before they'll give you a home'; her daughter, the intended subject of the interview, immediately tries to defuse the situation by saying, 'Don't get her off on politics'.[127] But it would be unwise to conclude that this silence reflected general taboos around the expression of intolerance. The comment 'Don't get her off on politics' is arguably rather too light-hearted to fit this interpretation, but evidence from other studies is also suggestive. Not just Robb's late 1940s fieldwork from Bethnal Green, which after all targeted areas of known fascist organization, but also Firth's research in Bermondsey (which was conducted at the same time as Robb's work). Firth and his fellow anthropologists recorded many examples of popular antipathy to the non-white 'Other'. Barbara Ward recorded a teenage girl being shocked to realize that Ward's job could mean having to sit with a black man to take down his family tree, while Kenneth Little observed that in the local argot anyone non-British was labelled 'Irish', recording in his notes: 'The word "Irish" is apparently a "teknonym" for Jewish as the Jews and other "outsiders" are apparently looked on as less desirable, and this appears to apply more definitely to coloured people.'[128] On the other hand, Firth found local families displaying 'no particular attitudes' to in-laws from minority ethnic backgrounds (hostility appears to have been directed most fiercely at the *unknown* 'Other').[129] Given that Bethnal Green had considerably stronger historical associations with anti-Semitism, Young's silence on the question therefore seems likely to reflect his broader deafness to vernacular voices which challenged his celebratory account of 'community'.[130]

Especially for older residents, any change was generally synonymous with decline. Mrs Hadrian, an elderly widow who had lived all her life in Bethnal Green, complained that 'people were not as they used to be', citing the failure to organize a local Coronation party, and the lack of flags and bunting as proof.[131] Similarly, Mrs Whiteside complained that 'people in the East End seem to keep more apart than they used to; young married couples keep to themselves'.[132] When Firth's team returned to Snowsfields in 1958 they met many elderly residents who keenly felt the loss of family and friends. Mr Dyer was said to be 'very sad' that he 'neither sees nor hears from any family now except his own children', two of whom were also on the brink of moving away.[133] Mrs Buckland insisted that the Buildings were less friendly than before, and cited the decline of borrowing and small favours between neighbours.[134] People also complained that the organized 'Beanos' to the seaside had ceased, that the Social Club was now barely used, and that the Buildings' darts, boxing, and football clubs had all been wound up (although there was also a suggestion that new facilities elsewhere meant that people were less reliant on the Guinness Trust).[135]

There was a natural tendency for people to transpose their feelings of sadness and isolation outward, but new social networks were almost certainly being constructed as the older ones decayed. The Irish newcomers may have been 'strangers' to Mrs Warden, but it's unlikely they were all strangers to each other. Sadly, Firth didn't interview any of the new Snowsfields tenants in 1958, but the original study included families of Irish descent, and it is striking that they perceived sharp differences between their own social codes and those of their English neighbours. Edgar Scully and his wife had moved to Britain before the Second World War. More recently, two of his brothers had also come to Bermondsey. It was a classic migration pattern, and one that helped ensure that newcomers quickly developed their own networks—their own lived community. Scully judged the English, including his middle brother's new English wife, to be 'greedy', unsociable, and neglectful of both family and neighbours. He claimed to be shocked to find that at Snowsfields neighbours often did more for the elderly than their own relatives.[136] In turn, when Firth interviewed Edgar's brother Paul and his English wife, Jean, he was struck by Paul's ability to name his seventh cousins back home in County Cork (so was Jean, who remarked, 'It's quite different over here, Paul').[137]

In fact, as part of their 1958 work in Bermondsey, Firth's researchers conducted a focused project on what they termed Rotherhithe's 'Catholic Community', apparently recognizing that organized religion offered a valuable way to gain access to local social networks. One of the researchers, a woman in her late twenties, became a regular at the whist drives and socials organized by the local Catholic church (it seems pretty clear that her main contact, 'Mrs H', was trying to set her up with a recently widowed man struggling to look after two young children).[138] Although attendance at Mass was said to be poor, local people identified strongly with 'their' school; only those who had attended the local Catholic school were felt fully to 'belong' to the community—everyone else was viewed as more or less a 'stranger'.[139] The whist drives were a recent innovation and seem to have helped to integrate newcomers into local Catholic social networks. Speaking about two young couples from outside the area, one witness claimed that 'no one spoke to them for three years until the Whist Drives started and they got to know them then' (although this aloofness may have been compounded by the fact that their husbands were police-men as well as 'outsiders').[140] But if religion did not provide an instant, unproblem-atic sense of community, it could act as an important social bond, connecting some neighbours whilst excluding others. Unfortunately, most post-war enquiries into community were resolutely secular in their framing, making it hard to judge the importance of these lived communities of faith, and how they may have cut across the supposedly fixed communities of residence that so interested social scientists like Young. The novelist Jeanette Winterson's adopted parents may have been unusual in connecting only with their co-religionists at Accrington's distant Elim Pentecostal Church, whilst having nothing to do with their 'heathen' neighbours, but they were only an extreme example of a more general pattern: the desire to assert personal choice over social life, rather than be defined entirely by the local and immediate.[141]

The point is therefore not to suggest that 'real' community existed among Irish migrants, or Catholics, or in the west of Ireland, and was somehow absent among London's indigenous white working class. Recalibrating the myths of community should not mean abandoning the idea of community altogether. Rather, we need to recognize that community always existed in two forms within everyday life. In the mind—as an imagined vision of how social relations should be—but also in the micro-level interactions people experienced in their everyday lives. Imagined com-munity and lived community always existed in tension with each other. The crucial reason for this was that at any given time there were many overlapping *lived* communities, not one community that could be said to be 'in decline', or, for that matter, growing in strength. Over the chapters that follow we will trace shifting patterns of lived community, but it is also important to reconstruct changing popular conceptions of *imagined* community. In so doing, we need to avoid repeating the mistakes of Young and Willmott by superimposing our own idealistic preconcep-tions about real 'community' on to people's testimony. But we also need to avoid simply puncturing rosy vernacular myths of community when we find them; our task must be to understand what community meant to people in their daily lives.

Different voices

Perhaps the best way to illustrate the diversity of lived community, and in the process end this exploration of post-war working-class London, will be to focus on a group of Bermondsey families visited intensively by Firth's researchers during 1958–9 as part of a study of the experiences of expectant mothers. Detailed notes survive on eleven households which were visited repeatedly over many months either side of the child's birth.[142] Again the diversity of lifestyle and outlook is striking—any attempt to reduce these to some composite model of 'working-class' (or even popular) urban culture would be a travesty. But patterns *are* discernible. Looking closely at these households can provide useful insights into the different ways in which people understood, and lived, community by the late 1950s in a supposedly traditional working-class district like Bermondsey as it stood on the brink of radical social and economic changes associated with affluence and large-scale migration.

Again, the degree of population churn in this supposedly static community is underlined by the fact that five of the eleven families moved house between their first and last visit (an average interval of just eight months). Three moved locally, including Mrs Peters, the woman delighted to be returning to Rotherhithe's 'Downtown' district, and two left the area (one to buy a house in suburban London, the other to take up the offer of a job and house in Thetford under the Government's expanded towns scheme, an adjunct of the 'new town' programme).[143] More than half the families could be said to have deep roots in the locality, and in most cases family played an important part in sustaining this sense of rootedness. Mrs Holden, a mother of two in her late twenties, described herself as being part of a 'very local family', claiming that '[I] never go anywhere when I don't see some family'. Both she and her husband were strong Labour activists, and had grown up in local Labour families. He had recently been elected as a local councillor. A trained electrician, he now worked as librarian for a major trade union. Though more prosperous than many (they had taken foreign holidays and were saving for a car), the Holdens identified strongly with Bermondsey and had no wish to leave.

In some respects the Holdens (like most political activists) were decidedly untypical of the people they lived amongst. They did not believe in christenings or godparents, had only reluctantly agreed to get married in church, and did not believe in 'churching' a woman after childbirth (this was a ritual blessing of mother and newborn child then still widely practised in working-class London).[144] Perhaps most unconventionally of all, they had holidayed together in Austria before marrying (Mrs Holden's sister was also about to go to Vienna for a 'final fling' before marriage, although she was going *without* her fiancé). They had also both taken evening classes to improve their job prospects. But if they were self-consciously independent, self-improving, and 'modern', they nonetheless still had much in common with their neighbours. Mr Holden was a regular at Millwall FC, they could still only afford to rent one floor of an old terraced house, and they now took their summer holidays at an English seaside holiday camp.[145]

Despite many stereotypical accounts of working-class family life which might suggest the opposite, the Holdens were also far from unusual in enjoying a close, home-centred married life.[146] Many of the women interviewed claimed to socialize only with their spouses, who in turn were said to lead quiet, home-centred lives. They also claimed to take joint responsibility for the household finances. In some respects this poses a challenge to sociologist Elizabeth Bott's famous 1957 study *Family and Social Network*, with its influential argument that couples embedded within 'close-knit' social networks lived very separate, sex-segregated lives (her account was based on an intensive study of twenty London families, although notably only *one* of these was said to be unambiguously enmeshed in a close-knit social network).[147] Viewed case by case it is always possible to find ways to explain why a family's circumstances might not qualify as 'close-knit'. The Holdens' shared commitment to socialism could be said to trump both the appeal of same-sex socializing and the social pressure to conform to the expectations of others. Other close, home-centred working-class marriages might also be claimed not to fit the model. For instance, the Peters family, who we saw had been bombed out of Rotherhithe's 'Downtown' district in the war, might be exceptionally close (mother and daughter spent most of every day together), but their sense of living in exile from Rotherhithe may have weakened their connections with non-kin.[148] Contrastingly, whilst the Burns and Church families might present themselves as deeply embedded in local support networks, they both claimed to have only loose ties to family.[149] But arguably in their diverse types of exceptionalism what these families really demonstrate is the unhelpfulness of schematic models of 'traditional' close-knit working-class networks. In their different ways all these families were both deeply embedded in local social relations *and* sufficiently autonomous from them to exert personal discretion over how they chose to interpret the vows of matrimony (and doubtless much else besides). By the late 1950s people deeply enmeshed in local face-to-face networks could nonetheless still assert the right to live as they chose.

Indeed, exploring the Burns and Church families' lives in greater detail sheds considerable light on the dynamics of personal, lived community at this time. Both couples seemed to place more emphasis on socializing with friends than with family, to have mostly shared friends, and to socialize with those friends mostly at home. Not for them the idea that the home was a special place reserved solely for family, as both cultural critic Richard Hoggart and Young and Willmott suggested.[150] The Churches lived in a Victorian tenement block on Tower Bridge Road. Almost all Mrs Church's family had moved out to estates such as West Norwood and Tulse Hill, while her husband's family had moved to a seaside resort on the north Kent coast. It was neighbours and friends, not family, who visited

Mrs Church when she came home from hospital—indeed one of her neighbours drove her home, while another was 'scrubbing out the flat' when she got there. Seven more neighbours popped in to see her over the next twenty-four hours along with close friends who lived at Richmond, but no relatives. She remained close to her elderly mother—making the 4-mile journey to visit her every Tuesday and Thursday—although the relationship was clearly volatile. Mrs Church reported that nine years earlier her mother had refused to come to her wedding because of a quarrel; all but one of her siblings had also stayed away. Mrs Church saw almost nothing of her wider family. Her mother was said to have twenty siblings, but Mrs Church only knew the names of four, and had never seen most of them. Perhaps significantly, she reported having spent the previous Christmas with her friends in Richmond rather than with family.[151]

In many ways the Burns family was similar. Mrs Burns's father died when she was a baby and her mother gave her up to be raised by a grandmother and aunt. These had been the important people in her life. Contact with her wider family, including her mother, was sporadic. She was closer to her husband's family, especially his siblings, who had offered considerable help during her pregnancy. But as a family they preferred to socialize with friends rather than relatives, challenging many stereotypical accounts of post-war working-class life.[152] When they threw a party to celebrate the birth of their daughter it was ten friends who came round to their flat to drink and dance to rock and roll and Cuban 'cha-cha'. Mrs Burns explained, 'It's better like that, all your relatives have got their eyes on you.' The Burns had a party most Saturday nights, usually with her husband's friends, most of whom were dockers.[153]

But researchers also visited households that could rely on neither friends nor family for social support. These took radically different forms. The Davidsons appear to have been largely *self*-isolating. Mrs Davidson maintained close relations with her mother, and saw her siblings frequently, mostly through daily visits to her mother. However, they had few if any visitors, partly because their flat was badly overcrowded. The Davidsons were in the process of buying a house at Abbey Wood, and seem not to have had much contact with neighbours. This could reflect deliberate social exclusivity—Mr Davidson worked as an accounts clerk—but Mrs Davidson's explanation was that the lady upstairs complained whenever her children made a noise. Certainly they weren't well off; even though they were now a family of seven they planned to take lodgers at Abbey Wood in to afford the mortgage.[154] The Murrays, by contrast, had no local connections, having ended up in Bermondsey largely by chance when Mr Murray found a job in a local brewery. The Murrays had almost no contact with their respective families in

Scotland; Mr Murray had not seen his family for more than ten years after dropping out of university and then refusing to take a job alongside his father in the local shipyard. Mrs Murray had been brought up in a care home after her father died and her mother abandoned her. Mr Murray's job had not lasted long, and he had been unemployed for some time. They had five children under 9 and life was clearly very tough (they had large debts, the children were poorly clothed, and there were suggestions of mental health and alcohol problems). During the study the health authorities referred the Murrays to the local Family Service Unit as a 'problem family' in need of help.[155] Their problems were merely compounded by social isolation. The Murrays claimed to have no support from neighbours. No one visited Mrs Murray either in hospital, where she was kept for many weeks before the birth, or later when she came home. Even her husband struggled to visit her in hospital because he could find no one to take care of their children.[156]

Mrs Moran, by contrast, was isolated by a combination of weak family ties and a bullying, possessive husband. Not only were her family in Northern Ireland, but they had disapproved of her decision to marry a Catholic docker (her sister, a member of the Protestant Orange Order, had disowned her). Unable to get an adequate allowance from her heavy-drinking husband, Mrs Moran had borrowed from friends to prepare for the birth, but this only increased her isolation because her inability to repay these debts led her to drop contact with the few friends she had. In the end her husband barred her from cooperating with Firth's project. The researcher noted, tragically, that the husband would not let her leave the house without the children 'in case she runs away & leaves him with them!' The file ends with a sombre note saying that the Health Office had been informed and asked 'to keep an eye out on Mrs Moran'. There is little sign that anyone else was going to do so.[157]

Finally, we need to consider the Miltons—the family that decided to relocate to rural Norfolk. In many ways they conformed closely to the model of a traditional close-knit working-class family. Mr Milton was a Thames barge-builder whose yard was so close to their flat that he could come home for a morning tea-break as well as for his midday dinner. Mrs Milton had been born locally, and many of her family still lived close by. She claimed to visit her mother at least three times a week, although she knew little of her wider kin (her mother had eleven siblings but she could name only one). They also saw a good deal of her husband's family, especially his mother, even though she lived over the water in Bow. Mrs Milton also had good relations with neighbours. After the birth a neighbour drove her home from the hospital as a favour because Mr Milton regularly gave him offcuts of wood from work. But Mrs Milton was unhappy with her council flat: it was 'too cut off', there was nowhere for her children to play, and they were not allowed to keep a dog (she had promised to buy one for her disabled son). Mr Milton was also unhappy—barge-building was in decline and he was often on short time. He also voiced anger at immigration, denouncing 'the Blacks' for 'taking all the work'. In May 1959 this cocktail of discontents came together in the sudden decision to tear up their roots and move to the small Norfolk town of Thetford under a Government-backed scheme to disperse people and industry away from London. The attraction, as the Government intended, was the guarantee of a job and a new house (to rent). In fact Mr Milton got two job offers, allowing him to bargain for a higher wage. The Miltons were hopeful that the move would not mean a complete break with close family. As they left, both sets of parents were said to be thinking of joining them in Norfolk, but it's clear that they were going regardless.[158] Even for the closest knit of families, the pull of a better life could be too strong to resist. As we will see in Chapter 3, the Miltons were far from alone in post-war Britain—arguably the 1950s witnessed internal population movements on a scale not seen since the early years of industrialization.

CHAPTER 3

MOVING OUT

In relocating from Bermondsey to Thetford in 1959 the Milton family joined a mass exodus from Britain's major urban conurbations taking place in the immediate post-war years. More than a million Londoners moved to new 'overspill' towns, and the movement out of Britain's other major conurbations such as Tyneside, Merseyside, Glasgow, the west Midlands, and Greater Manchester was on a comparable scale. The population of Thetford itself quadrupled in barely a decade, while the planned new towns grew at an even greater rate. Basildon, in Essex, increased from 25,000 to 157,000 in its first forty years, and Stevenage in Hertfordshire saw its population rise from under 7,000 to over 81,000 in the same period.[1] In total more than 2.5 million new homes were built in the decade and a half after 1945, and the majority of these were constructed by local authorities and new town corporations on greenfield sites that were often located at a considerable distance from their residents' former homes. The scale of this internal migration, and the extent to which it was actively planned by government, at both national and local levels, made it a unique social experiment. Perhaps inevitably, it drew close attention from social scientists and policymakers keen to know if the experiment—or rather the many *different* experiments dotted across the landscape—had been successful.

In 1953 Michael Young interviewed a sample of former Bethnal Green residents who had moved to the new post-war council estate at Debden in suburban Essex, 14 miles out on the underground's Central Line (he called it 'Greenleigh'). Built by the London County Council as one of a series of large 'out-county' estates to help ease overcrowding in the capital's war-torn central districts, by 1953 4,300 families had already moved to Debden, including 268 from Bethnal Green (see Map 4).[2] Young focused on a sample of forty-seven families, all of whom had at least two children under 15. In 1955, he returned to the estate, now accompanied by colleague Peter Willmott, to conduct follow-up interviews with the forty-one families still present and willing to cooperate.[3] Sadly, most of the Debden field-notes have been lost, but we do have details of more than thirty interviews conducted with a dozen couples who had moved out from Bethnal Green.[4] Although the number of cases is too small to draw sweeping conclusions about life on a new suburban council

Map 4. South East England showing the location of Debden and Stevenage and boundaries of Greater London

estate, the testimony is sufficiently rich to provide useful insights into the diverse ways in which people made sense of their part in the great post-war migration of urban Britons.

By contrast, 147 questionnaires survive from the survey of Stevenage new town organized by the young 'New Left' Marxist intellectual Raphael Samuel in the wake of Labour's 1959 election defeat (interestingly, the study was funded by Young and Willmott's Institute of Community Studies).[5] Samuel's primary aim was to under-stand the reasons for Labour's third successive election defeat, and in particular why so many working-class voters had apparently forsaken the party in prosperous southern towns like Stevenage. The interviews are less open-ended and exploratory than those conducted either by Young and Willmott in Debden or by Firth's anthropologists in Bermondsey, but fortunately they do touch on the vital issue of the new town as a giant experiment in planned community. In many ways, the post-war new towns were designed as the antithesis of the large, one-class suburban estates, both municipal and private, that had grown to cover large swathes of Britain's countryside between the wars.[6] Sited beyond the newly designated 'green belt' around Britain's conurbations, they were planned as 'balanced communities',

73

where people from a broad range of social backgrounds would live and work together. Based closely on the ideals of the garden city movement, they were imagined as self-sufficient communities where work and services would be close at hand and living densities would be low.[7] Twice as far from London, the move to Stevenage undoubtedly involved a greater break with one's roots than moving to an out-county estate like Debden (though not as great as relocating to many of the provincial towns scheduled for 'overspill' expansion at the same time—like Thetford in Norfolk, the Miltons' choice, which lies 88 miles from London, or Swindon in Wiltshire, slightly nearer at 80 miles distant).[8]

Debden and Stevenage had much in common. They were both post-war developments begun in the late 1940s to relieve the acute overcrowding of Victorian London. Both also met considerable resistance from established residents who feared that a large influx of 'outsiders' would reduce their own quality of life.[9] The newcomers therefore faced the challenge of a strange environment in which they had to learn how to live both with each other *and* with resentful locals. But the differences were at least as great. Debden was a residential housing estate set down between historic Essex towns and villages which had already become part of the London commuter belt. Perhaps inevitably this caused considerable social tensions, not least because, unlike Stevenage, Debden had relatively few amenities of its own, so that in the early years newcomers were dependent for services on nearby towns like Loughton, Chingford, and Epping. Debden was essentially a dormitory estate, with most of its residents still dependent on London for work and often for much of their social life—in 1953 some of the families visited by Young continued to do all their shopping in Bethnal Green, refusing to transfer their ration cards to the new estate in consequence.[10]

By contrast, Stevenage was a planned community, based around a civic centre and a series of smaller neighbourhood centres—or urban villages—providing schools, amenities, and local shops. The plan itself was far from perfect—the neighbourhood districts, with populations of approximately 10,000, were too large to become the familiar, walkable spaces that planners envisaged (as architects and planners subsequently acknowledged).[11] Nor did they become 'balanced communities' in which rich and poor lived happily together, side by side, although into the 1960s most residents continued to work locally; in 1960 Peter Willmott found 86 per cent of male employees worked within the new town's borders.[12] In practice both rich and poor were largely absent from the new town, but, ironically, this appears to have contributed considerably to residents' sense of belonging to a relatively cohesive, stable 'community'. For the most part Stevenage worked despite itself, but the key thing is that it worked.

The testimony collected from both Stevenage and Debden largely supports the arguments of social scientists and historians who have sought to challenge overly pessimistic accounts of the social consequences of post-war overspill policies.[13] Most people were happy with their new lives, probably partly because those who were not often moved on. More importantly, at Stevenage in particular many had clearly internalized a sense that they were part of a great social and political experiment; that they were pioneers of a new way of living in which the private hopes and ambitions of individual families could be realized through progressive social reform enacted on a grand scale. With spacious and convenient new houses, and a panoply of consumer goods to fill them, most felt themselves to be beneficiaries of what contemporaries were learning to call post-war 'affluence' (real disposable income per head rose by almost 60 per cent in the first two decades after the war). But it is not clear that the residents of post-war Stevenage recognized any fundamental tension between personal advancement and collective social progress. Understanding the social and political conditions that made this reconciliation of self and society possible in affluent post-war Stevenage can help to challenge overly deterministic accounts of the 'rise of individualism' which assume that affluence and the aspiration to 'better oneself' necessarily meant disregarding others and rejecting the claims of community.

Suburban blues?

For Young and Willmott the London County Council's Debden estate in suburban Essex represented the antithesis of 'community' as they claimed to have found it in Bethnal Green. Uprooted from familiar surroundings and close friendships, they argued that people retreated into privatized, isolated lives where neighbours were distrusted and held at arm's length. They wrote of a fundamental shift 'from a people-centred to a house-centred existence', and claimed that at Debden 'relations are window to window, not face-to-face'.[14] These stark contrasts depended on an idealized account of social relations in Bethnal Green, which, as we have seen, largely ignored the tensions that could run through relations between both neighbours and kinsfolk. They also depended on an overdrawn account of suburban anomie and the ills of the so-called 'affluent society' which once again ignored the complexity and diversity of people's everyday lives.[15] In Family and Kinship, Young and Willmott argued that 'bitterness', rather than 'a tacit agreement to live and let live', tended to dominate personal relationships at Debden.[16] When 'nearly everyone is a stranger', they argued, 'there is no means of uncovering personality ... Judgement must therefore rest on the trappings of the man rather than on the man himself.'[17]

For them suburban anomie was absolute; people thrown together with strangers from across the capital had responded by retreating into mutual suspicion, distrust, and even enmity. But was it fair?

Their Debden field-notes certainly provide examples of men and women bad-mouthing their neighbours. People with very different ideas about what it meant to be a 'good' neighbour were thrown together, and much as in new blocks of flats built in Bethnal Green and Bermondsey, this could generate considerable tension. Mrs Rawson complained that her next-door neighbour's children used foul language and stayed up till nearly midnight. She also complained that the family were always slamming doors, or coming home late from parties.[18] In a similar vein, Mrs Maggs spoke with vehemence about her neighbours 'at the back', complaining that their six children pulled up flowers in other people's gardens and used their own garden as a toilet.[19] Neither woman appears to have mobilized the language of 'rough' and 'respectable', but it is evident that they resented being forced to live next door to people with very different habits to their own.[20] To underscore her sense that she was 'normal' and her neighbours were not, Mrs Maggs mentioned that '3 of their neighbours have moved already', and criticized the father for neglecting his garden and failing to hold down a job: 'He works for 3 weeks and then packs it in.' Interestingly, she was also one of only three respondents (out of twenty-four) to complain that people were generally aloof and unfriendly at Debden, telling Young,

> We don't even know who lives opposite. We only know two couples on the whole estate by name. We say 'good morning' to many of them—but we don't know them from Adam. We didn't know that the husband of the woman opposite had died until we saw it in the local paper.[21]

But this family was unusual. After three years on the estate they insisted they were still hoping for a chance to get a house 'down home' in Bethnal Green. Indeed, their children were still going to school in London, and both parents travelled in daily for work. Their claim to be 'just lodging' in Debden rang true, and it is perhaps unsurprising that they had failed to put down roots.[22] Tellingly, they were the only family from the subsample who could not be recontacted in 1955—most likely they had gone 'home'.

Others reported having felt isolated and lonely on moving to Debden, but presented this as something they had managed to overcome. A number of women said loneliness had been an important factor encouraging them to go out to work, although they usually conceded that higher living expenses at Debden had also played a part. Mrs Usher claimed 'people think themselves a little bit above each other' at Debden, and told Young that she only took a job as a canteen assistant near Old Street 'because I'm so fed up with myself being on my own'. This was an understatement; as she went on to explain, she had recently been 'sent away' to Sussex for six weeks to recover from a nervous breakdown. She was convinced that the job had aided her recuperation, telling Young 'I feel better now, because of the company I suppose'.[23] Mrs Prince's story was similar, although she was adamant that she worked primarily for the company (her adult children brought home good wages). Interestingly, she was also particularly voluble in her complaints about unfriendly neighbours at Debden—proclaiming 'Some people down here have got big heads...It's only next door we speak to now. The rest ignore us and we ignore them now.'[24] Speaking in 1955, she explained the benefits of a new job at the local hospital almost exclusively in terms of her personal health: 'It keeps you in trim. Instead of sitting looking at yourself all day, you go out and see something of other people. Course my daughters help me a lot in the house.'[25]

But even Mrs Prince had no wish to return to Bethnal Green, and though she complained about neighbours being 'standoffish', she was glad that life was quieter in Debden than Bethnal Green. She told Young that in the early days there had been a 'terrible crowd' living near them, with lots of 'shouting and swearing', but things had since improved because most of the unruly people had returned to central London.[26] Two years later, Mrs Prince was even more positive about life in Debden, telling Young 'We like it here. We've always lived quiet. The only thing we do miss is the relations. I suppose it's the fares that does it. They can't afford to come down here and you can't afford to go down there. Everybody's hard at it these days.' She was particularly pleased that the estate now had its own supermarkets (a Sainsbury's and a Co-op), making it easier and cheaper for her to do the family's shopping (see Figure 11).[27] But Young was not much interested in the small things that made life at Debden pleasant for people like Mrs Prince. Interviewing Mrs Minton the following day he didn't even bother to record her list of things that had improved since his first visit in 1953. Instead he simply noted: 'There was the usual stuff about more shops, better bus services, more privacy, value of garden, improvement in children's health and in particular the advantage of the new house was stressed.'[28] It might be just the 'usual stuff' to Young, but this was life transformed for new suburban residents like the Mintons and the Princes.

Young and Willmott did recognize the genuine attractions of a new house and clean air, but they concentrated mainly on the problems of life at Debden, rather than the advantages. Besides suburban isolation, they emphasized the higher costs, poorer amenities, and above all the fractured family life associated with living on an out-county estate. Because their main aim was to encourage local authorities to

77

Figure 11. The Broadway shopping centre, Debden, *c*.1967 [private collection]

rehouse more families locally in Bethnal Green, they generally played down the positive reasons for wishing to move out. Indeed, they suggested that many families would be happy to return to Bethnal Green, but for the fact that they believed life at Debden was 'better for the kiddies'.[29] There were undoubtedly couples who saw things in these terms. The Rawsons, in particular, struggled to meet the higher rent and travel costs associated with life in suburban Debden. In 1953, Mrs Rawson explained that 'When we first came I thought we'd have to go back because the prices here were so high, and the rent nearly three times what we'd been paying, and the moving money was so heavy. Now I wouldn't go back any more. There's better air at Debden. It's better for the children.'[30] By 1955, Mr Rawson had given up hope of making a good living at his trade of French-polishing, and was working on the night shift for a transport firm in the City. His wife also worked full-time, explaining to Young, 'We really could not manage on £10 a week the way we live. We have a good standard.'[31] It is striking how often, in this period, people talked about living well *not* in terms of the things they owned, though most undoubtedly wanted new consumer goods like televisions and washing machines, but in terms of how they ate—as cultural critic Richard Hoggart famously noted, working-class people took pride in being able to keep a 'good table'.[32] With many foodstuffs rationed until 1954, and memories of the hungry thirties still strong, it was only natural to measure the good life as much by food as by things.[33] Couples like the

Rawsons accepted serious hardships in order to secure their 'good standard': Mr and Mrs Rawson hadn't seen each other at all during the week Young visited because of clashing shifts and long commutes. But their efforts were not just about securing a better standard of living; they were also focused on improving their children's life-chances. In 1953, Mrs Rawson told Young about their hopes for their 11-year-old son Paul: 'We want to give him the opportunity his father never had. My Hubby said, "he's not going to be a future van-boy of England". I sometimes look at Hubby and I say he goes out to work and he comes home. Well, Paul won't be like that.' In 1955, Mr Rawson also spoke of his ambitions for his son, telling Young: 'I'm hoping Paul will become an architectural draughtsman, certainly not manual work or a clerk. He'd worry too much if he did clerking work. When he gets started, even if it means working my nights off, I'm going to do everything to give him a good start.' Young promised to put their son in touch with an architect when he left school—noting 'I must remember that I have made this promise...Mr [Rawson] seemed very keen indeed on this and said he would keep up with me' (it was a striking example of social-science interviews being a two-way process in this new, more democratic age).[34]

Mrs Minton was no less ambitious for her children and was emphatic that Bethnal Green was no place to bring them up. As soon as the family returned from wartime evacuation they had applied for a house on one of the out-county estates, and in 1948 had been allocated one of the first houses to be completed at Debden. Her account of the conditions they returned to in post-war Bethnal Green underscored what geographers often call the 'push factors' behind moving out: 'Club Row, where we used to live, was very disgusting. After the [live animal] market they would throw dead dogs and chickens over the fence where the children had to play. The house was by a saw-mill so there was a terrible lot of dust in the air. The children had to play in the debris and one of my boys fell on it and cut himself bad on the glass.'[35] Others commented that the roads were safer, the schools better, and the temptations to petty crime fewer at Debden. Importantly, many stressed that this was also how their children saw things. Mrs Painswick reported that her eldest daughter 'cries her eyes out at the idea of going back to Bethnal Green. [She] doesn't want to go to London at all.'[36] Similarly, the Princes' grown-up son John told Young that, even though, like his mother, he found the neighbours to be too reserved, he would definitely prefer to live in Debden once he married, partly because he was a keen gardener, but also because the properties back in Bethnal Green were too small and cramped.[37]

But it wasn't all about 'the kiddies'. Some of the Debden residents welcomed the chance to make a new life, not just away from Bethnal Green, but away from family.

Others might voice regrets about breaking their old ties, but were clear that moving out was the best option for themselves as well as their children. Again, it is striking how uninhibited people could be when discussing their feelings about close family. Mr Rawson, the night-shift worker, told Young: 'There's never been a lot of love lost between us, because we've never had a good family life. Even as youngsters we never went round together. I don't miss my brothers or sisters.' He went on to explain, 'I've never been able to call on my relatives for anything. The same goes for my wife's side. As far as they care we might as well be off the earth. All that we've done we've achieved on our own.' Rawson claimed to have been brought up by a 'tartar of a grandmother' after his mother's early death, and said that his wife's upbringing had been even worse because of a heavy-drinking, brutal father (he told a story about how, when his wife was a child, this man had accused her of stealing ½ d (0.2p) from his pocket—when she denied it, her father had forced her leg on to an open fire).[38]

No one else felt quite so bitter about their families, but plenty stressed that weak kinship ties had made it easier to move to Debden. Mrs Sandeman's parents had divorced when she was young and she had largely lost contact with her mother, declaring 'We're too poor for my mother's people to pay any attention to, but perhaps we're rich in ways that they are not. We've got our children for instance.' Proud of her six children, she told Young that she could not have had such a large family if they had continued to live in cramped conditions in Bethnal Green.[39] Mr Damson, a disabled ex-serviceman, declared boldly of his relatives that moving had made no difference because he 'saw as little of them as possible when he lived in Bethnal Green', maintaining contact merely 'to "keep the peace" and be friendly'. He insisted that he did not 'depend on them in any way'. His wife declared herself 'thrilled to be away from the dirt of London', and was incredulous when Young told her that some families disliked the new estate and wanted to go back (she claimed to 'love Debden because it's the country').[40] Although some residents complained about the 'snobbish' attitudes of established residents in the surrounding townships, the Damsons displayed no self-consciousness about living on an out-of-town municipal estate. Indeed, there is little suggestion that living in 'social housing' carried the mark of social stigma in the early 1950s that it would carry later in the century. Certainly, the Damsons had no sense that they had been dumped in the suburbs to be forgotten; rather, they saw the new estate as evidence that there was a place for them in Britain's post-war 'New Jerusalem'.[41]

When Young revisited the Damsons in 1955, the first thing Mrs Damson said was 'we still love it here', before explaining that they were 'dreading' the possibility that their prefab might be demolished 'in case we have to move away'.[42] They had moved to Debden early (in 1949), and had evidently made good friends locally. It probably helped that Mr Damson's status as a disabled veteran meant neighbours liked to be helpful: one man parked his mobility vehicle each evening, while another came in and started blacking the Damsons' living-room grate in the middle of Young's first interview. Young observed 'if these had been siblings of the [Damsons] they could not have been more at ease in [their] house'; he also noted that the man appeared to be Jewish and pondered whether this explained the unusual intimacy since he also thought Mr Damson looked 'partly Jewish' (he wasn't, but Young always tried to find exceptional reasons to explain why people failed to behave according to his expectations, in this case ethnicity supposedly neutralized suburban anomie).[43] Mrs Damson was also close to her neighbours, claiming two as 'good friends' and observing that 'At night they shut their doors and all retire in to their homes, but in the day they are all friendly.' It was a pattern of female-centred, daytime sociability which we will also encounter at Stevenage a few years later, and one that survived, in modified form, into the twenty-first century. It was a form of sociability that could easily leave others, especially working women, feeling excluded (it is notable that the two interviewees who spoke most harshly about their neighbours were women working full-time). But the Damsons, at least, clearly belonged to an extensive social network on the estate. It is striking that, unlike many in Bethnal Green and Bermondsey, they also felt no social taboos about inviting non-kin into their home. In 1955, the Damsons celebrated the birth of their third child by throwing a party for friends and neighbours at which they reported everyone 'drank his health in champagne'.[44]

Residents boasting strong family ties generally managed to sustain their social connections, although distance undoubtedly made this more difficult and costly than when they had lived at Bethnal Green. Mrs Barnes, an Oxbridge graduate whose marriage to a self-taught Jewish building surveyor had increased her 'estrangement' from her own family, told Young that 'At week-ends a great many people visit their relatives; arriving with baskets of food and stuff, almost like visiting day in hospital.'[45] Additionally, those who still worked in central London often saw relatives after work, while others would catch up while making special shopping trips to buy things still hard to come by (or expensive) in suburban Essex.

It was in times of crisis that many felt the loss of relatives close at hand. Mrs Ruck was the most extreme case. When Peter Willmott visited her in 1955 she was preparing to leave Debden. Recently widowed, she found life in Debden impossible as a lone mother and was planning to return to London to live near her own mother in Islington (she had already found someone willing to swap properties and was waiting for council approval). As she explained to Willmott, 'As soon as I get back to London, near Mum, I'll be alright. I'll get a job and Mum will look after the kids.' She was bitter about the lack of support she had received from her neighbours, claiming,

> When I lost my husband they were all round—for about five minutes. Out here they come round to find out your business and then they don't want to know you. After I lost my husband I went up to stay with my Mum for a week. Before I'd gone they were all round asking me about it. But when I came back not a bugger spoke to me.[46]

Mrs Ruck had never fully adjusted to life on the estate. In 1953 she had told Young that she and her husband had spent the first two years having 'terrible arguments' about whether to stay. She explained that 'It's all pulling your roots up when you move, and I used to get terrible depressed...I used to say it's alright for you. I have to sit here all day.' But both she and her husband abhorred the prospect of living in flats, and it was this, plus the fact that her late husband had liked Debden, which had originally reconciled her to stay. As Willmott sagely noted, there were also reasons not to take her harsh indictment of her neighbours at face value. Two local people were actually visiting when he called; one was a neighbour, the other a female friend (and former Debden neighbour) who was staying over to keep her company. But if her harsh words might not be literally true, they powerfully conveyed the pain of trying to cope with bereavement when immediate family were not close at hand.[47]

By contrast, the Painswicks were very happy at Debden despite the fact that the father had had to give up a well-paid job (and future pension) because commuting had triggered a serious depression. He made jokes about having learned to enjoy gardening despite not knowing 'an oak tree from a flowerpot' before he arrived, and told Young 'I wouldn't want to go back to Bethnal Green even if it were rent free'.[48] But this family still registered the difficulties caused by separation, and, as so often, it was the woman who articulated these feelings most strongly. In October 1955 she told Young that although they were 'content' in Debden, and had 'always liked it', the one problem was that 'we do miss the relatives. Up there [Bethnal Green] you have got the relatives near.' This was partly about missing social contacts. Mrs Painswick described her family as 'a very united one', and argued that 'When you come from a united family you get used to company and you miss it when you don't have it. You want company.' But it was more than that. Having struggled with debilitating illness for some time, she had recently been told that she must have an operation. In previous years her eldest daughter had stayed off school to look after the home, but now that she was working this was no longer an option, and Mrs Painswick didn't know what she could do. She told Young, 'I can't pluck up the courage to go into the hospital. It is worse being ill out here because you're not near anyone who can come and give you a hand.'[49] But again things were not quite as they seemed. In the past

Mrs Painswick had felt able to turn to her Debden neighbours for help with childcare, reporting that she had been able to take a full-time job in Loughton because a friend across the road looked after her youngest daughter (she paid the woman a pound a week for her trouble). Perhaps more surprisingly, in an earlier interview she mentioned that even when she had lived in Bethnal Green she had turned, not to family, but to a paid home help during a previous period of hospitalization. Again, this is not to suggest that she did not feel the absence of family, merely to point out that what she missed may have been an idealized version of the family life she had once known.[50]

It was Mrs Painswick's eldest daughter who was said to cry at the thought of going back to Bethnal Green; it was one reason why she, like most Debden residents, had no wish to leave despite the lack of 'company'. But even among those who *were* keen to leave, very few were willing to countenance a return to their former haunts in Bethnal Green, despite Young and Willmott's suggestion that most had only left because of the acute shortage of housing. Out of twenty-four respondents, seven indicated a desire to leave Debden (although in some cases this was projected into the distant future; for instance, Mrs Barnes, the Oxbridge graduate, said she liked the estate 'very much' but imagined moving 'further into the country' when her children were older).[51] The only people who wanted to move back to Bethnal Green were Mr and Mrs Maggs, the couple who described themselves as 'just lodging' in Debden (the couple that had indeed left the estate when Young returned two years later).

Besides Mrs Ruck, who wanted to move to be with her mother in Islington after her bereavement, other dissatisfied residents merely wanted to try a *different* new place. In her account of moving to a new council estate as a child in the early 1950s, Lorna Sage has written that 'We all shared a sense of being out of place, on the move,' and it was probably this internalized sense not just of mobility but also of making choices which encouraged restless Debden tenants to think in terms of alternative new beginnings rather than 'homecomings'.[52] Mrs Paige, whose husband worked as a windscreen fitter in London, asked Young if he knew of any two-storey maisonettes going in Hackney, ideally near Victoria Park, and made it quite clear that she would never go back to Bethnal Green, saying 'I don't like the look of Bethnal Green'.[53] Mrs Usher hoped to move further from London. Lonely and unhappy in Debden (she was the woman who had taken a job after suffering a nervous breakdown), she hoped to move to the expanding town of Bletchley (later incorporated into Milton Keynes), partly because it would be nearer her relatives in the east Midlands, but also because she thought it would have better amenities than the Debden estate.[54] She was not the only person to think like this. The Mintons' adult son Bernie wanted his parents to secure a transfer to the nearby new town of

Harlow, which, he pointed out, already boasted a 'skating rink, cinema and better shops'. Although generally happy with Debden, his father was forced to agree, commenting that 'they got the jobs there before the houses and that seems the right way round'.[55]

For these people at least, the bold vision that underpinned Britain's post-war 'new towns' seemed more attractive than the ad hoc creation of suburban dormitory estates such as Debden. To them the ambitious scale of the new towns promised jobs and amenities close at hand—something that Debden still sorely lacked in the mid-1950s. But were they right to believe that the great social experiment which led to the creation of Harlow, Stevenage, and the other post-war new towns had solved the problem of creating viable communities from scratch? In the next section we turn to examine this question through the lens of Britain's first new town: Stevenage.

New towns, new lives

Conducted in the immediate aftermath of Labour's resounding election defeat in October 1959 (the third in succession), Raph Samuel's Stevenage survey focused mainly on exploring newcomers' attitudes to class, deference, and party politics (George Clark conducted a parallel study of Clapham in south London). Samuel, still only 24 when he began the survey, had an overtly political aim: to understand why Labour had apparently lost further ground in this expanding new industrial town. Stevenage did not become a constituency in its own right until 1983, but it already provided a sizeable chunk of electors to the Hertfordshire constituency of Hitchin, which in 1959 saw its Conservative majority increase from 965 to 4,375.[56] In political terms, Samuel's survey threw up few surprises. Voters who had switched to the Conservatives explained their choice mainly in terms of the Government's record of good economic management, which was often contrasted with the economic crises that had dogged the post-war Labour Governments (Labour also suffered from a widespread perception that it was disunited, and from fears about the possible impact of further nationalization).[57] Strikingly, some residents even reproduced recent Conservative election slogans as their own common-sense reasons for returning Macmillan's Conservatives for a third term. Eric Forrest, a technician in the plastics industry in his late twenties, told Thea Vigne (the future pioneer of oral history), 'we have done very well under the Conservative government, and people don't want to take a chance of Labour ruining it. The Labour Party could probably do as well or better but people aren't prepared to take the chance.' He also declared that the Conservatives had 'made it better' since taking office in

Figure 12. Conservative Party election poster, 1959: 'Life's Better with the Conservatives' [photo by The Conservative Party Archive/Getty Images]

1951—another reworking of the famous Conservative election posters designed by the advertising agency Colman, Prentis, Varley (Figure 12).[58] But there were also specifically local factors influencing the large swing from Labour to Conservative (Samuel calculated that in Stevenage itself there had been a massive swing of 15 per cent since the 1955 election).[59] Time and again, people reported fears that jobs (or overtime) would be at risk if Labour nationalized local firms or cut defence spending, while workers at the De Havilland aerospace company reportedly feared that Labour would cancel the ill-fated Blue Streak medium-range missile system (in fact it was cancelled anyway the following year).[60]

Finally, Samuel was particularly struck by the persistence of essentially deferential reasons for preferring Conservative politicians over their Labour counterparts even in a new town like Stevenage. In an article in the first edition of the radical journal *New Left Review*, he sought to drag the debate about Labour's electoral plight away from narrow economic rationalism and an obsession with consumption, to issues of ideology and culture. He argued that the Left needed to develop a strong counter-narrative to the Conservative claim that they alone governed in the 'national interest'—that it needed to revive the basis of Left patriotism and challenge the still widespread view that Conservative leaders represented a disinterested elite, born and educated to rule. Samuel stressed that deference was as widespread in Stevenage, 'one of the newest industrial communities in Britain', as in an 'ageing inner London borough' like Clapham.[61] Even in the new towns, he suggested, the weight of England's past sat heavy on people's shoulders.

Samuel's pioneering exploration of the relationship between deference and working-class Toryism reflected his determination to understand the broader social and cultural context of politics.[62] Thankfully, this meant that his researchers were instructed to ask a broad range of questions about people's experience of moving to a new town, including questions about neighbours, community feeling, and the prevalence of class distinctions. They were also encouraged to reflect on what Stevenage was like compared with where they had lived before. Most people were glad they had moved and claimed to like living in Stevenage. This is not especially surprising. Not only had people *chosen* to relocate to Stevenage, often because their existing living conditions were intolerable, but many of those who may have come to regret their decision would already have moved on. They were not around to be interviewed by Samuel and his colleagues.[63]

Mr Davies, the head teacher at one of the town's new primary schools, was a beneficiary of the Development Corporation's failure to persuade senior executives and other professionals to put down roots in the town. His family rented a large detached house which the developers had been unable to sell even at a heavy discount. Davies was a strong (if somewhat patrician) socialist and he deeply regretted that 'we don't get a true cross section living here', claiming 'there isn't enough stimulus for the people who could become really interested in things' (the interviewer commented: 'This is a good Socialist . . . We talked for hours, and I'm not going to write it all down because he said just exactly what any of the rest of us would have said'—the post-war 'New' Left still possessed a strong patrician belief that 'the masses' would be led to socialism through education and cultural enrichment).[64] One respondent, a plumber at English Electric, seemed to resent the fact that managers refused to live alongside their workers, saying 'They try to create a class distinction—between the management and the working class. They think they're a better class—they get a home outside where the workers come from.'[65] But the man's comment was made to reinforce his wife's observation that there was *no* class distinction where they lived. In essence, he too was saying that the failure to realize the planners' ideal 'balanced community', where managers and workers would live side by side, made Stevenage a better place to live, even if he didn't much like the reason.

We do hear from a few people who were in the process of leaving Stevenage, and their comments are suggestive. Liz Church, the wife of a sales manager in engineering, had moved to Stevenage 'to get a house', having previously lived in rooms in Bayswater. She liked the town, especially its 'very pleasant, friendly, family living', but explained that they had always intended to move on as soon as they could afford to buy their own house.[66] It was evidently inconceivable to her that they would buy in Stevenage despite the fact that by the early 1960s approximately 10 per cent of the housing stock was privately owned.[67] Betty Thatcher, a middle-class housewife in her mid-thirties, was also about to move and obliquely acknowledged that she was motivated by a desire to separate herself from other classes. Like many respondents she did this by making impersonal sociological statements about how 'people' felt (*displaced* snobbery was socially more acceptable). She told Stephen Hatch: 'A lot of people who live here because they have to [interviewer: "due to job"], dislike the attitude of having to live next to just anybody. They prefer to live next to people of their own kind. That sort quickly get out of Stevenage' (her husband's job with the Atomic Energy Authority had brought them to Stevenage in 1957).[68] Mrs Thomas, the wife of a structural engineer, arrived the same year, also because of her huband's job transfer. She too was determined to get out as quickly as possible. She complained that the town was 'dead at night' and that there was 'no social mixing'. Again there are strong suggestions that aspirations to class exclusivity were fuelling her desire to move, hence her comment that 'it keeps people working class anyway. Nobody who fancies he's anybody would live in a place like this.'[69]

Writing in 1961, Alan Duff, the former general manager of the Stevenage Development Corporation, acknowledged that not one in ten of Stevenage's senior managers chose to live in the town. Duff conceded that 'he [the senior manager] does not want to live cheek-by-jowl with his own work-people, nor they with him.... So either he buys or rents a manor house or vicarage in some country village as much unlike a New Town as it can possibly be; or else he takes a flat in London, where many of his business connections live.'[70] Duff, a distinguished career soldier before taking up the post, was also surprisingly frank about why the poor were radically under-represented in England's post-war new towns: they weren't wanted. Here it was the planners themselves who undermined the aspiration to create a 'balanced community'. Duff explained that the policy of requiring newcomers to complete a six-month trial with a local employer, and of insisting that *only* employers could nominate people for Corporation tenancies, was intended to exclude 'less welcome types' such as 'people with very large families, or suffering from chronic illness, or indifferent workers'. As he candidly explained, 'this *hidden process of selection* works towards an appreciable raising in the levels of skill and of character'.[71] Housing need alone was not sufficient to secure you a move to a post-war new town.

Initially Stevenage had been envisaged as somewhere to house the 'overspill' population of north London's outer boroughs including Tottenham, Wood Green, and Edmonton, rather than more central, inner-city districts.[72] In practice, some people came from much further afield, but Londoners always had priority in the allocation of jobs and housing, and the bias towards the outer London boroughs was still clearly evident in Samuel's 1959 sample. Less than 8 per cent of residents had moved from inner London boroughs, compared with 68 per cent from the rest of the London conurbation, including Middlesex and the metropolitan boroughs of Essex.[73] Only 11 per cent had come from outside the south-east region, and of these half came from other parts of southern England—East Anglia, the south coast, and the West Country. However, many of those moving out from London had originally been born elsewhere, and almost 30 per cent had been born outside the South East. Many of these (more than half) hailed from northern England, making Stevenage regionally less homogeneous than the official data on origins might suggest.[74] The average age for this group was 42, noticeably higher than for the sample as a whole, suggesting that many may originally have migrated to find work in the prosperous South during the 1930s Depression or the war.

Although rich and poor might be thin on the ground, Stevenage was far from a one-class town. Samuel's sample, which was drawn exclusively from wards in the new town, suggested that more than 40 per cent of heads of household had non-manual jobs, including 17 per cent in professional and managerial occupations.[75] As Duff had hoped, skill levels were high across the workforce: only three of Samuel's households (2.3 per cent) were headed by an unskilled worker, compared with 9.2 per cent nationally.[76] Willmott's 1960 survey the following year generated broadly similar results, with 35 per cent of male workers recorded as 'non-manual', and only 3 per cent as unskilled.[77] Contemporary sociologists made much of the social and cultural gulf between manual and non-manual workers, but here only managers and professionals seem to have felt (and been seen as) a class apart. Despite its mixed occupational structure, most residents insisted that people were more or less the same in Stevenage. Mrs Tufnell, a bricklayer's wife in her late thirties, actually thought there was less class distinction in Stevenage than in the East End, which she'd left in 1952, saying, 'Everyone having new houses makes everyone on the same level.'[78] Mrs Richardson, a painter and decorator's wife originally from the North East, took a similar view, arguing that 'when you come to a new town everybody starts on a new level. They have their own place to live and their own jobs. I don't think there is much class distinction at all.'[79] For them, at least, the town's newness trumped class.

When Samuel asked people more directly about social class he received answers which can easily appear contradictory. Some thought that having a modern house and a good job automatically made them (and their neighbours) middle class. So Gino Rossi, a young engineering fitter from central London, thought that 'middle class is people like myself. Really, nearly everyone on this estate. We all go to work but our standard of living is much higher than 20 years ago.'[80] But others thought that everyone in Stevenage was working class precisely because they all had to work for a living, or because they (almost) all had to rent their homes from the Development Corporation.[81] Mrs Tungate, the wife of an engineering inspector in her mid-twenties, thought that the world was divided between 'the people who work for a living and the people who don't!', and insisted 'well we're working people and I can't imagine we shall ever have any money without working for it'. The interviewer had no doubt that the family were 'definitely middle class', but Mrs Tungate was adamant that 'everyone's very much the same, we're all working people here, of course there's some earning more than the others, but that's all'.[82] As the sociologist Mike Savage has shown, in this era it was common for working-class people to embrace an inclusive language of 'ordinariness' when talking about social class. To be ordinary was to take people as you found them—it was the self-conscious antithesis of 'snobbery' or 'putting on airs'.[83] But in Stevenage, at least, this was the also the default position of workers in clerical, technical, and supervisory occupations. Mrs Tungate was far from a lone voice.[84]

Many people professed to see Stevenage itself as a place outside the English class system. For them, the modernity and progressivism behind the new-town vision stood in stark contrast to the rigidities of social class in the 'old England' that people had left behind. Even more than in Debden, many newcomers possessed an overt sense of themselves as the mobile pioneers of a new way of living—they saw themselves as 'starting afresh', as one rootless ex-serviceman put it.[85] In memoirs about the early days of the new town, people explicitly identify as having been 'pioneers' of a 'great social experiment'.[86] The testimony that Samuel collected is never this explicit, but we do hear people identifying strongly with the town as somewhere new and different. Mrs Burns, the wife of a skilled toolmaker, liked the fact that there was none of the social snobbery she had known living in Hendon, commenting that here no one 'looked shocked if your husband came home dirty'.[87] John Collins, a tool-room supervisor who described himself as coming from 'a working-class family in Bow', was struck by the unfamiliar 'maze of class' in Stevenage, and claimed that here 'I'm in a kind of unclassed position'.[88] Others praised the way house types had been mixed up, so that residents weren't rigidly segregated by income. Dennis Black, a draughtsman who had moved out from Richmond, liked the fact that it wasn't like Letchworth Garden City, 'where people are separated with the fifteen pound a week people on one side of the street and ten pound a week people on the other'. He was also adamant that he and the shop-floor machinist had 'the same standard of living. I don't consider myself any better. We're equal, actually in the same class, the skilled class' (though he was realistic enough to acknowledge that the machinist had to work heavy overtime to achieve this equality).[89] Similarly, Mrs Warren, the wife of a quality control inspector in her late forties, liked the social mix in Stevenage, particularly the fact that 'professional people live in amongst you, in the same houses as yourself' (she too identified her own family as 'skilled class').[90]

It is also striking how many people displayed a strong sense of being part of a shared project of self-improvement and self-making as residents of the new town.[91] It is here that we see most clearly how, at least in Stevenage, people's ambition to 'better' themselves, as so many of them put it, was intertwined with an awareness that this was also a *collective* endeavour—that they were all in the same situation, trying to make a new life in a place orientated squarely to the future rather than the past. June Baldwin, a clerk's wife from Tottenham with three young children, loved Stevenage and identified strongly with her neighbours as people who also valued the new life it offered. As she explained in response to the survey's question about class distinction, 'People are much of a kind here. They came down for one purpose: having a home in a country area, to be able to breathe and live, a garden for the children to play in.'[92] Others latched on to the fact that 'They'—those with power and authority—had finally begun to take an interest in ordinary people's lives and how they might be improved. A Labour-voting old-age pensioner was impressed to have seen Harold Macmillan visiting her street, and told Samuel that 'the Queen went into one of the houses along here, one of the flats; *they're* taking more interest in the working-class people' (see Figure 13).[93] But what really impressed people was how the new town had transformed their living conditions. Derek Harston, a draughtsman in his twenties, spoke in an abstract, sociological way about its impact on people who had previously only known poverty and overcrowding, but others spoke more personally about the joys of having their 'own front door' at last.[94] Of course it wasn't the door that people cherished, but what it stood for: domestic privacy, and especially not having to share their kitchen and bathroom with strangers (or parents) (see Figure 14).

Figure 13. The Queen visiting Stevenage to open the new town's shopping centre, 1959 [copyright Stevenage Museum]

It would be difficult to exaggerate just how bad housing conditions were for many young couples in post-war London, even in the suburban districts from which most Stevenage residents hailed. A couple who had moved from Ealing in 1953 had previously been trying to raise their young family in a cramped attic flat, while a junior manager's wife recalled that moving to Stevenage had made 'a world of difference', because before the family had lived in just two rooms with no running water in Leyton (this wasn't just a story about working-class hardship).[95] Dorothy Cotton, an aircraft technician's wife, was equally overjoyed to have a modern house, though for her the contrast was with the cramped and dilapidated country cottage she had left behind in Hampshire. She felt her new home was like living 'in a hotel'.[96] These comments strongly reinforce the picture we gain from contemporary studies of overspill developments. An early 1970s study of people who had moved out from Islington found that 87 per cent thought they had made the right decision, including an elderly couple who declared, 'This is like Paradise to us. It's as near to it [as] we've ever been and are ever likely to get!'[97]

Figure 14. All mod cons 1950s style; promotional image of a Stevenage new town kitchen [copyright Stevenage Museum]

The good life shared?

Some Stevenage residents feared that social divisions were sure to resurface with time. Mrs Warren ruefully acknowledged that her professional neighbours would probably move on to more prestigious districts including Stevenage's old town (something we've seen was already happening). But others displayed a more genuinely sociological mindset, like the skilled fitter who argued that the decision to build more houses for sale on his side of town was likely to breed 'snobbery' in the future.[98] There was also a fairly widespread sense that people would want to go on 'bettering' themselves. For most this meant improving their homes and buying more (or better) consumer goods, but the restlessness that had brought people to Stevenage also made many recognize they might move again. The urge to own rather than rent was an important factor here and, as we have seen, for professional and managerial workers this ambition was often linked to the urge to move out of the new town to a nearby village or historic market town. But others, like instrument-maker Richard Hopper, just wanted a better home. Evidently determined not to be labelled a social climber, Hopper declared, 'I'd like a better home and so on, but wouldn't like to be known as middle class. I've no illusions about myself.' He would probably have been pleased to discover that the interviewer recorded him as being a 'forthright cockney'.[99] A survey of Stevenage in 1966 found that 43 per cent of new-town tenants wanted to become owner-occupiers, and 93 per cent believed that the Development Corporation should sell houses to sitting tenants. Among the minor-ity of existing owner-occupiers there was even higher support for the right to buy, as well as an even stronger urge to keep moving: every owner-occupier surveyed said they planned to move to a different house at some point.[100] Nor was this just idle talk. Overall 39 per cent of newcomers to Stevenage had moved again since arriving in the town, including 33 per cent of Corporation tenants.[101]

One might imagine that this restless churn added to the sense of anomie on the new town's estates, but the evidence from Samuel's survey is more positive. There were certainly people who reported that they had little contact with their neigh-bours, but the majority found Stevenage to be friendlier than the place they had left. For some newcomers neighbours undoubtedly filled the gap left by now distant family. In his 1960 survey of the town Peter Willmott reported that half his sample had been visited by a friend or neighbour in the previous twenty-four hours and three-quarters at some point in the previous week.[102] Samuel asked just under a hundred of his respondents about the perceived friendliness of the new town. Just over 40 per cent felt that Stevenage was friendlier than the place they had left, compared with 25 per cent who felt it less friendly (the rest felt there was no real difference).[103] Clearly, in answering this question much depended on how people felt about where they had lived before. Interestingly, of those who found Stevenage less friendly none had moved out from the old inner London boroughs, which, as we have seen, were, at that moment, being celebrated as the epitome of close-knit community in studies such as Young and Willmott's *Family and Kinship in East London*. In fact there is no simple pattern among those who found Stevenage less friendly. Some were from predominantly working-class suburban districts such as Dagen-ham and Walthamstow, or northern industrial towns such as South Shields, and others were from small provincial towns in Cornwall, Somerset, and Kent, but there were also people from the mixed suburban sprawl around London that contem-poraries often assumed to be the antithesis of 'communal' living: places like Enfield, Edgware, and Willesden.[104] Mrs Black, a retired policeman's wife from Brixton, regretted that there was 'not the same companionship and community' as she had known in London, but viewed her new house and access to 'Beautiful country' as compensation (although the 'community' she missed was partly occupational—the couple had previously lived in police accommodation).[105] The man from South

Shields found people 'a little chary of meeting each other' in Stevenage, but took comfort from knowing that 'there are quite a few Geordies here'.[106] If the planners' attempts to engineer community through design strategies such as communal spaces, neighbourhood units, and walkable journeys to school failed to register, this man could create his own sense of community from shared bonds to a lost (or perhaps simply imagined) 'community' elsewhere.

On health and environmental grounds, new town planners sought to maintain a strict separation between industrial and residential land usage, but they were also keen to recreate the communal cohesion widely associated with older industrial towns where large numbers had lived and worked alongside one another. Attracting large high-tech companies like English Electric and De Havilland, which each employed thousands of highly skilled workers, was seen as one way to do this whilst avoiding many of the environmental disadvantages of traditional heavy industry.[107] But not everyone was happy to live amongst their workmates, certainly not the technician from New Malden who complained that 'In London you don't live within half a mile of your workmates. Here I live with my workmates and feel like an ant in a trap.'[108] By contrast, an inspector at English Electric, who had grown up in Newcastle, welcomed the sense of 'close-knit community' (his words) that he gained from frequently meeting workmates about the town.[109] Interestingly, an electrical engineer who had grown up in Enfield and Harrow was convinced that the new town was friendlier 'because a lot of people in Stevenage come from the North and the Midlands—they are less reserved than Londoners'.[110] There may be something in this. Certainly when large numbers of Londoners began moving to Swindon under the Government's town expansion scheme, the council moved quickly to appoint full-time neighbourhood workers to help ease the process of mutual adjustment. Amongst other things this included reassuring anxious Londoners that although their new West Country neighbours might seem unusually friendly, this did *not* mean that they would intrude on their privacy.[111]

Certainly, those who found Stevenage to be friendlier than the place they had left were disproportionately likely to be ex-Londoners. Overall, Londoners comprised 76 per cent of respondents, but they represented 82 per cent of those finding Stevenage friendlier, and only 58 per cent of those who felt the opposite. People offered a range of explanations for Stevenage being friendlier. A painter's wife from Bexleyheath, who had grown up in Sunderland, observed 'I think people down here are young, [they] don't know anyone and they speak to you because they're lonely.'[112] For others, as we have seen, the key factor was that Stevenage was less 'snobby' and class-conscious. But some simply relayed tales of meeting everyday friendliness that they had not previously encountered. A woman in her mid-thirties, who had been born and raised near King's Cross, commented that 'in the short time we've been here [two years] we know as many people as we did in London'.[113] Marie Pearce, a labourer's wife in her forties who had moved from Harrow Weald in 1955, offered a powerful testimony about how being thrown together in an unfamiliar environment could itself build strong social bonds:

> I've had quite a lot of illness and the neighbours have been very helpful with the shopping; they've taken the children in and they sent me flowers when I was in hospital. We're all close together here: we all depend on each other for help because relations are so far away. I hope to stay here for the rest of my life.[114]

Studies of new council estates between the wars had found that identification with neighbours tended to be strongest in an estate's early 'pioneering' phase, when residents were thrown together both by hostility from established residents living nearby and by shared grievances such as poor amenities.[115] There is some evidence that this was also true for the post-war new towns. People were aware that many in 'Old Town' (as pre-war Stevenage now came to be known officially) had opposed the creation of the Development Corporation vociferously in the late 1940s, but perhaps because the new town's residents were already in the majority Samuel's survey found little evidence of lasting resentment (see Map 5).[116] Hostility was discussed as something from the past, and was explicitly identified with well-to-do groups in the Old Town. Rightly or wrongly, it was viewed as a hangover of the old class order that Stevenage had supposedly been created to wipe away. Jack Bannister, a young tool designer from Scotland described as 'an extra-metropolitan "Absolute Beginner"-type' by his interviewer, recalled avoiding dances in the Old Town because they were dominated by Young Conservatives who 'thought they were a cut above us'.[117] Subsequent oral histories have also played down the hostility between the old and new towns. Interviewed in the late 1990s, Kate Cope, who had moved to the new town in 1954 with her young family, commented that though she had read about hostility, 'I didn't come across it personally', while retired aerospace draughtsman John Amess was adamant that 'we didn't find any hostility towards us, it was more of a gentle leg-pull'.[118] Terry Carter's autobiographical account of growing up in Loughton paints a very similar picture, stressing that working-class locals like his mother identified with the newcomers at nearby Debden and sought to make them feel welcome in their unfamiliar new surroundings.[119]

Some certainly felt that after nearly ten years of rapid development Stevenage's early communal spirit was already on the wane. Mrs Ford, a labourer's wife who had arrived in 1953, complained that established residents were no longer 'as helpful to

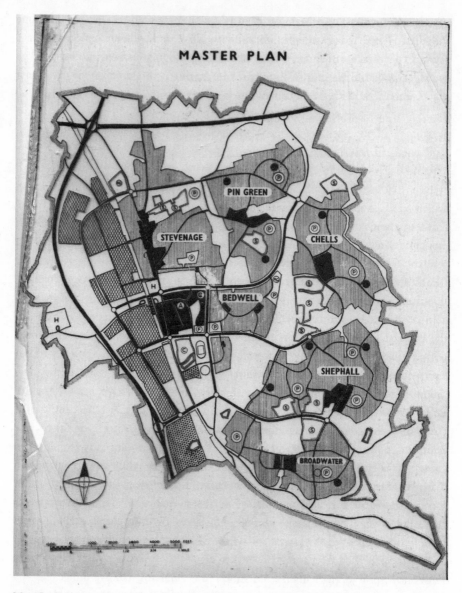

Map 5. Stevenage Town Plan, showing the planned neighbourhood districts; Old Town is here marked simply as Stevenage (from *The New Town of Stevenage, an illustrated account*, Stevenage Development Corporation, 1949) [copyright Stevenage Museum]

the very new people as they were at the beginning'. She also attacked the 'false snobbery' of people who bought cars when they were too poor to run them: 'they eat Oxo for lunch! And you hear the same people saying "Come in and have a drink, old chap".'[120] It was a jarring comment which reminds us that not everyone thought that Stevenage existed outside the old class system. Inevitably, we also hear people proclaiming 'we keep ourselves to ourselves', including a lorry driver convinced his neighbours were a bad lot, a skilled engineer who felt 'otherwise you have rows and people borrowing things all the time', and a technician who acknowledged his neighbours were friendly, before declaring 'they're just not my type; they always give the impression that they want to know one another's business'.[121] It was the same ingrained wariness towards strangers we encountered in Bermondsey and Bethnal Green, but here mobilized to help navigate a new social world where people from quite different backgrounds found themselves living side by side.

Doubtless personal temperament played its part in whether people felt at ease with their new neighbours, but there were also more structural factors at play. As at Debden, the people who spoke most warmly about their neighbours tended to be women with young children. In this group, the proportion saying Stevenage was friendlier, rather than less friendly, was almost three to one (compared with less than two to one overall). Mrs Tungate was a classic example. In her late twenties with two young children, she had built close ties to neighbours in the same situation, explaining, 'In Walthamstow we hardly knew anyone, here we swop children, me and the girls who live in the next house, we're always in and out.'[122]

Despite conscious attempts to build properties for people at different stages in the life course, new town populations still tended to be skewed dramatically towards young couples with children (at Stevenage 76 per cent of the population was aged under 40 in 1961 compared with 56 per cent nationally).[123] Perhaps inevitably, people without children could feel marginalized. Mrs Black, the retired policeman's wife, complained that there were 'too many children' because Stevenage was 'a young town'. The Carrolls, a childless couple in their late twenties, complained that at Stevenage 'none of your neighbours have got the time to spend their spare hours with you because of children', adding that 'in London friends and relatives were always popping round'.[124] As in Debden, mothers who worked full-time tended to be marginal to local female networks, and could feel deeply resentful. This was true of Mrs Ford, the woman who jibed that neighbours fed their kids Oxo for lunch, and also Mrs Szymański, a Polish labourer's wife, who worked full-time in a canteen despite having two pre-teenage children. She called her neighbours 'stand-offish' and insisted that because she worked all day she never mixed with them.[125] These women claimed they could be *better* mothers by going out to work—Mrs Ford's children didn't get malnutrition from living off Oxo cubes—but both seem to have felt keenly that it placed them outside the dominant culture of their respective neighbourhoods.[126]

Samuel's team was also interested to know whether life in a new town encouraged consumerism and the urge to 'keep up with the Joneses'. Their question lacked subtlety, and may well have helped generate some barbed comments about other people's consumption habits (like Mrs Ford's observation about neighbours with cars they could not afford to run). Researchers asked people: 'Do you think there is much competition between neighbours over washing-machines, T.V. sets, refrigerators and so on here?' Overall, 52 per cent agreed that there was, compared with 28 per cent who said no, although the question offered such a strong lead that this probably tells us more about respondents' suggestibility than anything.[127] What people actually said is often more revealing—the suggestion that they and their neighbours might be trying to 'keep up with the Joneses' sparked many lively responses. Some directly challenged the question's premise in one way or another, and a few clearly felt personally offended by the implied criticism of their status-conscious materialism (one interviewer noted that an engineer's wife 'made disapproving grunts at this question even being asked').[128] But there were also people who genuinely and strongly agreed with the anti-materialist sentiment at the heart of the question. John Collins, a tool-room superintendent and Labour Party member declared, 'it's tragic. A family's rated for what it owns. Everyone's trying to get that bit better; looking into one another's houses to see what fridges they have.'[129] Similarly, Mrs Ince explained her decision to carry on working in a clerical job at English Electric by commenting, 'You've just got to compete with the Joneses here, whether you like it or not.' Her husband, a semi-skilled wireman with the same firm, blamed women for the 'competitive spirit', explaining 'People have never had modern amenities before, and it's just the swank of people with good things for the first time.'[130]

Mr and Mrs Ince clearly felt uncomfortable in Stevenage. When asked whether there were class distinctions in Stevenage, Mr Ince replied, 'We hate communal life, and don't really fit in the New Towns. Everyone knows your business, though we try to keep ourselves to ourselves. Everyone says this—there's a lot of scandal mongering—for instance we can't go out separately without people spreading rumours about us'. But his wife then added 'I'm the only woman to work round here'—an odd non sequitur unless one assumes that this played its part in the couple's feeling that they did not 'belong'.[131] Certainly, others celebrated 'communal life' and saw the acquisition of new consumer goods as something not just to be celebrated, but also to be shared with friends and neighbours. In essence, they were describing the same behaviour, but assigning it a completely different meaning. Beryl Watts, the 23-year-old wife of a Luton car worker, told how, 'When I got my fridge the whole street came to look at it, and now they've all got one.'[132] She clearly took pride in having been a trailblazer for domestic refrigeration, but there is little sense here of competitive one-upmanship. For Watts, private consumption was something to be shared with friends who, like her, strongly identified with the pleasures of making their first home.[133] Peter Willmott's 1963 study of the massive Dagenham estate on London's eastern fringe drew similar conclusions, arguing that 'the process by which one family followed another's example was the result of friendly endorsement rather than rivalry', and concluding that 'in the main people on the estate seem to see their fellows not as adversaries but as allies in a general advance'.[134]

Others challenged the implications of the question more directly. Linda Jones, a hairdresser in her late forties, replied, 'Not really. Most of us have these things but I don't see where competition comes in' (note the use of 'us' here; in many ways it was a bigger challenge to the researchers' assumptions than her denial that people were competitive).[135] Mrs Pearce, an Irishwoman in her early thirties, took a different, more personal, tack by replying, 'For me there's not. I go out to work. We have them all.' But arguably her narrower, more individualist, outlook said more about her pride in contributing to the family's well-being than about her love of things. Certainly, her explanation of why she voted Labour suggested strong identification with her neighbours: 'Labour stands for me, and for next door, and for all the people in the street.'[136] Mrs Tufnell, a bricklayer's wife from Shoreditch, tried a different approach, arguing 'people don't compete, but they have room now, and they like nice things', while others simply pointed to practicalities: that young couples moving from furnished rooms to a new three-bed *unfurnished* house were bound to need to focus on homemaking.[137] Mr and Mrs Bridge were in exactly this situation, having moved to Stevenage as newly-weds in 1956. They tried to explain that paying to furnish their new home was the one downside of the move: 'We do get very short at the end of the week. If we didn't have everything to buy we'd be quite well off really.' Sadly, the interviewer, almost certainly Samuel, wasn't listening—having noted that all their furniture was new (was there even much choice about this in late 1950s Stevenage?), he commented: 'pattern of mass media imposed misery'.[138] It was the New Left's 'false wants' thesis about the corrosive effects of 'affluence' reduced to a soundbite. It seems unlikely that the Bridges would have concurred.

Many people resented the suggestion that they (or their neighbours) only wanted things because others had them. Margaret Richardson, a housewife in her late twenties, insisted that 'everyone wants them regardless of the neighbours', and Kevin Burnaby, a maintenance fitter originally from Cornwall, replied 'If they can afford it they get it. [They] used to be a luxury but now they're necessities.'[139]

Valerie Warren also stressed that young couples only bought what they could afford (she was in her late forties), and insisted that it was only 'human nature' that they should want things.[140] This was certainly the view of Mrs Tungate, the young woman who spoke of swopping children with her next-door neighbours; she replied 'yes definitely, you see you can't help knowing what everyone else has got and then you just naturally want the same thing'.[141] This emphasis on *naturalness* strongly echoed Beryl Watt's proud demonstrations of her new fridge, and underscored how consumption could be shaped as much by deep social connections as by the supposed social anomie of new estates.

Unlike Tungate and Watts, most people who offered personal responses to the question about competitive consumption reacted sharply against the implication that they didn't need the things that they (or their partners) had worked long hours to acquire. Mrs Burns, a toolmaker's wife and lifelong socialist, declared 'I'm not bothered by other people's possessions. Mainly people have what they can afford— if they can't afford it, they don't have it', while Iris Fry simply retorted 'I don't care what the neighbours have'.[142] Lionel Barratt, a London-based clerk in his late twenties who self-identified as 'working class', replied 'Not with us there's not. It's a question of finance.' Pressed about other people, he said, 'There may be striving, not competing.'[143] It was a nice distinction that too few Left intellectuals proved ready to hear at the height of the furore about the corrosive effects of post-war 'affluence'.[144] It was all too easy to perceive 'mass' consumption—that is, the acquisition of consumer durables like televisions, fridges, and washing machines by people previously too poor to do much more than feed and clothe themselves— as somehow a symptom of a new, more individualistic and materialist culture. Especially on the new estates, sociologists imagined that consumption was driven by status anxiety and the collapse of 'face-to-face' community. But, as Willmott came to recognize when conducting his study of east London's vast Dagenham estate a few years later, consumerism and community could easily go hand in hand among people who saw themselves as 'allies in a general advance'.[145] Returning to the testimony from Stevenage helps us to understand why. Not only did people like Mrs Watts and Mrs Tungate see the world of new consumer goods as something to be shared with friends and neighbours, but more fundamentally they understood post-war prosperity itself through the lens of wartime populism: as something that was at last to be shared by 'people like us'. Its ethos was at least as much communal as individualist.

This ability to reconcile self and society—personal 'betterment' and general social progress—appears to have been a distinctive feature of these new post-war communities. At both Debden and Stevenage, people appear to have perceived no tension between their ambitions for themselves and their children and the idea of state-led improvement for all. In part this may reflect the fact that almost all of them, whatever their social class, were the beneficiaries of new, high-quality social housing provided by local (Debden) or national (Stevenage) government action. After the war, as in the 1920s, the State built houses for 'general need', rather than prioritizing slum clearance, and this may explain why tenants do not appear to have internalized any sense of social stigma being council or Corporation tenants, despite the acknowledged hostility of well-to-do residents living nearby.[146] On the other hand, we should not assume that this situation was stable. Not only were there already signs of strong support for the idea that tenants should have the right to buy their properties, but the Conservative Government's 1956 decision to end building subsidies for 'general needs' housing signalled the prospect of a growing 'residual-ization' of social housing, especially in areas of new build (to some extent the shift to the prioritization of slum clearance in the 1930s had had a similar impact).[147] The apparent ability of Britain's post-war estates to reconcile individualist and collectivist impulses rested on a fragile new equilibrium. Forged in the optimistic afterglow of the 'People's War', and apparently consolidated by post-war rising living standards, it remained vulnerable, not only to shifts in political priorities, but also to the possibility that expectations of 'betterment' would come to overspill the still strongly paternalist instincts of post-war welfare politics.[148]

These studies also remind us that people could have radically different experiences of living in the same place. In both Debden and Stevenage the high concentration of young families helped foster a strong sense of 'community' for some, whilst others— the childless, the elderly, and working mothers—could easily feel that they did not quite 'fit in'. Here, as elsewhere, different 'lived communities' could exist side by side, with people experiencing place and social connection with their fellow residents very differently depending on personal circumstances as well as personality. It is striking that those who felt most isolated from neighbours also proved most likely to share their interrogators' assessment of post-war materialism—of the endless struggle to 'keep up with the Joneses' through competitive consumption. Those who lived, or felt that they lived, on the social edge of things saw mass consumption through the filter of their own internalized sense of isolation and anomie. In many ways they shared the outsider viewpoint of the New Left intellectuals who journeyed to suburbia to study the alienating, disintegrative effects of post-war prosperity. But others embraced a very different relationship both with their neighbours and with the material goods that were coming to define a new age of 'affluence'. More deeply embedded in local social networks, women like Mrs Watts and Mrs Tungate rejoiced in the 'comfort of things' not just as personal possessions, but also as objects that marked the journey that they *and their friends* had embarked upon towards a better life in the post-war era.[149] It is perhaps this apparent reconciliation of personal ambition with collective progress that is the most striking feature of the testimony from late 1950s Stevenage. People wanted more from life, but they were happy that others should share the rewards of post-war affluence: even the town's small minority of homeowners displayed no desire to defend their exclusive status, declaring themselves keen for others to have the right to buy too.[150]

In Chapters 4 and 5 we will follow this story of shared progress into the 1960s, when the pace of social change accelerated, increasing the strain on the social democratic settlement that had been forged in the immediate aftermath of the 'People's War'.

CHAPTER 4

GETTING ON

The Booming South

A new north–south divide had been growing in England since at least the 1920s, when southern commercial and industrial towns recovered quickly from the sharp post-war recession, while most of the North (like most of Scotland and Wales) did not. Especially in the 1930s, when regional differences grew even sharper, large numbers moved long distances to find work in the booming southern economy. Overall, it is estimated that London and the South East experienced net inward migration of more than 1.2 million people between the wars.[1] Despite significant government efforts after 1945 to divert investment towards the regions, both employment and wages continued to be more buoyant in the South throughout the 1950s and 1960s. In consequence, long-distance population movements continued, with workers from across the British Isles, and now also from Eastern Europe and the Commonwealth, heading to the region in search of security and prosperity. At the same time, as we have seen, post-war planners envisaged radically uprooting urban populations to reduce overcrowding. The Greater London Plan alone foresaw the relocation of a million Londoners to new or expanded settlements, mostly built beyond the city's newly designated protective 'Green Belt'.[2]

In this chapter we visit two very different southern towns (see Map 6): the ancient university city of Cambridge, where high-tech industries like electronics and scientific instruments sat alongside a traditional service economy dominated by paternalism and low wages, and Luton, just 40 miles away, where tens of thousands found work in booming industries including the massive Vauxhall car plant (see Figure 15), which employed over 18,000 people in the early 1960s. Just 15 miles from Samuel's Stevenage, Luton had much in common with the post-war new town. It had a strong, high-wage manufacturing sector geared towards new consumer industries including electrical goods and engineering components as well as cars, and it was growing fast (the population doubled between 1931 and 1961). But there were also important differences. Luton was three times bigger, with a population of 132,000 in 1961, and it had a longer history as an industrial centre

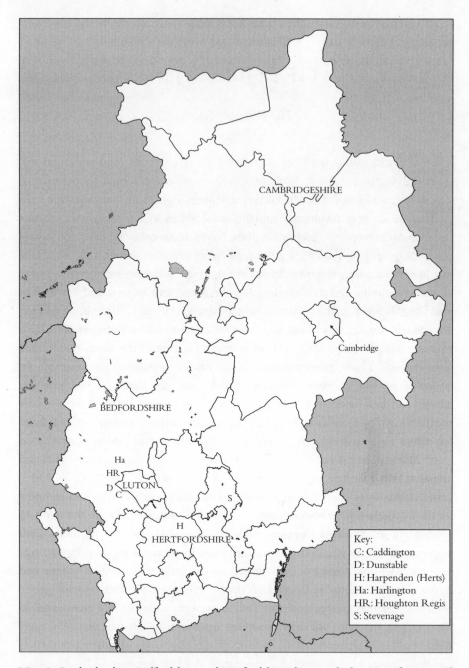

Map 6. Cambridgeshire, Bedfordshire, and Hertfordshire, showing the location of Luton and Cambridge and of local towns and villages mentioned in the text

Figure 15. Aerial photograph of Vauxhall works, Luton, *c.*1970 [Vauxhall Heritage]

(it had been twelve times bigger than Stevenage in 1931). Perhaps crucially, Luton was different because it was not a planned community. Rather, it grew rapidly across the twentieth century as job opportunities drew workers to the town from far and wide.[3]

Cambridge and Luton were both studied by the same team of Cambridge-based sociologists in the early 1960s. Led by David Lockwood and John Goldthorpe, who had both recently taken up lectureships in the University's Economics Faculty (as, briefly, had the Institute of Community Studies founder Michael Young), the team began by studying local male workers in a range of well-paid occupations. Their Cambridge sample was skewed towards different segments of the middle class, including bank workers, university technicians, teachers, and shopkeepers, but approximately one-third of the 316 interviews involved skilled manual and supervisory workers in industries such as electronics, aircraft engineering (Marshalls), and scientific instrument-making (Pye).[4] By contrast, their subsequent research at Luton focused predominantly on manual workers in skilled and semi-skilled occupations, with a small sample of clerical workers added late in the project. In Luton interviews were confined to married men aged between 21 and 46, most of whom had families.[5]

Both studies sought to understand the impact of post-war 'affluence' on lifestyles and class identities. Responding to the same debates that prompted Samuel to ask about competitive consumption among newcomers to Stevenage, researchers paid close attention to domestic furnishings, furniture, and electrical goods in an attempt to gauge not just relative affluence, but also whether workers' homes displayed signs of 'bourgeois' taste and pretensions. Like Young in Debden, interviewers frequently criticized households where the television was the newest and most expensive piece of furniture and family life appeared to revolve around 'the box'.[6] In turn they lauded workers who appeared to share their taste—whether for art, books, or interior design (where Scandinavian simplicity ranked highest). There was a paradox here. The principal objective of the research, especially in Luton, was to disprove the then fashionable theory of *embourgeoisement*, which held that rising levels of prosperity (which people were coming to call 'affluence') were rendering Britain's manual workers 'middle class' in lifestyle and values.[7] The paradox only makes sense when we realize that the researchers saw themselves as having transcended class in their own lives; workers who shared their values and taste were therefore by definition *not* 'bourgeois'.[8]

The Luton survey was longer and decidedly more sophisticated, exploring many issues besides the men's attitudes to class and consumption. It was also much more influential. But both studies register the strong popular sense of change that ran through early 1960s Britain. Some respondents railed against the threat of 'coloured' immigration, others lambasted an out-of-touch 'Establishment' judged incapable of overseeing the modernization of British economic and social life. But most displayed striking optimism about their own and the nation's future—the post-war dream of rising prosperity and technological progress had deep popular roots and continued to grip the public's imagination. There were also strong signs, particularly in Luton, that the struggle to lead materially richer lives was placing profound strain on social relationships. Widespread shift-working and heavy levels of overtime could make it difficult for workers to socialize with their own family, let alone with friends and neighbours. As in Stevenage, there were also signs that the increase in married women's work was weakening local social networks, partly because it created tensions between working and non-working women. But, once again, this was not a simple story of increasing isolation and the decline of 'community'. Compared with post-war Bermondsey and Bethnal Green, more people seem to have viewed the home as a place to socialize with friends as well as family. Indeed, some were actively reconfiguring their homes to make them better places for home entertainment—knocking down walls to create larger living spaces, installing drinks cabinets, and buying expensive sound systems. Change was not all in one direction.

Future lives

The Luton survey ended with a question in which respondents were asked to look ahead ten years and say 'what improvement in your way of life would you most hope for?' Since interviews could sometimes last four hours, and regularly lasted three, everybody involved was likely to be pretty tired by this point. Many answers are brief and confined to the wish for more money and/or shorter hours (although this still speaks volumes about the irreconcilable tension between these two goals in workers' lives). Some of this brevity probably reflects the interviewer's understandable urge to get away, especially when they were in danger of missing the last train home. But despite these constraints, the question threw up many fascinating insights into the hopes and fears that ran through people's everyday lives in the early 1960s. As sociologists remind us, asking people to imagine their future often tells us a great deal about how they understand their present lives.[9] In Bethnal Green and Bermondsey people had often commented on change across the generations, noting how their children's lives were radically different from their own. But in Luton we begin to find people articulating a sense that change was now so rapid that their own future was likely to be radically different from the present. Theorists such as Hartmut Rosa have written of the shift from a modernist expectation of *inter*-generational change, which first became established in the West in the eighteenth century, to a new, late modern sensibility based around a common-sense assumption that change will be *intra*-generational—my future will not be like my present and is intrinsically unknowable.[10] Seen on a global scale, this shift is generally associated with the decades since the mid-1970s and is connected to declining confidence in the inevitability of 'progress'.[11] But by the 1960s popular culture was already creating a strong sense that the pace of change made one's own future unknowable. In one of the more idiosyncratic answers to the Luton survey, John Ward, a shop-floor worker at the massive Skefko bearings plant, wryly commented that 'whatever the twist & shout [crowd] & Beatles are doing I suppose we shall have to be doing in 10 years' time—so if its wrought iron chairs for furniture . . . !'[12] Given it was only November 1963, and the Beatles had not yet released their second album, this was a statement about the growing power of celebrity and fashion rather than a prescient insight into how the Beatles would help spearhead a global transformation of popular culture over the coming decade. It spoke to a powerful desire to be 'modern' and 'with it' which presupposed change, but in the early 1960s that change was still largely understood in terms of 'progress'.

Despite this fundamentally optimistic mindset, it is striking how often people cited greater security as their main hope for the future. Luton might be one of the most prosperous towns in the country, but there was widespread resentment not just about the heavy demands of shift work and overtime, but also about the risk of short time, lay-offs, and sackings.[13] For sure, full employment helped, but particularly for older workers with responsibilities there was still a powerful sense of the precariousness of their affluent lifestyle. Ron Collins, a middle-aged Skefko worker, wanted 'more security at work', and complained that 'It's a crying shame that a firm can make you redundant at 50'.[14] Another Skefko worker simply wanted 'to feel that this present standard of living that we've got is secure'. Like this pair, most of the men raising the issue of security were over 40.[15] But younger workers could also feel insecure, especially if they had heavy financial commitments. A Skefko worker in his late twenties, who had recently moved out of London to be able to buy a house, hoped for 'more security as regards sickness & unemployment'.[16] Arthur Seaton, Alan Sillitoe's angry anti-hero from 1958, might fantasize about chucking in his job, or even blowing up his factory, but men with families tended to take a more sober view.[17]

There were a minority of workers who claimed not to want *any* improvement in their lives, declaring themselves wholly contented. An Irishman in his thirties simply replied, 'I don't think we could be much better off in 10 years' time than we are now—a little, but to keep on as we are'd be quite satisfactory.' Interestingly, he earned less than many of the town's 'affluent workers' (between £15 and £17 per week), and had not sought to buy a house, suggesting that more modest material ambitions may have been the key to his contentment.[18] Older workers who claimed to have all they wanted tended to suggest that their hopes for improvement were reserved for the young, and especially for their own children. For some this meant seeing their children 'settled' (a more precise and prescriptive term than 'happy', it might be suggested).[19] A Skefko worker in his forties declared himself 'quite happy to go on as I am now', but wanted 'the kids to grow up without . . . fear' of the H-bomb.[20] One of his workmates insisted 'We're very happy with our life at the moment', before declaring 'Be a grandfather . . . be a grandfather twice, put that down'. Interestingly this man went on to acknowledge that they could do with 'a new TV, new 3 piece suite' before adding, 'but they're the things that come along normally in life'. For this man at least, material progress was now part of everyday common sense.[21]

That said, the great majority did want to see material improvements in their lives, most commonly a new or better car and a bigger or better house. It would be easy to follow the lead of contemporaries and use their answers to paint a bleak picture of workers locked on a materialist treadmill—doomed always to want more than they could afford, always dependent on overtime and bonuses to pay their bills. But we should be wary of making such sweeping generalizations. For one thing, the question presupposed the idea of 'improvement' (and, one might add, of hope). There is every reason to believe that most workers shared this fundamental belief in 'progress', but this does not alter the fact that the question encouraged them to list material gains over less tangible things like health, happiness, and quality of life (especially given that it followed immediately after a set of questions about consumer goods, housing, and income). Even so, approximately one-third of answers did stress *non-material* improvements, with shorter hours, longer holidays, and 'security' most popular. It is also striking that a number of men mocked their own materialism, or otherwise sought to deny that they might be locked on a consumerist treadmill. A Skefko worker in his forties, who had grown up in South Africa, said that he most wanted his own house and a car, but then joked 'Oh what material values!' before talking about what he would like to do for his wife and children. Vauxhall worker Patrick Doyle, originally from Waterford in the Irish Republic, hoped most 'to have my own car' but quickly added 'not that I want to be above anybody . . . but it's useful . . . to take the families for trips'. Pressed for any other hopes, he added 'Winning the pools . . . [it] keeps you going really.'[22]

He was not alone. Fantasies of escape played an important part in helping men to reconcile themselves to the monotony of the production line, where men often performed the same routinized task for an entire shift without even being able to control the speed at which they worked.[23] Even men who claimed to be completely contented, like Ken Lewis, a Skefko worker in his late thirties who earned enough to buy what the interviewer called 'a very posh house indeed', still hoped for 'a win on the pools' to improve his financial situation. Migrants to Luton hoped for a big pools win so that they could return home in style; others just longed for the chance to get out of the factory while they were still young.[24] A worker in his late thirties at the Laporte chemical plant hoped 'to make a ruddy fortune' on the football pools, so that he could quit work while 'I'm still young enough to enjoy my retirement'.[25] Although, just a few years earlier, Castleford housewife Viv Nicholson had famously declared she would 'Spend, Spend, Spend' after winning over £150,000 on the football pools, Luton's affluent workers generally had more sober dreams, many of which revolved around buying a small business in a much-loved beauty spot.[26] When they rehearsed fantasies of escape, they spoke not of fast cars and fur coats, but of the village shops, country pubs, smallholdings, and even chicken farms which would whisk them away from the world of night shifts and time and motion studies.[27] However, somewhat bizarrely the survey also threw up an Irishman who had moved to Luton *after* winning £20,000 on the pools (he claimed to want anonymity after greedy neighbours in his old town had 'stripped his house clean' on hearing of his good fortune). It seems an unlikely story, but the interviewers were convinced the man was telling the truth—noting that though he had the money to buy his house and car for cash, breed pedigree dogs, smoke upmarket cigarettes, and had plans to set his wife up in a shop, he welcomed the camaraderie and sheer normality of his shop-floor job at Laporte.[28]

A Vauxhall worker's wife nicely captured the role that windfall fantasies played in working-class life, describing how 'Every Saturday night he builds me up and then we go flat till next week.... Oh the big ideas, the houses we're going to build.'[29] It should also be stressed that this was very much a working-class dream—or at least only shop-floor workers *acknowledged* that they longed for a pools win. White-collar workers had their own dreams of escape, including the accounts clerks at Şkefko who claimed that running an independent business is 'perhaps a secret of every man's heart', but none mentioned the pools.[30] In total, 56 per cent of clerical workers, and a remarkable 74 per cent of shop-floor workers, told researchers that they would like to set up in business if they could.[31] Often this meant the husband taking the risk of becoming a self-employed tradesman in a booming trade such as heating installation or car repairs, but there were also lots of couples who clearly envisaged running a small family business *together*, usually in retail, catering, or hospitality. A Skefko worker and his wife talked of their 'life-long ambition' to run a 'village general store ... preferably in Norfolk'. As he explained: 'I want to get out of engineering and it's something the wife and I can do together'.[32] A Vauxhall worker in his forties dreamed of 'being my own boss' by running a business in Devon, explaining 'that's always been our dream'.[33] Others simply hoped to save enough money—or amass enough equity in their houses—to be able to sell up and retire to the coast or the countryside.[34] And one, a Scottish shop steward at Skefko, who already owned a house in a desirable middle-class neighbourhood, hoped to be able to buy 'a caravan or a bungalow near the coast' so that they could take regular holidays. But even he wasn't absolutely confident that the good times would last, adding 'providing we keep prospering in this country'.[35]

At heart, fantasies of escape were about taking control of life and asserting some modicum of autonomy and independence. Men talked of wanting to use their initiative and be their own 'governor'—they hardly ever talked of wanting to make money.[36] Luton's affluent factory workers may have struck an instrumental bargain which demanded they sacrifice job satisfaction for high wages, but they only sustained that bargain by imagining a future life freed from the discipline of mass production. Their relationship with the materialist treadmill was more complicated than a simple assessment of their undoubted thirst for new consumer goods, cars, and houses might suggest. But in one important respect the testimony collected in Luton does signal a decisive shift towards not just a privatized but a status-conscious lifestyle. Compared with 1950s Debden and Stevenage, a much larger proportion of council tenants said they hoped to become homeowners, with many citing the perceived stigma attached to council housing as a reason. One factor here may simply be that in Luton the majority of workers—both manual and non-manual—were already homeowners by the early 1960s (among those surveyed by Goldthorpe and Lockwood 57 per cent of manual and 69 per cent of non-manual workers owned their homes).[37] Some of the town's large employers, including Skefko, even built houses and arranged mortgage finance as part of their recruitment strategy to attract workers from depressed areas of northern England and Scotland.[38] Asked about their hopes for the next ten years, almost half the manual workers renting a council house said they wanted to buy a house. The proportion was even higher among the small number of office workers who were council tenants (seven couples out of eleven hoped to become homeowners). Mrs Collins, the wife of the man who wanted to see firms barred from sacking older workers, said she most looked forward 'to giving my boy the deposit for his house', before explaining, 'We've always lived in a council house, and now it's too late for us to change.'[39] It was a powerful example of the post-war expectation that life should be different, and better, for the next generation, but her comment also underscored the changing social status of social housing by the 1960s, at least in the affluent South.[40]

Estate life

Goldthorpe and Lockwood tended to play down the importance of status factors among Luton's manual workers, but status sensitivities often loom large in the testimony collected from council tenants in the town.[41] Asked about his hopes for the next ten years, Ray Harrison, a Labour voter in his late thirties, declared, 'The thing we've most wanted is our own house or bungalow . . . that's our one big ambition'. Earlier he had said that they would like to move from their current neighbourhood—asked where to, he replied, 'Anywhere not on a council estate—I'd like this area if it was a private house—say in [NAME] Road; I think of this area as handy for work.' In other words, it wasn't the neighbourhood he wished to escape at all—just living on an estate.[42] Des Barnes, another Labour voter in his late thirties, was more explicit about what he didn't like about his council house. Partly it was the property itself, but he also wanted to reduce the danger of having bad neighbours. Looking to the future he hoped 'to own a little bungalow, a garage and trimmings—it'd have to be better than this. In the country. On a council estate you can have a bad lot put in next door. I'd like a detached bungalow.' This probably wasn't just an abstract issue for Mr Barnes. Earlier his wife had qualified her observation that they had 'good, quiet neighbours' by saying 'well her next door, she's got 8 children—she's dirty but she doesn't interfere. She's not bad. Yes she's noisy really, and dirty, but she's improving.' Like many local councils, Luton hoped that over time its more challenging tenants would learn to adapt their standards in line with those of their neighbours.[43] The only problem was that couples like Des Barnes and his wife had no wish to be the unacknowledged agents of social improvement. Given that Mrs Barnes had recently returned to work as a teacher, boosting the family income to more than £40 per week, it seems doubtful whether these two very different households would have remained neighbours much longer.

The Barnes family and their neighbour were perhaps an extreme example, but post-war council estates generally brought people together from diverse back-grounds. Respondents often drew attention to this diversity, perhaps hoping to challenge researchers' presumed preconceptions about their estate. Sensitivities were sharpest in Houghton Regis, the village between Luton and Dunstable that had grown rapidly after its designation as the site for a large London 'overspill' estate. A Skefko clerk's wife offered a good rendition of the prejudices with which residents of the estate had to contend. Her husband would say little more than that since the building of the estate they no longer liked living in the village, but she felt no such inhibitions, declaring 'we've got the worst that they could throw out of London—it's not pure snobbishness but they cause all kinds of trouble—for example a friend of ours had their girl beaten up in the High Street by two leather-jacketed girls'. And though the interviewer generally had no time for what he called her 'irrelevant, snobby asides', he agreed that the overspill estate was 'pretty rough' (earlier, after vandals had apparently stolen his parking light, he had written, 'I tremble for my car's safety whenever I have to park it on this estate').[44] On another visit he compared the estate to 'a chunk of Bethnal Green on a bright evening, with kids committing hopscotch and vandalism and grannies leaning over the garden-gates or sitting on the step'.[45]

Perhaps significantly, many who complained about the overspill estate and declared their determination to move were local-born. They were resentful that a large influx of 'outsiders' had quickly redefined local norms of community, challenging their sense of belonging. The newcomers were overwhelmingly white, and mostly English, but that did nothing to reduce the sense of clashing cultures. A Laporte worker who was in the process of moving to a newly built private estate said he disliked the fact that 'a big London County Council slum clearance' scheme had been built on his doorstep. And a Labour-voting Vauxhall worker, also Luton-born, wanted to move, even though he had not long arrived on the estate, after encountering problems with stone-throwing children.[46] But this was not all about locals versus outsiders. Even newcomers could find other people's children difficult to live with—especially when they had none themselves. Richard Walker, a Skefko worker in his early twenties who had recently moved to an overspill estate with his London-born wife, was already keen to move. He told the interviewer, 'What I'd like is a house [with] a garden in a select area, nice and quiet—the sort of place where if you [want to] have a quiet afternoon nap you can, without everyone waking you up. Somewhere where there aren't so many kids.'[47] 'Select', 'nice', and 'quiet' were all words plucked from the interview card Walker would just have been handed, and from which he was asked to choose the description that 'fits this area best'. Walker said his own area was 'very mixed' (almost no one chose 'pretty rough'—another of the options). Perhaps he was just suggestible, but it seems as likely that he had seized on the chance to conjure up an alternative vision of how he would like to spend his early married life. What he wished for was evidently a neighbourhood that would not feel like 'a chunk of Bethnal Green' whenever the sun came out.

By no means everyone reacted negatively to life on Luton's sprawling new council estates. A couple who had recently moved out of London, after thirteen years living in two rooms (latterly with three young children), acknowledged that 'some of the people up here are rough', but focused on the positives—the open air, the house, and the fact that they had 'nice' next-door neighbours. Similarly, a Skefko worker's wife who had come from the East End recognized that her estate had 'got a bad name from people', and conceded that some of the residents were 'dirty and rough', but insisted that their part of the estate was 'quieter' and more 'select'.[48] Des Miller, another ex-Londoner, offered a similar perspective, commenting 'I wouldn't like to live at the other end of the estate. That's what I was trying to get away from in London. Now they're making hovels of them. We came down here to better ourselves' (the same phrase heard so often from newcomers to Stevenage).[49] Such comments may have been special pleading (post-war studies often found residents disagreeing about which areas were supposedly 'rough'), but a few months later the researcher who had complained about his car being vandalized recorded being 'astonished' to discover that a clerical worker's house on a quiet road in Houghton Regis was also part of the council estate.[50] As recent work on the stigmatization of post-war council estates has shown, particular areas often acquired powerful reputations as housing 'problem' or 'slum clearance' estates. Residents fought against these processes of categorization and stigmatization, but often they also internalized the shame of being judged by others for where they lived.[51]

These powerful feelings could naturally complicate testimony about living on stigmatized estates, but it is striking that a number of people explicitly celebrated places like Houghton Regis for their friendliness and strong sense of 'community'. As in Stevenage, newcomers often stressed how much friendlier they found their new environment than the places they had left—especially when, as was the case for so many, that place was London. The Davidsons, a young couple who had moved to Luton to start a family, were delighted by the friendliness of the estate. Asked about relations with their neighbours, Mrs Davidson commented, 'We get on very well— they seem much more friendly than they were in London—there we didn't know their names, here they'd do anything for you.' She thought that the main reason was that everybody missed having their relatives close by, but her husband thought it was also something about the place itself: 'I think it's the change in the environment—it's like the war, everybody mucks in.'[52] By no means everybody felt defensive about living on an estate, let alone determined to move on.

Migrants' town

As the preceding discussion underscores, post-war Luton was a migrants' town. Only 30 per cent of the men interviewed for the Luton study had grown up in the town (and only 44 per cent of their wives).[53] Perhaps inevitably, this large influx could give rise to tensions between locals and newcomers, not just in the immediate environs of overspill estates but across the town. These tensions could, in turn, help bind newcomers together, blurring distinctions that might otherwise divide them. An Irishman who had recently moved from Southwark identified strongly with his fellow former Londoners, telling the interviewer 'We only mix with people who've come from London—and perhaps the Luton people resent us.' His wife agreed, adding that Londoners were 'the only ones you get to know'. A man from Tyneside said he liked living on a new council estate on the outskirts of town—almost certainly Houghton Regis—commenting that 'there are Scotch, Irish, Welsh & Londoners in one close'.[54] Because companies like Skefko and Vauxhall recruited extensively in particular depressed towns, migrants should not be assumed to be isolated individuals motivated solely by high wages: many were following well-trodden paths when they chose to swap low wages and poor housing for life in Luton. The 'affluent worker' study sample included three workers recruited from the same depressed Lancashire cotton town, and Margaret Grieco has shown that Vauxhall's recruiting officers hired 400 workers from a single employment exchange in northern Scotland between 1956 and 1960 (the depressed fishing port of Peterhead).[55]

Many of these newcomers were happy to voice complaints about local residents. A Welshman in his forties, who had lived in the town for six years, said Lutonians were unfriendly both at work and on the estate, explaining 'they're reserved people and thought we were foreigners taking something away from them'. He felt that locals were particularly 'jealous' that his Skefko recruitment package had secured him a brand-new council house.[56] A London couple, who had previously been living in one room, had chosen Luton because they had friends who had already moved there, but they were still pleased to find that 'The majority of people round here are Londoners', explaining that it meant they were 'easy to get on with'.[57] Eric Houghton, a recent migrant from Bethnal Green, also made it clear that he was glad to be on an estate dominated by fellow Londoners, saying the locals were poor 'mixers'. His wife agreed, saying they 'don't like Londoners'—she also claimed to find the locals 'very tight' with money, commenting, 'we've got a lot but we like to spend it'.[58] Living on an estate dominated by fellow Londoners they clearly felt no pressure to adapt their behaviour to the locals' ways. On the contrary, the Houghtons clearly took pride in the community spirit that had flourished on the estate. When Mrs Houghton mentioned that her husband was always using his car to run errands for the neighbours, he was quick to turn this into a general statement about the community's virtues: 'We seem to be more helpful than people are on other estates.' The interviewer commented that he displayed 'A true working man's pride in his own way of life, and a slight arrogance of manner to underline this.'[59]

As Rogaly and Taylor have astutely commented, attitudes to internal migrants could often be difficult to distinguish from reactions to migrants from overseas.[60] Certainly a number of the British-born migrants to Luton explicitly complained about locals treating them as unwanted 'foreigners'—one man's defensive retort was to insist that 'without us Luton would be a dead town'.[61] But the buoyant Luton economy was also attracting large numbers of workers from overseas, including by the early 1960s a significant minority from south Asia and the Caribbean. In 1961, there were more than 10,000 people living in Luton who had been born outside the UK, representing just under 8 per cent of the town's population. Of these more than 6,000 came from Ireland, and a further 2,216 came from outside the British Commonwealth (probably mostly Eastern and Southern Europe), slightly more than the total from the whole of the Commonwealth.[62] Although Goldthorpe and Lockwood felt that ethnicity could complicate their attempt to test the *embourgeoisement* thesis (apparently dropping plans to study Bedford because its population was considered ethnically too diverse),[63] they did not exclude minority ethnic households. However, nor did they ask direct questions about ethnicity, or even place of birth, which means we need to identify workers born overseas from their answers to other questions (or from interviewers' field-notes). The largest identifiable group by far were Irishmen, most of whom had come to Britain to find work in London or other major English cities before deciding to try their luck in Luton. Something like one in eight of the manual workers interviewed had migrated from Ireland.[64] This fits Colin Grant's picture of growing up in a Jamaican family in Luton in the early 1970s. In his poignant memoir Grant recalls that Caribbean families were greatly outnumbered by the local Irish population on the town's Farley Hill estate.[65]

In fact, most of the non-Irish overseas respondents were themselves of white European heritage, including refugees from Eastern Europe, a South African, and a Cypriot. In only one case (out of more than 200 examined) does the team appear to have interviewed someone from an identifiably non-white ethnic background.[66] Arun Banerjee had originally settled in a nearby cathedral city, but moved with his wife and four children to Luton to get a better-paid job and buy a house. Asked about the changes associated with moving to Luton, he replied, 'England has taken a lot of getting used to. There is always the colour question.' It was an answer which encapsulates why Banerjee was a unique case in the Luton survey. In the early 1960s many industrial firms, including major car companies, continued to operate de facto colour bars which confined black and Asian workers to the dirtiest and least well-paid occupations.[67] There might already be more than 2,000 migrants from the Commonwealth living in Luton in 1961, but only a small proportion would have secured the sort of highly paid industrial jobs selected for Goldthorpe and Lockwood's investigation of 'affluent workers'. Banerjee was clearly exceptional. Since coming to Skefko he had already been promoted to tool-setter, and sometimes earned as much as £30 per week (though usually it was more like £20). But if his was a singular case, it can still shed valuable light on aspects of the immigrant experience in early sixties Britain.[68]

As his comments about the colour bar demonstrate, Banerjee had undoubtedly faced race prejudice since coming to Britain in the mid-1950s, but overall his testimony offers a remarkably positive assessment of life as an 'immigrant' among the myriad other migrants of booming post-war Luton. Like many affluent workers, his life appears to have been strongly home-centred. When asked what improvements he hoped for in the next ten years, he replied, 'I want to make a beautiful room for the children to play in' (he was in the process of extending the house when the interview took place, and DIY work took up much of his spare time). Banerjee liked his neighbourhood, a private estate dominated by factory workers like himself, noting that he had 'nice people on each side' who would talk over the fence and occasionally visit. He clearly had a strong sense of himself as 'a working-class man' and 'a union man'—stressing both identities even before the interviewer had got to ask his detailed questions about class. Asked who he felt most at ease with, Banerjee said 'working-class people', explaining 'it's a lot easier for me when we sit down and talk'. The two friends he mentioned by name were both working-class Englishmen, one of whom had apparently made a point of befriending him 'when I was a stranger' (a human dimension of the everyday response to immigration that we too rarely acknowledge). He also demonstrated a strong sense of what Mike Savage has called the egalitarian, unpretentious spirit of the shop floor, declaring 'In the working class everyone should be the same [. . .] When the foreman comes up we want to respect him and he us. We're wanting to be the same class.'[69] But as his prominent pictures of Nehru and Bose testified, Banerjee also identified strongly with Indian nationalism. When the interview turned directly to his views about class Banerjee made it clear that he saw little difference between prejudice based on class and on race—both were social evils in urgent need of eradication. He stressed that prejudice must be changed because the colour of his skin could not be, and drew a direct parallel between someone barred from a restaurant by race prejudice and someone barred by poverty. As his interviewer acknowledged, these were not arguments that sat easily within contemporary sociological debates about *embourgeoisement*, but they nicely captured how the politics of class and of ethnic identity could be woven together in post-war Britain, despite claims to the contrary.[70]

The strongest example of someone resenting the rapid expansion of the town's non-white population came from a local-born man. Ray Jeffries was a Skefko worker in his forties and had recently moved away from central Luton, where he and his wife had grown up. He told the interviewer, 'it used to be respectable once but now all the coloured people live down there and that means noise and drunks— Oh it's such a change out here.' They regretted seeing less of their relations, most of whom still lived centrally, and felt it was harder to make friends in their new suburban neighbourhood, but there was no suggestion that they regretted their decision. From their perspective, the community they had known had already disappeared—made unfamiliar not just by newcomers from overseas, but also by the actions of private landlords profiting from the migrants' acute housing need.[71] Sociologists studying the elderly stress how it is often the disruption of memory, of the sense of a seamless connection between past and present, which most fuels resentment of newcomers as the perceived agents of unwanted change.[72] This was the case for white Lutonians like the Jeffries, though they had long been a minority in their own town.

However, there were plenty of local-born workers who spoke in more neutral terms about non-white migration to the town. Mrs Hargreaves, the wife of a Vauxhall worker in her forties, commented that though their neighbourhood was 'ordinary working-class' in character, 'it's getting a bit mixed as regards nationalities'. Seen in isolation, this comes across as coded racism, even though the couple indicated that they had no plans to move. However, a little later Mr Hargreaves mentioned that he sometimes invited 'coloured people' round to his house for dinner if they seemed isolated and lonely. Though he didn't say so, this activity was almost certainly connected to his involvement in the local Pentecostal church, where he was a Sunday school teacher and home visitor, roles which may well have brought him into contact with migrants from the Caribbean (where Pentecostalism had established deep roots).[73] Another Lutonian who had moved to a council estate six years earlier said he liked the fact that it was a friendly, mixed area, commenting 'The people are alright to get on with [. . .] They're not snobbish, but quite friendly. There are Irish, Scotch, & even one coloured family. There are private houses behind us, but we don't see so much of them.' Nor was he the only local to be unfazed by his new non-white neighbours. John Ward, the man who thought the Beatles might one day have everyone sitting on wrought-iron furniture, also liked the 'mixed' area he had moved to in the 1950s, explaining 'We've even got a coloured gentleman round the corner, you cannot distinguish his house from the rest'. The interviewer noted that what he meant by this was that 'just [a] family live there, not 10+'. It was a comment that certainly underscored the power of myths about 'dark strangers in our midst', but one that suggested people were quite capable of recognizing when reality and myth were at odds.[74]

Too few people discussed the issue to draw any firm conclusions, but it is striking that none of these respondents was still living in the area where they had grown up. They may have been local-born, but they were still newcomers in their neighbourhoods and for those who weren't overt racists this may have made change easier to accommodate. In a sense they were adapting to the melting-pot ethos of the new estates (council and private) that had sprung up around the town in the post-war boom. In the same spirit, a Skefko worker from Kent said he liked Luton because it was 'very cosmopolitan [. . .] the % of Lutonians I work with must be less than 15%, one in 10 perhaps'. And a Vauxhall worker in his forties, who had moved from Edgware in north London in order to buy a house, claimed to like his 'mixed' area, noting 'they come from all parts of the world, and all classes'.[75] More difficult to place is Des Miller, a Skefko worker in his forties from Hackney who had moved to one of the town's LCC estates a few years earlier. He too claimed to like living in a 'mixed' area, but his comments suggested that it was the *lack* of mixing he most liked about Luton. Miller said the town was 'like London', explaining 'There are areas where there are black men & foreigners. Here we're with Londoners.' But again this was not a simple case of white working-class racism. Elsewhere we learn that the couple had been fostering a mixed-race child for the previous two years, and that Mrs Miller had fallen out with a neighbour and been excluded from the street's informal women's social club, after the woman had picked on her foster-charge.[76] It was certainly evidence that social relations could be fraught on new estates, but it also reminds us not to assume a default white working-class racism in 1960s Britain. Fault lines ran through the white working class, not between white workers and immigrants, as we will see clearly in Chapter 5, where we examine the reaction of Tyneside shipbuilding workers to Enoch Powell's controversial attempt to whip up anti-immigrant feeling in the late 1960s.

On living in an old town

By contrast with Luton, Cambridge in the early 1960s was still very much a slice of old England, despite the presence of high-tech companies like Pye and Marshalls and the university's strong international reputation for science. In many ways, the university's ancient colleges still dominated civic life. Fourteen per cent of the workforce was employed directly in education (compared with just 2 per cent in Luton), and the spending power of university staff and students helped sustain a large retail and service sector, which represented 53 per cent of the total workforce compared with 21 per cent in Luton.[77]

It is striking how many Cambridge residents felt that life in the town was blighted by class snobbery. Bill Froggatt, an electrical inspector in his early thirties from the east Midlands, was convinced that there was more class conflict in Cambridge than elsewhere, blaming what he called the town's widespread 'snobbism'. Froggatt declared, 'This is the snobs' town. It might be the University but it applies all over—even on housing estates. Local people are snobs—they're noted for it—for example you find it in Joshua Taylors [an upscale department store]—it takes them all their time to serve you if you go in on the way home from work.'[78] An English teacher in his early twenties took a similar view, saying 'there's still a lot of what we call snobbery [. . .] I think there are a great many people who, by going into a shop, or buying a bus ticket, will demand it discourteously, ask for it without please or thank you, just take it for granted [that] that person serves them. A great many people have taken on themselves to feel they are above others, & believe that.' Like many young professionals he rejected this outlook as outdated and pernicious, and celebrated the fact that class segregation seemed finally to be breaking down (as evidence he cited the fact that many of his fellow teachers 'live opposite ordinary working people like barbers').[79]

Reg Barnes, a prosperous local grocer whose household income was more than double that of the young teacher, took a rather different view of the social geography of class in Cambridge. To him it was obvious that class divisions were written into the fabric of the city at every turn. 'They emanate by streets,' he said. 'Take Long Road. The inhabitants of Long Road are superior to those of, say, Catharine Street. Catharine Street is composed of manual workers and Long Road's inhabited by company directors and business executives. You have, there, two different classes: a paid man and a man who pays wages. There must be class there.'[80] For Barnes the geography of class in Cambridge was as palpable and fixed in the early 1960s as it would have been when the last terraced houses were being built on Catharine Street in the 1910s. Part of the strongly working-class district known locally as 'Red Romsey', Catharine Street (where I lived myself in the early 1990s when the area's gentrification was already in full swing) epitomized that strand of independent, unionized working-class culture which had long marked the area off from the rest of the city, both socially and politically.[81] According to Barnes, the city's pubs and clubs also encapsulated its class divisions, even when geographically they sat cheek by jowl. He explained to the interviewer that 'The Co-operative Club and the Labour Club are essentially working men's clubs. In Mill Road there is the Salisbury Conservative Club and not ½ a mile away is the Constitutional Club with a different class of people altogether. A lot of it is by choice—you wouldn't get a workman going into the bar of the Bath Hotel in Bene't Street any more than you'd get a company director going into the Earl of Derby at the foot of Mill Road bridge.'[82] In Cambridge people literally 'knew their place', to use a phrase resonant with the hierarchical assumptions that animated this powerfully status-conscious worldview. They also thought they knew *other people's* place—so our grocer went on to discuss the groups below what he called Romsey's 'steady workman' type: 'those in "Coronation Street", who'll never get beyond beer and skittles [. . .] and are content to live in a hovel' and 'the ragamuffins of Newmarket Road' (here he added that he only meant 'the lower part' of Newmarket Road—his mental geography of class was a precise science).[83]

By displaying his expertise about the city, Barnes managed to place himself outside the old hierarchical class system he dissected with such confidence. Mike Savage has argued that Britain's post-war middle class developed new ways of conceptualizing class which placed greater emphasis on the personal characteristics, such as expertise and knowledge, deemed necessary for success in a more 'meritocratic' society.[84] Barnes had no time for snobbery or deference based on fear, but he celebrated those who displayed 'industriousness and ambition' (making it pretty clear that he believed these qualities explained his own success).[85] As Savage suggests, the city's teachers and university technicians also tended to define themselves against older, more fixed understandings of class rooted in ideas about birth and upbringing ('breeding'). However, though they looked forward to a very different future, they insisted that most of Cambridge still lived by the old ways—like Bill Froggatt, these young professionals saw it very much as a 'snobs' town'. A big factor here was the long shadow cast by the university, and especially its more privileged undergraduates. Indeed, it may well have been the distorting influence of the university that ultimately determined the research team to look further afield to study changing attitudes to class (they ultimately abandoned the Cambridge project entirely, despite having conducted over 300 interviews).

Perhaps the most dramatic account of what it was like to live in a town dominated by socially privileged young men came from Brian Reynolds, a skilled instrument maker who was himself still in his early twenties. Trying to explain why relations between the classes were poor in Cambridge, Reynolds touched on how it felt to be 'cut' socially by people who assumed they were his superior. He explained, 'if I go down town and go to a party, or pay for a drink with some of my friends, and I'm introduced to people who, say, have got their own business, or students, or people like that, they tend to ignore the ordinary working person because they feel (I suppose) we're not good enough to talk to or mix with'. Pressed to amplify his comment that there were 'so many things I could say' about class conflict in the city, Reynolds offered the example of how, if he was out on his own and met 'stuck-up people like students in Sunday suits walking in threes and fours, they'll knock me off the pavement because I'm inferior'. Encouraged by his female interviewer to say more about what Sennett and Cobb call 'the hidden injuries of class,' Reynolds went on:

> it's mostly a university town, so wherever you go you're bound to meet university types, and they're given first chance and you're not, you're pushed around. I mean all this is not very good for the person who wants to get on; you really believe you are inferior in the end, these types sort of glare at you . . . It seems to be a lot of different feelings, hard feelings, between all those different sets and types, no-one's friendly, they just keep to their own circles and don't want to know anyone else.[86]

A skilled machinist in his forties—who incidentally insisted he could earn twice as much doing the same job in Luton—felt that people were held back in Cambridge by the predominance of the 'college servant' type, who was 'accustomed to patronage'. He contrasted Cambridge with the industrial North, where workers had not been 'kept down', but also believed that classes were inevitable, that those with 'breeding' always 'treat you much better,' and that 'There's more snobbery among the working class than anywhere else'.[87] In many ways he both inhabited the Cambridge class system and stood outside it as critic.

Even middle-class critics of the university's influence often found it difficult to sustain a stable 'outsider' perspective when criticizing snobbery and hierarchical ideas about class which implied their own supposed inferiority. A grocer in his forties felt that what he called 'pompous snobbery' was endemic in Cambridge, claiming 'you come into contact with it every day—they become indoctrinated or impregnated through contact with the colleges—it's the area they live in'. But he clearly looked up to the 'upper crust' himself, and felt that their influence helped people 'to see through the superfluous snobbery of the lower middle class'.[88]

Gerard Field, a geography teacher in his late twenties, felt the injuries of class more personally. He blamed the university for intensifying class feeling in the town, saying 'In Cambridge especially the university being there creates classes, mainly the hangers-on, you feel a social outcast if you're not in, [if you] have been to a school in the town & not got to university.'[89] Similarly, Bob Smith, a clerk at the university in his forties, felt that although 'Class distinction has disappeared a bit in recent years', this welcome change was least noticeable in southern university towns like Cambridge. He felt that whereas in the North you could be on first-name terms with a company director and buy him a drink in the pub, in Cambridge this was unimaginable because class distinctions ran too deep. He commented, 'I don't know whether they know they do it: the little action, the gesture that indicates "We are U, you are non-U". Of course as you get older it doesn't matter; when you're younger it hurts.'[90] Here he was alluding to the U/Non-U controversy that Nancy Mitford had sparked in the mid-1950s with her mischievous essay about the defining features of upper-class ('U') speech, and the code words that betrayed people as social outsiders ('Non-U').[91] Deeply sensitive to the 'social snub', Smith longed for a more classless society, but felt little confidence he would see one in his lifetime.

Smith attributed the main softening in class attitudes to the improved economic position of manual workers, commenting that 'the boss class have had to accept less civility'. He was convinced that, but for the disruptive impact of the war, change would have been much slower 'if it happened at all'.[92] In fact, older residents often portrayed the Second World War as marking a watershed in local class relations. A former skilled worker now in his forties and in management recalled that as a young man his neighbours had ignored him if they met him wearing his work overalls: 'That's snobbery and not class distinction—just snobbery. The people around here work in shops and offices—there's no difference in class. They went to the same schools as I did—at that time [i.e. the 1940s] they were just "better" than I was in their own eyes. It was only at weekends that we were accepted.'[93] George Chapman, an electrician in his late forties whose mother had run a lodging house for undergraduates between the wars, felt that the university itself had changed. He commented, 'when I lived with my mother, you used to get that [snobbishness] especially with the undergrads—but college now is open to anybody if you can get there. Once upon a time when you had these Lords and Sirs and Princes who came up to college . . . well, money was money!' Chapman also suggested that class segregation was weakening in the town, commenting that he had just visited a property 'in one of the best roads in Cambridge' where the owner was 'nobody, just ordinary working class, [she] has a damn great place and she's letting to undergrads—you used not to find that'.[94] Similarly, Donald Bates, a head of maths in his forties, recalled being 'acutely aware' of class before the war—'in our village there were two people, Them & Us, I could name the families. I don't think that any longer exists.' By contrast, he found life in Cambridge more anonymous and relaxed: 'one can lose one's identity—of the people in the road, probably half don't know what I earn, who I am, where I come from, & I prefer it that way'.[95]

Arguably Bates underestimated how much his personal journey from labourer's son to senior teacher had informed his transformed experience of social class. As we have seen, other Cambridge residents still keenly felt the sting of class associated with living in an old town. Men like Bates might feel that they had transcended an older, more rigidly hierarchical class system through education and mobility, but many townsfolk clearly felt that the old injunction to 'know your place' still held sway. If Cambridge was a town in transition, it was changing more slowly than much of the rest of the country. Eventually, the university would drive the city's transformation into an economic powerhouse deeply embedded in international networks of knowledge exchange, but in the immediate post-war years the university seemed to many the antithesis of modernity. It was an anchor fixing the city firmly in a nineteenth-century world of social deference and minute attention to status.

High-speed society

Compared with Cambridge, post-war Luton was in many ways the epitome of the emerging high-speed mobile society—and not just because its economy was dominated by vehicle manufacturers like Vauxhall and Commer (commercial vehicles). The population itself was also highly mobile. Not only were the majority of residents newcomers to the town, but more than a third had lived in the town for five years or less; respondents' average length of residence at their current address was less than seven years.[96] As in Stevenage, large numbers of newcomers had moved again since arriving in Luton. In total, 70 per cent of the total Luton sample had moved at least once since arriving in the town or since marriage, and more than a fifth had lived in their present home no more than two years.[97] A couple who had come as newly-weds four years earlier because houses were unaffordable in Enfield, claimed to like their neighbourhood, but regretted that 'there was an awful lot of coming and going' as people cashed in on rising house prices.[98]

In many ways, the Luton study's design radically underestimated mobility levels, because (for reasons that were never fully explained), the team decided only to interview workers living in Luton and neighbouring Houghton Regis.[99] This probably reflected the residual influence of the waning community studies tradition, or perhaps it was simply a matter of practical convenience given that the researchers had to conduct home as well as workplace interviews and rarely had access to private transport. But of course the consequence, intended or otherwise, was to exaggerate the homogeneity of the study's working-class sample.[100] In turn this made it easier for the book's authors to draw bold conclusions about the lessons of their study for party politics when writing up in the late 1960s: namely that Harold Wilson's struggling Labour Government could easily recover the popularity it had enjoyed in the mid-1960s if it reasserted (and demonstrated) its political commitment to working-class interests.[101]

Given that in 1959 sociologist Ferdynand Zweig had found only 60 per cent of Luton's Vauxhall workers actually lived in the town, and that one in four commuted more than 10 miles, the exclusion of working-class commuters was not a small matter.[102] In fact three of the men interviewed by Raph Samuel's team in Stevenage were working at Vauxhall's massive Luton works, despite the 30-mile round trip. All three were former Londoners who had moved to Stevenage to secure a house, in one case just fifteen months earlier. Samuel didn't ask many questions about work, but like the Vauxhall employees surveyed in Luton, they were all semi-skilled assembly workers. None was obviously affluent. One, a man of Irish descent from the East End, made a point of emphasizing that 'people down here [Stevenage] are struggling', while another was said to have a home that was 'not very well furnished according to Stevenage standards'. All three were Labour voters.[103] This group was distinctive only to the extent that their tiring day on the assembly line was extended further by a long commute. Even so, choosing to exclude them from the Luton study necessarily meant underestimating the impact of increased mobility on workers' lives.

In fact the Luton study did include some commuters. Although among shop-floor staff at Vauxhall and Skefko the researchers confined interviewing to local residents, the smaller samples drawn from among Laporte's chemical workers and from clerical staff at both Skefko and Laporte did include workers living in nearby towns and villages. More than one in six of Laporte's manual workers lived outside the town, including one in the desirable north Hertfordshire market town of Harpenden, two in Dunstable, and two in nearby Bedfordshire villages (Harlington and Caddington).[104] Interestingly, these people were no more likely to be car owners than those still living in Luton, and only marginally more likely to be homeowners. But there were other ways to get to work. Harlington and Harpenden were on the main north–south rail line through Luton, and there were also regular bus services. In his contemporaneous study of the rise of commuting in rural Hertfordshire, Ray Pahl argued that the rapid post-war industrial expansion in towns like Stevenage and Luton had provided employment for large numbers of local working-class men who might otherwise have been forced to migrate away from rural villages. He commented that 'The ancient cars and motor-cycles parked outside the council houses of many of the villages of the area are in many cases the necessary links of the wage earners with their places of work.'[105]

We don't know if any of the Laporte workers ran a motorbike, but we do know that some still did heavy overtime despite also having a long commute. John Carr, who lived 7 miles from Luton at Harlington, claimed to do fifteen hours' overtime a week. He ran a car, voted Conservative, and was in almost *every* respect unlike the researchers' model of the typical 'affluent worker'. Mrs Carr also worked full-time, they had no children, and their household income was over £30 per week (the highest category). The interviewer commented that they were 'the first couple I've had who were in any sense middle-class'.[106] Asked why they had moved out to Harlington, Mrs Carr was blunt: 'We don't like Luton, and we were fortunate to find this place which doesn't look like a row of council houses.' She insisted that village life was 'friendlier' and less 'impersonal' than town life, and described Harlington as 'an active little community'. However, it is noticeable that their close friends—the people they saw regularly and invited round for meals—lived elsewhere: they were definitely not a couple tied to community as place.[107] Perhaps if the researchers had not radically under-sampled workers living outside the town they would have found more couples like the Carrs who came close to fitting the contemporary stereotype of the 'bourgeois' worker.

In recent decades, sociologists have identified the growth of 'elective belonging' as a feature of affluent, mobile societies, where those with access to the greatest resources come to see connection to place as an extension of their sense of self—as an expression of identity, and crucially as something *chosen* rather than something determined by the accident of birth.[108] In many ways couples like the Carrs were already pioneering this new way of living in the early 1960s, and doing so despite remaining not just objectively 'working class', but in many ways subjectively so as well. Mrs Carr stressed that their friends were 'people who don't look down on you just because you work with your hands', and the interviewer noted 'the genteel mockery that crept into her voice' when she discussed people who exhibited pretensions to superiority. They might be middle class in his eyes, but the Carrs were uncomfortable being classed at all. In fact Mrs Carr, who was more vociferous on the subject, was adamant that 'class is in-bred snobbery—that's all it is'.[109] Nor, despite the project's strong bias towards Luton residents, were the Carrs a lone case. The two Laporte workers living in Dunstable also claimed to be planning to move further from Luton to escape the expansion of overspill estates. In both cases they named specific villages about 10 miles from Luton where they were looking to buy a house.[110]

Many people undoubtedly found this increasingly mobile high-speed society unsettling and unfriendly. A Laporte worker in his forties, who had moved out from Shoreditch five years earlier, complained that 'Down here you get the young Vauxhall workers; they get their car and don't seem to be the same.' His wife agreed. She acknowledged that they were 'the same working-class people' she had known in London, but felt that here 'you could be dying' and still they wouldn't help—'as long as they've got a car and can get out' nothing else mattered. The couple had bought a big pre-war semi three months earlier, and claimed that so far no one had spoken to them. The interviewer thought that the man was of 'stereotyped Jewish physiog-[nomy]', so it is possible that their experience was partly about racial prejudice, but if so there is no corroborating evidence.[111] Certainly this focus on the alienating pace of life was unusual for migrants from the capital—as one might expect, it was mostly newcomers from rural districts who equated the pace of life in Luton with a broader sense of social anomie.

Ron Hodge, a Laporte worker in his forties who had lived in Luton for more than twenty years, still recalled being scared by 'the crowds and the bustle' when he first arrived from rural south Lincolnshire.[112] More recent migrants from the country-side also felt the change keenly. Two Skefko workers from Suffolk expressed mixed feelings about the move. Bob Green, from a Suffolk coastal town, acknowledged that there was 'a better chance to get on', and also liked the fact that (unlike at home) people with 'better jobs' like doctors 'treat you as equals'. But he felt that in Luton people were much less willing to mix and have fun: 'the people are not so much free here. They're always working or redecorating. They don't enjoy themselves so much.' Mr Green also put much of the difference down to car ownership: 'Down there, there were no cars—they can't afford them—so they mix more'; his wife agreed, recalling how they 'used to have a party every week'. But they ran a car themselves (and had also bought a house)—and asked about the future they talked about better pensions and owning a detached bungalow; there was no suggestion of returning to what Mr Green called 'depressed' Suffolk.[113] Sid Ransom had also come from coastal Suffolk, in his case after being put on short time by his Lowestoft employer. Asked what had changed coming to Luton he said 'everything', adding 'I think we was a lot happier in ourselves down there, in ourselves I mean, but we're better off in the money way [in Luton].' His wife agreed, explaining that in Suffolk 'we weren't in the rat race'. The interviewer noted that 'all the family spoke with distaste of Luton's obsession with money'. Mr Ransom accepted that people were generally 'very nice', but complained that they 'make money their God. Talk about keeping up with the Joneses'. Perhaps tellingly, his closest friend was a man from home who had taken a job at Vauxhall and now lived some distance away at Harlington (the same village as the Carrs). But when he talked about having had more friends 'down home', his teenage daughter was quick to point out that what he really meant was that 'they had lots of relatives there'. Later, Mrs Ransom acknowledged 'we didn't have any friends at home', explaining that coming from a 'big family' meant 'we was more or less one unit'. Doubtless, it was the loss of these intimate kinship bonds that they felt most strongly in Luton; certainly, unlike the Greens, they hadn't conspicuously embraced Luton's famed materialism. They were living in private rented accommodation, and had no fridge, phone, or car.[114]

But it wasn't just mobility and population churn which many felt compromised social life in Luton. It was also work itself. As we have seen, securing an 'affluent' lifestyle often depended on men working antisocial shifts and large amounts of overtime; it also often meant their wives taking paid employment to boost the household income.[115] This inevitably had an impact on people's ability to socialize with friends and neighbours, even when they were temperamentally inclined to do so. For Graham Turner, who published a chatty, anecdotal account of Britain's car workers in the early 1960s, Luton was 'Gadgetville, U.K.'—a town dedicated to money and materialism. Turner wrote that 'the influence of T.V., wedded to a long working-week and the endless drive for money, goes far towards killing social life in Luton'.[116] Turner quoted a Vauxhall shop steward's complaint that younger workers 'spend their lives keeping up with the Joneses—cars, cocktail cabinets, tape recorders, the lot'. More sober, sociological accounts of the town also stressed the emergence of a new family-centred, 'privatized' culture based around television, home life, and—for a growing minority—the car.[117] The argument relied on an idealized model of 'traditional' working-class life that played down the extent to which home and family had long been the centre of most workers' social world.

Wariness of neighbours, a reluctance to socialize with workmates, and a selective approach to kinship could all claim a much longer history than these accounts suggested (as the field-notes from post-war Bermondsey and Bethnal Green confirm). People had long found ways to reconcile privacy and personal autonomy with local expectations about what it meant to be a 'good' neighbour.[118] The same was true in 1960s Luton. This is not to minimize the importance of heavy overtime, high levels of mobility, and the increase in women's paid employment, but merely to suggest that these factors shaped the specific local context in which this familiar story played out. We need to study social relationships in affluent Luton on their own terms, rather than in comparison with an idealized model of 'traditional' communities that were supposedly more neighbourly and gregarious.

Social life in a boom town

It isn't difficult to find evidence of Luton workers complaining that long hours and irregular shifts made it difficult to have a normal social life. A Luton-born Laporte worker living on a new council estate commented, '[We] don't have much to do with anyone, being on shift-work, & with [the] wife working, but we see the neighbours next door'. Similarly, a Skefco worker commented, 'We don't entertain, not what you can call have people round at all, shiftwork cuts that out.'[119] The Luton study reported a strong negative correlation between shift-working and entertaining at home: half those on shift work entertained less than once a month, compared with only a third of those working regular hours. Heavy overtime had a similarly negative impact on workers' ability to socialize.[120] But there is little doubt that many of Luton's workers felt a strong urge to entertain at home, even if work often made this difficult. Stan Newlands, a Londoner who had moved to the town on the promise of a new council house and a well-paid job at Skefko, told his interviewer, 'If we had this house in London we'd entertain our friends. Here at the moment we haven't found the people to do it with. And shift work stops social life.' But he was also adamant that he found people 'a lot friendlier' than in London, explaining 'There's not so much bickering.' He missed his old friends, but not London life more generally. Newlands then outlined his philosophy for good neighbourly relations, commenting, 'If you get too thick at the beginning, and get to know too much about each other, it leads to jealousy. You try to keep up.' But the Newlands were on good terms with their neighbours, visiting, offering help, and citing one good-humoured, friendly neighbour as the epitome of 'the type of person you'd like to have all round you'. There was nothing very new about this model of good neighbouring—many in the older parts of London like Bermondsey and

Bethnal Green had also expressed a desire for friendly, helpful neighbours who would also respect the privacy of domestic family life. Arguably, what was novel about the Newlands' testimony was the emphasis on wanting to 'entertain' their close friends together at home, and the sense that this was a natural reaction to having a spacious home for the first time (rather than anything loaded with status implications). Mrs Newlands commented that their new home allowed them 'to live decently', while her husband's lament about their restricted social life hinged on the irony that they had only secured a spacious house by moving away from the close friends they would choose to share it with.[121]

Interestingly, in the late 1950s Zweig found that Luton's Vauxhall workers were more likely to be on visiting terms with their neighbours than affluent workers in Sheffield, Birmingham, Workington, or south-west London. He explained this partly in terms of the absence of close family, and partly by the fact that many Vauxhall workers lived in small Bedford villages where social life remained intimate.[122] Certainly many of the workers interviewed by Goldthorpe and Lockwood did what the Newlands only hoped to do: they invited friends round in the evenings either to share a meal or to just chat, play music, and enjoy themselves. Many of the consumer goods held up as epitomizing the selfish, materialist ethos of 'Gadgetville, UK', things like record players, tape machines, cine projectors, and cocktail cabinets, were actually central to this culture of domestic entertaining. Doubtless the Newlands weren't alone in identifying with the culture without actually doing much entertaining, but even the idea that couples would have mutual friends they invited into the family home was novel. In his classic 1950s account of working-class life Richard Hoggart had insisted that 'the living-room is the warm heart of the family . . . It is not a social centre but a family centre; little entertaining goes on there, or in the front room if there happens to be one.'[123] Hoggart's picture is one amply confirmed by the testimony from post-war Bermondsey and Bethnal Green.

But it is important not to exaggerate the transformation. In all, just over 62 per cent of Luton manual workers claimed to have friends (as opposed to relatives) visit in the evening. The comparable figure for non-manual workers was 78 per cent.[124] Manual workers were also more likely not to entertain at all—15 per cent claimed never to have anyone round in the evenings (twice the figure for non-manual workers). It seems likely that shift-working, longer hours, and heavy overtime played their part here. It also needs to be remembered that the Luton sample was skewed towards men with young children since it included only married men aged between 21 and 46 (many workers commented that they used to have people round more often before they had children). But 85 per cent of manual workers did 'entertain', and on average they claimed to have guests round about twenty times a year (slightly more often than non-manual workers).[125] Intriguingly, they were also much more likely to have people round to eat. Asked how they usually spent their evenings with guests, less than a quarter of non-manual workers mentioned having a meal, compared with 44 per cent of manual workers.[126] This surprised me, and may well tell us more about the relative affluence of the two groups than anything else. Most of the clerical workers interviewed earned less than shop-floor workers, and were quite conscious of not being in a position to entertain in a lavish manner. By contrast, as in working-class London, many manual workers prided themselves on keeping a 'good table' and on being generous, open-handed hosts. Visiting a Vauxhall worker's house, one of the interviewers (almost certainly a hard-pressed postgraduate) noted how he had 'craftily' declined the offer of sandwiches, in the hope that he would get dinner instead—and sure enough he was fed a good steak followed by dessert.[127]

Manual workers were more likely to feed both friends and relatives when they visited, but the difference was less marked in relation to friends (30 per cent compared with 22 per cent for non-manual workers) than for relatives (31 per cent against 14 per cent).[128] The taboos around inviting non-kin into the home had not disappeared, but they do seem to have become much attenuated as homes became places where it was easier to envisage entertaining. But if manual workers were more likely to feed their guests, they remained less likely to entertain them with card games, music, or cinefilms. More than half of white-collar workers mentioned either playing cards and board games or entertaining their guests with music or films (56 per cent). The comparable figure for manual workers was 32 per cent. However, white-collar workers were equally likely to mention activities which the researchers considered characteristically 'working-class', such as watching TV or going to the pub, and more likely to mention gendered social activities in which husbands and wives did different things.[129] In fact, manual workers often made a point of stressing that they turned the TV off whenever they had guests—as a Skefko worker in his thirties put it, 'First thing we do is switch the TV off, because I think it's bad manners to have it on when you've got company.'[130] Overall, class differences undoubtedly remained, but they were less sharply defined than one might imagine—or than contemporary sociologists suggested (especially once one recognizes that more 'informal' styles of entertaining had also become the norm in well-to-do homes by the 1960s).[131]

In the original study, researchers noted that manual workers who could be said to have 'white-collar affiliations' (either through family connections or their own past employment) were more likely to entertain non-kin at home, and also entertained people more frequently. Borrowing a term from Marxism, they called these workers 'déclassé', and argued that workers who lacked such cross-class connections remained true to more traditional patterns of working-class sociability. Given that the differences involved were minor,[132] and that more than *two-thirds* of their manual sample (69 per cent) possessed 'white-collar affiliations', it is perhaps strange that they were keener to refute claims that manual workers were becoming 'middle-class' than to understand what, if anything, was distinctive about the people who entertained at home. The first thing to stress is that in many respects they were just like the workers who didn't entertain. They had the same politics (approximately two-thirds Labour), they were equally likely to be migrants to the town, and equally likely to want to live in a different area. Those who were migrants (the great majority) had, on average, lived in the town for exactly the same length of time. But the 'entertainers' were different in a number of key respects. Firstly, as we might imagine, they tended to work less overtime, and their wives were less likely to have a job (at the margin, having extra time was more important than having extra money).[133] They were also more likely to be in the youngest or oldest age groups. Whereas 54 per cent of men aged between 25 and 40 claimed to invite friends home, the figure was 100 per cent among the under-25s and 65 per cent among the over-40s. This was almost certainly the young-child effect. Finally, it also mattered where people lived. The 'entertainers' were significantly more likely to be home-owners. Whereas 67 per cent of owner-occupiers claimed to have friends round in the evenings, the figure was 56 per cent for council tenants, and 43 per cent for private tenants. Relatedly, the entertainers were also more likely to say that they lived in a 'nice' or a 'select' area, rather than an 'ordinary' or a 'mixed' one (79 per cent of the former compared with 57 per cent of the latter said they had people round).

It is important to stress that these are only *tendencies*. With the understandable exception of those in private rented accommodation (who may often have lacked the space to entertain), almost whatever way one subdivides the data one usually still finds a majority of workers sharing evenings at home with non-kin. For sure, many did this less than once a month, but it nonetheless offers an important corrective to the idea that families were becoming increasingly isolated and 'privat-ized' as they became more prosperous.[134] But who did they tend to invite into their homes? The Luton study reported that 80 per cent of shop-floor workers' guests consisted of kin, neighbours, or workmates (compared with 76 per cent for white-collar workers), and concluded that 'they would appear to build up their friendship relations largely on the basis of social contacts that are in the first instance "given"'.[135] But the claim seems somewhat forced. For one thing, neighbours were defined very broadly to include anyone living within a ten-minute walk, despite the fact that most people considered only those living next door (or sometimes opposite) to be 'neighbours'. They also included *former* neighbours and workmates in this category of 'given' relationships. But to the people concerned, continuing to socialize with former workmates and neighbours was all about the expression of personal preference. Luton's affluent workers didn't invite people round in order to *make* friends, but they did take pleasure in being able to entertain special friends they had made by other means. Hence the man who commented that his new house was ideal for entertaining but he had yet to meet the right people. Hence, too, the particular wariness about being on intimate terms with immediate neighbours— people who had not been chosen, and who could all too easily undermine the family's sense of domestic privacy if they spread 'gossip' or unilaterally assumed the rights of special friends.[136]

Here we do seem to be dealing with the adaptation of established customs to new conditions: to prosperity, to better housing, and also to the physical mobility which meant that many people were often living far from close family. As we have seen, wariness about becoming too close to neighbours could be as strong in old working-class districts like Bethnal Green and Bermondsey as on Luton's new estates. And nor was the desire to assert personal autonomy—to live as one chose—a purely post-war or suburban phenomenon. The defence of family life and domestic privacy had long been a way to resist coercive pressure to conform to the expectations of others.[137] By the interwar period, there were already signs that this was beginning to mutate into a more radical belief in the right to live as one chose, in public as well as in private.[138] It wasn't just Bloomsbury intellectuals who declined to live by the restrictive codes of the nineteenth century. We also find remarkable figures like Lillian Rogers, the interwar wife of a garage mechanic, described by James Hinton as the 'Birmingham flâneuse' for her advanced views on women's sexuality, and her strong emphasis on personal fulfilment and the pursuit of pleasure.[139] And though it may often have been difficult to resist the pressure for social conformity within close-knit neighbourhoods, there were always independent spirits determined to defy convention in the name of personal free-dom, and others adamant that no one had the right to judge how others lived their lives.[140] New levels of prosperity and mobility may have strengthened these ten-dencies, but they did not create them.

But this was more than a simple story of continuity. Although we have no comparable data to work with, as Hoggart's comments and the evidence from Bermondsey and Bethnal Green both suggest, something *had* changed in terms of the dominant patterns of social interaction in post-war Luton. Here improvements in housing were key—hence the much lower levels of entertaining among those in private rented accommodation—although as Stefan Ramsden has suggested, there was doubtless also a broader cultural dimension rooted in generational change.[141] And though feeding a visiting friend might be presented as a spontaneous act of generosity (like the interviewer's impromptu steak), rather than as a pre-planned dinner party, it still represented a distinctive pattern of domestic sociability. But perhaps the clearest indication that the meanings attached to home life were changing in the 1960s was the vogue for home improvement—or 'DIY' as it came to be known.[142] We have heard Bob Green complaining that, unlike in Suffolk, Luton people seemed to do nothing but work or redecorate, and sure enough we do often find interviewers commenting that the house they are visiting is in a state of upheaval thanks to some ambitious DIY project. They also frequently comment on the 'garish' contemporary colour schemes favoured by Luton's affluent workers, including one where every wall had a different coloured wallpaper and another with a 'terrifying granite-wall motif on wallpaper over fireplace'.[143] They also called on a number of homes where the family were in the midst of more radical DIY alterations, either building an extension or knocking through their downstairs rooms to create a large living space.[144]

In the 1940s many people had complained when councils built homes to this design, preferring the traditional 'parlour house' pattern, with smaller downstairs rooms, one of which could be designated a 'best' room reserved for guests and special occasions, or for use by courting couples.[145] As Hoggart observed, where possible even quite poor families maintained the tradition of keeping a 'best' room—it was a symbol of their refusal to be demoralized by economic hardship (in his 1936 novel *Keep the Aspidistra Flying*, George Orwell suggested that even in the poorest street the hardy aspidistra in the front-room window advertised the English cult of domestic respectability to the outside world).[146] Many Lutonians preserved this tradition on the town's new estates. In both manual and non-manual homes, interviewers complained about being ushered into 'drab', 'soulless' front rooms.[147] However, they also visited many homes where the 'best' room had already been transformed into the family's TV room, meaning the interview had to take place in the kitchen or back room so that the viewing of other family members would not be disturbed.[148] Knocking through the downstairs rooms merely completed the symbolic revolution against Orwell's aspidistra that had been begun by the incursion of television. It was a revolution against social codes which said that respectability and the opinions of others were more important than getting the most out of life. But this wasn't all about creating a better space for 'entertaining'. First and foremost, it was about creating more room for the family to be together, including more room to enjoy the new generation of larger television sets. As we have seen, Arun Banerjee was building a large extension to his living room so that his children would have more room to play. But others installed expensive sound systems and cocktail bars in their new knocked-through rooms: for them this was definitely about embracing a new, more modern, way of living in which entertaining at home would play a central role. Long before Mike Leigh's *Abigail's Party* and the droning sounds of Demis Roussos, people were adapting their homes as sites of social entertainment, though not necessarily to ape Alison Steadman's Beverly by throwing drinks parties for neighbours they hardly knew.[149]

If the 'best' room wasn't dead, its days seemed numbered in the boom-town economy of 1960s Luton. This could be painted as a victory for a brash, consumerist individualism over deep-rooted communal traditions and norms. It certainly reflected a widespread determination to assert a greater degree of personal autonomy—a rejection of the idea that one should live by the codes of others. But this revolution against social conformity was done in the name of living more integrated social lives— both within the nuclear family itself, and with friends and family one hoped to socialize with at home.

In the prosperous South most families had the financial resources to improve their homes, even if heavy overtime meant that many lacked the time or energy to enjoy those homes to the full. In Chapter 5 we turn our attention to the industrial North and ask whether similar changes were afoot in the rather different economic and social context of late 1960s industrial Tyneside.

CHAPTER 5

THE SWINGING SIXTIES
ON TYNESIDE

Wallsend, an industrial town on the River Tyne, 3.5 miles east of Newcastle city centre, is famous for its long history of shipbuilding and for being the birthplace of Gordon Sumner, better known to the world as the pop singer Sting. Sting grew up in a terraced house immediately behind the vast Swan Hunter shipyard, in a district of small, tightly packed terraced streets known locally as 'top of the bank' (see Figure 16).[1] In 1965, when a group of sociologists began an extended project studying the workers at the Swan Hunter yards, Sting would have been a teenager at Newcastle's Catholic Grammar School, Saint Cuthbert's (Wallsend had a reputation for being a strongly Catholic town, and parts of the Swan Hunter works were said to be predominantly Catholic).[2] Sting's father ran a local milk round and the budding musician would often help him on the milk float in his school holidays. The sociologists studying the Swan Hunter works must surely have seen father and son as they made their way to the shipyard early each morning to observe the welders, platers, shipwrights, and others who together built the great tankers and cargo ships that dominated the local skyline (see Map 7). Like many of the men who worked in the shipyards, Sting's family left the area in the late 1960s, moving to a modern semi-detached house near the coast. By the 1980s the whole riverside district had been cleared of housing, revealing the footprint of Segedunum, the large Roman fort which once marked the eastern end of Hadrian's Wall (from which the town gets its name). The ruins have now been excavated and transformed into an important tourist attraction.[3]

Overseen from 1966 by the industrial sociologist Richard Brown of Durham University, most of the fieldwork in the Swan Hunter yards was conducted by Peter Brannen, a social anthropologist trained at Manchester University, and Jim Cousins, a recent Oxford history graduate from Chiswick in west London who would settle in the area, becoming a local councillor and from 1987 to 2010 the Labour MP for nearby Newcastle Central.[4] Both men were from working-class backgrounds. Cousins's father was a skilled printer, and Peter Brannen had grown up on the

Figure 16. Leslie Street, Wallsend, looking towards Swan Hunter, 1975; Sting grew up in the next street and recalls how such tankers 'blotted out the sun for months' before they were launched [Images are copyright Peter Loud and must not be copied or used without permission from Peter Loud]

nearby Durham coalfield; most of Brannen's extended family continued to work in the local mining and engineering industries.

Brannen and Cousins conducted extensive observation around the shipyard, sometimes organizing informal interviews, but often simply recording what was said and done around them (usually by hand, sometimes—when conditions allowed—using portable tape recorders).[5] Some workers suspected the pair of being company spies, but most appear to have accepted that they were academics keen to understand more about working-class life.[6] Drawing on their early fieldwork, Brown's team drew up a seventy-page questionnaire which was completed by nearly 270 shop-floor workers from different sections of the Swan Hunter workforce. The discussion that follows draws mostly on Brannen and Cousins's rich ethnographic field-notes in order to explore the shipyard workers' world-view and 'structures of feeling', although the questionnaires are also used where these help to contextualize workplace discussions.[7] From these surviving field-notes we can build a fascinating picture of how workers on Tyneside experienced the social and cultural flux of the 'Swinging Sixties', living, as they did, 250 miles from its iconic

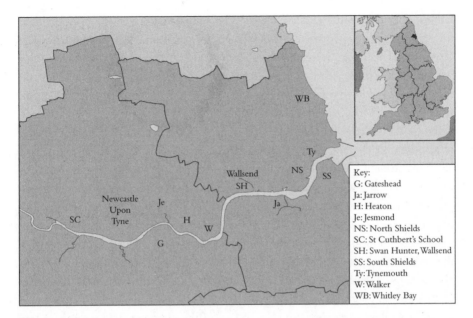

Map 7. Tyneside area showing location of Swan Hunter's Wallsend shipyards and of local places mentioned in the text

London hotspots like Carnaby Street and Chelsea's King's Road. What did 'the sixties' mean in provincial working-class England; how did working-class Geordies respond to talk of the 'permissive society', to the rising tide of consumerism, to the furore over immigration ignited by Enoch Powell's speeches, or to disillusionment with the Labour Governments of 1964–70? These may not have been the questions that originally brought Brown's team of industrial sociologists to Tyneside, but during many months in the shipyards they recorded fascinating material about each of them, and about much else besides.

For Brown and his team Wallsend was interesting because it represented a classic example of the type of nineteenth-century industrial district that post-war sociologists had begun to call 'traditional' (often drawing an explicit contrast with modern, affluent places like Stevenage and Luton when they did so).[8] Wallsend was dominated by heavy industry (shipbuilding, mining, and engineering), tight-packed Victorian housing, and deep-rooted traditions of trade unionism and Labour voting. From the start the researchers sought to complicate this model of a 'traditional' working class, and their published findings laid considerable emphasis on the shipbuilding workers' 'varied' lifestyles and 'complex' attitudes.[9] From the field-notes we see that the shipbuilders themselves also stressed diversity and individuality. None more so than Ronnie Morris, the man I have come to think of as the 'philosopher plumber'.[10] In October 1968 he confronted one of the researchers in the shipyard, saying: 'You're out trying to put us all together and look at us as one group, aren't you? But we've all got different opinions. There's nothing in common with us at all.' Having been interrupted before he could say more, Morris waited till the end of the shift to track down the researcher and resume where he had left off: 'What do have we in common after all?' he asked. 'Just money and shagging. Money is the root, no matter what's said. We're all individuals outside that. Each has their own opinion.' The researcher was impressed, noting that 'underneath an air of apparent stupidity which he puts on semi-deliberately to cover himself at work, Morris is very shrewd. He is on at me again about the fact that I am trying to force plumbers into being a group rather than being individuals.'[11] Nor was Morris the only one to challenge the sociologists' impulse to generalize. One of the ship's joiners, a keen local historian who had taken a different evening class every year for the past thirty years, told a researcher that he hoped he 'wasn't one of those Southerners with the cloth cap, Andy Capp image of the North East' (the *Daily Mirror*'s cartoon series began in 1957).[12] And when the same researcher tried to explain sociological concepts of class to two of the plumbers, he found them less than convinced; they told him it was all 'a load of piss'.[13]

Unlike the other community studies we have considered, the Wallsend project focused only on working-class men. Its subject was the world of work, and particularly the experiences and attitudes of different types of male manual worker in heavy industry. The formal interviews were conducted at home, often with the men's family present, but in contrast to the Luton study, *only* the man was interviewed. This made sense to the researchers because their principal aim was to test the hypothesis that work played a major part in shaping shipbuilding workers' social attitudes—or, in the phrase of the time, their 'images of society'.[14] In late 1960s Britain the debate about social class remained primarily a debate about men, and therefore no attempt was made to interview the minority of women workers at Swan Hunter in a variety of office, canteen, and cleaning jobs.

But if women were largely absent from the study, *gender* was not. The men had a great deal to say about sex, marriage, and what it meant to 'be a man'. They had even more to say about work—of all the sources considered in this book it is here that we gain most insight, not just into the experience of work, but also into the ways in which work could itself provide a powerful sense of community for many. But the picture is complicated. Not only did employment conditions vary greatly for different groups of workers, particularly between the steelworking or 'black' trades and the ships' outfitting trades, but there were also sharp generational and cultural differences among the men. Fortunately, the surviving testimony from this project is so rich and extensive that revisiting it can offer valuable insights into workers' perceptions of the social changes of the 1960s in a supposedly 'traditional' working-class area like industrial Tyneside.

Some of the most distinctive features of the testimony from Swan Hunter, notably the incessant swearing and sexual banter, surely reflect the fact that so much of this material was collected in the workplace, rather than at home. We should not assume that it tells us something unique about this time or place. We don't hear men swearing in our other surveys because they were generally being interviewed in their own homes, often in front of their wives and children. The same workers we hear effing and blinding (and worse) throughout this chapter would probably not have sworn at home, especially if family members (or a female interviewer) were present. This may explain why an elderly Tyneside woman interviewed in the mid-2000s could adamantly declare that men had not sworn when she was younger—as she told sociologist Yvette Taylor: 'My father worked in the shipyards and he never swore. Nothing sexual!'[15] Context was all-important. As transport worker Dick Sexton had explained to the Bermondsey researchers in the late 1940s, 'I can swear too—I've been in the army—but there's a time for such things. My wife has never heard me swear yet, and I hope she never will.'[16] Accordingly, the transcripts from interviews conducted in men's homes contain none of the obscenities that frequently pepper their speech at work. Nor do we see the same fascination with sex that runs through the workplace encounters, during which the young academic researchers were shown pornography they found 'revolting' and were repeatedly quizzed about stories of free love and orgies among university students. On a number of occasions men even asked the researchers for tips on how to talk to (that is, chat up) female students, although one young blacksmith was deeply pessimistic about his chances, complaining, 'I couldn't go down Jesmond way with all the intellectual women. But you and people like you could talk to them.'[17] Not everyone was so reticent. An apprentice joiner was described as 'one of these types who smoke cannabis and gate crash parties in Jesmond'; a plumber claimed to be going out with a female graduate, although he still asked the researcher for tips on 'what intellectual women were like'.[18]

The shipbuilding workers were convinced that new social mores around court-ship and sex were sweeping the land, but believed that these new ways of living (and loving) were happening somewhere else—in the universities, 'down south', and locally in more bohemian districts like Jesmond, but not in Wallsend. One of the plumbers reckoned that 'It's all fun down south, isn't it[?]'[19] But if the Swinging Sixties of their imagination were happening elsewhere, and the backdrop to their own lives was more *Get Carter* than *Sergeant Pepper*, it does not follow that nothing was changing in the shipyard workers' lives. Quite the contrary; change was very definitely in the air.

Arguably, for the first time, great swathes of the population were embracing the idea that they were radically free; that they were answerable, first and foremost, to themselves for everything they did—rather than to the dictates either of scripture or of local opinion. A classic sitcom set in the North East at almost exactly this time nicely captured this feeling. In the first episode of Clement and La Frenais's *Whatever Happened to the Likely Lads?*, Terry Collier (played by James Bolam) can't believe the changes that have swept over Britain while he's been away in the army. Meeting his old friend Bob Ferris on the train home to Newcastle, Terry complains:

> When this country goes through a social transformation I'm not here to see it. I missed it all…Death of censorship, the new morality, *Oh! Calcutta!*, topless waitresses…Permissive society, I missed it all.

When the programme first aired, in January 1973, Britain was still in the grip of unparalleled social and cultural flux. It was not without reason that Christopher Booker's excoriating critique of the post-war 'revolution in English life', first published in 1969, was called *The Neophiliacs*. It seemed as though everything old was discredited; that Britain must invent itself anew to face its post-colonial future as a medium-sized country suddenly keen, at least for the time being, to seek its destiny in partnership with Continental Europe.

As Terry Collier would discover, his native Tyneside was as much in flux as the rest of Britain. But what did flux mean in this context? Dick Clement and Ian La Frenais were gifted writers, and *The Likely Lads* arguably offers a more plausible rendition of everyday life than many kitchen-sink dramas, but it was still a work of fiction. By contrast, in Brown's shipbuilding study we hear working men grappling with social change in their own words. We also gain insights into how their everyday lives were changing. By 1970 less than a third of the men still lived close by the yards in Wallsend, and even those that did were beginning to display a keen awareness of new ways of thinking and living. Some questioned locally dominant ideas about what it meant to 'be a man', some questioned the area's historic allegiance to Labour politics, and everywhere people professed their determination to think for themselves rather than follow the herd, though crucially most did so *without* abandoning the idea that friends and family mattered as much as self.

Work, friends, and family

Brown and his team argued that the main reason that Wallsend's shipbuilding workers complicated the classic model of 'traditional' solidaristic, class-conscious workers was that their work experience was highly sectionalized, with a history of friction between trades over demarcation (who could do which job) and differentials (how much each trade would be paid), as well as big differences in pay and conditions between skilled workers with a trade (often still called 'journeymen' locally) and labourers and other workers who had never served a craft apprenticeship. But this situation was not simply taken for granted. One of the blacksmiths' labourers denounced what he called 'the class system' at Swan Hunter, arguing that it degraded labourers and unskilled men. Certainly in the shipyards class could divide workers as easily as it brought them together.[20]

Among the outfitting trades, such as plumbing and joinery, labourers complained that they were excluded from bonus schemes and treated as second-class workers, though it should be stressed that relations between individual skilled men and their labourers were often very close, even affectionate (indeed the widely used term 'mate' arguably encapsulated this closeness).[21] It's striking that when the blacksmiths went on their annual outing, with one of the researchers in tow, the event was dominated by smiths, foremen, and inspectors, with only a smattering of strikers (the blacksmiths' semi-skilled assistants) and no labourers at all.[22] Though considered less exclusive than some of the ancient shipbuilding trades such as platers or shipwrights, blacksmiths enjoyed considerable privileges within the yards. They still negotiated the price for each job individually with their foreman, paying their striker's wage from the agreed sum at the fixed rate of 60/40 (in their favour, naturally).[23]

Relations *between* the skilled trades could also be fraught. Mixing was limited, with groups such as the platers and shipwrights particularly known for their social exclusiveness. Waiting in the yard before work, men gathered in their trade groups, with only relatives and close friends breaking up the segregation.[24] On board ship, trade groups generally ate separately, and some bragged about their exclusiveness— blacksmith Johnny Macpherson boasted to the researchers that he 'wouldn't sit with plumbers'.[25] But it is important not to exaggerate these divisions. Although sectional disputes could cause real anger if other workers lost overtime or, worse, were laid off without pay, there was a general recognition that the shipyards had been much more bitterly sectional in the past.[26] Perhaps significantly, less than one in five men reported having been involved in a demarcation dispute in the previous five years.[27] The same man who refused to eat with plumbers acknowledged that 'everybody works in with one another', citing the way in which workers in other trades often made a point of tipping off the blacksmiths when they saw a job that might need a smith, knowing they were on piece rates (indeed he hinted that sometimes men in other trades deliberately created work for the smiths through judicious bits of vandalism around the ship).[28]

Some of this camaraderie almost certainly stemmed from the recognition that men shared a dangerous working environment where their lives could literally depend on each other. More than half of shop-floor workers reported having witnessed a serious accident at work, and a staggering 94 per cent had themselves been injured badly enough to have to visit either a doctor or the company ambulance room.[29] During the fieldwork one of the burners was killed, knocked from the ship's staging by a poorly riveted plate, leading some of the men to walk out in protest against poor safety.[30]

Perhaps partly because death hung over them, trades such as blacksmiths, riggers, and platers all prided themselves on being the most fun-loving, sociable workers in the yard. They often looked down on other trades for being 'dead' or 'snooty'; 'They never laugh or have a daft carry on like us,' as a blacksmith said of the plumbers, before adding, 'The joiners! They don't even talk to one another.'[31]

The researchers' field-notes are awash with descriptions of boisterous horseplay between the men, *including* the plumbers. Much of this horseplay was overtly sexual. A plumber known to his friends as 'Johnny Big Cock' was famous not only for his generous endowment (which his mates had measured with ruler and flange), but for amusing his workmates with pranks such as inserting said member in an apprentice's ear while the lad was eating his lunch: 'My God didn't he squeal! Johnny's the most popular man in the squad, we're all proud of him' (the fact that the plumbers could nonetheless be seen as 'dead' probably gives a good sense of just how lively things were elsewhere in the yards).[32] Among the blacksmiths it was common for men to try and pull down each other's trousers as a joke, and to make surprise attacks on the apprentices to kiss or grope them, and even to pretend to bugger them.[33] On one occasion Geordie Den, a blacksmith's striker, told a researcher, 'I nearly touched you up then. I thought you were one of the boys.'[34]

The researchers wrote about the role of 'horseplay' in moulding a strong 'occupational culture' in the yards, mentioning 'mock fighting, mock kissing, mock embracing', but they did not acknowledge that it could also be used as a strategy for asserting hierarchies of masculinity in which apprentices, academics, and sometimes even foremen were fair game for physical harassment.[35] Nor did they acknowledge the possibility that this sexualized horseplay may have been part of a broader culture of same-sex intimacy within the workplace. Gender historian

Helen Smith has recently argued that sexual intimacy between men remained commonplace in northern industrial districts up until the late 1950s, partly because popular culture lacked any fixed concept of 'the homosexual' until this point.[36] The behaviour of men like Geordie Den may have been a hangover from this older culture of male intimacy, though if so workmates certainly did now possess a vocabulary for labelling such behaviour as 'deviant'. On the blacksmiths' workshop outing men discussed asking a workmate's wife if he was 'queer' because he was always touching men up at work, but their courage failed them.[37]

The apprentices themselves clearly resented being the butt of sexualized horse-play, recognizing that it was about denying their claim to full manhood.[38] Paddy Foley, an apprentice plumber, described his shock at first meeting Macpherson: 'you come into the yard feeling like a man, and you find men blowing kisses and touching one another up'.[39] But there is no suggestion that anything was done to stamp out the practices, either by management or by the trade unions. On the contrary, they were widely viewed as a necessary rite of passage into full manhood. Riggers, by reputation the 'wildest men on the ship', were said to 'make or break a shy lad and have your trousers off in no time'.[40]

But there was another dimension to workplace 'matedom'. Men would do favours for each other, even when they were no more than acquaintances. Welders would help men with their car maintenance or DIY, carpenters would make furniture for people from offcuts, and so on. Sometimes they seemed barely to know the men they were helping—beating the system and helping a fellow worker were more important.[41] Shipbuilding workers valued this relaxed cooperative atmosphere. Two welders in the prefabrication sheds, who had both earned much more working outside the shipyards, explained this succinctly: 'We...always come back. It's the matiness here. You know everyone. They'll tell you things like what rate they're on. In the construction industry they're clannish. They won't tell you anything.'[42] Overall, more than 60 per cent of shipyard workers felt that shipbuilding was better than factory work for having 'good mates'.[43] But it is important not to romanticize this comradeship. There was also plenty of suspicion and distrust in the yards. One of the joiners said that he didn't like to talk about his valuable collection of coins when at work because there had recently been a spate of targeted burglaries.[44] Another complained that 'the likes of platers and welders' were so dishonest that if you were out working on the ships you had to 'lock up your tools even when you go to the toilet'.[45] And a foreman joiner, who was also a local Labour councillor, scathingly commented: 'Here you have to work with men you wouldn't touch with a barge pole socially.'[46]

In many respects this division reflected a deeper schism that ran through the shipyards. Many contemporary sociologists would have seen it as the division between the 'traditional' and the 'new' working class—with the former characterized as more solidaristic, with strong rituals around work-based male bonding, and the latter as more instrumental and home-centred (their word was 'privatised'). However, we should be wary about assuming that this division was either new or clear-cut. Workers had always been faced by the challenge of how to prioritize the competing claims of family and workmates over both their leisure time and their earnings. In the nineteenth century, both political radicalism and evangelical religion had celebrated the virtues of the domesticated family man—the responsible paterfamilias who was worthy of the vote in this life and salvation in the next.[47] Many men had always sought to live up to this ideal, setting themselves apart from fellow workers who chose to prioritize their own pleasure over their families' well-being (like Robert Potts, a ship's plumber at Swan Hunter, such men took great pride in the label 'family man').[48] Even before the First World War, social commentators like Martha Loane had insisted that most working-class men were caring, home-centred fathers and husbands despite stereotypes to the contrary.[49] Perhaps significantly this cultural schism between respectable and pleasure-seeking masculinities plays a central role in two of the classic historical accounts of the origins of working-class industrial politics in the north-east of England in the nineteenth and early twentieth centuries: Robert Moore's *Pit-men, Preachers and Politics* and Huw Beynon and Terry Austrin's *Masters and Servants*.[50]

In real life most men probably sat somewhere between the two extremes; depending on the context they could appear either as the fun-loving roisterer or the respectable family man. This was something that Clement and La Frenais captured brilliantly in their sitcom *The Likely Lads*. Ostensibly the sitcom portrayed Terry Collier (James Bolam) as the unreconstructed 'traditional' working-class man, and his best friend Bob Ferris (Rodney Bewes) as the aspirational, would-be family man keen to put the old ways behind him (see Figure 17). But what raised the programme above the run-of-the-mill sitcoms of the era was the fact that both men hankered for aspects of the other's life; neither was reducible to a crass social stereotype.[51]

In *The Likely Lads*, Bob Ferris is shown becoming geographically as well as culturally distant from his working-class roots when he buys a new suburban house on the Elm Lodge Housing Estate. As we have noted, something similar was also happening in the shipyards. As one of the foreman joiners explained, historically the men had all lived close to the yards ('at the top of the bank'), but the combination of improved transport, higher wages, and new housing developments meant that many now chose to live further afield—as he dryly observed, the 'dinner at home men [are] becoming a minority'. This man had himself been born just along

Figure 17. James Bolam as Terry Collier (right) and Rodney Bewes as Bob Ferris (left) in *Whatever Happened to the Likely Lads?*, 1973–4 [Pictorial Press Ltd / Alamy Stock Photo]

the road from the yard, but now lived 6 miles away on the outskirts of the coastal town of Whitley Bay.[52] Similarly, a welder who claimed to earn £30 to £32 a week with heavy overtime had moved out to Tynemouth, also on the coast, having bought a house for £4,000 (approximately the average price for a house nationally in 1968).[53] It was the same move that Sting's family made when they abandoned Wallsend and the shadows of the Swan Hunter cranes in 1967 for a semi-detached house in Tynemouth with a garden and distant view of the sea.[54]

Like Sting's family, most chose to move away to get a better house in more pleasant surroundings, but some deliberately chose to live away from the shipyards in order to draw a clear line between work life and home life. 'Geordie' Price, a well-paid welder, called shipyard work 'the lowest of the low', adding 'I'm glad I live in Gateshead. When I'm out of the yard that's the finish.'[55] According to a foreman this was the general attitude among the famously exclusive shipwrights. He claimed that by the late 1960s barely 2 per cent of these elite craftworkers still lived at the 'top o' the bank'.[56] Overall, approximately half the men interviewed felt that shipyard workers could be described as 'close-knit', though a number stressed that this was only true for those still living in Wallsend (now roughly one in three), and barely more than a third (37 per cent) said they sometimes went for a drink with workmates after work. Asked if they *preferred* to socialize with fellow shipyard workers, only one in ten said 'yes'; and of those who explained their reason, most commented that they preferred to avoid talking shop outside work. A shipwrights' foreman was probably exaggerating when he claimed that 'Once the buzzer blows the men don't care about Jack who works alongside him,' but even on Tyneside many men clearly drew a firm line between their work and non-work lives. Despite the horseplay and camaraderie, they worked to live; even among the yard's elite craftsmen few lived to work.[57]

Interestingly, the study also found high levels of socializing within the home—much higher than contemporary accounts of the 'traditional' working class would predict.[58] More than half claimed to have friends round for a meal or drinks. And though some workers still confined home entertaining to their extended family, as at Luton, many did not. As the determination to protect home life from prying eyes diminished, so patterns of working-class socializing began to change in the industrial North as well as in the prosperous South. Here too, it was probably still unusual for working-class people to have friends round for a pre-planned meal—though by no means unheard of among younger workers—but having them round for drinks, or for a party, appears to have been normal. A few even claimed to host managers and professionals such as accountants on a regular basis.[59]

But there were still men who insisted that it was a man's prerogative, even his duty, to go drinking with his workmates on a regular basis. In their mind, anyone who did not do so was somehow less alive; less a 'real' man. For such men the hard-drinking, misogynist cartoon character Andy Capp was a comic hero, not a calumny on Geordie manhood (though being from Hartlepool, 30-plus miles south of the Tyne, Andy wasn't *technically* a Geordie at all). When the blacksmith Johnny Macpherson sought to explain the scandal of labourers' low wages he cited the example of a man who earned 'so little he's just tied to the house'. Macpherson was clear: 'That's not living, that's only existing.'[60]

Ideas about what it meant to be a 'family man' were themselves in flux in the 1960s. An exchange about nappies brought this out particularly vividly. When one of the blacksmiths contrasted his own parenting with his father's by observing '[my] father never even saw a nappy never mind changed one', Johnny Macpherson immediately leapt in to assert his own unreconstructed version of masculinity: 'Get away! You don't change nappies do you? I've never touched one, would I fuck!'

Many of the shipbuilding workers appear to have been conflicted over the role to play within modern marriage, as though torn between being barfly Andy Capp or the home-centred Bob Ferris of *Likely Lads* fame. Rob Monks, a newly married blacksmith's striker, was a case in point. Having recently bought a house at Heaton, he complained of feeling 'tied down', and declared that when the holidays came he might have to 'go off for two days on my own with my motor bike'. But this was no Tyneside version of *Easy Rider* (Hopper and Fonda's cult road movie had been released just a few months earlier). Rob made it clear that he'd have to get his wife's permission. Others made fun of the idea that they were lords and masters in their own home. One of the blacksmiths claimed that he had had such a hard day at work that he was planning to go to the club for a drink on the way home. Conjuring up a scene straight from the *Daily Mirror*'s Andy Capp cartoon strip, the researcher recorded their exchange as follows,

'And I hope wor lass has got supper ready.'
Pause.
'Aa'll flop her if not.'
Pause.
'—if I stand on a chair!'[61]

Ronnie Morris, our philosopher plumber, was another conflicted case. On one occasion he's recorded mocking a welder for handing over all his wages to his 'career woman' wife, only getting back 'pocket money' to cover his daily expenses. Morris boasts that in contrast he always secretly keeps back a pound from his own wife, plus any bonuses he might earn. But on another occasion he praises his wife for doing a factory job she dislikes, proclaiming 'she's a genius with money and we pool it'. We also see Morris taking pride in the fact that his earnings go mainly towards improving their domestic life—or, as he puts it, on buying things for 'the wife' like 'a car, a house, a washing machine and fitted carpets'.[62] If change was afoot—and the evidence on attitudes to domestic chores, nappy changing, and women working would suggest that it was—then it was slow and messy. Most men appear to have been living less rigidly segregated married lives than their fathers, but like Bob Ferris in *The Likely Lads* they had not abandoned the idea of male privilege within marriage and could easily revert to type.[63]

'Us and them'

The picture is no simpler when we turn to examine how shipbuilding workers talked about what class and social justice meant to them. Again we see signs of change, particularly among younger workers who tended to be more radical and questioning of tradition, but across the shipyards many workers had evidently internalized a hierarchical world-view in which 'the likes of us', as they often described themselves, were anchored firmly at the bottom of society.[64] Even someone as outspoken and extrovert as the blacksmith Johnny Macpherson turned to this submissive phrase when he tried to explain how it felt to be a working man at the mercy of arbitrary managerial authority. In a powerful comment he explained:

> I can't think of the words to say what I want. That's where the likes of us always get fucked. What I mean is you [the researcher] can't really know what we feel. Like going in to Pearson [their manager] when there's a cut on our bill [payslip], and he knows and I know that there's no one we can appeal to. You ought to get a job and really see.[65]

Though of course Macpherson *did* manage to say this, even if it was only to a researcher rather than to his manager. The feelings of this hyper-masculine man are not entirely lost to us. What's more, in discussing how it felt to be powerless, Macpherson must have known that he was challenging the central premise of the researchers' project—if they really wanted to understand working-class life they should take a job on the shop floor rather than wander about the yards observing the workers and asking questions.[66]

It is particularly striking how often men described themselves as 'thick' when talking to their university-educated interrogators. After a few too many drinks on the blacksmiths' outing, Rob Monks confessed that his well-off father had wanted to send him to a private college, but he had refused, saying it would have been a waste of money because he was 'the thick cunt' of the family.[67] Similarly, an apprentice plumber explained that he had had to give up his apprenticeship as a patternmaker because he was 'too thick', declaring himself lucky to have secured a second chance in plumbing—'Up here you're an apprentice or on the dole.'[68] Another man explained that he was a plumber, while all his siblings were teachers, because he had lost eighteen months' schooling to illness as a child (in essence he was saying: 'I'm not "thick", just poorly educated').[69]

Some men had been labelled failures in school and carried the stigma with them, but the process did not stop at 15 (the school-leaving age until 1972). Few appear to have doubted that the ability to train for high-status skilled jobs such as draughtsman, patternmaker, or toolmaker reflected concrete, objective measures of relative worth. Nor was this just a personal story about an internalized sense of failure. Men routinely labelled each other in this way, and not just in casual workshop banter. Bumping into a group of workers in a Tynemouth pub, the first thing that the researcher's drinking companion, a ship's plumber, thought to

148

say about the men was that one of them was a miner because he had not been 'clever enough' to qualify as a fitter.[70] The tyranny of what Michael Young termed post-war Britain's 'meritocracy' was deeply ingrained in the lives of shipbuilding workers, but since it was anchored in their working lives as much as in formal education we may doubt whether it was simply a product of the selective education system. Yes, the 1944 Education Act and its '11-plus' examination determined whether a child would go to a grammar school or secondary modern, but arguably the nineteenth-century traditions of the apprenticeship and the evening class still had an equally strong influence on popular understandings of merit.[71]

Considering its reputation for troubled industrial relations, the workers at the Swan Hunter yard generally had a fairly positive overall view of management. It seems to have helped that the firm had a long tradition of promotion from within. This led to widespread suspicion of favouritism based on religion or membership of semi-secret associations such as the Masons or the Buffaloes, but it also meant that large swathes of management had had direct experience of the shop floor.[72] This was especially true among prestigious groups like the platers, where in one group the foreman, his boss, and his boss's boss were all ex-platers or shipwrights.[73] Not everyone would have agreed with the blacksmith who declared 'They're canny gaffers here', but there was a widespread sense that, as another blacksmith put it, 'they are better than at most places'.[74] In the main survey 59 per cent said that Swan Hunter's management was good compared with other firms; just 3 per cent thought it bad.[75] Some men even tried to portray Sir John Hunter, the company chairman and managing director, as a self-made man despite the fact that he was the third generation of his family to run the firm and had been educated at Oundle School, and at Cambridge and Durham universities. When Sir John walked past during a works interview, a foreman painter said, 'He often does it, he never bothers anyone. He's a good man. He worked his way through all the trades. Not the soft way for him.'[76]

But like the privileges of skill, those of management did not go unquestioned. One of the blacksmiths denounced the class snobbery that meant a storekeeper would always keep a workman waiting if a clerk turned up. To underline his argument that such attitudes were outdated he stressed that he had no problem being friends with men who worked in the prestigious, white-collar drawing office.[77] Another compared his experiences at Swan Hunter with those of a friend employed as an engineer in America. He claimed that whereas his friend could have a frank discussion with a draughtsman if a drawing was wrong, at Swans class barriers made this impossible with the consequence that workers had to sort things out for themselves on the job. But this division was not just between white-collar and blue-collar, staff and works. A tack welder said much the same thing about working with shipwrights, complaining that any opinion he offered would be resented and dismissed with the refrain, 'I'm the shipwright you're just a tacker'.[78]

Overall, most workers agreed that there was less fear and deference in the shipbuilding industry than before the war. Stories about harsh treatment, like the man who recalled being forced to shave off his greying beard to avoid the sack, were generally mobilized to illustrate how bad things *used* to be.[79] As blacksmith Tommy Walker put it, when telling one of the researchers that he didn't care if the man was a management spy, 'The workman doesn't run when the gaffer comes now. A man of 50 isn't scared because the Social Security will look after him.'[80] In fact men frequently took pleasure in telling stories about how they had manipulated or otherwise disrespected their foreman, and plenty of foremen gave evidence corroborating this picture.[81] For instance, one of the blacksmiths told how his mate Bob had gone about negotiating an improved piece rate:

> One time he [the mate] wanted a bit extra for a hard job. I told Bob to use a bit of tact. Not him. He went straight up to the foreman who was with some apprentices and said 'Hey, Cuntie!' Tact! The foreman told all the apprentices to move away, and just said don't talk like that in front of the apprentices and gave us the money![82]

In the same discussion it was claimed that another blacksmith had a different approach: he tried to kiss his foreman whenever he saw him. Rather than face disciplinary sanction the man claimed to be left alone to work unsupervised most of the time.[83]

But change was afoot in the late 1960s, and it seemed likely to herald a worsening of industrial relations in the yards. There was considerable dissatisfaction that the recent amalgamation of Tyneside's shipbuilding firms under a new consortium headed by Swan Hunter risked suppressing wages and reducing men's freedom to switch employers. Potentially transferable tradesmen like the plumbers were particularly unhappy, talking of men being reduced to 'robots', and complaining that 'It's all one firm and they've got us now'.[84] There was also bitterness that old paternalistic traditions were dying out. When one of the burners retired after thirty-three years at Swan Hunter his workmates complained that he would not get a penny extra in his pay packet and that none of the 'gaffers' would come down to shake his hand. One of the men turned to the poetry of Walter Scott to sum up their situation: 'That's it . . . unwept, unhonoured and unsung. We're just cogs in the machine'[85] (in the late 1960s there were still many autodidacts among Tyneside's shipbuilding workers).[86]

There seems to have been a growing mood of militancy in the yards at this time, just as there was across much of British industry. Interestingly, shop stewards told researchers that whereas in the past militancy had always been driven by left-wingers, 'amongst the youngsters, whether left, right or centre, they're all militant'.[87] In fact even young foremen were becoming radicalized at Swan Hunter, spurning the firm's approved staff association in favour of a proper union pledged to push their demands for higher wages.[88] There was also growing disillusionment with trade-union leaders and Labour Party politics, even before Barbara Castle published her controversial white paper *In Place of Strife* in January 1969, with its call for radical reform of trade-union powers. Some of the misogynistic attacks on Castle may have been intended to shock the researchers, but if so they nonetheless remind us of the dark, brutal side of male workplace culture. In a note from October 1968 a researcher records: 'Larry Dixon produces a picture of Barbara Castle and says he would like to get her in the dock, do her and drown her.'[89] Although this was core Labour territory, and had been so for generations, there was a deep sense of outrage against the Wilson Government for turning its back on working people and threatening to undermine their bargaining position with employers.[90] As one of the joiners put it, 'They're going to start sending the bailiffs after an honest man who withdraws his labour. I ask you.'[91] Others denounced Labour Party leaders as 'bastards' and 'fifth columnists'. Their underlying message was simple: the Government had turned on the people who created the nation's wealth rather than target those who lived off the labour of others. As an angry plumber put it: 'we're the producers. There are too many being carried in this country.'[92] The labour theory of value, which held that all wealth was ultimately derived from the labour of working people, had a long life on the British shop floor. Although its roots lay in nineteenth-century radical movements now long forgotten, it helped to inject righteous moral indignation into the new-found militancy of the late 1960s.[93]

This lionizing of 'the producers' was not confined to the shop floor on Tyneside. The head of piecework inspection at Swans took a similar line, declaring 'the wealth of this country is its workers' and lamenting that too many lived off the workers' backs. In the USA, he noted with approval, 'an electrician gets more than a teacher'.[94] Among shop-floor workers the cause of the producer was more personal, as one of the researchers discovered in October 1968 when he jokingly called a group of workers 'parasites living off my brain' after finding them playing an improvised game of football on board a half-built ship. The men themselves retaliated with banter about idle students and campus demos, but later a plumber who had not even seen the incident tracked the researcher down to tell him, only half in jest,

> You've let the side down now. Living off you! We're the producers! Come the revolution you cultural lads will have to work for top place. All the students will be at their desks all day long. We'll have the whips out on you then.[95]

When the researcher responded by suggesting that perhaps the cultural lads would organize a counter-revolution, the plumber retorted, 'You wouldn't have the strength. When we're on top we'll stay there.' Here, behind the jocular banter, one sees echoes of the revolutionary rhetoric of Paris 1968 and of the ensuing penetration of a bowdlerized Marxism into shop-floor culture, at least among the young. In fact a number of the younger men claimed to be Trotskyists and identified with fringe revolutionary groups such as IS (the International Socialism Group, which would eventually become the Socialist Workers Party or SWP).[96]

But producer-consciousness could be turned against the non-working poor just as easily as it could be turned on the idle rich or layabout students. A few days before the impromptu football match one of the plumbers had been railing against the generosity of social security, declaring that 'The wages of a man at work should be higher than on the dole. They should get fuck all. In the firm we're carrying too many' (by which, he made clear, he meant lazy workers who didn't pull their weight rather than managers).[97]

As the cultural critic Richard Hoggart pointed out in his seminal 1957 book *The Uses of Literacy*, British workers often mobilized the dichotomous language of 'us and them' to make sense of the social world. This, Hoggart argued, was a fatalistic rather than a conflictual language—in Hoggart's Leeds 'them' denoted 'the world of the bosses... [and] public officials'; people to be mistrusted and avoided, not confronted.[98] By inference, 'us' were all those without power and authority over the lives of others—the 'working classes' broadly defined. Among the shipbuilding workers we see echoes of this sentiment in the frequent use of phrases such as 'the likes of us', but, as Hoggart observed, such thinking was declining among the young, along with the fundamentally deferential outlook it signalled. But even young militants were keen to determine who was, and was not, '*one* of us'—this was a much less deferential formulation. Discussing why one of their foremen was 'OK', a plumber explained that 'unlike the others he's still working class, he's one of us, he'll still talk to you and carry on and send a pint over if he sees you in a pub'.[99]

By staying true to the codes of 'matedom', such as 'carrying on' and standing drinks, this man was seen as remaining faithful to his working-class roots—he had not 'put on airs'. Similarly, one of the apprentice plumbers explained that he got on with his brother-in-law, despite the man's high-status position in the company's drawing office, because 'He's not like some of them who try to be above you'.[100] By contrast, Tom Carroll, who was one of the men to call himself a 'Trotskyite', denounced an in-law who was a local miners' official for being 'a big head' who had 'risen above us, hobnobbing with middle class people and out five nights a week'.[101] In Carroll's eyes this man was resolutely no longer 'one of us'. Intriguingly,

Carroll himself regularly 'hobnobbed' with the researchers, going drinking with them in Tynemouth, and even taking one to a Newcastle United match at St James' Park.[102] Perhaps it wasn't keeping middle-class company he objected to, just assuming middle-class affectations.

The shipbuilding workers also had a good deal to say about race and immigration, and opinion was sharply divided on the subject. It is not difficult to find examples of men spouting rhetoric reminiscent of Conservative politician Enoch Powell's notorious tirades against non-white immigration which had exploded across the British media while the Wallsend fieldwork was in full flow (Powell's so-called 'Rivers of Blood' speech, which saw him sacked from Edward Heath's shadow cabinet, had been given in Birmingham in April 1968).[103] But racist views never went unchallenged in the shipyard; one cannot argue that being 'one of us' necessarily meant being white in 1960s Wallsend. One of the earliest recorded exchanges involved a blacksmith explaining to one of the researchers that there were 'Black Geordies' in the nearby town of North Shields, part of a historic black community linked to seafaring which was actually centred on South Shields, on the other side of the River Tyne. According to Laura Tabili, non-English migrants to South Shields had historically been well integrated in the local community, especially in the nineteenth century, an idea nicely encapsulated in the blacksmith's phrase 'Black Geordies'.[104] Welders in particular were said to like frequenting the cosmopolitan Northumberland Arms on the quay at North Shields. Known locally as 'The Jungle', it appealed precisely because, as a sailors' pub-cum-hostel with a worldwide reputation, it was livelier and more cosmopolitan than the ordinary pubs and clubs of North Tyneside. As a middle-aged welder in the blacksmiths' shop explained: 'They're a great bunch of lads [welders]...Any time you want to meet someone you haven't seen for years you go up the Jungle for a couple of nights and he'll be in. The Jungle is for welders. We've had some great times up there.'[105]

I have only found one worker in the Swan Hunter study explicitly identified as black: a general labourer called Sam whose family were originally from west Africa. He was deeply disillusioned with life in England, although there is no suggestion that he felt discriminated against by his workmates. He told the researcher,

> I'm sending my four kids with an education back to Sierra Leone. There's nothing here for them. There's too much discrimination in class and race, but all they think about is pop stars, guitarists or being shipyard workers! They don't want to be a professional man.[106]

In essence, he was complaining that his children had integrated too fully into local working-class culture—adopting the low aspirations which he felt were endemic in English popular culture.

Even workers who endorsed the Powellite line on immigration were usually quick to distance themselves from overt racism (the English racist's urge to *appear* liberal is not a new phenomenon). In a discussion among the blacksmiths which began with Paul Waites declaring that 'The Irish are all ignorant—only interested in drink', the conversation quickly moved on to the emotive question of immigration. Waites declared, 'We ought to keep the blacks out. They're no worse than me but they ought to stay in their own country.' One of his workmates, Dave, claimed he agreed but then offered a striking caveat which exposed both the myths about immigration that were fuelling these fears and his own instinctive liberalism: 'But if they work a year before drawing National Assistance I don't mind that.'[107] Here we see the strong hold of contractual models of welfare on popular thinking. We also see the historic legacy of popular liberalism, which served to contain, and to some extent tame, instinctive prejudices against outsiders—racialized or otherwise. We too often fail to recognize that liberalism was more than a hypocritical veneer across English society—it was a powerful and deeply ingrained script which helped to delegitimize intolerance and prejudice in the eyes of many working people. As historian Raph Samuel counselled, the myths we live by have great power over us, and historians must seek to study the power of those myths rather than simply debunk them.[108]

Waites's response to these liberal objections was to shift the conversation to a different stereotype which played on workers' class loyalties. He claimed that he particularly objected to Pakistanis because 'They hire rooms off at 24 to a room; and they all have their own businesses.' In short, they could not be 'one of us' because they were exploitative petty capitalists rather than 'real' workers. Now I am not trying to suggest that these comments weren't racist, but it is significant that to try and sustain his dislike of immigrants Waites was forced to mobilize an argument rooted in popular hostility to capitalist profiteering. He knew that race alone could offer no common ground. Indeed it is important to recognize that many politicized shipworkers were actively *anti*-racist in the late 1960s. In an argument about race with a fellow plumber of Irish descent, Tom Carroll, the self-confessed Trotskyist, proclaimed passionately: 'We're all one. They're not the real enemies.'[109] And at a branch meeting of the Wallsend Young Socialists a 19-year-old apprentice commented:

> Every night I argue with my mates about blacks. I used to think they were worse till I thought about it. Everyone has got an underdog they keep in place. The workers have the blacks. There are four classes: The upper, the middle, the lower, that's us, and the blacks. We've got no right to blame the others till we treat the blacks right. We want it but we won't give it. We don't want to be worse but we'll hold them down.[110]

This was vernacular, class-conscious anti-racism on the streets of an overwhelmingly white, declining industrial town at the height of the Powellite controversy over immigration. Yes, many of the apprentice's 'mates' clearly took a different view, but the fact that the argument was raging *within* white working-class communities should remind us of the need to avoid lazy stereotypes which assume that English ideas about class were inherently racialized, and that white working-class people were somehow predetermined to be racially intolerant and exclusive.[111] Popular culture was not monolithically racist, let alone white supremacist, in the 1960s. On the contrary, it was riven by intense arguments over the meaning of immigration. In the late sixties and early seventies, the scenes played out on the sofa between racist East End docker Alf Garnett and Mike Rawlins, his anti-racist, left-wing son-in-law in the controversial sitcom *Till Death Us Do Part* (1965–75), were taking place daily in workplaces across Britain.

It was not working people who racialized the idea of the English 'working class', but academics and journalists.[112] The sooner we recognize that the 'white working class' is not a *thing*, but instead simply an unhelpful media construction, the better.[113] Not only does it deflect attention from the virulent racism in other parts of English society, but it reinforces the idea of working-class people as unchanging, anachronistic, and 'left behind'. The 'racialization' of class in Britain has been a *consequence* of the weakening of 'class' as a political idea since the 1970s. Indeed, it was this political version of class, more than liberal morality, which gave force to vernacular anti-racism in Wallsend at the height of Powellite populism.

The pleasure of things

Perhaps the most widely discussed change in working-class life in 1960s Britain was the rapid growth of consumption driven by rising real wages. This was the continuation of a story that had begun in the late nineteenth century, when branded foodstuffs, toiletries, and ready-made clothes had first found a mass market as working-class living standards began to rise.[114] As we have seen from the studies of Stevenage and Luton, from the late 1950s Britain was gripped by feverish debates about the social and political effects of what came to be known as mass 'affluence'. On the Left, in particular, there was much soul-searching about how consumerism and materialism were supposedly corrupting the working classes.[115]

The conversation among Tyneside shipbuilding workers clearly registered these debates, and it is striking that most sought to deny that there was any link between wanting new consumer goods and social status; they self-consciously presented themselves as wanting things for their *use value*, not for display as status objects. Of course, we cannot treat such statements as windows on the soul, but the very fact that manual workers in late 1960s Britain sought to present themselves as untainted by the shallower motivations of consumerism is significant. A 60-year-old black-smith, who had only just started working at Swan Hunter, epitomized this professed rejection of materialist striving, declaring: 'With £20 a week, a house to live in and a car a man's a liar if he says he wants more.'[116] Others felt the same. Besides owning the motorbike on which he wanted to take to the hills, the blacksmith's striker Rob Monks also drove a 1950s MG, but he was anxious not to seem 'flash'. Monks stressed that the MG had been given to him by a friend who had emigrated, adding 'Some bring their cars to work to show off but I don't.' Monks was more interested in a different sort of bragging, asking the researcher: 'Don't you get frustrated, with no car—don't the other blokes get the fannys? In my car the roof is marked. That's a sign of pleasure.'[117]

Although Ron Morris, our philosopher plumber, claimed that he worked primarily so that he could provide his family with new consumer goods, he nonetheless insisted that things were less important to him than experiences, and the chance to share these with his wife. He insisted that he wanted a new car 'not for showing it about, but to get in it and take wor lass to Wales or Scotland'.[118] On another occasion he claimed that 'What I want to work for is to take wor lass abroad and show her the things I've seen.'[119] Similarly, a labourers' shop steward talked about giving up drink to buy a 'car for the missus', and regretted that it meant that his workmates now assumed he was well off and so constantly asked to borrow money.[120]

But, as all these examples demonstrate, though men may have professed indifference to materialism, they were acutely conscious that consumer goods conveyed symbolic status. Their stance was about distancing themselves from this materialistic value system. When one of the plumbers sought to explain his opposition to overtime he acknowledged that his attitude annoyed his workmates because, unlike them, he already owned a car thanks to his wife's earnings. His initial response was to insist that 'we don't live on my wife's money', and then to point to one of his workmates, a driller, and say: 'he's got a £125 camera and his wife doesn't work'.[121] Not only did men know about each other's possessions, but this knowledge was also clearly charged with considerable social significance.

If shipbuilding workers were more enmeshed in the world of consumer goods than they cared to acknowledge, their attitude to what we might call the broader 'aspirational culture' of the late 1960s was decidedly cool. When asked in the questionnaire whether they would 'like to belong to a different class', two-thirds of manual workers replied 'no'; and of those who took the opposite view almost all simply said they'd like to have more money.[122] As so often, the philosopher plumber summed up the dominant attitude very nicely, declaring: 'I'm happy to go on as we are or get a packet and be the idle rich. I'm not bothered about sweating for a £40 a week job.'[123] Striving for just a little bit more was seen as a mug's game; as social historian Selina Todd has argued, what mattered to working people was knowing how to enjoy life—how to have a bit of fun.[124] Although poor timekeepers risked being laid off if trade turned bad, many shipyard workers still routinely took days off work when they felt like it. After a hard-drinking 'bachelor party' at a young plumber's house, twenty of the men (but not the researcher) missed work the next day.[125] The party itself was also interesting, and not just because it took place at the man's house rather than a pub. During the evening it became clear that the bachelor in question was still a virgin, but instead of generating the sort of ribald humour seen on the shop floor, his friends tried to tell him what to expect when he did have a sexual encounter. The researcher records: 'Everyone joined in this [...] there was very little crudity, curiously in fact rather informative.' It was another example of the contrast between the culture at work and at home, even when that domestic space was all-male.[126]

Foremen sometimes connived in absenteeism, as long as it was kept within bounds. It was accepted, for instance, that crane drivers would take at least one day off each month as respite from their lonely job, perched high in a cab above the yard (see Figure 18). High-earning welders, especially if young, were particularly noted for their pleasure-maximizing behaviour, as the stories about The Jungle testify. We find a welders' foreman commenting: 'I asked one man why he only worked four days a week, and he told me "Because I can't live on three".'[127] Again the philosopher plumber was the man who best summed up this attitude. When he talked about wanting a new car to go travelling with his wife it was part of a remarkable extended monologue in which he set out his personal credo for freedom and happiness. The researcher noted he had 'done nothing to provoke' the outburst, suggesting that Morris had again sought out the opportunity to get things off his chest. It was another example of how the researchers' presence could act as a spur to self-reflection and the generation of what we might call vernacular sociology. The researchers' alien presence encouraged men (and elsewhere women) to try and explain how their lives were different from, and in many ways better than, the lives of the socially mobile scholars who came to study them. Seeing the researcher armed with his tape recorder, Morris's opening gambit was to suggest how he differed from a fellow ship's plumber:

Figure 18. Wallsend, the *World Unicorn* tanker, and the cranes of the Swan Hunter shipyard, 1973 [Images are copyright Peter Loud and must not be copied or used without permission from Peter Loud]

> I often wonder what life's for. Greavsey lives for work, but I don't. I'm happy to go on as we are or get a packet and be the idle rich. I'm not bothered about sweating for a £40 a week job. I'm happy now. I could do with £50,000 but I'm happy as I am. Are you? How can you be? You're far from home. You can drink but that's not real happiness. You're going to lecture and do teaching, the same things one time after another. That's just talk. We put up with bad conditions. But we're more free than you. We do something different each day. We can move about. We know how to have fun, we don't try to worry or try to keep up with the Joneses. That's my ideal—to be independent. I'd like to have a new car, not for showing it about, but to get in it and take wor lass to Wales or Scotland. We wouldn't need caviar. We prefer a fish and chip supper. I'd [like] to own property so my brothers and sisters and wor lass's people could live there just for the rates. Then I'd be able to put me mates up when they wanted it.[128]

Morris placed freedom and autonomy at the heart of his personal philosophy, but in doing so he nonetheless explicitly rejected versions of individualism which placed striving to 'get on' ahead of the pursuit of personal (and family) happiness. In this exchange Morris sets himself up as a spokesman for the men. It's striking that his monologue begins with eight strong ego statements (including three statements that 'I'm happy'), but after a bridging section where he interrogates the researcher

158

directly, he moves on to talk about what 'we' want and enjoy, before closing with a mix of ego statements which are explicitly about others (his family and his 'mates') and more 'we' statements. The social psychologist Carol Gilligan advocates constructing 'I poems' when reading personal testimony, but here we learn most from paying attention to how Morris mobilizes a range of *different* pronouns to assert a position which is simultaneously intensely individualist yet also strongly communitarian.[129] Not only did Morris explicitly reject 'keeping up with the Joneses' (itself a concept imported from consumerist America), but he was adamant that, in so far as he wanted things like a new car or property, it was for the benefit that loved ones would get from them; hence too his rejection of rental income. The rejection of profit, the prioritization of family, and the assertion of personal independence—these values gave dignity and meaning to Morris's life. It may also be that in conversation with a university graduate, himself from a working-class background, the assertion of these values offered Morris a defence against any suggestion that, given his evident intelligence, he should have 'done more with his life'.

Fantasies of escape

But not everyone was content with life as it was. As elsewhere, many cherished dreams of a different life, and some were determined to escape shipbuilding, Wallsend, and even the North East altogether. Asked 'Have you ever considered moving permanently to another part of the country or abroad?', 43 per cent of shipworkers replied affirmatively (exactly half of these explicitly mentioned emigrating, mostly to former British territories such as Canada and Australia).[130] Blacksmith Sam White longed to win the pools, declaring 'The first thing I'd do would be to leave here [Swan Hunter]'.[131] Others spoke of big money to be made 'down south' or abroad, anticipating a theme that would be made famous in the Clement and La Frenais comedy-drama *Auf Wiedersehen, Pet* (1983–6), in which Geordies formed the original core of a group of British workers taking their chances on the building sites of Germany in order to escape low wages and unemployment at home. Dave Potts, a plumber, claimed that 75 per cent of the men at Swan Hunter were 'unsettled' since the recent mergers, and that he was considering moving to Pembroke where his uncle was earning £60 a week building oil refineries in safer, better conditions than the shipyard.[132] Similarly, joiners swapped stories about men who had taught themselves welding and were now earning more than £50 a week on oil-rig construction at Grimsby, or had gone to Germany supposedly to earn more than £100 a week in their own trade.[133] But for many, stories about the possibility of escape were counterbalanced by the strong pull of home. During a strike by stagers in June 1968, one young married man commented that, if he wanted it, he had a job waiting for him on the Isle of Wight which would pay a much higher basic wage, before adding 'but hell, why should I leave my home town and go somewhere strange?'[134] A heating engineer, who was worried about the insecurity of shipbuilding, wanted to move to Birmingham or the south of England, but acknowledged that it was impossible because, as he put it, 'the wife won't leave her mother'.[135]

The great hope for many was that a car factory might come to Tyneside, bringing with it high-paid and secure manufacturing jobs. Alf Cuthbert, a plater's mate, declared, 'I'd move to a car factory any day. 9 out of 10 people here would…Better conditions and better pay.' When the researcher asked 'would you lose something if you did…You'd have to take a semi-skilled job?', he replied: 'Well, that's the way it's moving here. And there's the insecurity. In 1963 a lot of men were paid off. It could happen again.'[136] A number of workers repeated the story that, as a plumber put it, 'Sir John Hunter stopped Fords coming to Jarrow so that he'd have us trapped.'[137] Carpenters and joiners were especially keen to find alternative employment, even if it meant abandoning their trade. Tom Wright was thinking about taking a job as a customs officer, John Robinson had the offer of a semi-skilled factory job in Somerset, where his son now lived, and his mate was planning to move to Stevenage where he had found a job as a caretaker.[138] Two other joiners cursed ever having learned their trade and swore that they would not let their children have anything to do with it.[139]

Overall, less than one in three of the men interviewed said they would advise a boy just leaving school to go into shipbuilding, and only 35 per cent said they would make the same choices themselves.[140] However, most remained relatively sanguine about the industry's prospects, perhaps because of the recent spate of contracts for supertankers (the 250,000-ton *Esso Northumbria* was launched during the project's fieldwork) (see Figure 19). Only 19 per cent of shop-floor workers expected the firm to be less prosperous in ten years' time; nearly half (47 per cent) expected increased prosperity.[141] On the eve of the 1973 oil crisis (which would all but kill the industry in the North East), the optimism instilled by the long post-war boom remained broadly intact, even if most felt that other trades now offered better prospects. Even among the principal shipbuilding trades many were glad that their children had not followed them into the yards.[142] A welder with grown-up children rejoiced that his son was working in computers for a major bank, explaining 'there was never any security…A shipyard was always what was called "a day and a dinner"' job. A job with a bank was cherished, not because it brought status as a 'white collar' occupation, but because in 1968 it was still a job for life.[143]

Figure 19. Swan Hunter workers assisting the launch of the *Everett F. Wells*, the last super-tanker built on the Tyne, 1976 [Images are copyright Peter Loud and must not be copied or used without permission from Peter Loud]

Some saw becoming a works foreman as a way to escape harsh conditions and insecurity, although the loss of paid overtime was a powerful disincentive. As at Luton, foremen generally suffered a cut in take-home pay when promoted. In the home interview 39 per cent of men said they would like to become foremen, although many of these considered their actual chances to be 'hopeless'.[144] They were not asked directly why they did, or did not, want to be foremen, but again we get some clues from the fieldwork in the shipyards. One of the foreman welders explained: 'I took a reduction to become a foreman in order to exercise my brains and get away from the health hazard.'[145] A tool-shop foreman made a similar point, and perhaps significantly also remained as fearful about job insecurity as many shop-floor workers: 'There's variety and independence in this work. You have a responsible job. You're an individual. Mind, we're getting out of it now. We're afraid of pay-offs in the consortium. The firm can do anything they like.'[146] Like this man, most foremen appear to have felt closer to 'their men' than to management, and this could make the job very difficult, particularly if lay-offs were demanded.[147] They also had to put up with the suspicion that, having joined the 'staff', they were no longer 'one of us', as well as snide comments from craftsmen about leaving the shop floor, as one blacksmith put it, 'because they're frightened of their tools'.[148] If a man wished to get out, or even 'get on', this was not the easiest route to take.

New horizons

These fragments of workers' recorded speech from the Tyneside shipyards of the late 1960s cannot be woven together to produce any single, overarching model of working-class life and culture. Even here, in shipyards that had their roots deep in the nineteenth century, in an area that everyone agreed was overwhelmingly working class, diversity and individuality loomed large in workers' testimony. It's important, when writing their history, that we respect that diversity; we must shun the urge to force their words to fit neat models which suit our theoretical or political impulses. There is a moral imperative here—we have a duty to hear these voices on their terms, not ours, but there are also strong historical and political imperatives. If we fail to recognize the complexity and contradictions that ran through popular 'structures of feeling' even on Tyneside, then we are sure to fail to understand how people responded to, and in turn helped shape, the rapid social and cultural changes of the era.

Certainly a number of the shipbuilding workers were acutely conscious that previously unwavering loyalties to Labour were shifting, and not just because of the Wilson Government's short-term unpopularity. In typically reflexive mode Morris, the philosopher plumber, commented: 'I vote Labour, but I'm not Labour, I was just bred to it. Neither lot are much good for us. Both are feathering their nests.'[149] His cynicism might be formulaic, but his sense of the difference between 'being' Labour and merely 'voting' Labour went to the heart of changing attitudes. Johnny Macpherson, the boisterous blacksmith, went further, declaring publicly that he intended to break with Labour at the next election: 'I believe in thinking for myself about politics. When I was young in Walker, it was all Labour, you had to be Labour, everybody was Labour. Now I believe in thinking for myself, and next time I'm going to vote Conservative.'[150] Overall, 164 of the men interviewed (73 per cent) claimed to have voted Labour at the previous election, but only 100 of these said they would do so again.[151]

In the 1970s political scientists such as Ivor Crewe would register this shift as ushering in a new era of what they called 'class dealignment' in which voters increasingly *chose* their politics rather than being *born* to them.[152] But the Wallsend field-notes remind us that for men like Morris and Macpherson, class remained a powerful presence in their lives and in their political attitudes. Both men remained deeply rooted in local working-class life and overtly hostile to many of the changes taking place in wider society. Macpherson belligerently defended traditional male gender roles, and Morris was similarly forceful in his rejection of materialism and social striving. Yet both registered a deeper transformation of their world-view which might be summed up as the shift from habit to self-reflection. They presented themselves as making a journey from a world where politics (like other aspects of identity and selfhood) were determined by external forces to a new world of personal choice where they could think for themselves. Social scientists and historians have both identified a similar story about the rise of choice (or some would say the *illusion* of choice) since the 1950s, and have gone on to chart its corrosive impact on customary patterns of behaviour and belief. But what we see from Wallsend is working people's powerful sense that *they* were making this change, consciously and deliberately, in their own lives. Before most social scientists had even recognized that the 'traditional working class' might be a myth, they were consciously exploring new ways of living. But crucially, although they took great pride in their individuality and their rejection of habit, they were not turning their back on community or the traditions of social solidarity that working people had built up on Tyneside over generations. Like the pioneers of Stevenage new town, they still imagined a world in which personal freedom and community could be reconciled as twin pillars of a good life. But this was the late 1960s; the question would be whether this optimistic outlook and determination to reconcile self and society could survive the economic shocks and political upheavals that would soon be unleashed with the collapse of the long post-war boom.

CHAPTER 6

THE DREAM IS OVER

As we have seen, close observation of Tyneside shipbuilding workers in the late 1960s suggests that here new, more reflexive sensibilities reinforced industrial militancy. Paternalism was breaking down, and young workers, in particular, increasingly challenged the prerogatives of management. Among Geordie shipbuilding workers, a heightened emphasis on personal autonomy went hand in hand with strong traditions of workplace solidarity and collectivism. But things were rather different on Kent's remote Isle of Sheppey, even though this too was a predominantly working-class district with strong shipbuilding and maritime traditions. Historically, the island's economy had been dominated by the Admiralty dockyard at Sheerness, where management paternalism was said to have fostered a culture of docility and political Conservatism. The dockyard had closed in 1960, but sociologist Ray Pahl, who studied the island intensively for almost a decade from the late 1970s, was convinced that its ethos continued to shape island culture long after the arrival of new industries such as electronics, steelmaking, and plastics and the rapid of expansion of the Sheerness container port (see Figures 20 and 21).[1] Pahl was struck by Sheppey's strongly independent, individualist culture, and by the continued importance of working-class Conservatism.[2] More than 70 per cent of islanders owned their own homes even before Margaret Thatcher's programme of council-house sales got under way in the 1980s (compared with 55 per cent nationally). Many had built or part-built their houses on plots of land staked out, almost frontier-style, on the wilder parts of this remote, sparsely populated island in the Thames estuary (see Map 8). And a few (though far fewer than Pahl had originally expected) seemed to live almost entirely outside the formal economy.[3]

With its extensive areas of farmland, marsh, and foreshore, and its acres of holiday parks at resorts like Leysdown on the island's north-east coast, Sheppey offered more scope for irregular employment than most industrial districts. In the summer the island's population was doubled by holidaymakers, mostly Londoners, flocking to the beaches and the amusement arcades.[4] After some colourful encounters in local pubs, Pahl initially believed that such environments were generating new ways for less skilled workers, increasingly squeezed out of employment in the

164

Figure 20. Sheppey foreshore, Sheerness looking towards the Isle of Grain, *c.*1982 [photo by Ray Pahl, reproduced thanks to the kind permission of Graham Crow and Dawn Lyon]

Figure 21. A factory building inside the former Admiralty dockyard, Sheerness, *c.*1982 (the woman with her back to camera may be Claire Wallace, the project's principal researcher) [photo by Ray Pahl, reproduced thanks to the kind permission of Graham Crow and Dawn Lyon]

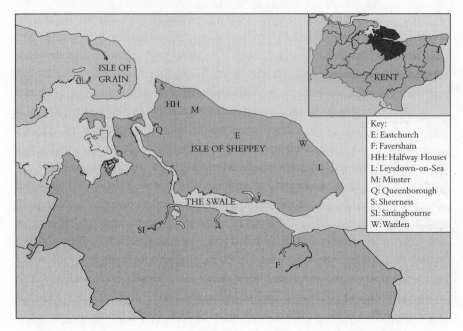

Map 8. The Isle of Sheppey and the north Kent coast showing principal settlements

formal economy by deindustrialization, to 'get by'. He speculated on the emergence of a new breed of 'urban pirate' able to survive, if not prosper, by supplementing State welfare benefits with various forms of self-provisioning, barter, cash-in-hand employment, and sometimes low-level criminality. As Pahl observed, it was a compelling theory spoiled only by the fact that his Sheppey fieldwork demonstrated conclusively that, with a few colourful exceptions, those marginal to the formal labour market also tended to have the least access to *informal* sources of employment, either paid or unpaid.[5]

But if 'urban pirates' were thin on the ground, the ravages of industrial decline were not. Indeed Pahl was originally drawn to the island precisely because he believed it epitomized the problems associated with 'deindustrializing Britain', albeit in what he acknowledged to be an extreme form.[6] Its modest population (*c.*33,000 in 1981), relative isolation, and the dislocation caused by the early closure of its main industry (shipbuilding) made it seem an ideal place to explore how people were coping with the severe economic problems associated with the end of the long post-war boom in the 1970s: rising unemployment, unprecedented inflation levels, and falling real living standards.[7] Pahl started interviewing islanders in 1978, but most of the fieldwork for his classic study *Divisions of Labour* took place in 1982–3, by which time the sharp recession associated with the Thatcher Government's short-lived experiment in monetarist economics had greatly intensified Sheppey's economic woes. Unemployment on the island rose to over 20 per cent, with school-leavers and older workers who lost their job in the shake-out of 1980–1 hit especially hard. Pahl interviewed many people living at the sharp end of deindustrialization, but he was also interested in those who were doing well in the 1980s—highly paid manual workers, self-employed tradesmen, public-sector professionals, and the owners of small businesses. Since the early 1970s, Pahl had been arguing that politics and economics had been working in tandem to increase social polarization in Britain, increasingly dividing a prosperous 'middle mass' of well-paid manual, clerical, and technical workers from an impoverished minority of unskilled and marginalized households.[8] This interest in 'polarization' meant not only that researchers collected testimony from those who were 'getting on' as well as those merely 'getting by', but also that issues of social cohesion loomed large in many interviews. The testimony from Sheppey therefore allows us to explore the impact of rapid economic change on the lives of individuals and on their social relationships with those around them.

In the late 1960s, Tyneside's shipbuilding workers had been convinced that a social revolution was tearing up the old ways, but they saw this as happening somewhere else, and involving people leading lives very different from their own. On Sheppey a decade later, Pahl encountered many people self-consciously living their lives by new social codes, despite the island's remoteness and its predominantly working-class character. Particularly striking were the number of working- and lower middle-class women directly registering the influence of the women's movement and its feminist critique of male power to articulate what we might call a new vernacular feminism.[9] Pat Clark was a twice divorced woman in her early thirties who described herself explicitly as a 'women's libber' who didn't want 'to be anybody's wife'. Convinced that it was 'a catastrophe' for women to stay at home and raise children, she declared herself determined to maintain her 'independence' and to 'better herself', whispering to Claire Wallace, her young interviewer, 'it is the most demoralising thing to be dependent on a man, it's most women's downfall'.[10] Among younger couples this language of 'freedom' and personal 'self-realisation' was commonplace, although, unlike Clark, most still found ways to reconcile the language of personal self-realization with ideas about romantic love and shared marital lives.[11] There was no simple pattern here. Plenty of Sheppey couples still lived largely separate lives, with strict gender demarcation of domestic chores, and sometimes separate friend-ship networks and leisure activities, but *how* one chose to live was increasingly coming to be seen as a matter of personal choice rather than social custom. The Baileys, a couple in their forties, suggested that in their youth they had only felt comfortable sharing the domestic chores because, as they put it, '[we] kept ourselves to ourselves', but they were sure that attitudes had now changed sufficiently that no one would think twice about fathers changing their child's nappy.[12] Again the emphasis was on an increased sense of personal freedom since the 1960s.

Particularly astute observers, like midwife Mrs Spillett, recognized that this greater personal freedom was, at least in part, the product of feeling less pressure to conform to the expectations of friends and family. Raised in a Derbyshire mining village, Mrs Spillett found Sheppey to be less friendly, but also less constricting and socially conservative than her birthplace, helping her to feel free to pursue a career whilst also raising a family. Her Sheppey-born husband agreed, telling Pahl's researcher that in his wife's home village men were expected to drink together and have the same hobbies: 'You've got to fit in with that style of life up there [. . .] I'd get my throat cut for doing the housework up there.' Mr Spillett acknowledged that islanders could be as nosey and suspicious of outsiders as the people from his wife's village, but he insisted that the big difference was that on Sheppey 'you can live your own way of life, the way you want to live it'.[13]

This strain of what Mike Savage has termed working-class 'rugged individualism' went hand in hand with a strong sense of local identity, and, for some at least, a strong sense of 'community'.[14] As an island, albeit one connected to mainland Kent by road and rail, Sheppey retained a strong sense of itself as a place apart. Even couples like the Spilletts, who valued privacy and the right to live as they chose, remained deeply embedded in local social networks. Mr Spillett reported regularly doing the decorating and repairs for neighbours, many of whom were elderly, and explained that in turn neighbours gave them fresh produce or acted as babysitters. His wife went further, saying that she felt closer to her neighbours than to their respective families.

But if Pahl's subtle fieldwork practice sheds light on the ways people found to reconcile new-found personal freedoms with a continued sense of place and social connection, it also illuminates many other aspects of everyday life at the end of the post-war boom. Some of the most interesting comments relate to the meanings people attached to their homes, and especially to home ownership. People who had built (or part-built) their homes tended to identify especially strongly with the bricks and mortar around them, but their sense of self-validation from home ownership was by no means unique. Pahl's interviews show how Margaret Thatcher's policy of selling council houses to sitting tenants could capture the imagination, not just of well-to-do, so-called 'aspiring', workers, but even of people struggling at the sharp end of the 1980s recession. They also shed light on the frictions that could develop between tenants who chose to buy and those who continued to rent; housing, as much as employment, could be a potent source of polarization in 1980s Britain. But we start this chapter by looking more closely at social change as it was lived, and understood, in the late 1970s and early 1980s. Some self-consciously identified themselves as trailblazers for a new way of living, perhaps influenced by the powerful ethos of self-making that had saturated Western popular culture since the 1960s, finding potent expression in 1970s Britain first in the radical alter egos of pop stars like David Bowie and Marc Bolan and then in the DIY spirit of the punk movement.[15] Others simply adapted their lifestyle pragmatically to fit new economic imperatives, but they too were doing things differently, and, perhaps crucially, they *knew* that they were.

New ways of living

As Helen McCarthy has argued, the increase in women's paid employment across the post-war decades altered the dynamics of married life, increasing women's financial autonomy and elevating their status.[16] Both social scientists and working women came to present female paid employment, not as a social problem, but rather as a pragmatic response to 'material aspirations and personal social and psychic needs'.[17] With good reason, feminist commentators in the 1970s complained of the double burden that paid employment could bring to women who were also assumed to remain the principal (even the 'natural') providers of housework and childcare.[18] With its close focus on 'divisions of labour' (paid and unpaid), Pahl's study of Sheppey confirmed that women continued to perform the majority of domestic labour in the vast majority of households (the main exception being households where husbands were caring for incapacitated wives). However, on the basis of a survey of over 500 couples, he concluded that this unequal division of labour was not fixed. Older couples, and couples where the wife worked full-time, tended to report the highest levels of domestic sharing, and Pahl identified a general pattern that 'The more hours the female partner is in employment, the less conventional is the domestic division of labour'.[19] This did not mean that there was no 'double burden', but it did, at the very least, suggest that couples tended to renegotiate the contours of married life when women became independent earners.[20]

Pahl conducted a series of in-depth interviews with couples who claimed to share domestic tasks equally, and their comments shed light on how people organized gender divisions within the home (and the extent to which they did so consciously). In *Divisions of Labour*, Pahl observed that women in professional occupations whose spouse was a manual worker experienced the most equal division of labour

169

(perhaps because in such households they were most likely to be economic equals or even the principal breadwinners).[21] This was certainly midwife Mrs Spillett's experience, although it also helped that her fireman husband's shift pattern meant he was often at home for long stretches. Mr Spillett spoke with pride about his ability to play an equal part in raising their daughter, and claimed to have forgone promotion at work precisely because it would mean being at home much less.[22] As we have seen, he explicitly rejected the traditional model of marital relations that predominated in his wife's native mining village. But even so, his wife seems to have played the more active role in shaping their egalitarian domestic division of labour. Recounting a conversation with an in-law whose husband did no housework, Mrs Spillett recalled telling the woman: 'Well, you didn't train him right when you first got married to him, that's why!' At another point, she acknowledged that when first promoted to the demanding job of ward sister, she and her husband had had 'tiffs' over who did what at home. He made a joke about it, commenting '[I'd] find I used to do the housework in a rage, and I used to get it done twice as quick!' But it is perhaps significant that, later on, when discussing how they had struggled financially when first married, Mrs Spillett commented: 'And then I was promoted to Sister, and I was the breadwinner!'[23] It seems likely, not only that status issues played their part in the couple's marital 'tiffs', but that Mrs Spillett's sense of herself as the family 'breadwinner' shaped their renegotiation of the domestic division of labour. This was about recalibrating what was 'fair' between economic equals, rather than adapting to wider shifts in the understanding of women's position in society (or to the expectations of neighbours). In short, it was about applying old standards of equity and 'fairness' to new situations.

Although she had only recently had a baby, Mrs Spillett had already applied to return to nursing, though initially only as part-time cover to keep her hand in. In some ways Mrs Chittenden told a similar story. A trained maths teacher, she returned to work part-time when her daughter was 2, and went full-time as soon the girl had started school. But the big difference was that by returning to work Mrs Chittenden made it possible for her husband to follow his dream of becoming a professional musician. They were both clear that without the security of her salary he would never have taken the risk of giving up a well-paid job as a draughtsman. On the other hand, they were equally clear that the family could not survive on her salary alone. In fact Mrs Chittenden joked that her husband had 'always had a thing about earning more than me anyway! (Laughs)'.[24] By the time of the interview he was earning good money, better than he had earned as a draughtsman, and he also had more time to be at home with his family. This was why he had taken on responsibility for cooking weekday meals and for much of the daily housework. But this transformation in their lifestyle had been possible only because Mrs Chittenden had underwritten the whole venture with her stable (if inadequate) teacher's salary. Interestingly, she also claimed that their new, more egalitarian domestic arrangements were essentially pragmatic, commenting 'we only sort of share like that because of our jobs. You know, I mean, the fact that [Richard] is out at a different time to me'. But in practice their set-up was not purely pragmatic. Asked the admittedly rather loaded question of whether they still held the 'old-fashioned view of the woman's place in the home', Mr Chittenden replied 'Oh no . . . I think that's criminal, when a woman can be . . . has got the talent to be a teacher or a nurse or something like that. Maybe for other jobs it might be different.' His wife agreed, saying she sometimes wished she did just want 'to stay at home and look after a family and that sort of thing, but . . . er . . . I'm just not that way inclined anyway'.[25] Continuing to work as a teacher was central to her sense of self, and both she and her husband were clear that being true to oneself was more important than conforming to the expectations of others.[26]

It was Pat Clark, the self-professed 'women's libber,' who articulated these new ideas about personal freedom and self-expression most vividly. Living all her life on the island, there is no suggestion that Clark had had any formal contact with organized feminism. It was life, she insisted, that had made her 'an ardent women's libber' and 'anti-men'. At the time of the interview Clark was working as an office temp and taking courses to improve her accountancy skills, but previously she had worked in local factories and bars, and as a school crossing attendant. Described as a 'working-class women's libber' in the project files, Clark surprised the interviewer sufficiently that she told her it was 'unusual finding someone as outspoken as you . . . living in a traditional area'.[27] By her own reckoning, Mrs Clark had been brought up 'a very old-fashioned girl that believed that once you got married that was it—that they didn't cheat on you, and that it was all lovely—cos that what I was brought up in'. But two failed marriages, the first to a man she called 'a real pig', and the second to someone who had cheated on her, convinced her that marriage was a con trick. She explained, 'in the end I just felt I didn't want to be anybody's wife. I don't want to be here just because I am expected to be here . . . I just started to have a good time'.[28] Though she now lived with a self-employed lorry driver, she stressed both her sexual freedom and her economic independence and took pride in being the sole owner of the house that was home to her, her two school-age children, her boyfriend, and his 11-year-old daughter (she had bought out her second husband when the marriage ended).[29]

Though it might seem unorthodox to tell someone they are 'unusual' for their community, this was precisely what Pat Clark *wanted* to be told. Earlier in the interview Clark had herself wondered if she was a suitable subject for such a survey, declaring: 'you see, I'm not normal. You've not really picked on an average person, I don't think, talking to me.'[30] These comments displayed a strikingly sophisticated understanding of social-science methods, and the profession's investment in 'average' rather than individual lives.[31] It also amply demonstrated the satisfaction Clark drew from feeling *different* from those who lived around her. When the interviewer tried to reassure her that everyone said this, she conceded that 'Everybody's different' but then insisted that she was more different than most: 'um, well I've been divorced twice and I don't believe in marriage', adding 'somebody told me the other day I wasn't normal actually'.[32] Clark's recent experience working with the Citizens Advice Bureau had reinforced these feelings. She talked of being amazed at the 'ridiculous' situations women put up with—lamenting that 'some women really believe that they can be turfed out of their home' and that they seemed to think men were a ruling class.[33] Similarly, she talked about young housewives who gave up work being 'stuck at home all day', socially 'isolated' apart from 'clothes parties, and Tupperware parties and now it's sex-aid parties isn't it?' According to Mrs Clark it was 'just a completely different world, once women stop working and raising children [. . .] it's a catastrophe. I think it's terrible.'[34] It was after this early, blunt exchange that she first declared herself an 'ardent women's libber'.

Mrs Clark probably *was* unusual for a woman in her early thirties living in a working-class neighbourhood far from big-city life, but the fact that she could turn to new social movements like second-wave feminism to help shape a distinctive and powerful sense of personal identity was itself a remarkable testament to the cultural eclecticism of the 1970s and 1980s. She knew that friends and family disapproved of her liberated, hedonistic lifestyle, her new-found indifference to good housekeeping, and her ambition to 'better herself' through education, but she had no intention of changing her ways to please them.[35] Nor was she a lone voice, even on the remote Isle of Sheppey. If anything, Helen Wood, 25 and working full-time in her family's successful concrete mouldings firm, was even more hostile to marriage and housewifery. To her, marriage meant dependence, and she was having none of that. She told interviewer Claire Wallace, 'I couldn't bear to 'ave me independence took away from me', or 'the thought of not being meself'. To Wood, marriage meant not just a loss of independence but also a diminution of self. Her boyfriend was keen to move in with her, but she baulked at the idea of sharing her space, declaring 'it's my home, I gotta couple of homes of me own, and there's somebody there, locked in my home, I just couldn't stand it.' But it was the idea of losing her financial independence that Wood rejected most vociferously, declaring: 'I just wouldn't want anybody to mention marriage. Not sort of saying, oh: "I'll give you housekeeping" – that's all out, you know. I've always worked for me own living. I suppose we've followed Mum and Dad, and I don't want anyone to 'elp me.'[36]

Not everyone felt equally free to reject the expectations of others. Even the Spilletts, who talked with pride about sharing domestic duties equally, remained sensitive to what neighbours might think. Or rather, Mr Spillett cared what the neighbours would think, and in turn his wife cared about his feelings. In the middle of a discussion about the various jobs he routinely did about the house she noted one key exception: 'I always used to wash the paintwork down on the front because he didn't want people seeing him doing that! (Laughs)'. Mr Spillett ignored the comment entirely, choosing instead to continue explaining how they worked out who would do which jobs through the week.[37] Sensitivities of this sort could be especially acute among men who were out of work. In his survey Pahl found that unemployed men actually did less, on average, about the house than those in work—and his interviews certainly threw up a number of cases where it was taken for granted that an unemployed husband would still do nothing about the home.[38]

Nor were such sensitivities focused solely on concern to protect men from the judgement of others. Jenny Ellis's husband had been unemployed for two and a half years in the early 1980s, during which time she chose not to return to work as a secretary, even though it would have boosted the family's income, because she knew her husband would feel humiliated to be supported by her earnings. As she explained to Pahl, 'it wouldn't have been worth what it would have done to our marriage. That would have . . . that would have split it. Reversal of roles wouldn't have done for us [. . .] if I'd been working, he'd have been asking for *my* money, and that wouldn't have worked with us.'[39] But this had nothing to do with what other people might think—it was all about preserving what she called her husband's 'self-respect' (with her approval, he had even taken temporary jobs that left them worse off because he preferred to work for his living). As Mrs Ellis explained, the outside world ceased to matter when they were struggling to survive—unemployment, she claimed, 'makes you sort of more narrow [. . .] it was me, [Mike], the kids, the house, and everything outside that, as long as it didn't really touch us, didn't matter. They could get on with their lives, as long as it didn't really affect me.' But the Ellis family was not as isolated as this comment might suggest. Yes, they took pride in displaying a strong sense of independent self-reliance and financial competence, but Mrs Ellis recognized that the main reason her children had not 'gone without' during her husband's prolonged unemployment was that she had been able to rely on the generous support of close family members who also lived on the island.[40] One might even argue that though she *performed* self-reliance and individualism within the interview, she *lived* a more complicated life in which reciprocal support networks based largely on the extended family continued to loom large. Once again, individualism and community were more deeply intertwined than conventional accounts of the period acknowledge.

Finally, Pahl's research did turn up a few households that could be said to be pioneering new ways of living outside the formal economy, though none conforming closely to his original hypothesis about a new breed of 'urban pirates' surviving on a mix of benefits and 'self-provisioning'.[41] Perhaps the most striking were the Dunkleys, who had moved to Sheppey from the Midlands to live the 'Good Life' on a smallholding near the sea after chronic ill health had forced Mrs Dunkley to abandon her teaching career in her late twenties. When Pahl visited the family in the summer of 1982 (the couple had had a son since moving to Sheppey), they had two pigs, two lambs, and flocks of ducks, bantams, and chickens on their small plot. They also claimed to grow enough fruit and veg to be self-sufficient throughout the year. Pahl, who knew his stuff, was deeply impressed by their achievements, commenting that 'to all intents and purposes they are a small peasant family engaging more in barter and exchange than wage labour'.[42] But it wasn't quite that simple. What ultimately made their lifestyle possible was the flexible shift pattern, and the cash income, associated with Tim Dunkley's job as a fireman on the mainland. Pahl calculated that Tim spent more time working his smallholding than he did on duty with the fire service.[43]

When the Dunkleys moved to Sheppey in 1977, *The Good Life*, the BBC sitcom about escaping the rat race through self-sufficiency, was at the height of its popularity. But whereas Tom and Barbara Good continued living in their large, detached suburban home, and simply dug up their garden, the Dunkleys not only uprooted themselves completely by moving to the island, but also took on a small, poorly converted barn with only an outside toilet. Their surveyor's report consisted of a single sentence: 'It's a dump, don't buy it.'[44] But because it was cheap and close to their families on the Kent mainland they ignored his advice and took the plunge. Locally, their social contacts were minimal. Tim maintained good relations with the neighbouring farmer, doing work for him in exchange for free wood, building materials, the loan of tools, and other favours, but otherwise the family lived an isolated existence. Asked whether the demands of the smallholding stopped them from going out or seeing friends, Tim replied dryly, 'Well it doesn't worry me because a) we haven't got any friends, and b) we don't go out.' Kate, his wife, protested that they did have 'one or two' friends but confirmed that they didn't do much socializing.[45]

Their immediate neighbours lived very different lives; one was said to have built 'a flashy type of residence' after demolishing the site's original property.[46] Relations went no further than an occasional chat, 'if we see them'. Asked what these neighbours made of them, Kate thought 'cranky'; Tim said, 'lunatics I should think'. Kate told a story the local farmer had passed on to illustrate 'what they think of us'. Having spotted that they were growing a large patch of sunflowers, one of the neighbours had apparently told the farmer, 'They're going to make their own margarine now.'[47] But they had no interest in what other people thought of their lifestyle—when Kate declared 'We don't care what anyone thinks', Tim echoed her thoughts: 'We don't really worry what people think of us. You know, we try to achieve as best we can with our resources.'[48] Pahl was impressed, commenting 'It was striking how far this couple managed their lives based on their own thinking and their own initiatives.'[49] Though powerfully 'individualistic', and only loosely connected to their local community, the Dunkleys completely rejected the materialist culture most saw as the driving force behind post-war consumerist individualism. Indeed, it was their radically ecological lifestyle which seems to have strained relations with their neighbours, though not with the local farmer, or with their own families. The couple claimed to see Kate's parents twice weekly, and though Tim's visited less often (they lived almost an hour away), they provided invaluable support to the venture. In particular, Tim's mechanic father helped service and repair the vehicles which made it possible for them to live so remotely.

Finally, there was Stan Cummings, the man the Sheppey researchers labelled 'the urban peasant'. He came closest to Pahl's original archetype of the post-industrial 'urban pirate', although in many respects his lifestyle wasn't urban at all. Not only was his house located on the rural fringe of a small council estate, but he had secured the council's permission to incorporate waste ground into his garden so that it was now large enough for him to grow his own veg and keep chickens and a goose. Like the Dunkleys, he hankered after a proper smallholding big enough to keep sheep, but in the meantime he eked out his disability pension by exploiting the island's marshes, foreshore, and other wild places for food and resources. Cummings, who was in his early fifties, took pride in knowing which wild plants, mushrooms, and seaweeds would make a good meal, how to gather shellfish, and how to catch rabbits and hares with a snare. He was also a keen fisherman and hunter.[50] But unlike the Dunkleys he was a jack-of-all-trades, always looking to make a few pounds buying and selling (at various points in the interview he mentioned dealing in scrap metals, antiques, and building materials as well as cultivated, foraged, and poached foodstuffs). Highly reflexive, he presented himself as 'a bit of a rogue', but insisted he knew where 'to draw the line' between a bit of thieving and serious criminality.[51] Explaining that his grown-up sons had refused to speak to him after he put his earring back in, Cummings declared, 'I'm reverting to the gypsy in me you see and that's it. I'm one on my own in my family, they all call me the black sheep. Half my uncles and that, when they go to a wedding, they just sit there quiet, whereas I get to know everyone before the evening's over.'[52] Undoubtedly one of a kind, Cummings might present himself as Sheppey's answer to 'Del Boy' Trotter from the BBC's *Only Fools and Horses* (first aired in 1981), but in his refusal to conform to the expectations of others, and in his knowing, playful sense of self-identity, he was nonetheless more typical of his time and place than appearances might suggest.

Place and belonging

Cummings had lived in the same house for over twenty years. Most of his immediate neighbours had moved in at the same time, when the houses were newly built, but he insisted that there was very little sense of community among them. Seeing himself as naturally gregarious, Cummings blamed his neighbours, arguing 'the people round here, they are not really the sort you get, you know, in a really close-knit community where they all mix. You've got a job to make people mix like that round here'; although, in keeping with his rogue persona, he then conceded 'I might be the awkward one. It depends on how people look at me.'[53] Born on the island, paradoxically Cummings was convinced that this was part of the problem: people knew each other too well, making people anxious to guard their privacy; 'if you are an islander, you've either gone to school with them or one of their sisters or brothers, and I know the biggest bulk of her family next door'. He claimed that even within families, local people often kept their distance: 'on the island you have got to be forced really to make friends, to make actual friends. [. . .] I've got aunts and uncles and I only see them for funerals and weddings. Well, some of me own children don't even know their own cousins, yet they are all on the island. It's just that you don't mix somehow.'[54]

According to Cummings it was often easier for incomers to mix and make friends: 'you get your people come down here from the north or something, and they don't want to leave the island. They get on so well with the people here, it's surprising, really.'[55] Perhaps predictably not everyone agreed. Mrs Spillett, the midwife from Derbyshire, was convinced that she would have found it very difficult to be accepted on the island if she had not married a local man. She told Wallace, 'if you came here on your own and you didn't know anybody, then you were going to be pretty much on your own – probably forever'. In response her husband conceded that islanders were stand-offish and always knew who was an 'outsider', but he insisted that once 'they realise that you're quite human' you are accepted for who you are (it was this discussion which prompted him to argue that, by contrast, in his wife's mining village to be different in any way was to be 'an outcast').[56] Rob Birch, who had come to the Island as a 10-year-old, spoke warmly about the friendliness of 'local people'. He told Wallace, 'since I've been on the Island [. . .] I've made a hell of a lot of friends. I mean, I've got a hell of a lot of friends.'[57] Similarly, the Chittendens, who had moved to the island shortly after the birth of their daughter in the early 1970s, liked living there, and found it hard to imagine leaving. Mr Chittenden, the professional musician, compared the island to 'an old pair of shoes', adding 'you get used to a place and . . . well, the Island doesn't change, but you just become part of it'.[58] Geoff Quayle, a foundry worker who described himself as 'from a London family' though he had been born on the island, was similarly poetic about the appeal of Sheppey. Speaking in 1978, he told Pahl that, though they had once looked to emigrate, he 'wouldn't leave the island now'. He loved its sense of history (he commented 'it's got a bit of nostalgia about it'), but most of all he liked the people, and how they got on together. According to Quayle, 'you can get two classes of people on the island. You've got either the class I come from or the higher class, but they all seem to mix in together.'[59] For Quayle, place seems to have trumped class as a marker of identity. He might remain conscious of coming from a 'non-island' family, but he clearly possessed a strong sense of belonging. He told Pahl, 'It's such a closely knit place that if anything goes on somewhere, you can always turn to the bloke next door and talk about it and he'll know what you're talking about. It's a close community.'[60]

Probably the most strident criticism of islanders came from Mrs Fallaci, an ex-Londoner who had moved to the island a few years earlier. She told Pahl, 'they don't like outsiders, I think that's what it is on this island.' She denounced islanders as spiteful and jealous, and said that she and her husband tended to socialize only with old friends from London, adding 'you never let them [islanders] know too much about yourself.'[61] But this was an odd case. Mrs Fallaci had also lost all contact with her own family back in London, commenting 'my family don't really know what goes on. We don't really see them.'[62] Dryly noting that their large house was full of good furniture, ornaments, and electronic devices despite neither having worked for many years, Pahl speculated that they could be 'ex-criminals lying low on the island', adding 'it would certainly explain why the Islanders don't accept them and it maybe that other members of the gang also from London are round about'. Certainly the audio recording bears out Pahl's assessment that it was an interview framed by 'difficulty and suspicion'.[63]

Of course, Pahl's musings also reflect his own positive take on island life—his book's frontispiece carried the dedication: 'For the people of the Isle of Sheppey'.[64] But even if he was right about the Fallacis, their comments probably still provide insight into what it felt like to harbour secrets in a 'close community'. Nor, as we have seen, was Mrs Fallaci the only person to make sweeping statements about the unfriendliness of people on the island. We cannot hope to triangulate these divergent accounts to draw definitive conclusions about how accepting islanders may have been of newcomers (or of each other for that matter). Different people clearly had different experiences of island life as well as different temperaments. But paying close attention to their testimony can help us to understand the meanings they attached to 'place' and 'community', and crucially the rather different things they hoped to get from social contact with those around them.

Once again, stage of life often played its part in how people viewed the wider community. For instance, island-born Mrs Ogden told Pahl that some years before she had swapped her Queenborough council house because 'it was nearly all old people round us, and it wasn't ... you know, they were nice enough, I got on very well with them, but there's nothing for the children'.[65] They moved when their two children were still of preschool age, and eight years later reported having strong friendships with many of their near neighbours. Asked by Pahl if she spent more time socializing with friends, neighbours, or relatives, Mrs Ogden replied, 'Friends probably [...] Which, you know, are my neighbours.' This answer clearly surprised Pahl, as did her subsequent comment that when she and her husband went to the local social club every Saturday it was as part of a large group with other couples from the estate (it's not clear why Pahl was surprised, possibly because this was not the leisure pattern he associated with non-traditional couples who shared the domestic chores, especially given that Mr Ogden had a white-collar job and the couple were buying their council house).[66]

Mr Harris, a carpenter, had also been born on the island and reported similarly strong connections to both friends and family. When Wallace interviewed him in 1982 he had just been made redundant (signing on for the first time in his life) and was convinced that his personal contacts would be much more likely to help him find a new job than the local Job Centre. Wallace assumed he meant friends from work, but Mr Harris, who was in his mid-fifties, was scornful, saying his friends were 'Certainly not from work'. Rather, he had in mind friends made in his local community, where he had built his own house more than twenty years earlier. As an example he mentioned friends made when his children attended the local school, adding 'these are the friendships that seem to stick over the years'.[67]

Though an islander, Harris had not been born into this community. He came originally from a terraced street in Sheerness, the main town on the island, which he described as 'like a *Coronation Street* set up'. He claimed to have wanted 'to get away from that situation' from the age of 13 or 14. Initially he and his wife had moved to a new-build estate, but in the early 1960s Harris used his own carpentry skills, and the help of friends and family, to build a large bungalow in one of the most desirable parts of the island, on what Wallace described as 'a leafy, windy road—very, very pleasant indeed'.[68] For Harris, this house meant 'freedom and independence' and 'a nice lot of privacy', but though his lifestyle was certainly domestic and 'privatized' (in Pahl and Wallace's sense that he and his family were largely self-provisioning), he was not socially isolated.[69] He might see his old Sheerness friends no more than 'once every couple of years', but Harris and his wife had an active social life, helping to run a local badminton club and being involved in a ramblers' group dedicated to keeping local footpaths open. Harris observed, '[you] tend to sort of make friends, and stick with friends, in the immediate area where you're living'.[70] Like the 'affluent workers' from Luton who chose to live in attractive Bedfordshire villages, in many ways Harris was an early exponent of what sociologists call 'elective belonging'.[71] The fact that, like the Luton workers, his mobility was geographic rather than social—he remained a manual worker all his life—also warns us against assuming that *only* those with significant cultural and economic capital could hope to exercise such choices.

In a way Mrs Iles practised a different sort of 'elective belonging'. Although she had lived on the island only a few years and had no relatives there except her immediate family, she told Wallace, 'I love it here. I wouldn't move. [...] The people are so nice! You know, they're not nosey, they're friendly ... they're friendly to *be* friendly.'[72] Later, explaining why she did voluntary work at the local baby clinic, she commented: 'I think we all help each other out on this Island, don't we, you know. I've got some great friends on here. Since I've been here, I've really ... and they are friends, you know, you could go to them for anything.' The secret to her strong, almost instant, friendship with islanders was, she explained, simple: 'Horses! (Laughs) Well, horses. You know, Lisa's got horses and we meet down the field.'[73] In fact, both Lisa and another friend dropped in during the interview, along with a neighbour's child and 'several' friends of her own teenage daughters.[74] When Wallace asked if these friends would help out 'if you're in trouble', Lisa was there to chime her assent when Mrs Iles replied: 'Yes. They'd be the first here, Lisa and Katie.'[75]

For sure, Mrs Iles was, as Wallace noted, a 'happy, gay and cheerful' woman who was clearly 'very sociable', but her good fortune was nonetheless to find herself living alongside other women who shared her interests and outlook on life.[76] But not, interestingly, *directly* alongside—Mrs Iles was unusually explicit about this. Realizing that Wallace believed that Lisa and her other close friends were immediate neighbours, Mrs Iles sought to clarify things:

> Oh, not *them*, I don't . . . they're [inaudible whisper] . . . we get on, we speak, but I mean, I never have my neighbours in. I don't . . . you know, I don't have them in . . . I think it's nicer to have friends that don't live next door, isn't it, really. Oh yes, I see Lisa every day. If we don't see each other weekends, we're ringing up, aren't we?[77]

It was a conscious rejection of community as something imposed by circumstances, i.e. by geography, but it was still a celebration of community for all that.

Neighbours and neighbourhoods

Although Mrs Iles and her horse-loving friends were not part of it, the Sheppey researchers developed a substantial sub-project focused specifically on the question of relations between neighbours. Stan Cummings, the 'urban peasant', was interviewed as part of this research, which focused on neighbouring in two very different places: a small post-war council estate on the west of the island (we will call it Weston), and a 1970s private estate on the other side of the island ('Easton'). Only a few interviews, like the one with Cummings, survive in full, but we have fragments of many more, along with some informative working papers written by Claire Wallace and Jane Dennett.[78] In structure and approach the study had many parallels with Philip Abrams's work on informal patterns of caring and the local Good Neighbour initiatives of the 1970s, though conducted on a smaller scale.[79] Neither Easton nor Weston was found to have a single, dominant understanding of what it meant to be a 'good' neighbour. Both were internally fractured. Indeed, even within families there could often be sharp disagreements about the friendliness of neighbours, and even about what constituted a 'good' neighbour. As one might expect, gender played the biggest role here, but it was by no means the only factor.[80]

Weston, like many estates, appears to have been internally divided between its 'rough' and 'respectable' ends—or between the 'friendly' and 'unfriendly' ends, depending on the respondent's point of view (but unlike on some estates the basic spatial distinction was agreed by all).[81] Neighbourly relations were both more intimate and more fractious at the supposedly 'rough' end of the estate. Self-selection must have played its part here, with some tenants relocating to find micro-environments that more suited their temperament, but social coercion—the pressure to conform to local norms—was also a factor. Wallace argued that the culture of the 'rough' end was personified in Janet, who had lived at both ends of the estate, and whom she described as a 'fantastically good respondent'.[82] According to Wallace, this 'rough' culture involved the 'common sharing and pooling of resources by women who are in daily contact'.[83] Janet's assessment of the 'respectable' end certainly conformed to type. She told Wallace, 'down there they are all looking at each other's houses and they say to themselves, I want one of them as well, and all that: it's beat the Joneses'.[84] She also conformed to type in having no qualms about saying that she was closest to her immediate neighbours, or in celebrating the fact that these neighbours/friends did regular favours for each other, including watching out for, and feeding, each other's children.[85] However, she also spoke frankly about the coercive undertow to this type of intimacy, acknowledging: 'You are under pressure to socialise here, otherwise you will be sent to Coventry.'[86] In fact, despite her celebration of her end of the estate as friendlier and more open, Janet claimed to feel lonely much of the time, claiming that in many ways she remained an 'outsider' because she did not conform fully to her neighbours' ways. She told Wallace, 'They all leave their kids in with their keys in the door, but I keep my front door shut so that I let in who I want. They go in and out of each other's houses and people might only be in their bras and drawers a lot of the time. I like a bit of privacy though.'[87] She also acknowledged that neighbours frequently fell out with each other, particularly over their children's behaviour, and that husbands often fought in the street.

In all these aspects Janet's testimony, though unusually vivid, covered familiar territory—across the post-war period careful studies of relations between neighbours had offered similar accounts of the thin line between social intimacy and social conflict.[88] Less usual was Janet's willingness to discuss how sex and sexuality could complicate relations between neighbours. In her early thirties, and herself a divorced woman, Janet was conscious that she was seen as a threat to other women's marriages. There had been a sixfold increase in the divorce rate over the previous two decades, so that by the mid-1980s it was estimated that approximately one in three marriages would end in divorce.[89] Janet commented on the dissatisfaction that ran through most of her friends' marriages, and hinted that shifts in sexual mores had exacerbated the problem:

> at my age, it's an awkward age really. The couples at my age are all dissatisfied, they've all got families with children, and they're all on the edge of getting older. They're married but they're not really sure if that's what they want from life. It's all sort of a mad panic to get things in. For the men, they need to get other women to boost their egos. They think they're missing out otherwise. They need to go out every so often. All the available men my age are married you see, and that causes problems.[90]

Leslie, Janet's closest friend, was also single. Recently widowed, she reported that neighbours had become less close after her husband died, and said she thought it was because they now saw her as a sexual threat to the stability of their own marriages. Both women recognized that there was a strong local assumption that any man doing favours for a single woman must be receiving sexual services in return. This made them wary of accepting help from men, and where this was unavoidable they devised ways in which they could be seen publically to repay the men—such as leaving payment with their wives. They also reported having developed strategies for protecting each other from the unwanted advances of sexually predatory tradesmen.[91]

The researchers claimed to have identified five distinct lifestyles among the residents of Weston, which they mapped on to different approaches to neighbouring. At one end of the spectrum were 'the roughs', who lived in daily contact with each other and pooled resources; at the other were the 'privatised affluent workers', who were said to form a clique who 'cut themselves off from the community'. They also identified a group of 'community leaders', mostly unemployed men, 'who put all their energy and resources into organising activities and groups for the community', and another group, the 'respectable unemployed', who struggled to survive by their own efforts, in the process maintaining 'fairly distant relations with neighbours'. Finally, in a class of his own, was the 'urban peasant', whose relations with neighbours were characterized as distant and contractual—based largely on buying and selling, and informal barter.[92] As we have seen, although Stan Cummings had lived at Weston for over twenty years, he found his neighbours aloof and unfriendly, even those who had lived there just as long. Asked if he saw more of people since he had been unable to work, he replied scathingly: 'Oh yeah, I see them. I don't go round speaking to them though. Oh no, no, no, no! You could walk up and down the road sometimes and you might just as well be a bit of paper blowing about for what someone would speak to you.'[93] He claimed that when he was out gardening his next-door neighbour generally retreated inside rather than speak. But they weren't enemies. On the contrary, Cummings stressed that if they met in the pub they would be sure to fall into a 'good conversation', before adding, 'if you see him next day in the garden he runs indoors'.[94] Everything depended on social context—in the street, or over the garden fence, neighbours preferred to be seen to 'keep themselves to themselves'.[95]

Ironically, Cummings took pleasure in articulating, more bluntly than most, the social prejudices which helped to police neighbouring. Asked whether some people 'pop in and out of each other's houses round here', Cummings insisted that it was only a few, before explaining,

There are some that live in one another's houses, and there's some that don't. You'll find that the roughest ones, who don't do bugger all indoors, seem to be the ones that live in one another's houses, you know what I mean? They seem to get up in the morning and sod the work, they go round someone else's house for a cup of tea. I'm a straightforward so and so aren't I?[96]

By contrast, most islanders tended to emphasize their own respectability rather than other people's failings. They often did so by describing how they remained *friendly* with neighbours without actually becoming friends.[97] Mr Archer, a retired shipwright living in a block of council houses at Minster, represented a classic case. When Wallace asked him 'do you see much of your neighbours? Are you close to them?' he replied:

No, not really. We're not that type. I mean, we've been here 24 years—something like that—I can . . . she's never been in here, that neighbour. Well, nor 'as that one. Never been in this house, and we've never been in theirs! [Laughs] We speak to them, we're really good friends, like, and we speak over the garden fence, but we don't sort of go in each other's houses for cups of tea or anything like that. [. . .] No, we don't . . . we're friendly with the neighbours but we don't sort of . . . er . . . go too far with them.[98]

The well-to-do Chopras were even more emphatic on this point. After decades running their respective businesses, they were now enjoying a wealthy semi-retirement by throwing themselves into a vast array of organized social activities including golf, dancing, and wine-making. They were part of a strong group of fourteen friends who met regularly throughout the year at social events or at each other's houses for dinner. But they were keen to stress that they never simply called on one another: 'we don't go into one another's houses. [. . .] we don't see them again, now, until the next wine meeting . . . unless one of them's doing a dinner party. [. . .] we have nice times. But we're never in one another's . . . in and out of people's houses.' As Mr Chopra put it, 'They're very close, but they're at a safe distance'—'none of them live locally around here'.[99] They were even more adamant about avoiding casual socializing with their immediate neighbours, even though they had known some of them since childhood. Mrs Chopra declared boldly, 'we don't have anything to do with any of the neighbours [. . .] we never go in and out of one another's houses, ever'. Mr Chopra repeated her emphatic statement for effect, and then his wife added: 'Never. She never comes in for a couple of tea, or anything like that.' But there was no animosity towards the neighbour in question. Mrs Chopra stressed, 'I always speak to her over the fence, and . . . and we would always buy, like, the kiddies birthday and Christmas presents, for instance, and he'll pop round with some flowers out of the greenhouse'.[100]

Unlike Young in Bethnal Green or Abrams in the Yorkshire woollen town he studied in the late 1970s, the Sheppey team found no evidence that people said one thing and did another, despite carrying out extensive observation of neighbours' behaviour in both Easton and Weston.[101] For most islanders, the defence of domestic 'privacy' seems to have required maintaining a clear distinction between 'friends' and 'neighbours'. Indeed, some who refused this distinction, such as Janet, could still place a high value on domestic privacy. This, after all, was why she declined to follow the example of her neighbours by keeping an open door. But as Philip Abrams's contemporaneous research underscored, the defence of privacy could go hand in hand with 'neighbourliness'—that is with a friendly, helpful attitude to those with whom one lived in close proximity.[102]

This was certainly true of the Jebbs, a wealthy, double-income family who had built themselves a large detached house in the late 1950s, which now included a swimming pool. They made a point of stressing that in their neighbourhood 'we don't tend to live in each other's pockets' (a vivid phrase that Abrams also found to be part of the vernacular in his work on patterns of neighbouring in northern England).[103] But Mrs Jebb, who was a teacher in her mid-forties, was adamant that 'there isn't a neighbour here that I wouldn't go to in an emergency. I'm not saying I see an awful lot of my neighbours, but there isn't one neighbour here that, in an emergency, you would feel that you couldn't go to.' She then gave examples of neighbours who had rallied round in past emergencies, before underscoring how having 'good neighbours' provided her with a powerful sense of security: 'there's always been this sort of . . . this sort of support, which is . . . you know, which is great. As I say, it's not that they necessarily do a lot, or, you know, spend their time with you, but there is always the thought that you do have the support of the neighbourhood, yes.'[104] Abrams found a similar sense of deep security among the residents of a Cumbrian farming village in the late 1970s, reporting that 'Many people did not see their neighbours for weeks but were confident that they could be relied on in a crisis.'[105] As with the Jebbs, mutual long-term residence was a key part of this sense of security.

Though much less advantaged, Mrs Simpson also found her neighbours offered a sense of security in times of crisis. The Simpsons featured prominently in Pahl's publications on Sheppey because the husband's colourful lifestyle of poaching and informal employment had played a prominent part in shaping Pahl's original thesis about the survival strategies of post-industrial 'urban pirates'.[106] Unfortunately, he was also a violent drunk when in money, and on a number of occasions Mrs Simpson's neighbours had had to protect her from assault.[107] Having previously lived in a flat in Sheerness, she was clear that people were much friendlier and more helpful on the estate. When Pahl asked her if it was a 'nice neighbourhood' she replied, 'Nobody likes them next door, but I found when I had "Susan", the difference having a baby here, to having one in a flat in Sheerness is worlds apart. It's a community feeling, I think, round here. You can usually . . . it doesn't matter when, you can usually find help, if you need it.'[108] But if Mrs Simpson felt accepted and supported we must assume that 'them next door' did not (sadly Pahl did not explore how this family had sinned against the 'community feeling' Mrs Simpson celebrated).

The interviews from Weston throw more light on the question of exclusion and social isolation. We have already encountered Janet's fear that she would be 'sent to Coventry' if she did not embrace her neighbours' ways. Stacey Smith's case was more complicated. She had lived in Weston for two years and had made a number of close friends in the area. She was always running out of things and having to borrow from her next-door neighbours, and on one occasion she forgot to buy any meat for the Sunday lunch and had to 'borrow' a frozen chicken from a friend up the road.[109] But perhaps partly because she had grown up in the countryside, Stacey was clear that she wanted more from neighbouring than reciprocal borrowing—she wanted friendship. Like Cummings she complained that 'Apart from the little kids, people don't tend to mix around here', but unlike him, she was keen for more people to just 'pop in'. She complained that most people on the estate were 'just acquaintances, people I say hello to', and that she had only three real friends, which she defined as 'people I'd actually visit'. Whereas most people wanted neighbours who kept their distance, her complaint was that 'Not many people stop by for coffee here. I'd like more people to stop by.'[110] But this was about more than just different expectations of neighbouring; Stacey was also clear that one of the problems on the Weston estate was that the popularity of the Government's right-to-buy policy had introduced new divisions between neighbours. She felt that those who had chosen to buy their homes tended, as she put it, to 'keep themselves off'. According to Stacey: 'The ones who bought their own houses, they just tend to think, you know, "We've bought our own house, we're better off".'[111] Here was a classic example of the social polarization which Pahl identified as increasingly pitting working people against each other. Despite the island's strong sense of distinctiveness, its powerful myths of community, and the popularity of self-building, unemployment and the growing stigmatization of those reliant on social housing placed great strain on social cohesion in the 1980s.

Work, home, and polarization

The Isle of Sheppey had been suffering from deindustrialization and unemployment for decades; that was, after all, a major reason why Pahl had chosen it as a suitable place to study people's strategies for 'getting by'. Hit hard by the closure of its naval dockyard in 1960, the local economy had never fully recovered. Unemployment was already a significant problem, especially for the young and the unskilled, even before the sharp recession associated with the Conservatives' monetarist experiment of the early 1980s.[112] But things did get considerably worse in these years, with many households finding themselves forced to rely on benefits for the first time. With unemployment at around 20 per cent, school leavers found it especially hard to find secure employment. Although only a small minority had never worked, in a sociological study of local youth Wallace showed that more than half had been unemployed at some point within a year of leaving school.[113]

In *Divisions of Labour* Pahl chose to highlight the issue of polarization by contrasting the lives of two working-class couples, one hit hard by the husband's loss of work in 1980, the other enjoying rising prosperity with two good incomes and money in the bank.[114] Pahl first met Linda and Jim, the couple at the sharp end of the recession, in 1978 and he interviewed them multiple times over the next fourteen years.[115] He portrayed them as decent, hard-working people who were 'puzzled' by what life had thrown at them, stressing that in comparison to the 'affluent' Beryl and George, '[they] had more enterprise, initiative and determination to achieve, yet they were oppressed by circumstances they could not control'.[116] In this way Pahl emphasized the arbitrariness of polarization, and highlighted the strains it placed on the social fabric, commenting that 'the two households do not live next door to each other, but they quite easily could do so'.[117]

Plenty and want had always existed side by side, but in the early 1980s the Government's radical economic and social policies made it much more likely that adjacent households, otherwise socially and culturally broadly similar, would experience radically different economic fortunes. There were certainly many islanders happy to peddle hostile myths about the unemployed: that they were all either work-shy or fiddling the dole by working on the side.[118] Even Cummings, who lived in an area of high unemployment and relied on benefits himself, claimed that 'half of them round here wouldn't want a job if it was offered to them'.[119] In turn this fed fear among the unemployed that their neighbours might report them on the mere suspicion of wrongdoing. Amy Cartlidge, whose husband had been unemployed for eighteen months during 1981–2, felt that people had become less 'spiteful and nasty [. . .] about people on the dole' since the recession, but she still claimed 'you can't even cut someone else's lawn' without risking being reported. Cartlidge commented that 'the majority of them still think that the dole give you a lot of money, and they are jealous because their husbands have to go out and earn it [. . .] especially in the summer when they see them walking around getting a sun tan'.[120]

Similarly, Rob Birch, an unemployed young mechanic, was convinced that neighbours had reported him for working on friends' cars, and told a boastful story about taking public revenge on his prime suspect by, as he indelicately put it, kicking him 'straight in the nuts' after he saw the man kick a dog in the street.[121] Linda and Jim were also convinced that neighbours would report them if they knew about their casual earnings, indeed Jim had to drop a 'fiddle' involving making advertising boards after people started asking questions at the local estate agents.[122]

But polarization could also take more subtle forms. Pahl noted that Beryl and George found it difficult to know how to offer help to unemployed neighbours without causing offence.[123] Their next-door neighbour had recently been out of work for six months, and Beryl said that she had been worried about the impact on his young children. She told Pahl that they tried to 'offer them things [. . .] in a roundabout way so they don't think we're giving them things because of that'. Pahl commented that they recognized 'the social burden and complexity of giving'; Beryl explained it more prosaically: 'you've got to be very tactful and very [. . .] cautious [. . .] Sort of . . . as a joke, you know, try and make it a joke, you know: "I'm fed up with this. I'm going to chuck it out", sort of thing.'[124] Similarly, the Beerlings, who were also prospering in the early 1980s, described how, when an unemployed neighbour refused to accept any payment for paving their front garden, they made up a Christmas hamper packed with sweets, biscuits, and fruit for his children; 'He couldn't refuse that, but he was wild about it.'[125]

Judging by what many unemployed families said, Beryl was probably right to be cautious about offering charity. Mrs Ellis told how her husband had felt uncomfortable socializing with his friends because he hated to have them buy him drinks, explaining: 'he could never take anything without giving back'.[126] Mrs Brakefield was convinced that some of her neighbours avoided her after her husband lost his job as a lorry driver. She thought it was probably because 'they felt they couldn't help, and that we would be looking for favours all the time', although she also acknowledged that other neighbours took to paying her husband for the many little jobs he did, knowing that he needed the money (she joked that he was the local 'Jack of all trades').[127] She also discussed how her husband had found it 'lowering' to have to claim welfare benefits, explaining 'It's so degrading when you've been used to a good wage coming in, then suddenly it's cut off altogether.' In fact he only agreed to accept social security when they had exhausted their finances and 'sunk to rock bottom'.[128] It is striking that in each case we hear about the man's feelings indirectly, from his wife, and also that both women are describing a traumatic phase in their life that has now passed (if only recently)—both husbands were back in work by this point (as was Mr Cartlidge, who had taken out a large loan to buy a taxi cab).[129]

The interviews with Linda and Jim are rather different. Firstly, they are much more extensive. Between 1978 and 1983 Pahl conducted seven lengthy interviews with the couple. From the second interview, in October 1980, when Jim learned that he was going to lose his job with a local marine transport company, they effectively became an extended study in the social effects of unemployment.[130] In his inimitable style Pahl told Jim that his experiences and feelings were important because he was 'a kind of guinea pig that's going through the system'.[131] Jim always remained more taciturn than Linda, but he was happy to cooperate and over time opened up more about how it felt to be unemployed. After eighteen months looking for work he confided to Pahl that he was 'more or less resigned to it now, to just doing odd jobs. I don't go down the Job Centre anymore, I just don't bother.' He was not yet 50. A year later, he was talking about feeling increasingly disappointed that nothing had turned up, and acknowledged that he often asked 'is it me?'. He assured Pahl that he would be 'quite happy' if Linda could get a full-time job to support them both, telling him: 'I'd be free and then I wouldn't be on social security . . . and I could do little jobs'.[132] But it was still Linda who spoke most frankly about feelings, both her own and Jim's. She talked about how unemployment had made Jim 'very edgy', whereas in the past he had always been the calm one in their relationship, and acknowledged that she 'got depressed a lot', and asked herself 'is it worth it?'[133]

Most striking, however, was Linda's refusal to take solace from the fact that, thanks to the recession, millions were in the same situation as them. When Pahl asked if it felt any better now there were a lot more unemployed, she was dismissive of the idea, telling him, 'I don't feel that, I feel the opposite. I don't want to be the same as anyone else.'[134] It was Linda, rather than Jim, who freely expressed her anger and bitterness about their situation, though she may in part have felt empowered to express emotion on Jim's behalf. In December 1983, when Jim had been out of work for over three years, she launched into a fierce attack on the people who used Sheppey's unemployed centre, calling them 'yobs' and 'bums' who had 'never done a day's work—never wanted to go to work—lived off the State all their lives'.[135] The immediate cause of her anger was that the centre had received significant government subsidies whereas she and Jim had been refused help with their scheme to set up a local meals-on-wheels service for the elderly on the island. But there was more to it than that: Linda was worried about being judged by those in work. She declared that she wouldn't go to the centre because of what 'everyone will think', and then explained her strong language about the unemployed by saying:

> they're looking at them as a different class of people, I think, now, you know, they're not looking at *them* as, ordinary people—doing a decent day's work and earning a

living, they're looking at *you* as people that are out of work, and the more you read in the paper, the more they turn it round to [be] that people don't want to go to work.[136]

Her pronounal shift here (from 'them' to 'you') underscored Linda's fear of being seen, not as an 'ordinary' person, but as one of 'them': the unemployed. It is perhaps significant that in explaining what it would mean to them to be able to set up in business she stressed, first, that Jim would be 'keeping us again' and second that 'you get back all your pride and your confidence and everything [. . .] 'cos you're back to *being people again*'.[137] The implication was clear—while they remained unemployed they were not fully 'people' in their own eyes, and perhaps not in the eyes of those around them either. It was a particularly stark testament to the psychological effects of 'polarization'.

Linda and Jim's answer to their problems—to try their luck in business—was a choice made by many desperate to escape unemployment or casualization in the 1980s. It was a choice positively encouraged by the State, not just through the Thatcherite rhetoric of 'entrepreneurship', but through direct monetary incentives. When Jim finally took the plunge to create a meals-on-wheels business in 1984 it was partly because the Government's Enterprise Allowance scheme, unlike 'supplementary' benefits for the unemployed, was not means-tested so that both he and Linda could also earn extra money from 'little jobs' without fear of repercussions.[138] Nationwide, the proportion of the workforce classified as self-employed increased by half between the late 1970s and the mid-1980s, and the Isle of Sheppey played its part.[139] But not everyone chose self-employment as an alternative to the dole. Pat Clark, the 'women's libber', said that she had encouraged her boyfriend to go self-employed because, as she put it, 'he worked so hard so he might as well work for himself [. . .] you might as well do it for yourself as for somebody else'.[140] This was also the philosophy of the Wood family, who had built up their concrete mouldings business from scratch—the family all agreed that there was 'no future in working for somebody else'.[141]

Most self-employed workers were rather more pragmatic, inspired less by Thatcherite rhetoric than by the lack of alternative ways to 'get by'.[142] Amy Cartlidge's husband had already failed as a self-employed plumber after losing his trucking job, and was now having to find £80 per week (a typical worker's wage on the island) to pay off the loan for his cab. She told Wallace that these days most of the vacancies at the Job Centre were for self-employed salesmen and the like, and it was all 'a big con'. As she explained, 'it's all "self-employed", "self-employed", "self-employed", which not many people wanna do. It's risky really, isn't it, being self-employed. It's risky in [Pete's] job. Very risky really, because there is so many taxis now on the Island.'[143]

Cartlidge thought that 'nine times out of ten' it didn't work out to go self-employed, but perhaps inevitably there were some for whom it did provide an escape, not just from unemployment, but from the whole gruelling cycle of 'getting by'. Mrs Ogden, herself the wife of a well-paid supervisor at the docks, told how her brother had been hit hard by the recession. First, higher interest rates pushed his mortgage to the point where it was almost half his weekly earnings, and then he got the sack. But he had used his redundancy money to buy into his brother-in-law's double-glazing business, and a year later was bringing home twice what he had earned in his old job and his home was safe.[144]

Mrs Ogden claimed that all her friends and family had bought their own homes and she regretted that she and her husband, a former dock worker, had come late to home ownership themselves. The Ogdens, who were in their early thirties, had rented their council house in Weston for eight years before exercising the right to buy under the Conservative Government's 1980 Housing Act. This was the couple who liked to meet up with friends every Saturday to go to the local social club, and they were adamant that becoming homeowners had in no way altered their relationship with neighbours. Mrs Ogden insisted to Pahl:

> I haven't bought it so that I can say I've bought it. I mean, I've bought it so that we can live in it, really, because we're fed up with the increase in the price of rents [. . .] obviously I could have gone elsewhere and bought one, you know, if you wanted to be like that, but I mean, I like it down here. [. . .] We like the house, you know, so that's what we decided to do. I mean, I haven't got any intention of even thinking of selling it and moving somewhere else . . . we just bought it to live in really.[145]

Pahl was convinced (it probably helped that during the interview two of her friends dropped in 'for a cup of tea, a chat and a cigarette'). In his notes he wrote, 'it's quite clear from the whole interview that the family really does enjoy living in this area and many of their neighbours are also their friends'.[146]

But if the Ogdens remained deeply embedded in local social networks, as we have seen, other similar households were labelled 'privatized affluent workers' who had 'cut themselves off from the community'.[147] Certainly, Stacey Smith wasn't the only Weston resident to think that people who bought their own homes tended to 'keep themselves off' from their neighbours. Cathy Taylor was convinced that her next-door neighbour had become 'a bit high and mighty' since opting to buy her house from the council. She insisted that 'It didn't bother me. I couldn't care less', adding 'I wouldn't buy this house anyway. No, I don't like the houses down here.' But it clearly hurt. She complained, 'One minute they'll talk to me, and the next minute . . . well, I think, please yourselves, I know where I can go for a cup of tea, down Sandra's.'

She listed a number of other neighbours who were buying their houses before commenting, 'They think they are better than you, but they are no better because they was in a council house too.'[148] Nor was it just women who felt looked down on by their home-owning neighbours. Rob Birch, the unemployed young mechanic, complained of neighbours regularly 'having a go' at him because his was now the only council-owned property on their side of the road. He claimed 'they think they're superior...because ours is only Council.' Though in his early twenties and unemployed, Birch declared, 'eventually we're going to put in to buy it, then they can't say anything.' Perhaps fearful that this sounded too defensive, he added: 'And we ain't gonna let them know that we're buying it, so when the next time they have a go at me, and say "Well, yours is a Council house" or something' (his thought was left unfinished). Birch seems to have been a particularly obstreperous character, constantly in battles with neighbours about his unruly dogs, his car-breaking, and his CB (Citizens' Band) radio transmitter, but even so it is a striking example of how government-inspired changes in housing tenure could serve to fuel social polarization on 1980s council estates.[149]

The Beerlings saw things from the other side. They had lived on the Weston estate for over twenty years, and had done a lot of work improving their house since deciding to exercise the right to buy. With four full-time incomes coming in (and four cars) they were much better off than most of their neighbours, many of whom were living on benefits. Jim Beerling prided himself on being a good neighbour, always willing to offer a helping hand and on friendly terms with everyone, but he was convinced that his neighbours resented the family's prosperity. He told Pahl, 'they come to us because they are jealous. You can see the state of our house and they are jealous of it. What we've done to it, it gets up people's noses, and they think "Why should they have done that?" But we have worked for what we've done. We've worked for all of it.'[150] It was the same pride in hard work and independence that also ran through the testimony of Tyneside's shipbuilding workers, but here turned against less fortunate working-class neighbours.

Asked to sum up their neighbourhood, Mrs Beerling was blunt: 'If I 'ad a choice I wouldn't live 'ere,' adding 'But you can't change what's around you, can you?' She deeply regretted that twenty years earlier she had chosen a new council house at Weston rather than accept her father-in-law's offer to cover the deposit on a small terraced house.[151] She insisted that she and her husband would never drink at the local community centre, adding 'They're not our kind of people. You know, they run around with no tax or insurance. With scruffy houses.'[152] Interestingly, later, when her husband joined the conversation, he too illustrated the family's distinctiveness by stressing that all four of their cars were 'legal', unlike '80 per cent of the cars round 'ere'. Along with paying their bills, keeping their windows clean, and not using foul language, it was one of the things that marked out the Beerlings' sense of their own respectability and *difference*.[153]

Like many homeowners, the Beerlings had a strong psychological investment in property. Mr Beerling took pride in having improved their house, including building his own kitchen, and his wife spoke of taking comfort from having 'a nice 'ome and a nice garden'.[154] Jill Lawrenson was similar. Although she had recently given up work to have a baby, she had waited until she and her husband had bought and furnished their small terraced house in Sheerness (see Figure 22). She explained that it had been her ambition to make a home of her own since childhood, even though her mother and sister both thought she was 'mad' to want to settle down. She told Pahl: 'since I've been about twelve I've always wanted to have my own home and my own family'.[155] At the other end of the age spectrum Mr Lewry, a widower in his late seventies, spoke with pride of having bought the house where he still lived half a century earlier, despite only having a labouring job: 'it was really a wonderful achievement to do that'.[156]

Figure 22. Clyde Street, Sheerness, *c*.1982 [photo by Ray Pahl, reproduced thanks to the kind permission of Graham Crow and Dawn Lyon]

If anything, the island's self-builders spoke with even greater pride about the meaning of home. Mr Harris, the carpenter who built himself a luxury bungalow, tried to convey his sense of personal satisfaction, saying: 'it gives you a different attitude to a property than when you . . . if you just went out and bought it . . . you know, you visualise it from when it was just a piece of field and . . . you're starting from scratch, putting the first spade in!'[157] In turn, he denounced the post-war estate of 'ticky-tacky boxes' where his married son lived, and explained that the couple were 'looking for something a little bit more individual now'.[158] It was a telling phrase underscoring how personal identity and property were tightly intertwined for many of Sheppey's rugged individualists.

But it wasn't all about self-expression and personal pride. Home ownership was also about security and independence—just as it had been for self-respecting South Wales miners a century earlier.[159] This was an especially pressing thought for workers in dangerous trades like foundry worker Geoff Quayle, who told Pahl that he was glad they were buying their own home in Sheerness 'because if anything happened to me I know that there's something left for the wife and children, apart from the insurances, and that they've always got a home that they can call their own'. Having already suffered one serious industrial injury which nearly resulted in them defaulting on the mortgage, this was not an unfounded fear.[160] Perhaps significantly Quayle was also a strong trade unionist, acting as the shop steward at work, and he spoke warmly of the 'close community' on the island.[161] He was no crass individualist interested only in himself and his family, but he was nonetheless enmeshed in social processes that were deepening polarization on the Island and potentially threatening the 'close community' he so cherished.

Conclusions

Perhaps the most striking feature of the testimony from Sheppey is the evaporation of the easy optimism about 'progress'—about life getting better from decade to decade and generation to generation—which had dominated the testimony collected in earlier post-war surveys. The long post-war economic boom was over, and so, it seemed, was the social-democratic dream that all might share equally in the nation's growing prosperity. People could still be strongly future-orientated, even at the sharp end of the economic downturn, but there was now much less talk of 'progress' as an anonymous social force lifting everybody equally. Instead, the emphasis was squarely on personal or familial strategies to secure a better life, or at least to 'get by'. With one in seven islanders unemployed, it was already difficult to sustain the optimistic post-war view of 'progress' when Pahl first visited the island in 1978. For sure, many residents continued to uphold mutualist, non-market values, sometimes in conscious defiance of the newly assertive Thatcherite Right, but when they talked about improving their own lives the default assumption was that this would depend on individual effort; it was no longer something to be *expected*. Individualism was not new, nor did it somehow become all-pervasive in 1980s Britain, but the conditions of everyday life had altered in ways that made it harder to sustain communal and solidaristic strategies for forging a better life. Crucially, however, this did not mean that the hunger for social connection and 'community' had disappeared. This continued to burn brightly in much of the testimony collected on Sheppey between 1978 and 1983. As we will see, it would continue to be a powerful feature of personal testimony in the decades that followed, further complicating simplistic narratives about the 'triumph of individualism'.

CHAPTER 7

INTO THE MILLENNIUM

B y chance, in turning to the decades either side of the millennium we are able to interrogate testimony from social-science projects based on two areas already studied intensively by researchers in earlier decades: Luton in the South East (Chapter 4) and Tyneside in the North East (Chapter 5). Between 1951 and 2011, employment in British manufacturing shrank from 40 per cent of the workforce to just 8 per cent; at the same time Britain's share of world trade in manufactured goods fell from 25.4 per cent to just 2.9 per cent.[1] Luton and Tyneside played their full part in this story of Britain's radical deindustrialization. In the early 1960s, when Goldthorpe and Lockwood's researchers were in the field, Vauxhall Motors had employed 22,000 at its Luton and Dunstable plants; by the mid-1990s, when Hartley Dean and Margaret Melrose visited the town to study attitudes to welfare and poverty, that figure had fallen to under 5,000, and by the late 2010s it stood at just 1,500.[2] Similarly, there were still more than 26,000 workers employed in the Tyneside shipyards and marine engineering works in 1966 when Richard Brown and his team began their study of male shipbuilding workers' attitudes.[3] By 2007, when Yvette Taylor undertook a study of how women were coping with the area's rapid deindustrialization, all the main shipyards had closed and just a few hundred workers remained employed in small-scale ship repair and refitting along the Tyne.[4]

As well as dealing with radically different places a decade apart, the studies by Dean and Melrose and by Taylor are also very different in approach and methods, but taken together they can shed considerable light on the long-term social consequences of the economic restructuring Ray Pahl had found unfolding on the Isle of Sheppey in the 1980s. Both studies deliberately sought a cross section of class and income groups, securing this by selecting their samples from workplaces and institutions with distinctive demographic and class profiles. The result is that compared with Pahl's work on Sheppey, where people were selected according to their place of residence, these later studies are much less tightly focused on specific communities.[5] In many ways this reflects the growing separation between work and home that has been made possible by the proliferation of car ownership and the extensive development of high-speed, multi-lane road networks since the opening of the M1 in 1959.[6] But the testimonies from Luton and Tyneside, gathered either side of the millennium, also remind us that this new-found mobility was itself highly classed. Among Luton workers in the 1990s there was a strong correlation between income and distance travelled to work. Those earning over £30,000 per annum lived, on average, more than 30 miles from their place of work (excluding the Lancashire-based accounts manager who lived away from home during the week, and was the highest earner interviewed). Workers earning between £20,000 and £30,000 per year lived on average 10.7 miles from Luton, but everyone earning under £10,000 lived either in Luton itself or in Houghton Regis, the large overspill estate on the town's north-west border.[7] Working a decade later, Taylor's study is explicitly focused around the interaction of class and place. She argues that to be 'working class' is to be viewed as fixed in time and place: to be immobile and unchanging. Crucially, she explores what place meant to those labelled in this way; to those told they had been 'left behind', and how they, in turn, used ideas about belonging and rootedness to give meaning and value to their lives.[8]

But by the 1990s, even people living where they had been born often felt a strong sense of flux and impermanence—a sense that the place they knew was changing around them. We see this most clearly in the testimony from the residents of former Durham mining villages like Easington and Easington Colliery, where the *raison d'être* of the local community had collapsed with the closure of the district's famous under-sea pit in 1993. Even many people proudly proclaiming themselves 'born and bred' in such places openly acknowledged that they hoped their children would acquire the education and skills necessary to make a better, more prosperous life somewhere else. It was a brutal testimony to the hollowing out of community by deindustrialization and the failure of regeneration to provide jobs with similar rewards and security to those that had been lost (if it provided jobs at all).

Insecurity of employment was a backdrop to many of the testimonies collected both by Dean and Melrose and by Taylor. The growth of temporary, part-time, and self-employment accelerated rapidly from the 1980s onwards. In 1983, 19 per cent of employees worked part-time, 10.4 per cent were on temporary contracts, and 6 per cent of the workforce was self-employed. By 2012, in the aftermath of the 2007–8 crash, 27.3 per cent worked part-time (nearly one-fifth involuntarily), 15.2 per cent were on temporary contracts, and just over 14 per cent of the workforce was self-employed.[9] Many respondents in both studies took it for granted that they would be working on short-term contracts or have irregular hours. No one mentioned being on a zero-hours contract, but the seeds of the ultra-flexible 'gig economy' were clearly visible by the turn of the millennium.[10] For most, the idea of a well-paid job for life had disappeared.

Alongside increased insecurity of employment, many also reconciled themselves to increasingly frenetic and mobile lives. Even those apparently 'fixed' in place often travelled considerable distances for work, and sometimes had multiple jobs. Social theorists such as John Urry, Zygmunt Bauman, and Hartmut Rosa see the accelerating pace of everyday life as a defining feature of 'late modernity'.[11] According to Rosa social acceleration makes it impossible for people to imagine a coherent, stable future for themselves or their children, whilst simultaneously cutting them off from the certainties of the past.[12]

Rereading the testimony from Luton and Tyneside at the turn of the millennium certainly underscores the frenetic nature of modern life. Time and again men and women complain that busy working lives leave them too little time for friends and family, let alone for neighbours. But it would be wrong to imagine that they meekly accept that this is how things have to be; that this is the modern condition. Some imagine a time when they will be able to establish a saner work–life balance, demonstrating, at the very least, that they continue to imagine firm connections between present and future selves. More radically, others speak bitterly about the social dislocations of modern life and lament the loss of 'community'. Feeling themselves cast into a new world of greed and individual self-assertion since the 1980s, they rail against its inhumanity and callousness compared with the world their parents had known. By no means everyone feels socially cut adrift—young parents and the retired often have more time and reason to maintain close ties with near neighbours. But loss dominates the language of 'community' in recent social-science studies.

Rather than take this language of loss at face value—using it to reinforce bold narratives of a shift from community to individualism—we need to recognize the more positive message it conveys: that people cherish social connection, and revile the aggressive, antisocial individualism they see lauded in their culture. Free market economics have not—to paraphrase Margaret Thatcher—remade 'the heart and soul of the nation'.[13] Individualism was not new in the 1980s, nor was it necessarily incompatible with the desire to live socially connected lives. But the changes of recent decades have undoubtedly made it harder for many people to find an easy way to reconcile an impulse towards personal autonomy and self-realization with a wider sense of social connection. Taylor's subtle, open-ended interviews with women from the north-east of England prove particularly effective for exploring how people understand, and seek to reconcile, the competing claims of self and society in modern Britain. They also help us recognize the growing importance of *personal* communities in peoples' lives. Greater mobility and improved communications have integrative as well as disintegrative effects, making it easier to sustain meaningful relationships over significant distances. Once friendship, and even kinship, were strongly bounded by place—in the 1940s and 1950s sociologists found that most working-class people lost contact with relatives who did not live close by.[14] Place still matters, as Taylor's testimony from the North East underscores, but the richness of twenty-first-century social connections can easily be missed if we continue only to valorize an outdated model of face-to-face community.

Luton revisited (twice)

Hartley Dean and Margaret Melrose were not trying to replicate Goldthorpe and Lockwood's classic 'affluent worker' study of Luton when they conducted a series of semi-structured interviews in the town during 1996–7. Since the interviewers were interested to explore attitudes to poverty, inequality, and social welfare across the income spectrum, Luton workers loomed large in their study because their academic positions at the newly established University of Luton helped them to secure cooperation from local employers.[15] By contrast, Fiona Devine had gone to Luton in the mid-1980s precisely because she wanted to test the robustness of many of the key hypotheses of Goldthorpe and Lockwood's earlier 'affluent worker' project. She conducted her restudy despite failing to secure the cooperation of Vauxhall or other large-scale industrial employers in the town.[16] It will therefore be useful to explore Devine's analysis of how Luton changed between the early 1960s and the later 1980s before turning to the transcripts from Dean and Melrose's later study of social attitudes among Luton-based employees.

Devine conducted intensive interviews with Vauxhall workers and their wives during 1986–7. Sadly, the original transcripts of these interviews have been lost, but the published study nonetheless provides useful insights into how the town had changed in the twenty-plus years since Goldthorpe and his colleagues first visited. Devine argued that Goldthorpe and Lockwood had exaggerated the distinctions between old and new patterns of working-class life in post-war Britain, placing too much emphasis on supposedly new normative attitudes such as family-centred 'privatism' and economic instrumentalism. Devine found that secure employment and cheap housing had been more important than high wages in bringing most newcomers to the town. Crucially, even among migrants few were as socially isolated as Goldthorpe and Lockwood's model of the privatized 'new working class' would suggest. Close family members had often come to join the early migrants, reconstituting familiar networks of social support.[17] But Devine also argued that relations with neighbours, friends, and workmates played a larger role in people's lives than models of a privatized, narrowly individualistic working class would suggest. According to Devine, what had changed was not working people's attitudes and values so much as the social context of their lives. She stressed that cars and telephones made it possible to maintain social contacts over greater distances, whilst acknowledging that busy working lives could hamper social relations with neighbours. She also found that compared with the early 1960s, Lutonians were much less optimistic about the future. With unemployment standing at 14 per cent in 1986–7, they feared for their own jobs and had little confidence that their children's lives would be better than their own.[18] As on the Isle of Sheppey, the post-war dream of inevitably rising living standards for all had broken down, though Devine insisted that people retained a strong commitment to the desirability of *general* social progress, displaying few signs of internalizing the assertive, self-centred individualism often associated with 1980s Britain.[19] It was a subtle point that historians are only now coming to incorporate into their understanding of social and political change in the 1980s.[20]

Another striking contrast with the early 1960s was that Vauxhall declined to help facilitate Devine's proposed restudy, perhaps fearful that uncertainty about the further contraction of a workforce which had already fallen from a peak of 22,000 to just 6,000 would reflect badly on the company (in fact the company shed more than 3,000 jobs from its local van and truck division while Devine was conducting her fieldwork).[21] Instead, she turned to local organizations such as a community centre, a church, and the Workers' Educational Association to construct her sample, but this inevitably introduced a strong geographical bias towards people living in Luton itself.[22] Workers who had chosen to move out of Luton—or had never lived there—were effectively excluded from the study even though increased time spent travelling to work was one factor weakening workers' connection to their place of residence. By contrast, Dean and Melrose constructed their sample with the help of Luton Borough Council and a major national company, Whitbread plc, who put them in direct contact with employees from across southern England.[23] Of the twenty-eight workers based in Luton, only ten appear to have lived in the town itself. Generally speaking, those on higher incomes commuted into the town for work, sometimes over long distances. It is striking that workers living in Luton itself earned on average £8,700 per year—well below the national average—with only one person (a female site manager in her forties) earning over £20,000 per year. By contrast, those commuting into Luton for work had an average annual income of over £29,500.[24] Excluding a senior accountant from Lancashire, who lived away from home during the week, Luton's commuters travelled on average 36 miles a day getting to and from work. But again this varied sharply with income, with those living in households with an annual income in excess of £50,000 commuting on average over 70 miles per day.

In the 1990s, before high-speed Internet made it easier to work flexibly from home, higher earners across the UK experienced a sharper geographical disconnection between home and work than workers on average and below-average incomes.[25] Luton had jobs, though less plentifully than in the 1960s, but it did not have the amenities or social cachet to persuade high earners to call it home. As we have seen, this was not a new problem for industrial towns—Stevenage new town had faced the same problem in the 1950s—but the rapid growth of the motorway network across the South East and beyond undoubtedly exacerbated the phenomenon (the M25 London orbital motorway was completed in 1986).[26] David Johnson, a senior manager in his late forties, joked that in thirty years with his firm he had lived all over the country, but having 'ended up in Luton [...] probably like you I have no intention of moving to Luton'. Johnson, who was on £55,000 a year plus benefits, clearly felt that Luton was so strongly classed that it was inconceivable that his interviewer would live there despite working at the town's university. Johnson lived near Maidenhead, 45 miles away, and was adamant that he got to work quicker than colleagues who commuted from nearby Bedford because he was travelling against the traffic. But even by his own estimation, the price of continuing to live in leafy Berkshire was spending two hours each day on the South East's congested motorways. He did it because he and his wife loved where they lived and hoped to be free to enjoy their retirement there within five or six years (his wife also worked—bringing in an additional £15,000 per year). Place and belonging mattered to Johnson, even if work radically weakened his practical, day-to-day connections to friends and neighbours where he lived.[27]

The same could be said of Brian Hamnett, an accountant in his early forties who was also earning over £50,000 a year, but only by living apart from his wife and two young children in Lancashire. Hamnett felt he could live comfortably on less, and implied that it was his wife who was determined to live in a big house in a desirable area even though it meant taking on a large six-figure mortgage which left them with very little money to spare each month.[28] Neither Johnson nor Hamnett talked about how it felt to be long-distance commuters, perhaps because they had internalized gendered ideas about male breadwinning and female nest-building. Helen Kelly, a senior computer analyst in her late thirties, displayed no such reticence about her 120-mile daily round trip to work in Luton. Contributing £43,000 to a joint household income of over £100,000 a year, Mrs Kelly enjoyed the highest living standard of anyone in the Luton sample, but she was clear that her high-pressure, high-reward lifestyle had many downsides. Asked if she thought of herself 'as a citizen', Kelly lamented that commuting left her no time to get involved in things where she lived:

> I would like to play a sort of part in the community, and certainly I mean in London I did a fair bit. I find now the reality is I leave home at half past six in the morning and I get home at half past seven at night and I cook supper and then we go to bed, (laughs) there's, you know, there's not an awful lot of time at the moment, but this is just a phase in life...[29]

This final comment echoed Johnson's argument that soon he would retire and be able to live a more settled life in the place (and house) of his choosing. For professionals like Kelly and Johnson, living a full and satisfying life had to be deferred in the name of work and the large financial rewards it could bring. In fact later in the interview Kelly returned to this theme, commenting that in London, when she had only worked part-time, she had been 'in touch with the daily community far more often' and had therefore been much more aware of social inequality and the need to be involved with the local community. Tellingly, she acknowledged that she would probably have to wait till she retired before she could play her part again—she was 39. Interestingly, Kelly was adamant that she had been no less happy living in a three-bedroom terraced house in London, and sending her children to the local school; she insisted that she did not need the big house, the company cars, or the private education for her children that money bought—but nor did she intend to give them up. They were 'the fruits of hard work and commuting sixty miles a day and that sort of jazz'. But whilst she was adamant that 'life wouldn't be affected without them', she claimed that she could not imagine giving up her career.[30] Proud that she had done better at work than her female friends and acquaintances, Kelly presented her life as determined by her career rather than the other way around. She had done well through the economic vicissitudes of the 1970s and 1980s and had internalized the logic of the market that seemed to have emerged supreme: she knew her worth, and she knew that 'hard work' (and commuting) brought rewards to people like her—even if the personal cost was high.[31]

Many of the workers interviewed for Dean and Melrose's project had rather different experiences of Britain's newly liberalized economy. Not only did many find themselves working on temporary contracts, without pension rights or job security, but some had also been hit hard by the sharp recession of 1990–1. Michael Callaghan had lost both his job and his house in the early 1990s, unable to cope with the doubling of his mortgage payments as the Bank of England base rate rose to almost 15 per cent. In theory he still owed the building society £37,000, having been forced to hand back the keys at the bottom of the market (house prices fell by more than 35 per cent in South East England between 1989 and 1992).[32] Now he was earning a little over £16,000 a year in marketing, but, only able to secure temporary employment contracts, he worried that he and his wife would 'drift into the gutter again when we're over sixty-five years old'. They had no pension provision, and no prospect of ever becoming homeowners again.[33]

Still only in his late forties, Callaghan would already have lived through three sharp recessions during his working life (1973–5, 1981–2, and 1990–1)—it was hardly surprising that he lacked the confident expectation of social progress that had characterized Luton's 'affluent workers' in the 1960s. But Callaghan was by no means reconciled to the new economic order. He spoke of having 'ducked and dived...to survive' and lambasted the Conservative Governments since 1979 for allowing the gap between rich and poor to become 'far, far too wide'.[34] He also rejected the idea that he and his wife should both go out to work to boost their standard of living, commenting that people who hand their child over to someone else after three weeks 'might as well not have one. I think we're again looking at "I've got a Rolls Royce, I've got a nice house, I've got two point five children" and whatever else...I think at that stage children become acquisitions.' However, he was quick to stress that when he was unemployed he had been the one to stay at home and look after their children while his wife worked—his stance was anti-materialist more than it was socially conservative.[35] Callaghan was struggling to hold on to his ideal of a good life in an unforgiving economic and political climate.

Judy Walker, an accounts clerk in her late fifties, had been on a rolling six-month contract for two years, but claimed not to mind the lack of security. She understood the advantages that contract work offered employers, and seemed to accept that this was how things would be from now on:

> That's the way the world's going now, everybody's on contracts, I know people that work for Matrix Marconi in Stevenage and they're on contracts, and when I worked for British Aerospace which was [...] about five years ago they were employing on contracts [...] it's easier from the company's point of view because they don't need to pay sick pay and there's no redundancy involved should you finish, so erm, you know, I think that's the way, I personally think that's the way the world's going, job wise.[36]

But Walker's acceptance of casualization didn't spring simply from fatalism or an unhealthy internalization of the logic of the market. She claimed never to have worked for a better company, commenting 'they look after their employees [...] nothing seems to be too much trouble for them'. The firm might not be willing to make her permanent, but she praised their generosity at Christmas, the summer outings they organized to farms in Kent and Sussex, and the fact that they offered employees free counselling and legal advice. Walker called them 'a very forward thinking company' and told her interviewer 'I like working for such a company'.[37]

Walker might be reconciled to the new, less secure labour market, but she was far from content. She and her 'partner' (as she called him) had a combined income of £20,000 a year and lived in private rented accommodation because they were too old to get a mortgage. She claimed that they would need to earn another £10,000 a year 'to have a proper standard of living', and said that in many ways she felt like one of the poor even though they were far from destitute. She worried about the future and 'getting poorer', but said she still dreamed that their fortunes might change, commenting 'everybody dreams, you have to have a dream to hold on to because I think living now is really difficult'.[38]

On paper, living standards had roughly doubled since Goldthorpe and Lockwood had chosen Luton for their study of 'affluence' in the early 1960s, but that wasn't how it felt to many people reliant on short-term contracts or self-employment. Deborah Thompson wore both hats, combining a part-time clerical job with running a small business as a 'colour and image consultant' offering people clothing advice. Thompson, a widow in her late forties, estimated that she probably earned about £8,000 a year after tax to support herself and her boyfriend, whom she said was in the process of launching his own business, but currently earned nothing.[39] It helped that her mortgage had been paid off by her late husband's insurance policy, but even so life was tough for Thompson, who complained of feeling socially isolated. Worse, she claimed to feel unsafe walking about the town, even during the day, commenting 'I don't feel safe in Luton but then most people who live in towns don't feel very safe these days'. Thompson felt that society had become more selfish and uncaring since her childhood in the 1950s. She blamed a decline in 'family values', and told her interviewer,

> care for other people an' that has, has got really low down in people's priority because it doesn't pay you, if you like, to be honest and care for other people. The only people that seem to get away with it or get on [...] are the ones that just take or, or you know, do whatever they wanna do.[40]

Later, asked who she thought of as 'people like you', Thompson backtracked on the claim to be an 'average person' just like everybody else, by drawing attention to the weakness of her own family ties: 'I haven't got any family attachments of course, I've never had children, I've got a father who's quite old who lives [in Devon], apart from him I've got no other family at all, so the old values of sort of families helping each other out doesn't happen to me.' She acknowledged that it was difficult not having any support 'network' to turn to, but did not expand on her feelings about living 230 miles from her only close relative (though since she had grown up barely 15 miles from Luton, we must assume that it was her father who had moved away).[41] Once again, we see the tendency for testimony subtly to elide the personal and the sociological. Thompson felt the absence of family in her own life and assumed that this was why society at large appeared to have become more selfish, uncaring, and violent.

The Luton study also included six workers at the bottom of the income scale: bar workers, shop workers, and cleaners, mostly working part-time and generally earning between £2,000 and £4,000 per year, depending on their weekly hours. Significantly, only one displayed signs of what sociologist Beverley Skeggs has termed 'dis-identification' with class: the tendency of socially disadvantaged workers, especially young women, to disown supposedly stigmatizing class identities in favour of more highly valorized identities organized around concepts such as respectability and femininity.[42] Jeff Howard was a shop assistant in his mid-thirties earning about £50 a week. He wanted to work full-time, but complained that, apart from the manager, everyone at his firm was on part-time contracts, working morning, lunchtime, or afternoon shifts (in the name of labour flexibility the Conservative Government had recently secured an opt-out from the EU's Social Policy Protocol partly to ensure that employment rights would not be extended to part-time workers).[43] Howard found life on low, part-time wages to be a 'big struggle', and had no doubt that he was one of the 'struggling' poor. But if he felt class in his daily life, the concept itself had little meaning to him. Asked to say what class he belonged to, he replied, 'Erm, what classes have we got?' Given a list of different options he chose 'middle class' but then immediately conceded: 'if you look at it properly, I'm lower class'.[44] But it was clear that the idea of social class had little meaning for him; this was less 'dis-identification' than non-identification.

Of the remaining five service-sector workers on low wages, one, a divorced woman in her forties working two part-time jobs, claimed to be 'just a middle class person', and the others all identified spontaneously as 'working class'.[45] Part-time bar worker Claire Brown, in her early twenties, thought that perhaps she was 'upper working-class' because she had recently graduated from Luton University (she had grown up in a working-class family in the North East).[46] By contrast, Jane Baines, a divorced woman in her early thirties, thought that being a part-time cleaner probably meant she was 'lower working class'. But it is not clear that she attached any stigma to the adjective 'lower'. She claimed to have learned her class position from studying sociology at college, where she had been told that 'working class' meant 'somebody who, like, works in Vauxhall', and she felt that her job came lower on the social scale.[47]

In November 1996, Baines was living with her parents, having quit the run-down flat she had shared with her boyfriend to escape difficult neighbours and a poor local school (she had an 8-year-old daughter). Until recently she had depended on social security, and had no illusions about the stigma attached to welfare. She told the interviewer, 'boyfriends' mums were a bit like that. "Divorced woman on social security, not for my son dear", do you know what I mean?'[48] She also claimed to 'feel better' now she was working rather than claiming benefits, even though she had less money (though she made a point of stressing that she did *not* mean she felt better than people on benefits—just better psychologically).[49] But in fact Baines didn't think of herself as poor because, as she put it, 'I don't mix with people who are poor'. Her boyfriend had a good job in the aircraft industry, and so, when she wasn't looking after her daughter, she could still have a good time.[50]

At one level Baines had a sharp, reflexive sense of class identity. She joked that she knew not to speak to her boss as she spoke to her workmates, but insisted that this did not mean she would ever 'suck up to him'. She explained, 'they think they've got respect off the cleaners, but in reality they haven't, 'cause we just [...] want to be paid at the end of the day'.[51] Later she claimed to feel sorry for the brewery managers who sometimes visited the pub. Dropping her voice to a whisper, she said,

> They're overweight, and they're, they're red-faced, and they..., they're like, hair's falling out, and they drive these gorgeous cars, and they're so stressed, and I'm standing there leaning on me broom thinking 'I'm glad I'm not you', because I haven't got any stress, have[n't] got any debts. I bet they're up to their eyeballs in debt, you know.[52]

Baines had made good friends with her fellow cleaners, and probably meant what she said about stress and debt, but it's striking that she still blamed herself for not being able to secure a better-paid, more rewarding job. Although she held her ex-husband partly responsible for making her poor, she told the interviewer: 'I blame myself mostly for not working harder at school. You know, 'cause if you [...] work hard at school you get the qualifications, erm, you'll get a better job than someone else. I mean you worked hard at school and you've got a better job than me, so you're richer than I am. Erm, in mone—, money-wise.' She went further; asked 'is anyone to blame for the fact that people are poor?', she quipped back, 'I think it's themselves. Wasn't the right thing to say was it?' (although a little later she asked if she could 'retract what I said before [...] it's not actually anyone's fault').[53] But there can be little doubt that Baines had internalized the idea that

205

qualifications and accreditation were the route to success, and that her own lack of these things represented a personal failing. This was why she had gone back to college to study for GCSEs, including sociology.

It would be easy to mine Baines's testimony selectively for quotations that pointed to a disidentification with class and an acceptance of the logic of the market and assertive individualism, but that would be to do violence to her complex, ideologically cross-cutting world-view. Baines remained deeply embedded in local social networks based on family and friendship, and she readily identified as 'working class'. On the other hand, this did not stop her from thinking that in large measure her poverty was no one's fault but her own. For Baines a strong sense of belonging and social connection coincided with an equally strong sense of individual responsibility for life choices and future prospects. Individualism and communalism, far from being polar opposites, were deeply enmeshed in how she understood everyday life. The same could be said for many of the women from the North East that Yvette Taylor would interview a decade later.

Deindustrialization and its consequences—Tyneside revisited

When Ron Brown and his team studied Tyneside in the late 1960s their focus had been on the workers of the region's iconic shipbuilding industry. Forty years later, that industry had entirely disappeared—as had the coal mining that had shaped the North East's identity for even longer (the *Oxford English Dictionary* records the proverbial pointlessness of taking 'coals to Newcastle' as having seventeenth-century origins). Indeed, by 2007, when social scientist Yvette Taylor began her study 'From coal-face to car park', the impact of deindustrialization on male life-chances and identities had become such a familiar trope that she chose to focus specifically on how the rapid change of recent decades had impacted *women's* lives. In this sense, Taylor's female-focused research nicely balances Brown's research, which had been concerned exclusively with male industrial workers. But if Taylor sought to approach deindustrialization from a fresh perspective, she had no intention of playing down its significance for the North East.

Taylor spoke to many women directly connected to efforts to regenerate areas that had been hit hard by the collapse of employment in shipbuilding, coal mining, and the region's other staple industries. She also spoke to women who lived in the areas that had been most affected by this brutal economic restructuring. Andrea's father had worked for Armstrong Vickers as an engineer, and had been heavily involved in unsuccessful campaigns to resist factory closures in the 1980s. Now in her mid-forties and living at Heaton, Andrea recalled how the riverside had once

Figure 23. The levelled site of the Swan Hunter main shipyard in Wallsend, 2014 [private collection]

been lined with thriving factories, 'whereas now, you've got one tiny little factory'.[54] Many of the women had strong family connections to the shipbuilding industry. Cathy, a business manager in her thirties, remembered her father getting up before six every day to catch the ferry to Wallsend where he had worked in the Swan Hunter yards (see Figures 23 and 24). Throughout her childhood, Cathy's father had been in danger of losing his job in the industry's periodic waves of redundancies, and he had finally taken voluntary redundancy in the mid-1980s. Angie's story was very similar. Her father had been a ship's joiner, and she recalled how he had been in and out of work during her childhood, as the industry suffered its long, slow decline.[55] Deindustrialization on Tyneside had been a process not an event. Debbie, who grew up in the shadow of the Swan Hunter yards in Wallsend, remembered how every dinner time crowds of men would fill her street 'like a football match coming out up the hill, it was absolutely amazing', but all that was long gone.[56] So too were the skilled jobs which had once offered prospects to local (male) school-leavers. According to Debbie, it was young men like her own son who were 'most disaffected' by the collapse of industry and the disappearance of the high-status, skilled jobs it had once provided. She was pleased that her son currently had a job labouring (he had been intermittently out of work since leaving school), but she

Figure 24. Swan Hunter site entrance, 2014 [private collection]

complained that he was trapped 'in this culture of just earning money, drinking, being with the lads [...] he's just not that aspirational'.[57]

The language of 'aspiration' was a distinctive feature of this early twenty-first-century testimony. No one had used the term on Sheppey in the early 1980s—in more than 400,000 words of transcribed testimony it fails to appear even once. We see it appear a few times in Dean and Melrose's 1996 Luton interviews (with five uses in 220,000 words). But in the North East a decade later it appears to have become part of everyday speech, with thirty-two uses in a little over 230,000 words of transcribed testimony (excluding two occasions where the word was used by the interviewer).[58] Ironically, Tony Blair's New Labour had embraced the language of 'aspiration' in the 1990s in an attempt to reset its relationship with the voters of southern England,[59] but the evidence from the North East would suggest a loop-back effect whereby, in turn, Labour's language influenced vernacular understandings of what it meant to live a good life. The paradox, of course, was that for many in the North East it had never been harder to turn aspirations into reality. (See Map 9.)

Many women spoke about the outsourcing of manufacturing jobs overseas, and the rise, in their place, of service-sector jobs in retail, leisure, and especially in call centres, for which the North East had become famous. Some stressed the positive aspects of this story—emphasizing the flexibility of the new employment models.

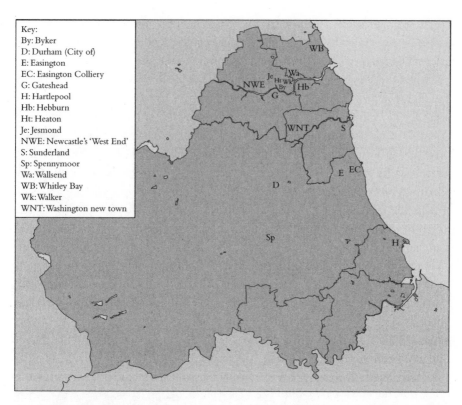

Key:
By: Byker
D: Durham (City of)
E: Easington
EC: Easington Colliery
G: Gateshead
H: Hartlepool
Hb: Hebburn
Ht: Heaton
Je: Jesmond
NWE: Newcastle's 'West End'
S: Sunderland
Sp: Spennymoor
Wa: Wallsend
WB: Whitley Bay
Wk: Walker
WNT: Washington new town

Map 9. North East England showing the location of places mentioned in the text

Carla, a medical researcher in her early fifties, recognized that many people 'detest working in the call centres', but stressed the attraction for people who wanted 'to go and do a few hours work a day' and insisted that working conditions were improving as companies recognized the importance of staff retention.[60] But most saw call centres as 'the new sweatshops' and insisted that they were no substitute for the jobs that had been lost. Esther, a family carer in her late sixties, felt it was much better for men 'to work with their hands' than to be 'sitting at a computer all day', although she recognized such jobs could be a useful source of income for people while they looked for something better.[61] Almost everyone stressed that the region had been hit hard by losing so many highly paid manufacturing jobs since the 1970s, even respondents who had found work promoting the region's economic regeneration.

Britney was a graduate in her late twenties who had grown up in a working-class family on the Durham coalfield. She had recently returned to her home town in a managerial role promoting local enterprise, but she had no illusions about the damaging consequences of globalization for local jobs. Her brother had been one of the last apprentices taken on by Black & Decker, the power-tool company, and had only kept his job because he had moved into design work just before the bulk of production had been relocated to China. Most of her brother's friends had been laid off when the factory closed, while she herself reported that 'the majority of my friends are in Scotland, Australia [...] they've moved away to do the jobs that they want to do'.[62] An important reminder that for many mobility was a matter of necessity rather than choice—we should not leap to the conclusion that workers who have followed the logic of globalized capitalism are indifferent to the appeals of place and belonging; that they are rootless 'anywheres' by *choice*, to use David Goodhart's implicitly judgemental term.[63]

The scars of deindustrialization were at their worst in the former mining villages scattered across County Durham. Nowhere more so than the villages of Easington and Easington Colliery—the clue is in the name. The village grew up around a deep-mine pit first sunk in 1899 near the Durham coast (see Figure 25). Famously, in its heyday, the pit's seams stretched miles out under the North Sea (I still recall my sense of wonder being taught about the colliery as a teenage geography pupil in the 1970s). Like many mining villages it was scarred by past tragedies, most horrifically an under-ground explosion in May 1951 which had claimed the lives of eighty-three men.[64]

Figure 25. Easington Colliery and the North Sea; used as a promotional picture for a *Billy Elliot* Walk in May 2017 [Charlie Hedley Photography]

Charlotte, a community worker in her mid-fifties, was proud that her grandparents had been 'one of the first four families that came into this community' at the turn of the previous century.[65] Although the pit finally closed in 1993, eight years after the miners' unsuccessful year-long strike against forced closures, Charlotte was adamant that decline had begun much earlier. For her the most significant moment had been 1976, when the pit had ceased to take on new apprentices. Until then, almost all the young men in the village had known there was a job for them at the pit, even if they and their families had what Charlotte called a difficult 'love hate relationship with the pit'.[66] She regretted the consequences of the pit's closure—especially the wasted lives of young people caught up in a cycle of joblessness, drugs, and petty crime—but she was still pleased that men no longer had to go underground, saying 'I don't think it was any way for men to work'.[67]

Although she identified strongly with Easington Colliery, on many issues Charlotte consciously placed herself outside its dominant mythology. She claimed to have been 'the one person who tried to stop *Billy Elliot* being filmed here', claiming it was 'wrong to bring the strike back' and bad for 'the image of the community' (sadly she didn't elaborate on why this bitter-sweet musical about a miner's son overcoming prejudice to win a scholarship to the Royal Ballet School might harm the town's image).[68] Although her husband stayed out throughout the strike, Charlotte made him promise never to join the picket line because she strongly disapproved of miners' leader Arthur Scargill and his reasons for calling the strike. Charlotte spoke powerfully about the strike as a 'horrible time', and of feeling 'mortifyingly embarrassed' at seeing miners reduced to begging in the streets to keep the strike going, and being forced to rely on communal food kitchens.[69] She knew that for many local women helping during the strike had been the proudest moment of their lives. Placing herself at odds with this sentiment clearly still caused her great pain. Having refuted the idea that her attitude to the strike might have caused social difficulties by declaring 'we were all in the same boat', Charlotte finally asked the interviewer: 'Can we move on now?'[70]

Grace was exactly the same age as Charlotte and echoed her comments about the strike as a time when 'everybody was in the same boat'. She also accepted that the strike had been an 'overwhelming' experience for all concerned, but chose to align herself with the more comforting narrative that it had nonetheless marked the high point of 'community' in Easington Colliery. Though like Charlotte she had personally not joined the local women's support groups—'I was just involved with my own family'—Grace celebrated the 'great sense of belonging, belonging to a community that was going through this hardship'.[71] Grace recognized that for many women the strike had been a moment of genuine awakening—when they had acted out, and thereby fully recognized, their centrality to the life of the pit village.[72] But Grace's own moment of self-realization came later, when she went back to college to study part-time for a Fine Art degree. She graduated in 1993, the year the village pit closed, and for her final year show she created a memorialization of the pit community and its traditions, which nonetheless encapsulated her mixed feelings: 'I was still sort of glad that the pit was closing and that my son doesn't have to go down there.' In the process she came to realize that somehow she had always resisted being identified with the pit; that going to university had been about trying 'to get away from being me, at home in this mining community, being a woman in a mining community and all the lack of expectation and the confinement of being a woman in a mining community'.[73] Grace explained how, scouring the beach for materials she could use in her project, she came to rethink her relationship with the community:

> being me here made me realise how…where I was and where I came from. And I became more proud of it. And I didn't mind the identity of it, and belonging to the mining community. Whereas I'd always sort of like struggled with myself, of not doing better than I had, because I'd always wanted to be a doctor, and I hadn't done better than fifteen and no qualifications.[74]

Like Charlotte, Grace had come to feel a powerful sense of connection with her community. As she put it, with characteristic power, 'for all I'd gone away, like I said, to find me, I found me right here, in [Easington] [...] I belong to the mining community, [to] the strength of it'.[75] But she had no illusions about the devastating consequences of the pit's closure. Like many long-established residents she lamented how the village had changed since 1993, and blamed incomers drawn to the area by cheap, run-down colliery houses that had been bought up by private landlords looking for quick profits. For Grace, Easington had become 'an area where you're neither one thing nor another' because of this influx of 'transient people' who 'will never have their roots here'.[76]

Similarly, for Diane, a local health worker in her early fifties who had grown up in the village, 'the closure of the pit really spelt the end of civilisation as we knew it, in [Easington]'. Both she and Mena, a pensioner proud to proclaim herself 'born and bred' in the village, drew parallels with life in Beirut, which was featuring prominently in British news bulletins at this time after a flare-up of brutal sectarian fighting across Lebanon.[77] Now in her mid-sixties, Mena said she now felt 'very vulnerable' walking about the village because so many people had left to find work and been replaced by people who 'don't contribute to the community at all'. She complained about the influx 'of drug addicts, of alcoholics, of all sorts of people' who lived by

212

different values to the hard-working miners who 'always kept their own home clean, spotlessly clean'.[78] Diane highlighted the same clash of cultures, describing how the newcomers liked to drag chairs into the street, open cans of lager, and have a spontaneous barbeque 'like a big street party'. She conceded, 'I suppose that's their sense of community really, but it's [a] queer sort of ... it would never have been like that, never' (although she did then concede that her mother had told stories about miners dragging pianos into the streets for a sing-song when she had been a little girl in the 1930s: 'so maybe it's come full circle, who knows').[79]

Most people recognized that Easington's problems ran much deeper than the influx of 'outsiders' with different, less 'respectable', lifestyles. Charlotte, always ready to challenge comforting shared myths, was adamant that

> these young people who are addicted come from our own families, and good families, you know, and if these young people get caught up in drugs it's horrifying [...] people from good families on drugs cause as much trouble as people from bad families on drugs.[80]

She also spoke warmly about incomers drawn to the area by its proximity to the coast, the countryside, and the cheap housing, including a Londoner who had told her that she felt 'relaxed' as soon as she turned off the A19 and knew she was nearly 'home'. At the same time, Charlotte was deeply critical of long-standing residents who 'put this place down, [who] don't see the good things'.[81] In a similar vein, Grace reported challenging local youths for 'trying to wreck the place' only to be told 'Well, it's crap here. Look at it, it's terrible.' When she claimed they were only making things worse, one retorted, 'We're not going to stay here when we grow up, we're moving on.' For Grace it summed up the hopelessness that had spread among the young since the pit's closure, but also the transformation in social attitudes since her own childhood in the 1950s. As she put it: 'I don't ever recall thinking like this when I was a child, that where I lived was crap. It was just accepted this is where you live.'[82] It was an insightful comment. In a highly mediated age, with websites and publishers competing to generate their lists of 'crap towns' where no one would want to live, it was all but impossible to be unreflexive about social conditions—to treat one's immediate environment simply as a given.[83]

Grace felt that local people had lost their self-respect; that vandals went unchecked because 'nobody cared any more'. Even she was beginning to lose hope, acknowledging that 'I've become disillusioned to a point [...] they can come and bulldoze my house down tomorrow, and they should have done it ten years ago [...] when the pit closed'.[84] In fact many streets had been cleared by the mid-2000s, including the ones that had been used to film *Billy Elliot* at the turn of the century, but even so the district's problems seemed to be deepening rather than the reverse. Grace was convinced that her daughter would move away as soon as she could afford to do so, commenting: 'there's no pull to stay here'.[85]

Drawing on her knowledge as a health visitor, Diane saw things differently, stressing that in practice established local families still provided 'a strong network of support' to one another. She contrasted the experience of young mothers from local families, who could rely on 'tight knit' networks of support involving not just mothers and sisters, but also 'aunties, uncles, [and] grandparents', with the experience of newcomers who often had 'no support' because they had left their family behind in London or South Wales. She had no doubt that drugs and dereliction meant that 'it's not got the sense of community spirit that it did', but she was clear that many of Easington's newcomers were simply 'running away from something, domestic violence, debt, social services'.[86] They were poor and desperate, and their lack of social resources left them even more vulnerable than the local-born population hit so hard by deindustrialization, for whom, in practice, 'community' still remained more than just a folk memory.

Place, belonging, and 'community'

Sadly, there are no interviews with Easington's nomadic newcomers, but many of the women interviewed for the wider study had been mobile, sometimes within the region, sometimes over much greater distances (although everyone appears to be white British, at least among those included in the deposited sample). Anna, who had moved to Newcastle from France as a young child, had interesting things to say about being an outsider with limited English. Initially her family had moved to the old working-class district of Byker, which had undergone radical redevelopment in the 1970s with the construction of Ralph Erskine's famous Byker Wall estate (see Figure 26).[87] Anna had fond memories of the estate; indeed, now in her mid-twenties she claimed that she and her boyfriend were determined to move back to Byker to escape the tedium of suburban life near the coast.[88] Although she claimed to be well acquainted with present-day Byker, her strong attachment to the area appears to have been rooted in her experiences as an immigrant child arriving there able only to speak French. Anna recalled how she immediately felt at home, in stark contrast to her experience a few years later when the family relocated to Whitley Bay. More ethnically diverse than most of Tyneside, Byker appealed to Anna as a friendly, accepting place where neither her ethnicity nor her class was a barrier to being socially accepted (the family had 'heirlooms' but no money after becoming bankrupts).[89] By contrast, at Whitley Bay she was bullied for being French, southern,

Figure 26. River Tyne redevelopment Ouseburn, with Byker Wall visible in background [private collection]

and 'posh' even though (or perhaps because) it was a much more suburban, middle-class area.[90]

For Anna, Byker represented the epitome of community; that was why she wanted to go back. She remembered it as somewhere safe, where friends and neighbours left their doors open, and looked out for each other, and where her mother could never get to the shops because so many people stopped her in the street to chat.[91] It is a warm, even romantic, picture of a district often perceived by outsiders as epitomizing urban decline and social deprivation. Anna herself talked about feeling angry when work colleagues made disparaging remarks about the area, mobilizing negative stereotypes which we also hear in the testimony of residents from the city's more affluent districts.[92] Nor were these views entirely groundless. Byker had the city's highest percentage of children living in low-income families at the 2011 census and the second highest level of long-term illness or disability. In addition, Newcastle City Council's 2015 residents' survey painted a fairly bleak picture of community cohesion in the area, with Byker ranked lowest among city wards for the percentage of the population believing that 'people from different backgrounds get on well together' or that people 'pull together to improve this local area', and second lowest for the percentage claiming 'friendships with other people in the local area'.[93] The friendly, accepting culture Anna claimed to experience whenever she returned to Byker, and which fuelled her plans to move back, was evidently not a universal experience. But it does not follow that Anna's sense of local 'community spirit' was illusory—rather, it was probably just less universal and less inclusive than she imagined.

Certainly we should be wary about latching on to survey evidence from Byker to feed stereotypes about working-class life as socially exclusive or illiberal. Poverty itself can make it difficult to sustain social connections, especially when populations are young and highly mobile, but it does not follow that people *want* to lead isolated, individualized lives (or that they are socially exclusionary). Perhaps significantly, although 10 per cent of the population identified as non-white, barely 3 per cent of residents registered prejudice based on race or ethnicity (compared with a city-wide figure of over 12 per cent).[94] The lack of minority ethnic voices in the archived sample makes it difficult to pursue this issue further. As one might imagine, none of Taylor's respondents let slip comments which would suggest hostility to minorities, and only a few made any comment about ethnicity or immigration at all. Angie, the student from Hebburn whose father had once worked as a ship's joiner, was a notable exception. Asked whether her father enjoyed working as a hotel odd-job man after the shipyards closed, she replied, 'Oh he loved it! [...] me dad's quite interested in different cultures and things like that.' Angie went on to explain that her father liked the hotel's diverse, international workforce: 'There's a lot of Polish people now, that work in hotels, and he often talks about them, he likes to see people coming and going.' Apparently her father was getting his workmates to teach him some basic Polish so that he could communicate with the Polish people who had recently moved into his native Hebburn: 'he's always shouting, what is it again? "Jindogury" [*dzień dobry*] which is Hello, and they like turn round, and they absolutely love him, all the Polish people!'[95] Doubtless Hebburn had other 'born and bred' residents who took a very different view of the new arrivals, but it nonetheless reminds us not to leap to conclusions about workers as somehow innately 'nativist' and hostile to immigrants.

In fact, Taylor's study includes a significant number of incomers to the area, but they are almost all middle-class professional workers or retirees living in desirable urban districts such as Jesmond, Heaton, and Durham City.[96] Intriguingly, of thirty women interviewed only nine self-identified as 'middle class', and, of these nine, all but three were incomers to the region. In turn, of the nine incomers to the region, only one, a care worker called Carrie who had grown up near

Liverpool, self-identified as 'working class'.[97] In many ways it is the same pattern that we see in Luton a decade earlier, with long-distance mobility and social class tightly interconnected. That said, only four incomers had been born outside northern England, and of these two had come to Tyneside as young children.[98] For many, therefore, a strong regional identity as northerners may have helped to facilitate identification with Tyneside. But the process ran deeper than this. Two of the women interviewed at an Over 60s club in leafy Jesmond described themselves as 'adopted Geordies'. Lillian had lived in Newcastle for sixty years, moving there from Cardiff as a teenager, but Cathleen had been born in the colonial Far East between the wars and only moved to Tyneside in her late forties to take up a professional administrative job.[99] Their friend Sandra, originally from Yorkshire, felt equally at home in Jesmond, commenting that she 'wouldn't want to live anywhere else [...] I've been here for so long and you know so many people [...] it's a very comfortable place to live'.[100]

Although quite a few Jesmond residents felt the area was becoming overdeveloped to cater for its expanding student population, it was generally perceived as a vibrant, socially diverse district with a lively nightlife.[101] As such it wasn't only incomers to the region who displayed a strong sense of 'elective belonging' when talking about living in Jesmond. Elisabeth, a counsellor in her late forties, had grown up in a mining district near Sunderland which she had no qualms about saying she had always hated. She described her childhood as 'horrendous' and 'absolutely horrible', with a depressed mother, an overcrowded home, and an unemployed father with a drink problem. She claimed that even as a child she had felt that she had been 'born into the wrong place, I felt I didn't belong'. Determined to move away, in her late teens she took a bedsit in Heaton, 15 miles away—relishing the freedom and anonymity of life in the big city.[102] For the past decade she had lived on 'a very sociable street' in Jesmond where people supported each other through illness or bereavement, and the atmosphere was generally 'very friendly'. She acknowledged that it would be an exaggeration to call it 'villagey', but insisted, like Sandra, that she 'wouldn't want to live anywhere else', explaining, 'it's just very different from sort of where I was brought up. It feels more like home than anywhere I've lived, really.' But she recognized that this community feeling was very much a micro-phenomenon. Things had been very different not just in the 'scary' district where she had grown up, but also in her previous Jesmond home— a flat where she had lived after separating from her first husband—even though this was less than a mile away. Here she had known no one in the street except the people who lived above her: 'It was a very different experience. It was much more...people were individuals, and there was a lot more passing traffic in the sense of people renting property.' As she put it: 'flat living tends to be more individualistic, rather than being part of a community'.[103]

Like many people, Elisabeth acknowledged being torn between the intimacy of 'community' and the anonymity of a more 'individualistic' way of living. She liked the fact that if an alarm went off on her street neighbours would 'go over and check that somebody was OK, you wouldn't ignore it'. But she was less comfortable with the flip side of face-to-face community, of feeling 'claustrophobic' and like 'you can't escape'. As she put it, 'the negative side is quite intrusive; you can't do anything without being seen...if you go out for a jog, the whole street knows you've gone out for a jog...sometimes you want to be anonymous if you're not in the mood. But it's swings and roundabouts.'[104] Like most of us, she lived this contradiction because, on balance, she valued the sense of living somewhere that was friendly and socially caring more than she valued social anonymity.

Elisabeth is also interesting because she found 'community' in a comfortable middle-class suburb, having grown up in a 'mining community' (her words) near Sunderland which many would imagine to be the epitome of face-to-face community. Coming from what she termed a 'well known' local family, she claimed to have 'hated everybody knowing my business'. For Elisabeth, her birthplace had all the worst aspects of 'community' with none of the advantages. As she put it: 'there were no role models of men or women, as neighbours, for me'; the women were 'long suffering, fatalistic', the men 'aggressive and violent', and everyone drank heavily.[105] But as with the newcomers to Easington, who horrified locals with their street parties, the drinking and fights Elisabeth abhorred may simply have been her neighbours' idea of how to 'have a good time' (probably best said in the drunken slur of Frank Gallagher (David Threlfall) in Paul Abbott's Channel 4 TV series *Shameless* (2004–13)). Certainly it would be wrong to slot Elisabeth's comments into a simple story of the 'decline of community'. Much better, surely, to think in terms of competing ideas about what constitutes social connectedness: different 'imagined communities'. Elisabeth expressed a clear personal preference for the reserved communalism of her adopted Jesmond. But not everyone could choose to belong so easily. In Easington, as we have seen, there was a clear schism between what sociologists Norbert Elias and John Scotson termed the 'Established' and the 'Outsiders'.[106] Something similar may also explain the apparent dichotomy between Anna's warm perception of community life in Byker and the picture of isolation and anomie painted in responses to the city council's residents' survey.

When Taylor conducted a focus-group interview with members of a Byker Over 60s club, she found plenty of people testifying to the persistence of community in the area. As Hannah, one long-time resident, put it: 'everybody's friendly from

[Byker] and no matter what's wrong with ye, ye know [...] Everybody is friendly and they try and help ye if they can. There's always been good neighbours in [Byker], always.' But Hannah felt things were beginning to change, observing 'some o' the young ones, like, keep theirselves to theirselves'.[107] Dorothy felt the same, commenting that 'younger people, they have their own life. There isn't that...I mean, I could knock on Amy anytime, but I don't feel as if I could knock on somebody younger.'[108] But others sounded a note of scepticism. Nina in particular stressed that 'this friendliness they're on about in [Byker] was a broader thing. It was the North East.' She also pointed out that in many ways people were now *more* gregarious than they had been when she was young: 'We didn't socialise as much as people do now. You were more within your family.'[109] Again, these were not necessarily contradictory comments, just different ways of understanding the same social experiences. Newcomers leading busy lives had less reason to prioritize social relations with rarely seen neighbours when they had social networks across the city, and quite possibly beyond.

There are also suggestions that families with young children often created their own parallel social networks based on playgroups, informal visiting, and the logistics of the school run.[110] Debbie, a community health worker in her early fifties from Walker, said that all her close local friends were people she had got to know while living in nearby Byker and attending the local toddler group. Trying to explain why she had not made new friends since moving to Walker she commented 'like the woman next...well both sides of mine, their community is their extended family [...] they all live within walking distance of each other, like their parents and their aunties and sisters and what have you, so I think that's their community.' Interestingly, she then added, 'But I think if you've got young children you'd probably get into a community, or if you're older and you've got more time.'[111] The key phrase here is 'a community'. Debbie recognized that it was easy for people to believe they lived in a strong 'community' without recognizing its exclusive, generational (or familial) character. Medical researcher Carla made a similar point, commenting about Jesmond that 'there is definitely a community spirit there, but I think you actually engage in that spirit at various parts of your life and then disengage and engage again [...] I'm sure when you've got small children up to the age of 11, you're very engaged'.[112] Both women offered striking examples of respondents' ability to articulate an acute, vernacular sociology of their own lives.

Speaking from the perspective of a community health worker, Debbie did not subscribe to the popular idea that 'community' was a thing of the past. She might feel that social connectedness often depended on a person's age and circumstances, but like Carla she recognized a broader 'community spirit' that people could tap into (or ignore) as they chose. Speaking about her adopted Walker, she commented, 'There is a community spirit because you get to know people that you just pass in the street.' She also felt that residential stability played a key role in the slow accretion of the social connections necessary to create this feeling of shared belonging. In this respect, she felt that there was a distinct difference between Walker and Byker, because of the higher population turnover in the latter:

> I think [Byker] is probably getting less of a community spirit because it's less stable now and more people are moving in and out and I think it's not as favoured as a community as it was. But where I live in [Walker] houses don't come up very often, you know, people don't move in and out very often.[113]

Few respondents were as reflexive, or sociologically insightful, as Debbie. Certainly most subscribed to the conventional wisdom that community had declined radically since the 1950s, whilst generally retaining the view that people were friendlier and more neighbourly in the North East than elsewhere (especially than 'down South').[114] This tension, between declinist accounts of neighbouring and a strong belief in the natural friendliness of Geordies, ran through many of the testimonies. Anna, the woman who longed to return to the Byker community she had known as a child, was a good example. She complained that Whitley Bay, by contrast, was snobbish and aloof, giving as an example the fact when she had painted the front of her house no one had spoken to her. She acknowledged that her next-door neighbours on both sides were 'absolutely lovely', but insisted that 'as a general rule I found that there's no community, no community spirit'.[115] Unusually, she offered some clues about what she meant by 'community spirit' and, crucially, her examples all revolved around other people's failure to recognize her personhood—their avoidance of intimacy and social connection. Besides ignoring her painting efforts, she pointed to the fact that probably no one in her street even knew her name, and no one said hello as she went about the town, even though she had lived there for twenty years. As she put it: 'I feel I'm making sweeping generalisations here, but people say hello to me when I'm in [Byker], they acknowledge my existence.' It was this recognition that really mattered to her, although she acknowledged that there were tensions running through her testimony. Not just the fact that her neighbours were lovely, and clearly did recognize her, but that most of her contact with people in Whitley Bay was as a commuter working long hours in the city, whereas when she socialized in Byker it was 'not during working hours'.[116] In many ways her comments epitomized the elusively subjective dimensions of 'imagined community'.

Jill, a part-time receptionist in her late fifties, had a similar attitude towards the Durham village she had moved to when her elderly parents became too frail to manage alone.[117] She found it a pleasant, convenient place to live, but regretted its lack of community feeling compared with the Northumberland mining village she had known as a child:

> [It's] not the community I grew up with. That isn't there anymore. That's where you left your back door open and your granny fetched you up, that doesn't happen. Not in my experience. In all of my married life, that hasn't happened but it did in my youth. I don't think so. I think people live behind...I can honestly say I don't know the names of anyone else in our street. After 12 years, that's sad! When I was growing up you would know everyone's name in the street. Even if you had to put a 'Mrs' in front of it, you knew who they were, and now you don't. And you can pass people on the street and say 'Good morning' and they look at you thinking 'What's the matter with her then?' you know? You have to be more careful.[118]

For Jill, social recognition again played a key part in feeling part of a 'community'. But here too we see tensions running through the testimony. Like Anna, Jill spoke warmly of her immediate neighbours. Living on one side was 'a lovely man' she viewed as the perfect neighbour: 'he doesn't bother [you]. But if you need him, he's there.' On the other side was a woman who had become a close friend and with whom she shared her nominally full-time job as a receptionist: 'we can fit the job in to suit ourselves'.[119] Jill also reported having previously lived in places which conformed more closely to conventional ideas about gregarious, face-to-face community. When her children were young she had lived in Newcastle's industrial West End. Despite being a working mother and a newcomer to the area she had got to know a large network of local women through the woman who lived below (this was a traditional Tyneside flat—a two-storey terraced property containing two flats, each with its own front door to the street; see Figure 27). She recalled, 'It was a long terraced street [...] and I knew 40 or 50 women and we used to go on a Wednesday night to the pub at the top of the street [...] And we would have like, birthday parties and things like that, just really good neighbours, and also looked after you [...] It was very nice, but the house was burgled four times.'[120]

One also has to acknowledge that Jill's child's-eye view of life in a Northumberland mining village may have been rose-tinted. This was something Chantelle acknowledged when recounting her positive memories of growing up in Easington Colliery in the 1980s. As she put it: 'It was great when I was younger, it was...It was a community. I mean, taking it from a kid's point of view, my Mum's point of view might be totally different.'[121] But not everyone shared Chantelle's willingness to reflect on the subjective nature of personal experience.

Figure 27. Upper Norfolk Street, North Shields, a classic terrace of Tyneside flats (note the side-by-side front doors and wide frontages) [Washington Imaging / Alamy Stock Photo]

Before moving to be near her parents, Jill had lived on the edge of Washington new town, close by the A1(M). She described it as having been 'a beautiful place to live', but socially she found it much less friendly than Newcastle's West End:

> There was no sense of community. It was a new town and there was people from all over lived in Washington New Town, people from everywhere [...] I didn't feel a sense of community at all. But then again, I worked; I wasn't there all day to be part of the community [...] I didn't have time to socialise with anybody. Got home, got out the ironing ready for the next day, you know?[122]

Doubtless people did socialize differently in the two areas, but Jill's experience would also have been shaped by her children being older and more independent, and by the fact that she now had to commute to work. When dealing with perceptions of community it can often be difficult to differentiate between the effects of place and those of personal circumstances. But Hebburn-born Cathy, the shipyard worker's daughter, was unusually well placed to comment on the contrasting 'spirit' of different localities. Now in her late thirties and living, as Jill had done, on the western fringes of Washington new town, Cathy regularly went back

222

to Hebburn to visit family and friends. She was adamant that Hebburn retained 'more of a community feel' than the new town. She explained that in Hebburn people would regularly greet her in the street, and sometimes stop to chat, whereas this never happened in Washington, even though it was only 10 miles away. Perhaps significantly, her comments make it clear that she had adapted her own behaviour to conform to the new local norms. She claimed still to say hello to people in the street, but otherwise 'I very much keep meself to meself [...] as far as neighbours and things are concerned.' Only when walking her dog did she break this local code of social reticence: 'the only community there is, really, is when, if I take the dog out, and people generally talk to each other when they've got dogs'.[123] In a place where everyone was a newcomer, dogs were a prop to allow social connection with strangers. Or so it seemed to Cathy, at least.

Chelsea, a manager in her mid-thirties living in the cathedral city of Durham, was one of the few people explicitly to reject talk of the decline of 'community'. Herself the mother of a toddler, she commented,

> you know, people talk about the decline of communities, I actually think we have a really strong community and I know that talking to the other mums that live in different areas of Durham, they're kind of sharing those same experiences. I talk to friends who live in London, they don't even know who their next door neighbour is, it's ridiculous![124]

Fortunately, she also tried to define what community actually meant to her—in the process drawing on her experience of growing up in Birmingham, where, after the 1985 riots, her family had moved from the gregarious inner-city district of Perry Barr to suburban Sutton Coldfield. Chelsea acknowledged that there was no easy way to define 'community' but insisted that 'you know when you've got it'. She did, though, try to put that sense into words, saying she felt community meant 'neighbours talking to each other, being involved in each other's lives, having that trust, for example, when my neighbour is going away on holiday, I'll go and feed their cats, water their plants...we all keep an eye out for each other'.[125] But once again lifestyle was a big part of this story. Before having her daughter she had frequently worked away from home managing major projects, and had therefore had no time to put into her local community. But everything changed when she became a mother, not because she stopped working, but because her life became more grounded in Durham. As she put it, 'once I'd had my daughter, that opened a whole network for me. So I've developed a whole group of friends now, through my little one.'[126] It was a perfect example of 'community' as a metaphor for personal connection; something both lived and imagined.

Hidden solidarities

At around the time that Taylor was interviewing women across the North East, sociologists Liz Spencer and Ray Pahl were publishing an important study claiming friendship to be the vital social glue holding modern 'individualist' societies together. They term friendship networks, and other similar informal associations, 'personal communities' to indicate that they are personally chosen, rather than given, forms of social connection. According to Spencer and Pahl, personal communities establish 'hidden solidarities' that are more than capable of offsetting any diminution in the power of solidarities rooted in place and kinship (although they acknowledge that these also remain vitally important in many people's lives).[127] In a sense this was what Byker pensioner Nina meant when she suggested that people now socialized more widely than they had done when she was young—when 'you were more within your family'.[128] Improved communications and greater mobility meant that friendship networks could be sustained over considerable distances. Andrea, a research manager in her forties with a strong, radical working-class background, explicitly described herself as having a 'wide social network', commenting that her close friends tended not to be 'people who live in the locality but quite a few people who live in Newcastle or down at the coast'.[129] Similarly, Cathy might claim to keep herself to herself in her prosperous commuter village, but she was clear that it was close friends (rather than family) who had helped her to cope with the recent break-up of her marriage: '[it was] my friends that kept us going and got us through them bad, them bad times. So I was out constantly, with one particular friend [...] just partying and getting drunk.'[130] Similarly, Carla was explicit that though Jesmond had a strong 'community spirit', commuting all day for work meant that she built her social life around established friendships rather than getting involved locally. For her this was a conscious and logical response to the demands of a busy, mobile life.[131]

Spencer and Pahl's 'hidden solidarities' are essentially secular, but for many women interviewed in the Tyneside study the bonds of religion continued to offer an important form of community that transcended place and family. Nor was this something that only older women recognized. Britney (28) recalled how she grew up knowing lots of people in the Durham former mining town of Spennymoor because her mother was 'heavily involved' in the local Catholic church: 'there was a big feeling there, everybody kind of knew everybody'.[132] Angie (25) also grew up in a large Catholic family, as did her boyfriend, and she liked the fact that because they were both from Hebburn their relatives 'all know each other through church and things like that'. In this study, only women from Catholic backgrounds talk about religion being central to their friendship networks (often through connections first made at denominational schools), but other faith groups doubtless function along similar lines for their adherents.[133]

On the other hand, there are also signs that personal friendship communities can often play a vital role in encouraging people to defy the customary expectations of family, neighbours, or for that matter organized religion. Because all Taylor's interviewees were women, the Tyneside material shows this most clearly in the form of what we might call vernacular feminism: women taking strength from other women to challenge expectations about how they 'should' live their lives. For some younger women, like Jody and Gaby, two local-born graduates in their mid-twenties, this could take a playful, postmodern form: both claimed consciously to mimic gender stereotypes in order to subvert them. When Jody was explaining that people often assumed she was 'stupid' because she was soft-spoken, attractive, and northern, Gaby joked that they used to call themselves 'the Baby-Faced Assassins', because people would misread their smiling demeanour: 'actually they've no idea how clever we are'.[134] But for most women transcending gender stereotypes was tough, and depended on the support and solidarity of close friends, usually other women. Debbie, the community health worker from working-class Wallsend, was quite explicit about her debt to other women, including the community worker in Byker who had originally inspired her to become a volunteer. Of such women, many of whom subsequently became friends, she commented, 'they've influenced us a great deal and encouraged us and I think women do get strength from women'.[135]

In fact one of the most striking features of the Tyneside interviews is many women's strong sense of themselves as harbingers of radical social change: that they were living radically different lives from their mothers' and grandmothers' generations. Feminist historian Lynn Abrams has identified women's sense of personal liberation from the expectations of others as a defining feature of the cohort of women born in the 1940s and coming to maturity in the long 1960s, but Taylor's testimony from the North East would suggest that here at least this feeling was often the hallmark of later generations of women.[136] For instance, Cathy, the recently divorced business manager living on the edge of Washington new town, felt that the position of women in the region had 'changed a lot' since her childhood in Hebburn in the 1970s: 'I think it is recognized that women can, erm, have careers and are an entity in themselves, they're not just attached to their husband or boyfriend or partner or whatever'. Earlier she talked about the generational change in women's expectations and life experiences, before declaring 'I couldn't have been a wife like that, a woman like that, I'm just too strong willed, I'm too independent. Erm...I would hate to try and rely on a man.'[137] Chantelle, now in her early thirties, had grown up in Easington Colliery in what she described as a house of 'strong women', who (unusually for a mining village) had 'always worked'.[138] Like Cathy, she prided herself on the fact that, in turn, she had 'always been independent and done my own thing'. By the turn of the century, vernacular feminism ran strong in working-class districts like Easington Colliery and Hebburn as well as among young, highly educated women like Gaby and Jody.[139]

Chantelle is also interesting for her complicated, and in some ways conflicted, attitude towards her roots, and towards the push-and-pull effects of growing up in a place like Easington Colliery. At one level she was evidently deeply proud of the strong women who had brought her up, of her own working-class identity, and of her personal connection to Easington. Recently separated, she had returned to Easington Colliery partly to be closer to friends and family, and partly because housing there was affordable.[140] Like many people from established Easington families, she spoke harshly about the 'complete losers' who had moved to the village since the pit closed, but her feelings of antipathy ran deeper.[141] Chantelle recalled how, as a child, she always wanted to get away to enjoy a better life: 'I wanted more, you know, to go out and do my own thing and I wanted better than that [...] I always wanted to have better stuff, better house, better money, have a car, you know, holidays, and to do that you need a better job really.'[142] But she also felt the pull of *place* very strongly, even though she was adamant that she had no wish to be connected to the *people* who actually lived in 'her' place (friends and family excepted). She recalled telling her ex-husband, 'I think the only place I can ever settle is [Easington Colliery]', before commenting,

> I don't know why because I've got all these negative points about it, why I don't like it. I don't want to be part of the community, I'm happy just going to work, coming home and having me own little house but it's home for me, even though the people are horrible...Not all of them are horrible and it probably does have its good points, but it's home.[143]

Britney, two years younger than Chantelle and from the mining and iron-making town of Spennymoor about 20 miles to the west, also had conflicted attitudes about her roots and the pull of family and place. Britney recalled feeling a strong urge to get away from her home town as a teenager, encouraged by an aunt living in the south of England whose own children had been to university.[144] After university, which took her to Scotland and then Newcastle, she moved south herself, building a career in the voluntary sector before taking a job back in the North East. At the time of the interview she was delighted to be living back with her parents, but struggling with the pain she knew she would cause them when, inevitably, she moved away again (she reported having plans to set up a business in Scotland where her boyfriend was working).[145]

Going away had not fractured Britney's connection to place, but it had certainly altered it. For one thing, most of her friends from school had not returned after university, and those that remained were now living very different lives to her own: married with young children.[146] To Britney they seemed fixed in place—lacking her sense of adventure and boundless possibilities (she recalled that as a teenager her parents had struggled to understand her desire to go away to university, and resisted her plans to travel to India).[147] Now, though she loved being 'home', and said she feared that it could suck her back into the 'comfortable' life she had grown up with, she asked herself 'am I going to kind of suddenly find myself living in [Spennymoor], having a family, settling down and getting into perhaps the public sector and staying there all my life[?] [...] it would be so easy for me to do that'.[148] In turn, Britney's childhood friends who had stayed in Spennymoor (Goodhart's 'somewheres', rooted more firmly in place and tradition) now teased her for being 'posh' because her accent had weakened. She disliked being made to feel 'different'— 'like they thought I was turning my back on my home and my family and that certainly wasn't how I wanted to feel'.[149] It was this conversation that prompted Britney to comment, 'it's going to kill my family that I'm going to move', before hesitatingly musing on how 'they' now viewed her. It is not clear whether 'they' meant her family or her old friends from the town, but either way the hurt was clear: 'In a way it's hard to live with. I always thought that they felt that I... I thought I was better than that or trying to be someone I wasn't, or trying to... and I think that's why it felt, yes it did feel, really hard.'[150] The idea of simple dichotomies between 'somewhere' people and 'anywhere' people obscures the complexity of feelings people have about place and belonging—the attachments that bind them and yet can also divide them. Strikingly, Britney ended her interview by declaring 'ultimately I'd like to live in the North East. [...] I'd like to have kids and I'd like my parents to be involved in their upbringing', but first she was determined 'to push it [her career] as far as I can and do it myself and travel a little bit more'.[151]

Britney's experience, of coming from a working-class family and going away to university, has become more common in recent decades. Overall, the proportion of school leavers attending university rose from 8.4 per cent in 1970 to 33 per cent in 2000, although children from poorer families remain radically under-represented in higher education.[152] Like Britney, some found themselves going to university from homes, not just with no tradition of higher education, but with no conception of what it meant or why it might be good for their child to take a degree. Andrea, now a research manager in her forties, recalled that her father had been 'mortified' when she first told that him she was giving up a good job to go to college. But this appears to have been as much about gender as class expectations. Like Britney, she was sure that her parents 'just wanted me to get married and have a family'.[153] Similarly, Angie, the 25-year-old Master's student from Hebburn, recalled that though her parents supported her efforts to go back to college, they had never pushed her academically and even now had no real idea what she did at college.[154] But this was not some modern-day version of cultural critic Richard Hoggart's account of the post-war 'scholarship boy', for whom education brought an irreparable rupture to family life.[155] Angie had only been able to return to college by moving back to live with her parents. And though she acknowledged that education marked her as different (she felt 'embarrassed' to discuss what she was doing with old friends in case they thought she was 'bragging'), she was adamant that college had not changed her on the inside. Indeed, she insisted that, even if she became a university lecturer, 'I would still consider myself as working class because of my background'.[156] Into the twenty-first century, place, family, and class were not things to be lightly shed, especially in the north-east of England.

Conclusions

By the turn of the millennium, the gap between community lived and community imagined could be vast. For many, long working days and their commitment to wider social networks could make it difficult to feel socially embedded within their immediate neighbourhood (although it is striking that even many of those who regretted the weakening of local social ties reported close relationships with near neighbours). People perceived the speed and flux of modern living as corroding traditional forms of community, and were generally less conscious of the multiple ways in which social change was also making it easier for them to sustain meaningful personal communities which transcended the limitations of physical space. Place remains central to community as it is imagined, so that even if personal communities can offer people powerful social bonds to resist the atomizing effects of modernity, they cannot fulfil all the psychic needs that gravitate around the idealized concept of 'community' in vernacular discourse. In particular, as we have seen, personal communities do not offer the casual affirmation of identity that comes from living among people who affirm your personhood, and your claim to belong, on a daily basis.

We need to take people seriously when they lament the loss of community. They are voicing a stubborn refusal to accept living in a society where their lives appear not to matter; where their personhood and individuality goes largely unrecognized.

In many ways, popular narratives about the decline of community tell us more about the present than the past (after all, even in post-war Bermondsey and Bethnal Green we found community feeling to be patchy and strongly influenced by personal circumstances and temperament). The longing for a lost golden age of community underscores how strongly many people feel the need for greater social connection in their current lives. In essence, an idealized mythic past is being mobilized to critique an alienating and dehumanizing present. It is a powerful antidote to glib accounts of the triumph of neo-liberalism which tend to assume that the great bulk of the public have become brainwashed by a tide of selfish individualism. Yes, they may have learned some of the shibboleths of the new order—like the modish language of 'aspiration' running through the Tyneside interviews—but we should not assume that in the process they have ceased to value place, belonging, and above all *social connection*.

POSTSCRIPT

Where Are We Heading?

Figure 28. Black Friday, north London, 2014 [REUTERS/Luke MacGregor]

So how can we reconcile the claim that community still matters with images like the one above from Black Friday 2014? (Figure 28) Aren't such images proof that people have been reduced to atomized, selfish consumers, happy to elbow old ladies and abuse staff in a desperate bid to get the latest gadgets at a knock-down price? Certainly that was the dominant take in the media at the time, with journalists denouncing frantic shoppers as 'animals' and 'barbarians', and suggesting that civilization stood on the brink thanks to a relentlessly rising tide of selfishness and greed.[1]

As ever, we should be wary of taking such scenes at face value. First, in 2014 the Black Friday phenomenon was a stage-managed media event; hence the large TV cameras being raised aloft towards the back of the melee in the still shown in Figure 28. The media were there because retailers were looking for a story that would help them introduce the concept of Black Friday discount sales to a sceptical British public. Unlike Americans, the British don't keep Thanksgiving and so don't have a long holiday weekend at the end of November in which to shop (the idea that people might be persuaded to feast on roast turkey twice a year has been deemed as unlikely to fly as the average supermarket turkey). This was why many of the 2014 bargains were both spectacular and strictly rationed. It was also why some shops chose to open at midnight on Black Friday. Most of all, it was why they tipped off the broadcast and print media and gave them permission to film on their premises.

Now that Black Friday has become more established, to the regret of many British retailers who have seen their pre-Christmas profits dented, such scenes have largely disappeared—or rather, the need to manufacture them has disappeared. In any case, there is nothing new in sales manias, nor in the appetite of the media to cover consumers fighting each other to secure a bargain. In 1986 the *Daily Telegraph* was reporting 'Frantic shoppers rampage through Regent Street' under a picture of two women tussling to buy the same scarf.[2] The story was a good deal more whimsical than accounts of Black Friday crowds, but its central message, that even the well-to-do lose all sense of civilized behaviour when faced by a bargain, was not so different.

However, it would be misleading to suggest that nothing has changed in recent decades. There are undoubtedly ways in which social life has become more atomized. Probably the most important is that people are almost twice as likely to live alone in the 2010s as they were in the 1970s. In 2017, 28 per cent of British households consisted of a single adult living on their own, compared with 17 per cent in 1971 (or, put another way, 7.7 million people, nearly 15 per cent of the adult population, lived alone).[3] Without wishing to play down the genuine scourge of loneliness in modern society, it is important to recognize that this massive increase in living alone is largely a consequence of personal choices made possible by increased affluence.[4] Historically, most single adults, whether young or old, lived as lodgers in someone else's household; with relatives if they could, with strangers if not. They did so because financially they had no other option. Until after the Second World War, they would also have had access to few sources of care or support beyond family and friends. It is no accident, therefore, that we find the highest figures for people living alone concentrated in affluent societies with comprehensive social welfare systems. In Europe, Sweden heads the list with an extraordinary 51.8 per cent of households consisting of a single adult living on their own.[5]

Even in the 1940s, older people, when asked, said that they wanted to continue living in their own homes, even if this meant living alone, because they wanted to retain their independence and allow their children to do the same. On the other hand, they were also clear that they wanted those children, or at least some of them, to live close by to provide company and, when needed, support. In the 1940s, this ideal was still relatively easy to achieve. So much so that gerontologist Joseph Sheldon argued that the concept of 'living alone' had little meaning for the elderly of post-war Wolverhampton, given how deeply their lives were enmeshed with those of their kin.[6] But the ideal became more difficult to achieve as young couples increasingly chose to move away from the parental home to enjoy the better housing and cleaner air of the expanding suburbs. Writing in 1967, Jeremy Seabrook painted a bleak picture of run-down, soon-to-be-demolished, inner-urban areas where the elderly were left 'stranded, isolated and helpless...exposed to an overwhelming sense of loss'.[7] Seabrook's picture was probably overdrawn even for large cities since, as we have seen, children often chose suburbs well connected to their old haunts; in smaller provincial towns it was even less relevant since the new suburbs were often just a short walk away—in practice kinship networks changed little where relocation took place on a local scale (the story was rather different for long-distance 'overspill' migrants such as the families we heard from who had moved to places such as Stevenage and Houghton Regis).[8]

One also needs to remember that the elderly could provide their own social networks; social support was never simply an intergenerational relationship. It is easy to forget that historically studies of the elderly regularly found that the majority of those who lived alone did *not* feel lonely.[9] From the time her only son left home around 1960, my widowed Great-Aunt May (see Figure 29) spent almost every evening visiting her sister Florence two streets away. Ostensibly, this was to watch TV, but everyone knew it was also for the company. Between them, the pair had five children, but these had all moved away from the Redfield district of East Bristol by the end of the 1950s. When Florence herself was widowed in 1963 the two sisters talked about living together, but, in the absence of pressing financial need, each felt too attached to their own home to take the plunge. Instead they maintained the same visiting ritual every evening until Florence's death in 1971. In short, post-war affluence, which for them meant little more than not being poor, allowed the sisters to reconcile the twin ideals of English popular culture: to be independent and yet also to maintain strong social connection to others—to uphold traditions of domestic privacy without becoming an island cut off from the wider world.

This desire to reconcile personal independence with social connectedness runs through the testimony that has shaped this book. It is in many ways the defining

Figure 29. Edith May Fowler on her wedding to Bill Nott in 1931; she was widowed in 1945 [private collection]

feature of English popular culture in the modern age. But it is not easy to achieve. Many struggle to find a happy balance in their lives between self and society. The country as a whole has also frequently struggled to reconcile the potentially competing claims of individualism and community, especially since the 1980s and the decisive shift in favour of markets as the principal arbiter of public good. But the fact that so many people lament the current bias towards individual self-interest, and mobilize powerful narratives about the decline of community to underscore their dissatisfaction with the status quo, reminds us that the ascendancy of economic liberalism may not be as securely based as is often imagined.

Yes, testimony collected from the mid-2000s registers the new-found purchase of terms such as 'aspiration' and 'self-improvement', with their roots in modern discourse about individual achievement and self-realization, but though the vocabulary may be new, it is not clear that underlying perspectives are equally novel. Long before the economic and political transformations of the 1980s, we find people blaming themselves, rather than society or 'the system', for not achieving more with their lives. On Tyneside in the 1960s, working men frequently claimed to regret not

233

being clever enough, or diligent enough, to secure the qualifications that would have been the passport to a better job and higher earnings. Within the working class, the gulf between apprenticed workers who had learned a 'trade' and workers who had merely learned 'on the job' had deep historical roots, and only really began to break down in the 1970s with deindustrialization and a general shift to modular, college-based training rather than time-served, on-the-job training.[10] Securing an apprenticeship was partly a matter of heredity, with sons following fathers, but the British class system was never a caste system and so there was always scope for personal 'aspiration', even if the word itself was rarely spoken. This was, after all, what kept the lucrative market in adult correspondence courses, evening classes, and technical education alive through the twentieth century.[11]

Just as individualism and concern for self are not new, nor is the desire to temper these impulses through social relationships based on family and friendship. Probably the single most important lesson to be drawn from reanalysing post-war social-science testimony is that people in the early twenty-first century are as determined as those in the 1940s and 1950s to find a healthy balance between self and society. It has probably become harder to achieve since the 1970s with the breakdown of the post-war social democratic belief in shared, near universal, progress—in the idea that everybody should be, and could be, on a shared journey towards greater security and prosperity.[12] But whether it is the Isle of Sheppey in the 1980s or Tyneside in the 2000s, we still repeatedly hear people either celebrating, or yearning for, meaningful social connection with others.

Crucially, it is clear that many do still find this social connection through micro-communities based either on shared interests or on their specific stage in the life cycle (youth groups, parent/toddler groups, Over 60s groups, etc.). Micro-communities rooted in the life cycle tend to remain quite closely tied to place, but this is much less true of other types of micro-community, many of which cater for highly mobile adults who are often already obliged to travel long distances for work. Both types of micro-community provide people with the social connection and social solidarities that can help them resist the atomizing pressures of modern society.[13] But people want more than this; they also want to feel that they 'belong' somewhere. The highly mobile are as likely to feel this yearning for place as people who can boast of being 'born and bred' where they still live—it is this impulse that sociologists have come to term 'elective belonging'.[14] Often what people crave most, as we saw clearly in testimony collected from women in the North East in the mid-2000s, are interactions in their immediate neighbourhood which can be said to affirm their personhood. People may find meaningful social connection elsewhere—at work, through leisure, or perhaps in organized religion—but they still feel the need for at least a minimal level of lived, face-to-face communal interaction. This may be little more than a passing greeting in the street or a casual word across a garden fence, but it symbolizes mutual recognition, a tacit acknowledgement about the bonds of common residence: a way of saying 'we both belong here'. When such greetings are withheld, people experience this as a social hurt—a type of symbolic violence, which denies their personhood and says: 'you do not belong'. The poignancy of this yearning for social connection and the pain of finding it missing is probably nowhere more beautifully captured than in Jon McGregor's 2002 novel *If Nobody Speaks of Remarkable Things*, with its kaleidoscopic picture of disconnected lives lived out on a single street in the north of England on the day of Princess Diana's death.[15]

Politicians probably can't do much to make us more civil to our near neighbours—though it might have a big impact on collective well-being if they could. Good Neighbour schemes flourished in the 1970s with official government support (they were the altruistic precursors of the 1980s Neighbourhood Watch schemes focused on crime reduction), and remain an important part of the voluntary sector in many rural areas, but the State has largely retreated from telling us how best to live together. In the 1950s it had widely been assumed that urban space could be organized to engineer social mixing and neighbourliness into the fabric of daily life, but by the 1970s the emphasis was already much more squarely on the need to facilitate community-building from below, through the mobilization of volunteers. In this sense the Good Neighbour movement was itself a strategic retreat from the mid-century patrician belief that experts could simply plan community into the lives of ordinary people. It also proved to be least effective where social need was greatest, something that is unlikely to have changed in the intervening decades.[16]

If we can't simply rely on reviving the call for everyone to be good neighbours, what might be done to help secure a healthier balance between individualism and community in daily life? We should certainly take heart from the fact that people clearly long for greater 'community' in their lives, often expressing this through a nostalgic language about how things used to be. This longing for greater social connection is a potentially powerful political force, but we should not let it blind us to the fact that there will be severe limits to the public's willingness to tolerate changes which might threaten to erode personal autonomy. Across the last seventy years the English have always sought ways to reconcile individualism and community in their lives; they have not become individualist in the last few decades. By exploring the recurrent ambivalences and tensions between community and self over the long view, this book reminds us that it has proved possible to develop communitarian projects that work with the grain of Britain's individualist popular culture; arguably this was what Raph Samuel found visiting Stevenage in the early days of the 'new town' project.

The vital lesson for the future is that any new politics of community has to enhance, rather than erode, the personal autonomy and independence that the majority of people have fought hard to secure for themselves and their families. It needs to focus on promoting the aspects of public life and culture that are open to all—bringing people together from diverse backgrounds, and at the same time enriching individual private lives. Today many of our public parks, libraries, museums and galleries, civic centres, and leisure venues are either starved of cash or run along purely commercial lines. But it is possible to imagine an alternative world in which these cherished public amenities not only flourish across the country, but re-emerge as the embodiment of civic pride and shared identities.[17] Writing in the 1950s, J. K. Galbraith famously denounced what he saw as America's emerging culture of 'private opulence and public squalor'.[18] His arguments retain their power today. Rebalancing the politics of individualism and community demands, above all, massive public investment in the amenities and spaces that can help to facilitate social connection and promote a general sense of living in an interconnected, shared social environment.

APPENDIX

NOTE ON ANONYMITY AND SOURCES

USE OF PSEUDONYMS

For most social surveys consulted here it is a condition of access that people's anonymity is preserved. It is also a condition of use that no attempt should be made to recontact interviewees or their descendants. Throughout the book I have therefore used only pseud-onyms. Where known, I have retained the researchers' original pseudonyms (e.g. the family names invented by Young and Willmott for their Bethnal Green and Debden families and by Pahl for his Sheppey study, or the given names invented by Yvette Taylor in her work with Tyneside women). Pseudonyms are consistent with the naming practices of the original project—i.e. sometimes just title and family name (Mr Jones), sometimes full names (Ron Jones), and sometimes only given names (Ron). Pseudonyms seek to retain any defining ethnic or regional characteristic of a respondent whilst ensuring full anonymity. This was done by using frequency lists of names from specific counties and countries. Where personal information might itself undermine anonymity, this has either been omitted or non-material changes have been made (e.g. a respondent's age may be altered slightly or, if they were from a very large family, the exact number of children may be changed). Researchers have not been named unless they were publicly associated with the work through publication, and even these named individuals are only identified with a specific interview if it is necessary to comment on the role that their class, gender, age, or ethnicity may have played in shaping the testimony under consideration.

QUESTIONS OF METHOD

The big methodological question for this project is: can we trust what people said when they were interviewed by social scientists? Especially given that these social scientists were usually from very different social and cultural backgrounds to the people being interviewed. Can we really talk about social-science field-notes offering insights into everyday speech, and, in particular, into how ordinary people understood their social world? For the past thirty years historians have tended to answer this question in the negative. Influential debates which began in the field of post-colonial studies have led many historians to accept that it is all but impossible to recreate what they call the 'subaltern voice'—that is, the ideas and world-view of people who have been unable to leave us a direct, unmediated account of their lives.[1] But it will surprise no one that, having spent the last decade working on the traces of contemporary vernacular speech to be found in field-notes, interview transcripts, and the recordings of encounters between social scientists and their subjects, I take a rather more optimistic view.

Partly this is on moral grounds—if we wholly discount such material, insisting that it is only capable of offering pale reflections of dominant social attitudes and values, we leave ourselves few options beyond the endless study of elite debates about the vast majority of ordinary people who leave little or no written record of their lives. More fundamentally, the absolutist position on reconstructing the 'subaltern voice' represents a refusal of the historian's responsibility to make the most of surviving traces of the past, especially when those traces can offer a perspective unavailable from other sources. Perhaps we cannot hope to offer a definitive account of popular attitudes and values, but we can and should try our hardest to construct the most plausible account of past lives that the evidence will sustain. The personal testimony that survives may all have been created through artificial encounters engineered by social scientists with their own research agendas, but by subjecting it to internal critical analysis, by contextualizing its creation and the reasons for its survival, and by triangulating with thousands of different surviving sources, we can shed light on facets of popular culture that would otherwise remain unknowable.[2]

Of course, it would be difficult to deny that it is the historian who decides how snatches of everyday speech from the archive should be woven together to create an overarching account of historical change. It is undoubtedly only historians who get to speak *unmediated* in such an exercise; only they who get the opportunity to orchestrate hundreds of separate, unrelated transcripts into a single, unified text (well that's the hope anyway). But that text does not expunge the voices it is made from; nor can it determine what meanings those voices will convey to the reader.

Additionally, we also have to confront the issue of representativeness. Here, a lot depends on what we want to achieve by returning to archived social-science testimony. If the aim is to critique a study's original conclusions, then issues of representativeness must loom large. This is also true if we want to make bold generalizations about structural socio-economic change. Indeed, in 1971 Jennifer Platt, one of the co-authors of the Luton 'affluent worker' study that is reanalysed in Chapter 4, famously launched a scathing critique of the unscientific methods deployed by Michael Young and Peter Willmott and their Institute of Community Studies to study social attitudes in Bethnal Green and Debden (studies reanalysed in Chapters 2 and 3). She dismissed the institute's work as largely impressionistic, arguing, in particular, that the samples taken at Bethnal Green and Debden were hopelessly inadequate for drawing robust sociological conclusions. I'm pretty sure I know what she will make of a historian reanalysing the project's *surviving* field-notes to build arguments about the past.[3]

So what's my defence? Well, in many ways it's similar to Young and Willmott's original response to Platt. They accepted many of her methodological criticisms, but argued that intensive, ethnographic research offered individual-level insights which offset deficiencies of sample size.[4] Having worked on the field-notes of ten different social studies spanning more than half a century, I have little doubt that it *is* the intensive ethnographic studies that throw up the most useful insights into popular attitudes and aspirations, rather than the large-scale, structured social surveys that Platt was championing in 1971. Surveys exist to answer specific questions based on a pre-existing sense of what matters. For instance, since 2005 the Government's Taking Part survey asks a random sample of people questions designed to measure their engagement with different cultural and leisure activities.[5] It is an invaluable tool for practitioners in these sectors, and for social scientists trying to map shifts in cultural and leisure activity. But if we want to understand what 'culture' means to people, or how they understand the idea of community engagement, a survey like this will not get us very far.

From my point of view the problem with surveys, even good ones, is that they strongly shape the terms of discourse, making it less likely that we will gain a clear sense of how people conceptualized social issues *for themselves*. By contrast, more open-ended interviews, and also ethnographic fieldwork observations like Firth's from Bermondsey in the late 1940s, tend to leave greater room for popular understandings to emerge through the research process. But with care even the driest, least promising social survey can be shown to elicit insights which are not simply imposed from without—any social-science encounter can be read for the clues it offers into popular, as well as elite, social attitudes.

THE CASE STUDIES

Unless stated otherwise, reanalysis involved repeated close reading of all surviving materials from the study in question.

<u>Bermondsey</u> (1947–1949 & 1958–1959), Sir Raymond Firth Papers, LSE Library, London

A vast collection of anthropological field-notes, research notes, and working papers from the original 1947–9 enquiry into community and kinship patterns at the Guinness Buildings on Snowsfields in Bermondsey. In all, at least twenty-two LSE-based anthropologists worked on this project at some point, and Firth collated much of their research material under topic headings, or integrated it into his own research notes. Firth's team included established researchers such as the Africanist Audrey Richards and Kenneth Little, who had just published a groundbreaking study of Black Britons, alongside graduate anthropologists who would go on to become major figures in the field, including Maurice Freedman, Derek Freeman, James Littlejohn, and Barbara Ward. The collection also contains Firth's personal field notebooks with detailed information about his visits to specific families in the Buildings and their relatives living elsewhere. Personal testimony from this collection consists mostly of snatches of recorded speech since there was no formal questionnaire or survey. Rather, the teams made repeated visits to selected households, using the exercise of compiling extensive family trees to elicit wider information about kinship ties, neighbouring, etc. In the early stages of the project, younger members of the team also got to know residents through activities associated with the Guinness Buildings Social Club, the Parent–Teacher Association, and other local groups. The late 1950s Bermondsey project was devised by Firth as a follow-up investigation of the buildings, but when it proved difficult to trace enough of the former residents the project evolved into a study focused on a small number of Bermondsey women, following them through pregnancy and the early stages of motherhood. The sociologist Pearl Jephcott, who had recently completed the fieldwork for her study of working women in Bermondsey,[6] helped facilitate this research. Detailed household case notes survive from both parts of this follow-up research.

Bethnal Green (1953 & 1955), Michael Young Papers, Churchill Archive Centre, Cambridge

This collection contains half the case notes from Young's original research in Bethnal Green for his 1955 LSE PhD, plus follow-up interviews conducted in 1955 as part of the research for *Family and Kinship in East London*. Some files are large and include Young's original scribbled notes in the field, and his subsequent written-up accounts of these interviews. Both the field-notes and the subsequent polished case histories contain snatches of reported speech; a few contain much more extensive testimony. This is consistent with Young's observation that they sometimes used portable reel-to-reel tape recorders in their Bethnal Green research. Most files also contain extensive biographical information collected via short structured surveys. Apart from one interview from 1955, the collection represents a continuous numbered series (cases 26 to 49 from the PhD project), suggesting no selection effects have influenced survival.

Debden (1953 & 1955), Michael Young Papers, Churchill Archive Centre, Cambridge

This collection, by far the smallest used here, consists of detailed interview notes for twelve families, with eleven interviewed both in 1953 and again in 1955 (sometimes by Peter Willmott in the latter case). This collection represents just over one-quarter of the interviews conducted at Debden. Most families were interviewed on multiple occasions, and the files are generally a little more detailed than those from Bethnal Green, though they are similar in structure. It is not clear why these cases survive (they do not form a continuous series), but there appear to be no obvious common features, and no systematic biases, and so it does not appear that they represent a deliberately selected subsample. Again there is evidence that a tape recorder was used for some interviews (still uncommon for social-science projects in the 1950s).

Stevenage (1959–60) [Raphael Samuel's] Ruskin Papers, Bishopsgate Institute, London

A collection of 147 completed responses to questionnaires about class, politics, and life in Stevenage conducted using a random samples of residents in the 'new town' wards of Stevenage during December 1959 and January 1960. The main sample consists of seventy responses to a survey with sixty-three questions, but there are, in addition, a further seventy-seven responses to pilot surveys, most of which had forty questions. The research was funded by Michael Young's Institute of Community Studies, and overseen by the young radical intellectual Raph Samuel, who conducted a number of in-depth interviews to supplement the main survey. Closest to a conventional opinion survey, though longer and with more open-ended questions, this study nonetheless touches on many vital issues in post-war social history including the experience of mobility and the meaning of affluence. Interviewers sometimes took down respondents' comments verbatim, but at other times they appear merely to have paraphrased their answers. Only Samuel's in-depth interviews appear likely to have been recorded and then transcribed.

Cambridge (1961–1962), Affluent Worker in the Class Structure, 1961–1962 Collection, UK Data Service, University of Essex

Conducted by John Goldthorpe and David Lockwood as a pilot study for the more famous study of affluent workers in Luton. Goldthorpe and Lockwood had both recently been appointed to social-science positions within the Department of Applied Economics at the University of Cambridge. In all there are 316 completed questionnaires. Respondents are predominantly from middle-class occupations, in contrast to the Luton study, but about one-third are skilled manual workers in trades such as plumbing, electrical engineering, aircraft manufacture, and scientific instrument making. These workers appear to have been contacted through their trade unions. The middle-class employees included teachers, bank workers, shopkeepers, university technicians, and clerical workers. Interviews were based around an eighteen-page questionnaire with open-ended follow-up questions and a lengthy semi-structured section exploring respondents' perceptions of social class. For this project I looked at a structured sample of 130 scanned interviews, over-sampling the manual workers to correct for their under-representation in the original study. These files have been deposited with the UK Data Archive at the University of Essex.

Luton (1962–1964), Affluent Worker in the Class Structure, 1961–1962 Collection, UK Data Service, University of Essex

This study involved 291 workers from three industrial firms: Vauxhall (cars), Laporte (chemicals), and Skefco (ball bearings). The published findings were based on a completed sample of 283 interviews. All respondents were aged between 21 and 46 and married. Older workers were excluded to ensure that any personal experiences of unemployment in the 1930s did not influence responses to post-war affluence. The sample was intended to include only men living in Luton or the overspill estate of Houghton Regis, though in practice this stipulation was sometimes relaxed (see Chapter 4). Manual workers were interviewed twice, first at work and then at home with their wives (some questions were specifically for wives). The non-manual sample of fifty-four workers was added late and confined to employees of Laporte and Skefco. These men were interviewed only once, at home with their wives, using a longer interview schedule. I have focused on the home interviews, reanalysing all non-manual interviews and 159 manual workers. The latter include the thirty cases transcribed by Selina Todd and Hilary Young and deposited with the UK Data Archive as SN: 6226. Questionnaires in shorthand were excluded from the sample. Todd and Taylor's digitization included workplace interviews, and in addition I read the questionnaires for a further thirty workplace interviews drawn from all three firms. Workplace interviews were twenty-six pages long and generally took about an hour to complete. Home interviews were forty-four pages long (fifty-three pages for non-manual workers) and generally took between two and four hours. Occasionally a return visit was required. As with the Stevenage survey, it is sometimes difficult to be sure when a respondent is being directly quoted and when paraphrased;

I have favoured unambiguous examples of direct speech when quoting from the study. Scanned questionnaires have been deposited with the UK Data Archive.

Tyneside (Shipbuilding workers), Wallsend (1967–1970), 'Qualidata: Shipbuilding workers', Modern Records Centre, University of Warwick

This study comprises two elements: a detailed questionnaire with 223 Swan Hunter shipbuilding workers from a variety of manual trades, and an extensive collection of ethnographic field-notes from 1968 to 1970 conducted partly to influence the design of the survey and partly to inform its interpretation. The project was directed by Professor R. K. Brown (University of Durham), and the ethnographic fieldwork was primarily conducted by Peter Brannen and Jim Cousins. My reanalysis focuses mainly on the fieldwork, but also makes use of the questionnaires which have been digitized by Selina Todd and Hilary Young and deposited with UKDA as SN: 6586. The field-notes are particularly extensive for three trades—blacksmiths, plumbers, and joiners—but there are also notes on other workers including labourers, prefabrication workers, and cranemen and stagers. In addition there are interviews with welders, foremen, welfare and safety officers, retired workers, and managers, and notes on trade disputes and the launch of a ship. Where possible the researchers used tape recorders in the field, but noise levels often made this impractical. Even when they could not make recordings the researchers placed a premium on capturing speech verbatim, writing extensive notes in the field, and transcribing these fully into their typed research notes. Only one-third of the men lived in Wallsend itself, where the yards were located, but most lived in nearby districts on either bank of the Tyne.

Isle of Sheppey (1978–1988), Pahl Papers, Isle of Sheppey Collection, UK Data Service, University of Essex

A massive collection of materials from Ray Pahl's ten years working on the organization of work (paid and unpaid) on the Isle of Sheppey. I have focused on transcriptions of taped interviews, including the ten pilot interviews from 1978–9, 58 interviews from the main study, and the remarkable series of nine interviews with the couple Pahl called Linda and Jim. These were digitized using the ABBYY12 OCR programme to allow full text analysis. In addition, UKDA digitized all the surviving tapes from the project; these included eighty-nine files from Sheppey household interviews (including the pilots and all but one of the Linda and Jim interviews). Interviews that had not been transcribed, or only partially transcribed, were listened to in full; others were used to explore ambiguities in the transcriptions, including questions of intonation and tone. There can be no doubt that reanalysis benefits from having access to the original recordings as well as researchers' transcriptions. The reanalysis also made use of miscellaneous research notes and also working papers written by Pahl and his colleague Claire Wallace, some of which contained extensive quoted material that had not survived in the archive. The interviews themselves were lengthy and were based around a series of loose topics rather than a structured survey. The pilot interviews and the interviews with Linda and Jim were particularly wide-ranging and exploratory, whereas the interviews for the main Household Work Strategies project tended to focus more directly on issues raised by the large quantitative social survey Pahl had already conducted on Sheppey. Indeed, these cases were selected as representative of different 'types' identified through preliminary analysis of the large random survey. Hence the fact that some were given quirky case identifiers like 'the urban peasant' and 'Bermondsey man', or shorthand codes like 'affwork' (affluent worker). In addition, I also read transcriptions of the fourteen interviews Pahl conducted with 'Linda' and her extended family in 1986, deposited with the UK Data Archive as 'Changing Sociological Construct of the Family, 1930–1986', SN: 4872.

Luton (1996), Poverty, Wealth and Citizenship Collection, UK Data Service, University of Essex

This collection consists of seventy-six transcribed interviews with workers from a wide variety of income groups who were asked about their attitudes to poverty, wealth, and social citizenship, and also about their reading habits. Of these, twenty-eight involved respondents working in Luton, approximately half of whom also lived in the town (mostly those on lower incomes). Thanks to improved mobility and more well-to-do respondents, this sample is geographically more dispersed than the Wallsend study, the only other project to be based on place of work rather than residence. The interviews tend to be between 5,000 and 10,000 words in length and follow a common format. Questions are open-ended, allowing a wide variety of responses. Interviews were recorded but only the transcriptions have been archived.

Tyneside women (2007–2008), From the Coalface to the Car Park Collection, UK Data Service, University of Essex

A deposited subsample of the interviews and focus groups conducted by Yvette Taylor and her researchers for an ESRC project on women's experiences of deindustrialization in the early twenty-first century. The collection includes transcriptions of twenty-five semi-structured, life-course interviews with women aged between 24 and 80, and also the transcriptions of three focus groups involving a total of seventeen women (two with Over 60s groups and one with a group of unpaid carers from the Newcastle district of Walker). These are drawn from a larger project involving five focus groups and more than seventy interviews, which forms the research base for Taylor's book *Fitting into Place?* (2012). Information about respondents' place of residence is taken from Taylor's book. The focus group with carers is disaggregated in the book, perhaps because there were follow-up interviews that have not been deposited. The criteria for selecting the deposited sample are not clear, but they are mostly the low numbered cases, suggesting no particular selection criteria were applied. Some sensitive material has been deleted from the transcriptions in preparation for deposit, including all identifying material. Most interview transcriptions contain between 7,000 and 11,000 words. Audio files are not available.

out, and thereby fully recognized, their centrality to the life of the pit village. But Grace's own moment of self-realization came later, when she went back to college to study part-time for a Fine Art degree. She graduated in 1993, the year the village pit closed, and for her final year show she created a memorialization of the pit community and its traditions, which nonetheless encapsulated her mixed feelings: 'I was still sort of glad that the pit was closing and that my son doesn't have to go down there.' In the process she came to realize that somehow she had always resisted being identified with the pit, that going to university had been about trying to get away from being me, at home in this mining community, being a woman in a mining community and all this lack of expectation and the confinement of being a woman in a mining community.' Grace explained how, scouring the beach for materials she could use in her project, she came to rethink her relationship with the community:

> being mature made me realise how, where I was and where I came from. And I became more proud of it. And I didn't mind the identity of it, and belonging to the mining community. Whereas I'd always sort of like struggled with it, self of not doing better than I had because so glory, I wanted to be a doctor, and I hadn't done better than fifteen and no qualifications.

Like Charlotte, Grace had come to feel a powerful sense of connection with her community. As she put it, with characteristic power, 'for all I'd gone away, like I said, to find me, I found me right here, in [Easington] [. . .] I belong to the mining community, [to] the strength of it.' But she had no illusions about the devastating consequences of the pit's closure. Like many long-established residents, she lamented how the village had changed since 1993, and blamed incomers drawn to the area by cheap, run-down colliery houses that had been bought up by private landlords and buy-to-let property projects. For Grace, Easington had become an area where 'you're neither one thing nor another' because of this influx of transient people who 'will never have their roots here'.

Similarly, for Diane, a local health worker in her early fifties who had grown up in the village, the closure of the pit really spelt the end of a vocation as we knew it, in [Easington]'. But she, and Mena, a pensioner whom I interviewed, herself, born and bred in the village, drew a parallels with life in Belfast, which was featuring prominently in British news bulletins at this time after a flare-up of brutal sectarian fighting across Leinster. Now in her nineties, Mena said she now felt very vulnerable waiting about the village because so many people had left to find work and been replaced by people who 'don't contribute to the community at all'. She complained about the influx of drug addicts or alcoholics or all sorts of people who lived by

NOTES

Introduction

1. Some passages from this chapter have previously appeared, in a different form, in Jon Lawrence, 'Individualism and community in historical perspective', in Shana Cohen, Christina Fuhr, and Jan-Jonathan Bock (eds), *Austerity, Community Action, and the Future of Citizenship in Europe* (Policy Press, Bristol, 2017), 239–54; and Jon Lawrence, 'The voice of the People? Re-reading the field-notes of classic post-war social science studies', in Mark Hailwood et al. (eds), *The Voices of the People: An Online Symposium* (2015), at https://manyheadedmonster.wordpress.com/voices-of-the-people/.
2. See Selina Todd, *Young Women, Work and Family in England, 1918–1950* (Oxford University Press, Oxford, 2005); and Selina Todd and Hilary Young, 'Baby-boomers to "Beanstalkers": Making the modern teenager in post-war Britain', *Cultural and Social History*, 9/3 (2012), 451–67.
3. David Vincent, *Privacy: A Short History* (Polity, Cambridge, 2016); Robert Roberts, *The Classic Slum: Salford Life in the First Quarter of the Century* (Manchester University Press, Manchester, 1971); E. Wight Bakke, *The Unemployed Man: A Social Study* (Nisbet & Co., London, 1933), ch. 5.
4. Zygmunt Bauman, *Liquid Modernity* (Polity, Cambridge, 2000).
5. Robert Putnam, *Bowling Alone: The Collapse and Revival of American Community* (Simon & Schuster, New York, 2000).
6. Sarah E. Igo, *The Averaged American: Surveys, Citizens, and the Making of a Mass Public* (Harvard University Press, Cambridge, MA, 2007). Arguably Mass-Observation's 'Worktown' project in Bolton represented the first sustained attempt at a full-blown British community study; see James Hinton, *The Mass Observers: A History, 1937–1949* (Oxford University Press, Oxford, 2013), and David Hall, *Work Town: The Astonishing Story of the 1930s Project that Launched Mass-Observation* (Weidenfeld & Nicolson, London, 2015); though see Hilda Jennings, *Brynmawr: A Study of a Distressed Area* (Allenson & Co., London, 1934).
7. Craig Calhoun, 'Community without propinquity revisited: Communications technology and the transformation of the urban public sphere', *Sociological Inquiry*, 68/3 (1998), 373–97.
8. Liz Spencer and Ray Pahl, *Rethinking Friendship: Hidden Solidarities Today* (Princeton University Press, Princeton, 2006).
9. Raymond Firth (ed.), *Two Studies of Kinship in London* (Athlone Press, London, 1956), 34.
10. Richard Hoggart, *The Uses of Literacy: Aspects of Working-Class Life* (1957; Penguin edn, London, 1981), 34–5; Bakke, *Unemployed Man*, 153–4; Melanie Tebbutt, *Women's Work? A Social History of 'Gossip' in Working-Class Neighbourhoods, 1880–1960* (Scolar, Aldershot, 1995), ch. 2; Ross McKibbin, *Classes and Cultures, England 1918–1951* (Oxford University Press, Oxford, 1998), 179–81, 204–5.
11. Jon Lawrence, 'Inventing the "traditional working class": A re-analysis of interview notes from Young and Willmott's *Family and Kinship in East London*', *Historical Journal*, 59/2 (2016), 567–93.

12. Deborah Cohen, *Family Secrets: Living with Shame from the Victorians to the Present Day* (Viking, London, 2013).
13. Stefan Ramsden, 'Remaking working-class community: Sociability, belonging and "affluence" in a small town, 1930–1980', *Contemporary British History*, 29/1 (2015), 1–26; Claire Langhamer, 'The meanings of home in postwar Britain', *Journal of Contemporary History*, 40 (2005), 341–62.
14. The methodological issues raised by reanalysing social-science testimony are discussed in the Appendix.
15. Eric Hobsbawm, *Worlds of Labour: Further Studies in the History of Labour* (Weidenfeld & Nicolson, London, 1984), chs 10 and 11; also Ross McKibbin, *Classes and Cultures*, ch. 4, esp. pp. 527–8, and Jon Lawrence, 'The British sense of class', *Journal of Contemporary History*, 35/2 (2000), 307–18.
16. D. L. LeMahieu, *A Culture for Democracy: Mass Communications and the Cultivated Mind in Britain Between the Wars* (Clarendon Press, Oxford, 1988).
17. See Jon Lawrence, 'Social-science encounters and the negotiation of difference in early 1960s England', *History Workshop Journal*, 77 (2014), 215–39; see also the important studies by Seth Koven, *Slumming: Sexual and Social Politics in Victorian London* (Princeton University Press, Princeton, 2004), and Mark Peel, *Miss Cutler and the Case of the Resurrected Horse: Social Work and the Story of Poverty in America, Australia and Britain* (University of Chicago Press, Chicago, 2012).
18. Mike Savage, *Identities and Social Change in Britain Since 1940: The Politics of Method* (Oxford University Press, Oxford, 2010).
19. For a sociological emphasis on listening, see Jane Elliott, *Using Narrative in Social Research: Qualitative and Quantitative Approaches* (Sage, London, 2005), ch. 2.
20. Mike Savage, 'Working-class identities in the 1960s: Revisiting the affluent worker study', *Sociology*, 39 (2005), 929–46, and Savage, *Identities and Social Change*; Selina Todd, 'Affluence, class and Crown Street: Reinvestigating the post-war working class', *Contemporary British History*, 22/4 (2008), 501–18; Florence Sutcliffe-Braithwaite, *Class, Politics, and the Decline of Deference in England, 1968–2000* (Oxford University Press, Oxford, 2018).
21. Raymond Williams, *The Long Revolution* (1961; Penguin edn, London, 1965), 64–70; also Raymond Williams, *Culture and Society, 1780–1950* (1958; Penguin edn, London, 1963).
22. Stuart Middleton, 'Raymond Williams's "structure of feeling" and the problem of democratic values in Britain, 1938–1961' (*Modern Intellectual History*, Feb. 2019), explores how this influence was mediated through Williams's engagement with the anthropology of Ruth Benedict.
23. e.g. James Hinton, *Nine Wartime Lives: Mass-Observation and the Making of the Modern Self* (Oxford University Press, Oxford, 2010), and *Seven Lives from Mass Observation: Britain in the Late Twentieth Century* (Oxford University Press, Oxford, 2016); William M. Reddy, *The Navigation of Feeling: A Framework for the History of Emotions* (Cambridge University Press, Cambridge, 2001).
24. For an overview of the community studies tradition, see Graham Crow and Graham Allan, *Community Life: An Introduction to Local Social Relations* (Harvester Wheatsheaf, Hemel Hempstead, 1994); for a critical introduction to the concept of 'community', see Gerard Delanty, *Community*, Key Ideas series (Routledge, London, 2003).
25. Robert S. Lynd and Helen Merrell Lynd, *Middletown: A Study in American Culture* (Harcourt Brace, New York, 1929); Robert S. Lynd and Helen Merrell Lynd, *Middletown in Transition: A Study in Cultural Conflicts* (Harcourt Brace, New York, 1937); Sarah E. Igo, *The Averaged American: Surveys, Citizens, and the Making of a Mass Public* (Harvard University Press, Cambridge, MA, 2007).

26. Lawrence, 'Inventing'.
27. Margaret Stacey, 'The myth of community studies', *British Journal of Sociology*, 20/2 (1969), 134–47; Colin Bell and Howard Newby, *Community Studies: An Introduction to the Sociology of the Local Community* (George Allen & Unwin, London, 1971); for an overview, see Anthony P. Cohen, *The Symbolic Construction of Community* (Ellis Horwood, Chichester, 1985), and Savage, *Identities and Social Change*, ch. 6.
28. Ray Pahl, 'Are all communities communities in the mind?', *Sociological Review*, 53/4 (2005), 621–40.
29. R. E. Pahl, *Divisions of Labour* (Blackwell, Oxford, 1984).
30. UK Data Archive, Essex, C. D. Wallace and R. E. Pahl (2004), *Social and Political Implications of Household Work Strategies, 1978–1983* [data collection], UK Data Service, SN: 4876 (http://doi.org/10.5255/UKDA-SN-4876-1) [Pahl Papers, Isle of Sheppey Collection].
31. Michael Young, 'A Study of the Extended Family in East London' (London University, PhD Thesis [LSE Library], 1955); Michael Young and Peter Willmott, *Family and Kinship in East London* (Routledge & Kegan Paul, London, 1957).
32. Lise Butler, 'Michael Young, the Institute of Community Studies and the politics of kinship', *Twentieth-Century British History*, 26 (2015), 203–24; Bishopsgate Institute, London, Ruskin Papers, RS1/301–6, 'Survey on Social and Political Attitudes in Stevenage and Clapham, 1959–1960'.
33. UK Data Archive, Essex, J. H. Goldthorpe and D. Lockwood (2010), *Affluent Worker in the Class Structure, 1961–1962* [data collection], UK Data Service, SN: 6512 (http://dx.doi.org/10.5255/UKDA-SN-6512-1); John H. Goldthorpe et al., *The Affluent Worker in the Class Structure*, 3 vols. (Cambridge University Press, Cambridge, 1968–9).
34. Modern Records Centre, University of Warwick, Shipbuilding Workers on Tyneside: Research Papers of Professor Richard K. Brown, 'Qualidata: Shipbuilding workers' (MSS.371/shipbuilding workers).
35. UK Data Archive, Essex, H. Dean and M. Melrose (1999), *Poverty, Wealth and Citizenship: A Discursive Interview Study and Newspaper Monitoring Exercise, 1996* [computer file], UK Data Service, SN: 3995 (http://dx.doi.org/10.5255/UKDA-SN-3995-1).
36. For a fuller discussion of each project's methodology, its archival traces, and how these have been reanalysed for this project, see the Appendix, which also discusses the procedures followed to preserve respondents' anonymity.
37. Goldthorpe and Lockwood, SN: 6512, LHI 083 (interviewer M7's comment).
38. Richard Sennett and Jonathan Cobb, *The Hidden Injuries of Class* (Vintage, New York, 1973).
39. Grayson Perry, *The Vanity of Small Differences* (Hayward Publishing, London, 2013); and the three-part television series *All in the Best Possible Taste with Grayson Perry* (Channel 4, 2012).
40. See esp. Pierre Bourdieu, *Distinction: A Social Critique of the Judgement of Taste*, trans. Richard Nice (Routledge, London, 1984), 169–225, and *The Logic of Practice*, trans. Richard Nice (Polity Press, Cambridge, 1990), 52–65.
41. Roberts, *Classic Slum*, chs 1–3.
42. *Saturday Night and Sunday Morning* (1960), dir. Karel Reisz, screenplay Alan Sillitoe; based on Sillitoe's 1958 novel of the same name.
43. Tebbutt, *Women's Work?*
44. Dolly Smith Wilson, 'A new look at the affluent worker: The good working mother in post-war Britain', *Twentieth-Century British History*, 17/2 (2006), 206–29.
45. Mike Savage, Gaynor Bagnall, and Brian Longhurst, *Globalization and Belonging* (Sage, London, 2005); Mike Savage, 'The politics of elective belonging', *Housing, Theory and Society*, 27/2 (2010), 115–35, and the response by María-Luisa Méndez, 'Elective

belonging, moral ownership claims and authenticity of place', *Housing, Theory and Society*, 27/2 (2010), 151–3.

46. Goldthorpe and Lockwood, SN: 6512, Luton Home Interview, 105 ('Carr'), pp. 1–2, 7.
47. Williams, *Culture and Society*, 289; see also his discussion in *The Long Revolution*, 378–9.
48. Savage, 'Working-class identities'; also Michael Young and Peter Willmott, 'Social grading by manual workers', *British Journal of Sociology*, 7/4 (1956), 337–45.
49. Lawrence, 'Workers' testimony'.
50. Mike Savage, 'Sociology, class and male manual work cultures', in John McIlroy, Nina Fisher, and Alan Campbell (eds.), *British Trade Unions and Industrial Politics*, ii. *The High Tide of Trade Unionism, 1964–1979* (Ashgate, Aldershot, 1999).
51. Jack Common, 'Pease-pudding men', in *Jack Common's Revolt Against an 'Age of Plenty'*, (Strongwords, Newcastle, 1980), 32–41, at 34 (first published in *The Adelphi*, vol. 10, July 1935).
52. Maurice Glasman et al. (eds), *The Labour Tradition and the Politics of Paradox* (Soundings eBooks, London, 2011); Rowenna Davis, *Tangled Up in Blue: Blue Labour and the Struggle for Labour's Soul* (Ruskin, London, 2011). Also Jon Cruddas (ed.), *One Nation Labour: Debating the Future* (LabourList ebook, London, 2013).
53. e.g. *The Independent*, 21 June 2016 ('In or out, this is what will happen to the Labour party after the EU referendum') and 23 Sept. 2016 ('Labour party faces mass exodus of members who voted for Brexit'); *The Guardian*, 7 Feb. 2017 ('If you think Corbyn's wrong on Labour's Brexit policy, voters say otherwise'). The analysis was not new; see James Bloodworth, 'Working-class voters and the "progressive" left: A widening chasm', *New Statesman*, 21 Aug. 2103.
54. David Runciman, 'How the education gap is tearing politics apart', *The Guardian*, 5 Oct. 2016; also David Runciman, 'A win for proper people? Brexit as a rejection of the networked world', *IPPR Juncture*, 23/1 (Summer 2016) at https://www.ippr.org/insights/ippr-progressive-review (last accessed 10 Jan. 2018).
55. David Goodhart, *The Road to Somewhere: The Populist Revolt and the Future of Politics* (C. Hurst & Co., London, 2017).
56. See Matthew J. Goodwin and Oliver Heath, 'The 2016 Referendum, Brexit and the left behind: An aggregate-level analysis of the result', *Political Quarterly*, 87/3 (2016), 323–32; Lorenza Antonucci et al., 'The malaise of the squeezed middle: Challenging the narrative of the "left behind" Brexiter', *Competition & Change*, 21/3 (2017), 211–29.
57. Geoffrey Evans and James Tilley, *The New Politics of Class: The Political Exclusion of the British Working Class* (Oxford University Press, Oxford, 2017), ch. 4.
58. Evans and Tilley, *The New Politics of Class*, 70–6, quoting *British Social Attitudes Surveys*, 1983–2015; and Jon Cruddas, Nick Pecorelli, and Jonathan Rutherford, *Labour's Future: Why Labour Lost in 2015 and How It Can Win Again* (One Nation Register, London, 2016), 18.
59. Alan Sillitoe, *Saturday Night and Sunday Morning* (1958; Pan, London, 1960), 120.
60. The Arctic Monkeys, *Whatever people say I am, that's what I'm not*, Music CD, Domino Recording Company, 2006; also NME, 6 Dec. 2006, where frontman Alex Turner discusses the inspiration of watching Albert Finney as Seaton in the 1960 film version: 'he says that line and the conviction with which he said it, it just rang a bell'.

Chapter 1

1. Tanya Evans, 'Secrets and lies: The radical potential of family history', *History Workshop Journal*, 71/1 (2011), 49–73.

2. Melanie Tebbutt, 'Imagined families and vanished communities: Memories of a working-class life in Northampton', *History Workshop Journal*, 73/1 (2012), 144–69; Alison Light, *Common People: The History of an English Family* (Fig Tree, London, 2014); Richard Benson, *The Valley: A Hundred Years in the Life of a Yorkshire Family* (Bloomsbury, London, 2014).

3. Robery Q. Gray, *The Labour Aristocracy in Victorian Edinburgh* (Clarendon, Oxford, 1976).

4. Chris Williams, *Capitalism, Community and Conflict: The South Wales Coalfield, 1898–1947* (University of Wales Press, Cardiff, 1998), 11–26.

5. Williams, *Capitalism, Community and Conflict*, 21–4; Steven Thompson, *Unemployment, Poverty and Health in Interwar South Wales* (University of Wales Press, Cardiff, 2006), 1–2, 13–44.

6. M. J. Daunton, *Progress and Poverty: An Economic and Social History of Britain, 1700–1850* (Oxford University Press, Oxford, 1995), 413–15.

7. M. J. Daunton (ed.), *Councillors and Tenants: Local Authority Housing in English Cities, 1919–1939* (Leicester University Press, Leicester, 1984), 8–15; M. J. Daunton, *A Property-Owning Democracy? Housing in Britain* (Faber & Faber, London, 1987), 26–30.

8. Mass-Observation [Anon.], *An Enquiry into People's Homes: A Report Prepared by Mass-Observation for the Advertising Service Guild* (John Murray, London, 1943), 181–2.

9. Peter Saunders, *A Nation of Home-Owners* (Unwin Hyman, London, 1990), 14–15; see also Annette O'Carroll, 'Tenements to bungalows: Class and the growth of home ownership before World War II', *Urban History*, 24/2 (1997), 221–41, esp. 238–41, and Peter Scott, *The Making of the Modern British Home: The Suburban Semi and Family Life between the Wars* (Oxford University Press, Oxford, 2013).

10. Matt Houlbrook, '"A pin to see the peepshow": Culture, fiction and selfhood in Edith Thompson's letters, 1921–1922', *Past & Present*, 207 (May 2010), 215–49; also Michael Saler, *As If: Modern Enchantment and the Literary Prehistory of Virtual Reality* (Oxford University Press, Oxford, 2012).

11. Selina Todd, *Young Women, Work and Family in England, 1918–1950* (Oxford University Press, Oxford, 2005).

12. For Bermondsey, see Raymond Firth and Judith Djamour, 'South Borough', in Raymond Firth (ed.), *Two Studies of Kinship in London* (Athlone Press, London, 1956), 45; for Bethnal Green, see Michael Young, 'A Study of the Extended Family in East London' (London University, PhD Thesis [LSE Library], 1955), 112–13, and Michael Young and Peter Willmott, *Family and Kinship in East London* (Routledge & Kegan Paul, London, 1957), 25.

13. On changing naming practices and taste more broadly, see Stanley Lieberson and Eleanor O. Bell, 'Children's first names: An empirical study of social taste', *American Journal of Sociology*, 98 (1992), 511–54; Stanley Lieberson, *A Matter of Taste: How Names, Fashion and Culture Change* (Yale University Press, New Haven, 2000).

14. 'Conservative Manifesto 1951', in F.W. S. Craig, *British General Election Manifestos, 1900–1974* (Macmillan, London, 1975), 172.

15. Peter Scott, 'Did owner-occupation lead to smaller families for interwar working-class households?', *Economic History Review*, 61/1 (2008), 99–124.

16. John Rule, 'Time, affluence and private leisure: The British working class in the 1950s and 1960s', *Labour History Review*, 66/2 (2001), 223–42; Selina Todd, 'Affluence, class and Crown Street: Reinvestigating the post-war working class', *Contemporary British History*, 22/4 (2008), 501–18.

17. Michael Young and Peter Willmott, *Family and Kinship in East London* (Routledge, London, 1957), 66–7, 90, 111–13; Raymond Firth (ed.), *Two Studies of Kinship in London* (Athlone Press, London, 1956), 60–1, noted the same pattern but stressed that distant kinship ties could be sustained when they were of mutual benefit. See also London School of

Economics Library, London, Sir Raymond Firth Papers, 3/1/14, 'Two Kinship Studies in London—Comments and Subsidary Notes': notes on 'Kinship Groups'.

18. Office for National Statistics, *Social Trends*, 40/1 (2010), 23 (figure 2.17); Office for National Statistics, *Births by Parents' Characteristics in England and Wales, 2015* (HMSO, London, 2016), 4.

19. Madge Dresser, 'Housing Policy in Bristol, 1919–1930', in M. J. Daunton (ed.), *Councillors and Tenants: Local Authority Housing in English Cities, 1919–1939* (Leicester University Press, Leicester, 1984), 155–216, at 195–7; also Rosamond Jevons and John Madge, *Housing Estates: A Study of Bristol Corporation Policy and Practice between the Wars* (University of Bristol, Bristol, 1946), 67–72.

20. On the wider phenomenon of working-class home ownership between the wars, see Scott, *Making of the Modern British Home*. Scott's primary focus is on new-build properties, both private and municipal.

21. Alan Bullock, *The Life and Times of Ernest Bevin*, i. *Trade Union Leader, 1881–1940* (Heinemann, London, 1960), chs 2–3.

22. Scott, *Making of the Modern Home*, 102–8.

23. Common, 'Pease-pudding men', 34. Common was specifically discussing the impact of trade unionism on railway workers' class status.

24. Light, *Common People*; Cassandra Phoenix and Andrew C. Sparkes, 'Being Fred: Big stories, small stories and the accomplishment of a positive ageing identity', *Qualitative Research*, 9/2 (2009), 219–36.

25. Robert Colls, 'When we lived in communities: Working-class culture and its critics', in Robert Colls and Richard Rodger (eds), *Cities of Ideas: Civil Society and Urban Governance in Britain, 1800–2000: Essays in Honour of David Reeder* (Ashgate, Aldershot, 2005), 283–307, at 283.

26. Analysis of 1911 Population Census Returns for St George (Bristol) enumeration districts 03 & 04, Gloucestershire.

27. On the shifting and performative aspects of 'respectability', see E. Wight Bakke, *The Unemployed Man: A Social Study* (Nisbet & Co., London, 1933), 156–9, and Peter Bailey, 'Will the real Bill Banks please stand up? Towards a role analysis of mid-Victorian working-class respectability', *Journal of Social History*, 12 (1979), 336–53.

28. Selina Todd, 'Phoenix Rising: Working-class life and urban reconstruction, *c*.1945–1967', *Journal of British Studies*, 54/3 (2015), 679–702.

29. See Stefan Ramsden, 'Remaking working-class community: Sociability, belonging and "affluence" in a small town, 1930–1980', *Contemporary British History*, 29/1 (2015), 1–26, and his *Working-Class Community in the Age of Affluence* (Routledge, Abingdon, 2017). For contemporary recognition of this mutability, see Colin Rosser and Christopher Harris, *The Family and Social Change: A Study of Family and Kinship in a South Wales Town* (Routledge & Kegan Paul, London, 1965), 220–4.

30. Surname distribution in 1881 using http://gbnames.publicprofiler.org/Surnames.aspx (accessed 31 July 2017), although this branch of the Strawbridge family have lived in Bristol for at least 250 years.

31. Timothy Jenkins, *Religion in English Everyday Life: An Ethnographic Approach* (Berghahn Books, New York, 1999), 119–37, 169–77, offers a powerful account of the continuing importance of place in Kingswood and Hanham.

32. David Goodhart, *The Road to Somewhere: The Populist Revolt and the Future of Politics* (C. Hurst & Co, London, 2017).

33. Goodhart, *Road to Somewhere*, 4.

34. On 'elective belonging', see Mike Savage, Gaynor Bagnall, and Brian Longhurst, 'Ordinary, Ambivalent and Defensive: Class Identities in the Northwest of England', *Sociology*, 35/4 (2001), 875–92; Mike Savage, Gaynor Bagnall, and Brian Longhurst, *Globalization and Belonging* (Sage, London, 2005), 54–77; and Mike Savage, 'The politics of elective belonging', *Housing, Theory and Society*, 27/2 (2010), 115–35.

35. Bob Jeffery, '"I probably would never move, but ideally I'd love to move this week": Class and residential experience, beyond elective belonging', *Sociology*, 52/2 (2018), 245–61, describes the 'prescribed belonging' of socially and economically marginalized working-class residents.

36. Chris Phillipson et al., *The Family and Community Life of Older People: Social Networks and Social Support in Three Urban Areas* (Routledge, London, 2001); J. H. Sheldon, *The Social Medicine of Old Age: Report of an Inquiry in Wolverhampton* (Oxford University Press, Oxford, 1948); Peter Townsend, *The Family Life of Old People* (1957; Pelican, London, 1963). For historical accounts, see Charlotte Greenhalgh, *Aging in Twentieth-Century Britain* (University of California Press, Berkeley and Los Angeles, 2018); Pat Thane, *Old Age in English History: Past Experiences, Present Issues* (Oxford University Press, Oxford, 2000).

37. John Barry, 'Overspill and the Impact of the Town Development Act, 1945–1982' (University of Cambridge, PhD Thesis, 2015).

38. Dale Southerton, 'Boundaries of "Us" and "Them": Class, mobility and identification in a new town', *Sociology*, 36/1 (2002), 171–93, paints a starker picture of status divisions in Yate.

Chapter 2

1. E. P. Hennock, 'The measurement of urban poverty: From the metropolis to the nation, 1880–1920', *Economic History Review*, 40 (1987), 208–27; Jon Lawrence, 'Class, "affluence" and the study of everyday life in Britain, c.1930–1964', *Cultural and Social History*, 10/2 (2013), 273–99.

2. See Geoffrey Field, *Blood, Sweat and Toil: Remaking the British Working Class, 1939–1945* (Oxford University Press, Oxford, 2011), ch. 2; Angus Calder, *The Myth of the Blitz* (Jonathan Cape, London, 1991).

3. Gareth Stedman Jones, 'The "cockney" and the nation, 1780–1988', in David Feldman and Gareth Stedman Jones (eds), *Metropolis—London: Histories and Representations Since 1800* (Routledge, London, 1989), 272–324.

4. Asa Briggs, *Michael Young: Social Entrepreneur* (Palgrave Macmillan, Basingstoke, 2001), 53; Anon., 'London under bombing', *Planning* (PEP Broadsheet), 169, 17 Feb. 1941.

5. UK Data Archives, Essex, P. Thompson, ESDS Qualidata (2014), *Pioneers of Social Research, 1996–2012* [data collection], 2nd edn, UK Data Service, SN: 6226 (http://dx.doi.org/10.5255/UKDA-SN-6226-3), Int013, Sir Raymond Firth [7 Jan. 2000], p. 104.

6. Firth Papers, 3/1/8, 'Kinship Report, Oct. 1947', p. 3; 3/1/13 [File 2], 'Researchers' details 1947' and 'Notes on Survey Organization'.

7. Firth Papers, 3/1/14, 'Two Kinship Studies in London—Comments and Subsidiary Notes': 'Bermondsey Kinship Study'. Margery Spring Rice, *Working-Class Wives: Their Health and Conditions* (Pelican, London, 1939).

8. Firth Papers, 3/1/11, 'Reports': 'Kin Study group' meetings, 28 Nov. and 12 Dec. 1947.

9. Jon Lawrence, 'Languages of place and belonging: Competing conceptions of "community" in mid-twentieth century Bermondsey, London', in Stefan Couperus and Harm Kaal (eds), *(Re)Constructing Communities in Europe, 1918–1968: Senses of Belonging Below, Beyond and Within the Nation-State* (Routledge, London, 2016), 19–44.

10. Lise Butler, 'Michael Young, the Institute of Community Studies and the politics of kinship', *Twentieth-Century British History*, 26 (2015), 203–24; Jon Lawrence, 'Inventing the "traditional working class": A re-analysis of interview notes from Young and Willmott's *Family and Kinship in East London*', *Historical Journal*, 589/2 (2016), 567–93. See also Alex Campsie, 'Mass-Observation, left intellectuals and the politics of everyday life', *English Historical Review*, 131 (Feb. 2016), 92–121.

11. Michael Young and Peter Willmott, *Family and Kinship in East London* (Routledge & Kegan Paul, London, 1957), pp. xiii, 87.

12. Ruth Glass and Maureen Frenkel, *A Profile of Bethnal Green* (Association for Planning and Regional Reconstruction, Report No. 39, London, Feb. 1946), 6 and 24. Their main arguments were reproduced for a wider audience in the essay 'How they live at Bethnal Green', *Contact*, 3 (1946), 'Britain Between East and West' (eds A. G. Weidenfeld and H. de Hastings), 36–43.

13. P. J. O. Self, 'Voluntary Organizations in Bethnal Green', in A. F. C. Bourdillon (ed.), *Voluntary Social Services: Their Place in the Modern State* (Methuen, London, 1945), 235–62, at 236; Young and Willmott, *Family and Kinship*, 87, 225.

14. For its importance, see Christian Topalov, '"Traditional working-class neighborhoods": An inquiry into the emergence of a sociological model in the 1950s and 1960s', *Osiris*, 18 (2003), 212–33; Nick Tiratsoo and Mark Clapson, 'The Ford Foundation and social planning in Britain: The case of the Institute of Community Studies and *Family and Kinship in East London*', in Giuliana Gemelli (ed.), *American Foundations and Large-scale Research* (CLUEB, Bologna, 2001), 201–17; Lawrence, 'Inventing', 568–9.

15. Raymond Firth (ed.), *Two Studies of Kinship in London* (Athlone Press, London, 1956).

16. Peter Malpass, *Housing, Philanthropy and the State: A History of the Guinness Trust* (Faculty of the Built Environment Occasional Papers, no. 2, University of the West of England, Bristol, n.d. [2000]), 17; James D. Stewart, *Bermondsey in War, 1939–1945* (Bermondsey & Rotherhithe Society, London, n.d. [1981?]), 19 and 41.

17. V. Leff and C. H. Blunden, *Riverside Story: The Story of Bermondsey and its People* (Bermondsey Borough Council, London, 1965), 59–60; Stewart, *Bermondsey in War*, 61. On Bethnal Green's war, see George F. Vale, *Bethnal Green's Ordeal* (Bethnal Green Council, London, n.d. [1945]).

18. Firth Papers, 3/1/13 [File 1], 1947 family reports, 'Thomas', p. 6, and 'Woodcock', p. 1; also 3/1/4, 'Occupations of locality', and 3/1/12, 'Scully' 1947 Family report, p. 1.

19. Firth Papers, 3/1/13 [File 1], 'Mrs Buckland' Interview notes, 10 Nov. 1947.

20. Firth Papers, 3/1/4, 'Politics', 26 Oct. 1947; 'Survey—attitudes to', p. 1.

21. Firth Papers, 3/1/1, *Field Notebook 1*, pp. 21–2.

22. Susan Pedersen, 'Gender, welfare and citizenship in Britain during the Great War', *American Historical Review*, 95 (1990), 983–1006.

23. Firth Papers, 3/1/8, 'Miscellaneous Notes and Reports', untitled paper [4 pp., 1947], p. 3; 3/1/11, 'Reports', 'Darts Report' [Geddes, 28 Oct. 1947].

24. On parental expectations as a motor of change, see Selina Todd, *Young Women, Work and Family in England, 1918–1950* (Oxford University Press, Oxford, 2005), and Selina Todd and Hilary Young, 'Baby-boomers to "Beanstalkers": Making the modern teenager in post-war Britain', *Cultural and Social History*, 9/3 (2012), 451–67.

25. Firth Papers, 3/1/4, 'Occupations' [Wright, 2 Nov. 1947], and 3/1/9, 'Ken Gorman', 5.

26. Firth Papers, 3/1/1, *Field Notebook II*, p. 5; cited in Firth (ed.), *Two Studies*, 48.

27. Firth (ed.), *Two Studies*, 48.

28. Firth Papers, 3/1/1, *Field Notebook 1*, p. 76.

29. Firth Papers, 3/1/1, *Field Notebook II*, p. 5.
30. Churchill Archive Centre, Cambridge, Michael Young Papers, Acc. 1577, 'Bethnal Green papers' [uncatalogued deposit, 2010], BG37b, 'Jefferys Family', pp. 3–4 (3 Aug. 1955).
31. Todd, *Young Women*, 209–14 (and 69–71 on education as 'escape' for some working-class girls); Selina Todd, *The People: The Rise and Fall of the Working Class, 1910–2010* (John Murray, London, 2014), 218–24; Todd and Young, 'Baby-boomers to "Beanstalkers"'.
32. Young Papers, Acc. 1577, BG44, 'Sartain family', p. 2 (10 July 1953).
33. Young Papers, Acc. 1577, BG44, 'Sartain family', pp. 2–3 (10 July 1953).
34. Firth (ed.), *Two Studies*, 34; Firth Papers, 3/1/1, *Field Notebook I*, p. 67.
35. Firth Papers, 3/1/1, *Field Notebook I*, p. 65, and *Field Notebook II*, pp. 4, 41–3, 56.
36. Firth Papers, 3/1/1, *Field Notebook I*, p. 67 (emphasis added).
37. Firth Papers, 3/1/4, 'Communal Help', pp. 1–2.
38. Firth Papers, 3/1/4, 'Communal Help', p. 2.
39. Nigel Henderson, *Photographs of Bethnal Green, 1949–1952* (Newstead Publishing, Nottingham, 1978), esp. 34, 36, 38, 40.
40. Phyllis Willmott, *Bethnal Green Journal, 1954–1955* (Institute of Community Studies, London, 2001), 50 [27 Jan. 1955].
41. Young Papers, Acc. 1577, BG39, 'Porter family', p. 1 (23 June 1953).
42. Young Papers, Acc. 1577, BG27, 'Heal Family', p. 2.
43. Firth Papers, 3/1/13 [File 1], 'Mrs Buckland', 28 Jan. 1959.
44. Firth Papers, 3/1/1, *Field Notebook I*, p. 85.
45. Firth Papers, 3/1/13 [File 1], 'Nicholson Family' 1947 Report, p. 1.
46. Firth Papers, 3/1/13a [File 1], 'Mrs Buckland', 28 Jan. 1959.
47. Young Papers, Acc. 1577, BG37b 'Jefferys Family', p. 1 (3 August 1955).
48. Young Papers, Acc. 1577, BG27, 'Heal Family', p. 2.
49. Young Papers, 'Debden Survey, 1953–1955', YUNG 1/5/1/1, Case D25, 'Maggs Family', 3 Oct. 1953, p. 1; also YUNG 1/5/1/2, Case D34, 'Ruck Family', 10 July 1953, p. 1.
50. Willmott, *Bethnal Green Journal*, 63 [18 Feb. 1955]. On this use of 'They' and 'Them', see Richard Hoggart, *The Uses of Literacy: Aspects of Working-Class Life* (1957; Penguin edn, London, 1981), ch. 3, '"Them" and "Us"'.
51. Willmott, *Bethnal Green Journal*, 63 [18 Feb. 1955].
52. In the 1950s sociologists mainly studied these processes of adaptation on new estates; see Leo Kuper, (ed.), *Living in Towns: Selected Research Papers in Urban Sociology* (Cresset Press, London, 1953) esp. 42–82; also University of Liverpool, *Neighbourhood and Community: An Enquiry into Social Relationships on Housing Estates in Liverpool and Sheffield* (University of Liverpool Press, Liverpool, 1954).
53. Anon., Mass-Observation, *An Enquiry into People's Homes: A Report Prepared by Mass-Observation for the Advertising Service Guild, the fourth of the 'CHANGE' Wartime Surveys* (John Murray, London, 1943), 205.
54. E. Wight Bakke, *The Unemployed Man: A Social Study* (Nisbet & Co, London, 1933), 153–4.
55. Young and Willmott, *Family and Kinship*, 85; see also Ross McKibbin, *Classes and Cultures, England 1918–1951* (Oxford University Press, Oxford, 1998), 181–3.
56. Firth Papers, 3/1/1, *Field Notebook I*, pp. 2 and 64–5.
57. Firth Papers, 3/1/1, *Field Notebook I*, p. 114; Firth (ed.), *Two Studies*, 26.
58. Mike Savage, 'Sociology, class and male manual work cultures', in John McIlroy, Nina Fisher, and Alan Campbell (eds.), *British Trade Unions and Industrial Politics*, ii. *The High Tide of Trade Unionism, 1964–1979* (1999).
59. Young Papers, Acc. 1577, BG26, 'Banks Family', pp. 3 and 5.

60. Young Papers, Acc. 1577, BG32, 'Kimber Family', pp. 4–5.
61. Young Papers, Acc. 1577, BG41, 'Quail Family', p. 3.
62. Firth Papers, 3/1/14, 'Family Co-operation' notes, 8 Dec. 1947. Although Judith Henderson records exchanges of fuel with neighbours during the big freeze: Henderson, *Photographs of Bethnal Green*, 36, 40 [15 Feb. and 13 Mar. 1947].
63. On the performative aspects of 'respectability', see Peter Bailey, 'Will the real Bill Banks please stand up? Towards a role analysis of mid-Victorian working-class respectability', *Journal of Social History*, 12 (1979), 336–53, and Alastair Reid, 'Intelligent artisans and aristocrats of labour: The essays of Thomas Wright', in J. M. Winter (ed.), *The Working Class in Modern British History: Essays in Honour of Henry Pelling* (Cambridge University Press, Cambridge, 1983), 171–96.
64. For uses of 'rough' as a marker of distinction, see Firth Papers, 3/2/2, Rotherhithe, '2nd Whist Drive notes', p. 1; 3/2/5, 'South Borough Case Papers, 1958–1959', "Smith", p. 4 [15 Dec. 1958]; Young Papers, Acc. 1577, BG44, 'Sartain family', p. 4 [10 July 1953]. For 'rough and ready' as self-definition, see Firth Papers, 3/1/11, 'Social Club Report' [Kaplan], 14 Nov. 1947; Young Papers, Acc. 1577, BG26, 'Banks Family', p. 9. On 'ordinariness', see Mike Savage, 'Working-class identities in the 1960s: Revisiting the affluent worker study', *Sociology*, 39 (2005), 929–46. For judgemental, stigmatizing uses of 'rough and ready' in twenty-first-century Nottingham, see Lisa Mckenzie, *Getting By: Estates, Class and Culture in Austerity Britain* (Policy, Bristol, 2014), 51 and 64–71.
65. See Martin Bulmer (ed.), *Neighbours: The Work of Philip Abrams* (Cambridge University Press, Cambridge, 1986).
66. Young Papers, Acc. 1577, BG43, 'Silverman Family', pp. 3–4.
67. Martin Bulmer, (ed.), *Neighbours: The Work of Philip Abrams* (Cambridge University Press, Cambridge, 1986), 50–1, notes the widespread tension 'between expressed and practised norms' on the question of 'visiting' without seeking to explain the 'contradiction'.
68. Young Papers, Acc. 1577, BG32, 'Kimber Family', p. 4; BG43, 'Silverman Family', p. 1.
69. Firth Papers, 3/2/1, 'Kinship Project', 'The Community' [draft report].
70. Firth Papers, 3/1/5, 'Structure of the Kin Universe'.
71. Firth Papers, 3/1/4, 'Buildings' [26 Oct. 1947], 2.
72. Firth Papers, 3/1/4, 'Religion' [26 Oct. 1947].
73. Calculated from Firth Papers, 3/2/8, 'Census Dec. 1957'.
74. Firth Papers, 3/2/5, 'South Borough Case Papers, 1958–1959', "Peters", p. 4 [14 Jan. 1959]. Rotherhithe is a district in the east of Bermondsey; on the historic distinctions between 'downtown' and Rotherhithe village, see http://russiadock.blogspot.co.uk/2015/02/rotherhithes-downtown-area.html (accessed 11 Feb. 2016).
75. For community as largely a retrospective myth, see Carolyn Steedman, 'State-sponsored autobiography', in Becky Conekin, Frank Mort, and Chris Waters (eds), *Moments of Modernity: Reconstructing Britain, 1945–1964* (River Oram Press, London, 1999), 41–54; Chris Waters, 'Autobiography, nostalgia and the changing practices of working-class selfhood', in George K. Behlmer and Fred M. Leventhal (eds.), *Singular Continuities: Tradition, Nostalgia, and Identity in Modern British Culture* (Stanford University Press, Stanford, CA, 2000), 178–95; for an emphasis on its contractual basis, see Joanna Bourke, *Working-Class Cultures in Britain, 1890–1960: Gender, Class and Ethnicity* (Routledge, London, 1994), ch. 5.
76. Robert Colls, 'When we lived in communities: Working-class culture and its critics', in Robert Colls and Richard Rodger (eds.), *Cities of Ideas: Civil Society and Urban Governance in Britain, 1800–2000: Essays in Honour of David Reeder* (Ashgate, Aldershot, 2005), 283–307.
77. Firth Papers, 3/1/2, *Field Notebook II*, p. 48; 3/1/4, 'Hop Picking', 21 Nov. 1947 [Scobie].

78. Young Papers, 'Debden Survey, 1953–1955', YUNG 1/5/1/2, Case D35 (Rawson), 25 Oct. 1955, p. 3.
79. Firth Papers, 3/1/11, 'Weddings', 26 Oct. 1947, [Ward]; 3/1/11, 'No title' [Royal Wedding], 21 Nov. 1947 [Richards].
80. Firth Papers, 3/1/11, 'Social Club report', [Little], 12 Nov. 1947.
81. Young Papers, Acc. 1577, BG36, 'Mountain Family', p. 7; Firth Papers, 3/1/7, 'Buckley Family', miscellaneous notes.
82. Firth (ed.), *Two Studies*, 12–21; Firth Papers, 3/1/1, *Field Notebook I*, pp. 89–93, 'Definition of kin groups'. See 'Appreciations of Sir Raymond Firth', *Anthropology Today*, 18/5 (Oct. 2002), 20–3.
83. Firth Papers, 3/1/1, *Field Notebook I*, pp. 12 and 17.
84. Firth Papers, 3/1/1, *Field Notebook I*, p. 18.
85. For a fuller discussion of these tensions, see Lawrence, 'Inventing'.
86. Young Papers, Acc. 1577, BG44, 'Sartain Family', p. 4.
87. Firth Papers, 3/1/13 [File 1], 'Corbett Family', 1947 report, p. 3.
88. Young Papers, Acc. 1577, BG49, 'Whiteside Family', p. 1; also BG46, 'Threader Family', p. 1, and Firth 3/1/1, *Field Notebook I*, p. 13.
89. Firth Papers, 3/1/13 [File 1], 'Corbett Family', 1947 report, pp. 3–4.
90. See Adam Kuper, *Anthropology and Anthropologists: The Modern British School* (3rd edn, Routledge, London, 1996), 123, 128. Firth was most famous for emphasizing the importance of economics to anthropological analysis.
91. Firth Papers, 3/1/13 [File 1], 'Corbett Family', 1947 report, pp. 4–5; and 3/2/5, 'South Borough Case Papers, 1958–1959', "Milton", p. 3 [2 Oct. 1958] and "Church", p. 7 [9 July 1959]; also Young Papers, Acc. 1577, BG49, 'Whiteside Family', p. 6.
92. Firth Papers, 3/1/13 [File 1], 'Woodcock Family', 17 Nov. 1958.
93. Firth Papers, 3/1/14, 'Sibling relations', 14 Nov. 1947, cited in Firth (ed.), *Two Studies*, 36.
94. Firth Papers, 3/1/13 [File 1], 'Buckley Family', 5 Dec. 1958.
95. Young Papers, Acc. 1577, BG42, 'Rushton Family', p. 3 (and form).
96. Young Papers, Acc. 1577, BG38, 'Nulli Family', p. 1.
97. Young Papers, Acc. 1577, BG49, 'Whiteside Family', p. 1.
98. Firth Papers, 3/1/13 [File 1], 'Henderson Family', 3 Feb. 1959.
99. Firth Papers, 3/1/13 [File 1], 'Henderson Family', 3 Feb. 1959.
100. Young Papers, Acc. 1577, BG44, 'Sartain Family', p. 4.
101. Firth Papers, 3/1/13 [File 1], 'Buckley Family', 31 Oct. and 7 Nov. 1958, 28 Jan. 1959; 3/1/1, *Field Notebook I*, p. 14.
102. Young Papers, Acc. 1577, BG35 'Shipway Family', p. 2; cited in Young and Willmott, *Family and Kinship*, 33.
103. Young Papers, Acc. 1577, BG35 'Shipway Family', p. 2. It should be stressed that other families maintained warm relations with relatives who moved away or experienced social mobility; see BG28, 'Hadrian family', p. 2, and BG29, 'Hinton Family', p. 1.
104. Firth Papers, 3/1/13 [File 1], 'Woodcock Family', 1947 report, pp. 2, 8.
105. Firth Papers, 3/1/13 [File 1], 'Woodcock Family', visits 11, 17, and 24, Nov. 1958.
106. Laura King, *Family Men: Fatherhood and Masculinity in Britain, 1914–1960* (Oxford University Press, Oxford, 2015).
107. Elizabeth Wilson, *Only Halfway to Paradise: Women in Post-War Britain, 1945–1968* (London, 1980), 64–5; Ann Oakley, *Father and Daughter: Patriarchy, Gender and Social Science* (Policy Press, Bristol, 2014), 58; also Carolyn Steedman, *Landscape for a Good Woman: A Story of Two Lives* (Virago, London, 1986), 19.

108. Willmott, *Bethnal Green Journal*, 13 [15 Oct. 1954].

109. Butler, 'Michael Young', 215–17; John Bowlby, *Maternal Care and Mental Health* (World Health Organization, Geneva, 1951).

110. Population census figures for 1911, 1951, and 1961 from www.visionofbritain.org.uk.

111. Dudley E. Baines and Paul A. Johnson, 'In search of the "traditional" working class: Social mobility and occupational continuity in interwar London', *Economic History Review*, 2nd ser., 52/4 (1999), 692–713.

112. Young Papers, Acc. 1577, BG45, 'Sarson Family', pp. 1–2 and form.

113. Firth Papers, 3/2/5, 'South Borough Case Papers, 1958–1959', "Smith", summary, and pp. 1–2 [1 and 8 Sept. 1958].

114. Firth Papers, 3/1/9, 'Munro', Notes on 'Ken Gorman' [7pp], p. 5.

115. Firth Papers, 3/1/4, 'Attitudes to Survey', 7 Nov. 1947 [BEW], p. 2.

116. Firth Papers, 3/1/4, 'Attitudes to Survey', 7 Jan. 1947 [MF], p. 2; 22 Jan. 1948 [KLL]; 3/1/14, 'Two Kinship Studies', subsidiary notes.

117. Firth Papers, 3/1/13 [File 1], 'Warden Family', 11 Nov. 1958.

118. Firth Papers, 3/2/8, 'Census Dec. 1957'; nearly a quarter of the new tenancies (thirty-one) had been assigned to people moving from north and north-west London, many with characteristically Irish surnames.

119. For anti-Irish comments, see Firth Papers, 3/1/13 [File 1], 'Bower Family', 14 Nov. 1958, complaining of how 'they spread', and 'Goodge Family', 22 Jan. 1959, calling them 'Clannish'; more neutrally, 'Dyer Family', 18 Nov. 1958, called them 'nice enough people', and 'Warden Family', 11 Nov. 1958, acknowledged they were good tenants.

120. Firth Papers, 3/2/8, 'Census Dec. 1957', 107 tenancies (39 per cent) had begun after Dec. 1952; see Tables 3 and 4 for details.

121. Young Papers, Acc. 1577, BG26, 'Banks Family', p. 7.

122. Young and Willmott, *Family and Kinship*, 81. In addition, the population of the borough continued to fall through the 1950s, declining by 19.3 per cent between 1951 and 1961 to 47,078. It had stood at 108,194 in 1931; General Register Office, *Census 1961 England and Wales, County Report London* (HMSO, London, 1963), 1 (table 2).

123. James H. Robb, *Working-Class Anti-Semite: A Psychological Study in a London Borough* (Tavistock, London, 1954), pp. xiii, 2–5; see also Glass and Frenkel, *Profile*, 14, 17–18.

124. Young and Willmott, *Family and Kinship*, 86–7, 225; Michael Young, 'Reflections on researching *Family and Kinship in East London*: Michael Young interviewed by Paul Thompson', *International Journal of Social Research Methodology*, 7/1 (2004), 35–44 at 36–7; Geoff Dench, Kate Gavron, and Michael Young, *The New East End: Kinship, Race and Conflict* (Profile, London, 2006). On the Tavistock Clinic and its offshoot, see Henry V. Dicks, *Fifty Years of the Tavistock Clinic* (Routledge, London, 1970), and http://www.moderntimesworkplace.com/archives/ericsess/tavis1/tavis1.html (last accessed 28 Apr. 2017).

125. Willmott, *Bethnal Green Journal*, 58–9 [9 Feb. 1955].

126. For examples exploring the stigmatiszation of internal migrants as 'outsiders', see Norbert Elias and John L. Scotson, *The Established and the Outsiders: A Sociological Enquiry into Community Problems* (1965; 2nd edn, Sage, London, 1994); Selina Todd, 'Affluence, class and Crown Street: Reinvestigating the post-war working class', *Contemporary British History*, 22/4 (2008), 501–18 at 511–12; Ben Rogaly and Becky Taylor, *Moving Histories of Class and Community: Identity, Place and Belonging in Contemporary England* (Palgrave Macmillan, Basingstoke, 2009), esp. 39–50.

127. Young Papers, Acc. 1577, BG39, 'Porter Family', p. 1 (3 June 1953).

128. Firth Papers, 3/1/4, 'Attitudes to Survey' (7 Oct. 1947, BEW); 3/1/11, Social Club Report, 21 Nov. 1947 (KL), p. 3. Kenneth Little, *Negroes in Britain: A Study of Racial Relations in English Society* (Kegan Paul, London, 1947).

129. Firth Papers, 3/1/1, *Field Notebook 1*, pp. 127 and 130.

130. Lawrence, 'Inventing', *passim*.

131. Young Papers, Acc. 1577, BG28, 'Hadrian Family', p. 4.

132. Young Papers, Acc. 1577, BG31 'Instone Family', p. 3 (Oct. 1953).

133. Firth Papers, 3/1/13 [File 1], 'Dyer Family', 18 Nov. 1958.

134. Firth Papers, 3/1/13 [File 1], 'Buckland Family', 28 Jan. 1959.

135. Firth Papers, 3/1/13 [File 1], 'Bower Family', 14 Nov. 1958; 'Dyer Family', 18 Nov. 1958.

136. Firth papers, 3/1/12, Notes on Scully Family, 2nd draft, pp. 2–3.

137. Firth 3/1/1, *Field Notebook I*, pp. 52–3; for his elaboration of these differences see Firth (ed.), *Two Studies*, 57 (based on this case).

138. Firth Papers, 3/2/2, Rotherhithe, '2nd Whist Drive Report', p. 1.

139. Firth Papers, 3/2/2, Rotherhithe, 'R.C. Community', p. 1.

140. Firth Papers, 3/2/2, Rotherhithe, '6th Whist Drive Report', p. 1.

141. Jeanette Winterson, *Oranges Are Not the Only Fruit* (Pandora, London, 1985). For discussions of working-class choice and resistance to the fixity of place before the supposed age of individualism, see Mass-Observation, *An Enquiry into People's Homes* (John Murray, London, 1943), pp. xxi–xxii, 190–8, 205–12; Rogaly and Taylor, *Moving Histories*, 15–18; Selina Todd, 'Phoenix Rising: Working-Class Life and Urban Reconstruction, c.1945–1967', *Journal of British Studies*, 54/3 (2015), 679–702.

142. Firth Papers, 3/2/5, 'South Borough Case Papers, 1958–1959'; the principal researcher was a young graduate called Miss H. Stocks.

143. The Town Development Act, under which Thetford sought to grow its population and industry, was passed in 1952. For its implementation and effects, see John Barry, 'Overspill and the Impact of the Town Development Act, 1945–1982' (University of Cambridge, PhD Thesis, 2015); Anon., *Thetford Historic Environment Assessment, Part 1* (Breckland Council, Thetford, 2009), 11–13, 23.

144. See Young and Willmott, *Family and Kinship*, 39–40. Some women explained churching in terms of pleasing their mothers, others believed it was a way to give thanks for a new life; contrary to Young and Willmott, no one suggested it was necessary to 'purify' the unclean mother.

145. Firth Papers, 3/2/5, 'South Borough Case Papers, 1958–1959', "Holden", pp. 1–6.

146. A point Richard Hoggart had stressed in his 1957 study *The Uses of Literacy*, esp. ch. 2.

147. Elizabeth Bott, *Family and Social Network: Roles, Norms and External Relationships in Ordinary Urban Families* (Tavistock Publications, London, 1957), 57–73 (the Newbolts). On Bott, see Mike Savage, 'Elizabeth Bott and the formation of modern British sociology', *Sociological Review*, 4/56 (2008), 579–605.

148. Firth Papers, 3/2/5 'South Borough Case Papers, 1958–1959', "Peters", 1–2 [1 and 5 Sept. 1958].

149. Firth Papers, 3/2/5 'South Borough Case Papers, 1958–1959', "Burns", pp. 1–5 and "Church", pp. 1–8.

150. Hoggart, *Uses of Literacy*, 35; Young and Willmott, *Family and Kinship*, 85.

151. Firth Papers, 3/2/5, 'South Borough Case Papers, 1958–1959', "Church", 1–7.

152. For a classic example, see the 1958 BBC Eye To Eye documentary *The More We are Together* on the Gladden family, where mother, father, and four married daughters live closely interwoven lives in the same Bethnal Green street.

153. Firth Papers, 3/2/5, 'South Borough Case Papers, 1958–1959', "Burns", 1–5.
154. Firth Papers, 3/2/5, 'South Borough Case Papers, 1958–1959', "Davidson", 1–6.
155. See Pat Starkey, *Families and Social Workers: The Work of Family Service Units, 1940–1985* (Liverpool University Press, Liverpool, 2000); John Welshman, 'In search of the "problem family": Public health and social work in England and Wales, 1940–1970', *Social History of Medicine*, 9 (1996), 447–65.
156. Firth Papers, 3/2/5, 'South Borough Case Papers, 1958–1959', "Murray", pp. 1–7.
157. Firth Papers, 3/2/5, 'South Borough Case Papers, 1958–1959', "Moran", pp. 1–2.
158. Firth Papers, 3/2/5, 'South Borough Case Papers, 1958–1959', "Milton", pp. 1–11 and summary.

Chapter 3

1. Mark Clapson, *Invincible Green Suburbs, Brave New Towns: Social Change and Urban Dispersal in Postwar England* (Manchester University Press, Manchester, 1998), 47.
2. Michael Young, 'A Study of the Extended Family in East London' (London University, PhD Thesis [LSE], 1955), 168, 242.
3. Young and Willmott, *Family and Kinship*, 170.
4. Young Papers, 'Debden Survey, 1953–1955', YUNG 1/5/1/1 and YUNG 1/5/1/2.
5. Stevenage Survey, RS1/301–6. In fact the team carried out two separate surveys between November 1959 and January 1960. Variations between the two surveys mean that only a minority of questions were asked of all 147 respondents. In 1960 Peter Willmott organized another, larger Stevenage survey in collaboration with the Birmingham School of Architecture focused on questions of design and urban planning: Peter Willmott, 'Housing density and town design in a new town: A pilot study at Stevenage', *Town Planning Review*, 33/2 (1962), 115–27. The records of this survey, which involved interviews with 379 new town residents, have not been traced.
6. Alan A. Jackson, *Semi-Detached London: Suburban Development, Life and Transport, 1900–1939* (Allen & Unwin, London, 1973); J. W. R. Whitehand and Christine M. H. Carr, 'England's interwar suburban landscapes: Myth and reality', *Journal of Historical Geography*, 25/4 (1999), 483–501.
7. See Standish Meacham, *Regaining Paradise: Englishness and the Early Garden City Movement* (Yale University Press, New Haven, 1998); J. B. Cullingworth, *Environmental Planning, 1939–1969*, iii. *New Towns Policy* (HMSO, London, 1979); Clapson, *Invincible Green Suburbs*, ch. 2; and Andrew Homer, 'Planned communities: The social objectives of the British new towns, 1946–1965', in Lawrence Black (eds), *Consensus or Coercion? The State, the People and Social Cohesion in Post-War Britain* (New Clarion, Cheltenham, 2001), 125–35.
8. Ivor H. Seeley, *Planned Expansion of Country Towns* (Geo. Godwin, London, 1968); Cullingworth, *Environmental Planning*, ch. 9; John Richard Barry, 'Overspill and the Impact of the Town Development Act, 1945–1982' (University of Cambridge, PhD Thesis, 2015).
9. For a classic (and pessimistic) account of this problem, see Norbert Elias and John L. Scotson, *The Established and the Outsiders: A Sociological Enquiry into Community Problems* (1965; 2nd edn, Sage, London, 1994), based on fieldwork conducted *c*.1960 in a Leicestershire township which remained poorly integrated after a rapid influx of newcomers beginning in the 1930s.
10. Young Papers, 'Debden Survey, 1953–1955', YUNG 1/5/1/1, Case D25 (Maggs), 3 Oct. 1953, p. 2; YUNG 1/5/1/2, Case D35 (Rawson), 3 July 1953, p. 1.

11. Willmott, 'Housing density', 124–6; Anthony Alexander, *Britain's New Towns: Garden Cities to Sustainable Communities* (Routledge, London, 2009), 96.

12. Homer, 'Planned communities'; Peter Willmott, 'East Kilbride and Stevenage: Some social characteristics of a Scottish and an English new town', *Town Planning Review*, 34/4 (1964), 307–16 at 309.

13. Notably J. B. Cullingworth, 'Social implications of overspill: The Worsley social survey', *Sociological Review*, NS 8/1 (1960), 77–96; Nicholas Deakin and Clare Ungerson, *Leaving London: Planned Mobility and the Inner City* (Heinemann, London, 1977), ch. 8; Clapson, *Invincible Green Suburbs*; Mark Clapson, 'The suburban aspiration in England since 1919', *Contemporary British History*, 14/1 (2000), 151–73.

14. Young and Willmott, *Family and Kinship*, 127 and 135.

15. Madeleine Davis, 'Arguing affluence: New Left contributions to the socialist debate, 1957–1963', *Twentieth-Century British History*, 23/4 (2012), 496–528; Stuart Middleton, '"Affluence" and the Left in Britain, c.1958–1974', *English Historical Review*, 129 (2014), 107–38.

16. Young and Willmott, *Family and Kinship*, 127 and also 134–6.

17. Young and Willmott, *Family and Kinship*, 134.

18. Young Papers, 'Debden Survey, 1953–1955', YUNG 1/5/1/2, Case D35 (Rawson), 3 July 1953, p. 3.

19. Young Papers, 'Debden Survey, 1953–1955', YUNG 1/5/1/1, Case D25 (Maggs), 3 Oct. 1953, p. 4.

20. Interwar studies of council estates often placed considerable emphasis on such conflicts, arguing that they were the main reason why better-off tenants moved away, e.g. Rosamond Jevons and John Madge, *Housing Estates: A Study of Bristol Corporation Policy and Practice between the Wars* (University of Bristol, Bristol, 1946), based on a survey conducted in 1938.

21. Young Papers, 'Debden Survey, 1953–1955', YUNG 1/5/1/1, Case D25 (Maggs), 3 Oct. 1953, p. 2.

22. Young Papers, 'Debden Survey, 1953–1955', YUNG 1/5/1/1, Case D25 (Maggs), 3 Oct. 1953, pp. 2–3.

23. Young Papers, 'Debden Survey, 1953–1955', YUNG 1/5/1/2, Case D37 (Usher), 1 Nov. 1955, p. 1 (although since the family's difficulties had apparently been primarily financial the increased income must also have helped alleviate her worries).

24. Young Papers, 'Debden Survey, 1953–1955', YUNG 1/5/1/2, Case D28 (Prince), 9 June 1953, p. 1.

25. Young Papers, 'Debden Survey, 1953–1955', YUNG 1/5/1/2, Case D28 (Prince), 22 Sept 1955, p. 1.

26. Young Papers, 'Debden Survey, 1953–1955', YUNG 1/5/1/2, Case D28 (Prince), 9 June 1953, p. 1.

27. Young Papers, 'Debden Survey, 1953–1955', YUNG 1/5/1/2, Case D28 (Prince), 22 Sept. 1955, p. 1.

28. Young Papers, 'Debden Survey, 1953–1955', YUNG 1/5/1/1, Case D24 (Minton), 23 Sept. 1955, p. 1.

29. Young and Willmott, *Family and Kinship*, 103–5.

30. Young Papers, 'Debden Survey, 1953–1955', YUNG 1/5/1/2, Case D35 (Rawson), 3 July 1953, p. 1.

31. Young Papers, 'Debden Survey, 1953–1955', YUNG 1/5/1/2, Case D35 (Rawson), 25 Oct. 1955, p. 1 and 1 Nov. 1955, pp. 3–4.

32. e.g. Young Papers, 'Debden Survey, 1953–1955', YUNG 1/5/1/2, Case D27 (Painswick), 1953 Form. See Richard Hoggart, *The Uses of Literacy*, 35, 37–9 and his *Everyday Language and Everyday Life* (Transaction, Brunswick, NJ, 2003), 59–60.

33. Mark Roodhouse, *Black Market Britain, 1939–1955* (Oxford University Press, Oxford, 2013); Ina Zweiniger-Bargielowska, *Austerity in Britain: Rationing, Controls and Consumption, 1939–1955* (Oxford University Press, Oxford, 2000).

34. Young Papers, 'Debden Survey, 1953–1955', YUNG 1/5/1/2, Case D35 (Rawson), 3 July 1953 visit, p. 2; 1 Nov. 1955, p. 5.

35. Young Papers, 'Debden Survey, 1953–1955', YUNG 1/5/1/1, Case D24 (Minton), 16 Apr. 1953, p. 1.

36. Young Papers, 'Debden Survey, 1953–1955', YUNG 1/5/1/2, Case D27 (Painswick), 28 May 1953, p. 3.

37. Young Papers, 'Debden Survey, 1953–1955', YUNG 1/5/1/2, Case D28 (Prince), 15 Oct. 1955, p. 1.

38. Young Papers, 'Debden Survey, 1953–1955', YUNG 1/5/1/2, Case D35 (Rawson), 1 Nov. 1955, pp. 1–2.

39. Young Papers, 'Debden Survey, 1953–1955', YUNG 1/5/1/2, Case D36 (Sandeman), 11 June 1953, p. 1.

40. Young Papers, 'Debden Survey, 1953–1955', YUNG 1/5/1/1, Case D14 (Damson), 1953 report, pp. 2–3, and 1953 Summary.

41. For powerful accounts of the stigmas that would subsequently cluster around social housing, see Lynsey Hanley, *Estates: An Intimate History* (Granta, London, 2007). As in the 1930s, the shift from general needs to 'slum clearance' housing policies played its part in this process: Rogaly and Taylor, *Moving Histories*, ch. 2, and Ben Jones, *The Working-Class in Mid Twentieth-century England: Community, Identity and Social Memory* (Manchester University Press, Manchester, 2012), ch. 3.

42. Young Papers, 'Debden Survey, 1953–1955', YUNG 1/5/1/1, Case D14 (Damson), [17?] Nov. 1955, p. 1.

43. Young Papers, 'Debden Survey, 1953–1955', YUNG 1/5/1/1, Case D14 (Damson), 1953 report, pp. 1, 3 (later, on the 1955 Form [p. 8], Mr Damson reported being 'C. of E.' and none of the names in his family tree suggested Jewish heritage).

44. Young Papers, 'Debden Survey, 1953–1955', YUNG 1/5/1/1, Case D14 (Damson), 1953 report, p. 2; [17?] Nov. 1955, p. 2; 1955 Form, p. 7. On the importance of women's networks creating a sense of 'community' on new estates, see Mark Clapson, 'Working-class women's experiences of moving to new housing estates in England since 1919', *Twentieth-Century British History*, 10/3 (1999), 345–65.

45. Young Papers, 'Debden Survey, 1953–1955', YUNG 1/5/1/1, Case D12 (Barnes), 1953 Note and 1953 Report, p. 1; partly cited in Young and Willmott, *Family and Kinship*, 112.

46. Young Papers, 'Debden Survey, 1953–1955', YUNG 1/5/1/2, Case D34 (Ruck), 1955 visit report, pp. 1–2.

47. Young Papers, 'Debden Survey, 1953–1955', YUNG 1/5/1/2, Case D34 (Ruck), 10 July 1953, p. 1; 1955 visit report, p. 2.

48. Young Papers, 'Debden Survey, 1953–1955', YUNG 1/5/1/2, Case D27 (Painswick), 28 May 1953, p. 1; Nov. 1955, p. 1.

49. Young Papers, 'Debden Survey, 1953–1955', YUNG 1/5/1/2, Case D27 (Painswick), 25 Oct. 1955, p. 1.

50. Young Papers, 'Debden Survey, 1953–1955', YUNG 1/5/1/2, Case D34 (Ruck), 1953 Form.

51. Young Papers, 'Debden Survey, 1953–1955', YUNG 1/5/1/1, Case D12 (Barnes), 1 Apr. 1953, p. 1; 1955 Report, p. 1.
52. Lorna Sage, *Bad Blood* (Fourth Estate, London, 2000), 97–8.
53. Young Papers, 'Debden Survey, 1953–1955', YUNG 1/5/1/2, Case D29 (Paige), 1 Nov. 1955, p. 1.
54. Young Papers, 'Debden Survey, 1953–1955', YUNG 1/5/1/2, Case D37 (Usher), 1 Nov. 1955, p. 1.
55. Young Papers, 'Debden Survey, 1953–1955', YUNG 1/5/1/1, Case D24 (Minton), 23 Sept. 1955, 1–3.
56. There was a constituency of Hertford and Stevenage between 1974 and 1983. The 1959 election saw the intervention of a Liberal candidate who secured 8,481 votes (13.2 per cent). Samuel's survey suggested that, unusually for the 1950s, Liberal intervention may have disproportionately hit Labour among Stevenage voters.
57. On the central importance of perceptions of economic competency to Conservative success, see Andrew Taylor, 'Speaking to Democracy: The Conservative Party and Mass Opinion from the 1920s to the 1950s', in Stuart Ball and Ian Holliday (eds), *Mass Conservatism: The Conservatives and the Public since the 1880s* (Frank Cass, London, 2002), 78–99, at 94.
58. Stevenage Survey, RS1/302, 'Eric Forrest', pp. 2–3; see Jon Lawrence, *Electing Our Masters: The Hustings in British Politics from Hogarth to Blair* (Oxford University Press, Oxford, 2009), 164–5.
59. Stevenage Survey, RS1/301, 'Stevenage Statistics'.
60. See Stevenage Survey, RS1/302, #52, 'Bill Blatchford', p. 3 and #28, 'Joan Darby', p. 3; RS1/303, #35, 'Richard Hopper', p. 1; RS1/304, 'Les Roberts', p. 4 (on English Electric telling workers 'they would lose their jobs if they voted for a government that would nationalise the industry'); RS1/306, Anonymous Samuel interview, pp. 3–4. C. N. Hill, *A Vertical Empire: the History of the UK Rocket and Space Programme, 1950–1971* (Imperial College Press, London, 2001), chs 5 and 6.
61. Ralph Samuel, 'The deference voter: A study of the working class Tory', *New Left Review*, 1 (Jan.–Feb. 1960), 9–13 (Samuel still used his childhood nickname of Ralph at this time).
62. The classic political science studies of working-class Toryism were published in the late 1960s: Eric A. Nordlinger, *The Working-Class Tories: Authority, Deference and Stable Democracy* (MacGibbon & Kee, London, 1967), and Robert T. McKenzie and Allan Silver, *Angels in Marble: Working-Class Conservatism in Urban England* (Heinemann, London, 1968). On Samuel, see Sophie Scott-Brown, 'The Art of the Organiser: Raphael Samuel and the Making of History' (Australian National University, Canberra, PhD thesis, 2015).
63. Cullingworth, 'Social implications'.
64. Stevenage Survey, RS1/304, #8, 'Davies', p. 1. See Alex Campsie, 'Mass-Observation, left intellectuals and the politics of everyday life', *English Historical Review*, 131 (Feb. 2016), 92–121.
65. Stevenage Survey, RS1/305, 'Cousins', 3 Jan. 1960, p. 1.
66. Stevenage Survey, RS1/302, #51, 'Liz Church', p. 1. Also RS1/305, 'Peter Norris', p. 1, a certified company accountant who declared he wanted 'a place of my own'. Norris was also one of the few people to talk about specific parts of Stevenage as 'lower class'.
67. Valerie Ann Karn, *Stevenage Housing Survey: A Study of Housing in a New Town*, University of Birmingham Centre for Urban and Regional Studies, Occasional Paper, no. 10 (University of Birmingham, Birmingham, 1970), p. xiii (12 per cent was owner-occupied in 1966).

68. Stevenage Survey, RS1/305, 'Betty Thatcher', 1–2 (comment in parentheses interviewer's). Hatch recognized that she veiled her personal feelings in this way.
69. Stevenage Survey, RS1/304, #10, 'Mr & Mrs Thomas', p. 2 (the interviewer commented 'obviously plenty of money').
70. Alan Duff, *Britain's New Towns* (Pall Mall Press, London, 1961), 72–3.
71. Duff, *New Towns*, 69 (emphasis added). For a brief account of Duff's deficiencies as a general manager, see Jack Balchin, *The First New Town: An Autobiography of the Stevenage Development Corporation, 1946–1980* (Stevenage Development Corporation, Stevenage, 1980), 31–2.
72. Stevenage Development Corporation, *The New Town of Stevenage* (Stevenage Development Corporation, Stevenage, 1949), 3; Harold Orlans, *Stevenage: A Sociological Study of a New Town* (Routledge & Kegan Paul, London, 1952), 52, 109–10.
73. In these calculations inner London includes St Pancras but not Islington. Willmott, 'Housing density', 116, found 68 per cent had moved from Greater London, but in 1966 Karn, *Housing Survey*, p. xiii, found nearly three-quarters of Development Corporation tenants had relocated from within the Greater London area.
74. Neither Samuel nor the Stevenage Development Corporation recorded data on ethnic diversity, but this appears to have been limited in the 1950s; only people of Irish, Italian, and Eastern European descent have been identified within the sample.
75. The 1961 population census recorded very similar figures on the basis of a 10-per-cent sample: General Register Office, *Census 1961 England and Wales: Occupation, Industry, Socio-Economic Groups Hertfordshire* (HMSO, London, 1965), 27 (table 5). The main difference was a higher proportion of unskilled workers (4.9 per cent), probably reflecting Samuel's exclusion of the Old Town.
76. This is broadly in line with findings for other London new towns at this time; Brian Heraud, 'Social class and the new towns', *Urban Studies*, 5/1 (1968), 33–58 at 39.
77. Willmott, 'Housing density', 117, with 24 per cent professional/managerial and 10 per cent unskilled or semi-skilled.
78. Stevenage Survey, RS1/304, 'Mr and Mrs Tufnell', p. 1 (Q23). On the relative ease with which building workers could get a house in Stevenage, see Anon., *Building a Community: Construction Workers in Stevenage, 1950–1970* (University of Westminster, London, 2011), 6, 8, and Bert Lowe, *Anchorman: Autobiography of Bert Lowe, Socialist, Trade Unionist and Stevenage Pioneer* (Bert Lowe, Stevenage, 1996), 49–50, 52.
79. Stevenage Survey, RS1/305, 'Mrs Richardson', p. 2 (Q23).
80. Stevenage Survey, RS1/302, #18, 'Gino Rossi', p. 1 (Q9).
81. Stevenage Survey, RS1/303, 'Mr Cross', p. 1 (Q23): 'We're all living in council houses. How can you be snobbish living in council houses?'
82. Stevenage Survey, RS1/305, 'Janice Tungate', pp. 1–2 (Q19, Q20, and Q23).
83. Mike Savage, 'Working-class identities in the 1960s: Revisiting the affluent worker study', *Sociology*, 39 (2005), 929–46.
84. See Jon Lawrence, 'Workers' testimony and the sociological reification of manual/non-manual distinctions in 1960s Britain', *Sozial.Geschichte online/Social History online*, 20 (2017).
85. Stevenage Survey, RS1/305, 'John Lindsay', p. 1.
86. Margaret Ashby (ed.), *Stevenage Voices: Recollections of Local People* (Tempus, Stroud, 1999), 107–8; Lowe, *Anchorman*, 52; *Talking New Towns* website, at https://www.talkingnewtowns.org.uk/: Michael Cotter interview, 1985.
87. Stevenage Survey, RS1/303, #5, 'Mrs Burns', p. 1.

88. Stevenage Survey, RS1/305, 'John Collins' [anon.], p. 1 (Q20). Biography may have played its part here: not only had he been promoted from the shop floor, but his father-in-law was a chartered accountant.

89. Stevenage Survey, RS1/306, 'Dennis Black', p. 2 (Q20 and Q23); a wireman at English Electric commented that 'Overtime is necessary to live normally, especially if you have a family', RS1/305, 'John Lindsay', p. 2 (Q12). See John Rule, 'Time, affluence and private leisure: The British working class in the 1950s and 1960s', *Labour History Review*, 66/2 (2001), 223–42.

90. Stevenage Survey, RS1/305, 'Valerie Warren', p. 4 (Q20 and Q23).

91. This was not just a southern English story; see Lynn Abrams et al., 'Aspiration, agency and the production of new selves in a Scottish new town, c.1955–c.1985', *Twentieth-Century British History*, 29 (2018), 576–604.

92. Stevenage Survey, RS1/306, 'June Baldwin', p. 3 (Q23).

93. Stevenage Survey, RS1/306, 'Continuation of interview in Stevenage with X', pp. 6–7 (emphasis added); also RS1/301, Samuel, 'The Conservatives as Elite'.

94. Stevenage Survey, RS1/302, 'Derek Harston', p. 1; RS1/305, 'Joan Simmons', p. 1. On the symbolic importance of the front door, see Anon., Mass-Observation, *An Enquiry into People's Homes: A Report Prepared by Mass-Observation* (John Murray, London, 1943), 171. Willmott, 'Housing density', 119–20, found that one of the main grievances among Stevenage residents was that the design of some estates compromised their sense of personal privacy; see also Leo Kuper, 'Blueprint for living together', in Leo Kuper (ed.), *Living in Towns: Selected Papers in Urban Sociology* (Cresset Press, London, 1953), 19–24.

95. Stevenage Survey, RS1/304, #42, p. 1; RS1/303, #4, p. 1.

96. Stevenage Survey, RS1/306, 'Dorothy Cotton', p. 1.

97. Nicholas Deakin and Clare Ungerson, *Leaving London: Planned Mobility and the Inner City* (Heinemann, London, 1977), 123. The fieldwork was conducted in 1971–2. See also J. B. Cullingworth, 'Social implications', and his 'The Swindon Social Survey: A second report on the social implications of overspill', *Sociological Review*, NS 9/2 (1961), 151–66.

98. Stevenage Survey, RS1/305, 'Valerie Warren', p. 4; RS1/306, 'Kevin Burnaby', p. 2 (Q23). On the effect of such policies on social segregation, see Heraud, 'Social class and the new towns'.

99. Stevenage Survey, RS1/303, #35, 'Richard Hopper', p. 1 (Q13).

100. Karn, *Housing Survey*, pp. xiv–xv.

101. Karen, *Housing Survey*, pp. xiii and 23.

102. Willmott, 'East Kilbride and Stevenage', 314.

103. Only the second survey asked explicitly about friendliness; the first survey asked a more general question about people's perception of Stevenage. Here twenty answers included comparative statements about friendliness, giving ninety-seven answers in total.

104. For a classic study emphasizing weak social ties in outer London, see Bertram Hutchinson, *Willesden and the New Towns* (The Social Survey/Ministry of Town and Country Planning, London, 1947), 43–6.

105. Stevenage Survey, RS1/302, #24, 'Mrs Black', p. 1.

106. Stevenage Survey, RS1/303, 'Paul Murphy', p. 1; also Stevenage Survey, RS1/304, 'Edgar Stokes', p. 1, an engineering supervisor who complained 'we don't even know the names of the people next door'.

107. Initially the hope had been for a majority of smaller firms, but the need to accelerate development ultimately shifted the focus: Orlans, *Stevenage*, 83, 86–7; Balchin, *First New Town*, 181–91.

108. Stevenage Survey, RS1/303, #14, 'Mr & Mrs Carroll', p. 1.

109. Stevenage Survey, RS1/304, #44, 'Lionel Black', p. 1.

110. Stevenage Survey, RS1/303, #9, 'David Cartledge', p. 1.

111. Wiltshire and Swindon History Centre, Chippenham, 'Manchester University Research into Overspill, 1958–1962', Swindon Borough Council, Finance, Law and General Purposes Committee Papers, G24/132/1036; Cullingworth, 'Swindon social survey'; and Michael Harloe, *Swindon: A Town in Transition. A Study in Urban Development and Overspill Policy* (Heinemann, London, 1975), 119–20.

112. Stevenage Survey, RS1/305, 'Mrs Richardson', p. 1.

113. Stevenage Survey, RS1/306, 'Edna Pomfrey', p. 1.

114. Stevenage Survey, RS1/306, 'Marie Pearce', p. 1.

115. Ruth Durant, *Watling: A Social Survey* (P. S. King & Son, London, 1939), 22–31, 36–46.

116. On this opposition, see Orlans, *Stevenage*, 67–70.

117. Stevenage Survey, RS1/303, #8, 'Jack Bannister', p. 1 (Q23); also RS1/305, 'Daphne Edgerton', pp. 2–3 (Q23); Colin MacInnes, *Absolute Beginners* (1959; Allison & Busby, London, 1980).

118. Ashby (ed.), *Stevenage Voices*, 102–6.

119. Terry Carter, *Post-War Loughton, 1945–1970: How We Were and How Loughton Changed* (Loughton and District Historical Society, Loughton, 2006), 38–9.

120. Stevenage Survey, RS1/305, 'Susan Ford', p. 1.

121. 'Stevenage Survey, RS1/304, 'Richard Robinson', p. 1 (Q7); RS1/305, 'Ray Turvey', p. 1 (Q4); RS1/305, 'Mr X', p. 1.

122. Stevenage Survey, RS1/305, 'Caroline Tungate', p. 1. Also *Talking New Towns* website: Barbara Metcalf on 'friendship'; and Clapson, 'Working-class women's experiences'.

123. General Register Office, *Census 1961 England and Wales, County Report Hertfordshire* (HMSO, London, 1963), 16 (table 6).

124. Stevenage Survey, RS1/302, 'Mrs Black', p. 1; RS1/303, 'Mr & Mrs Carroll', p. 1.

125. Stevenage Survey, RS1/304, 'Diane Szymański', p. 1.

126. Dolly Smith Wilson, 'A new look at the affluent worker: The good working mother in post-war Britain', *Twentieth-Century British History*, 17/2 (2006), 206–29; Helen McCarthy, 'Women, marriage and paid work in Post-war Britain', *Women's History Review*, 26/1 (2017), 46–61. Willmott, 'East Kilbride and Stevenage', 310, reported that almost 80 per cent of Stevenage mothers with children under 5 had no paid employment.

127. Of eighty-nine people asked, forty-six agreed (including three who said it was the same everywhere), twenty-five disagreed, eighteen claimed not to know.

128. Stevenage Survey, RS1/303, #9,'David Cartledge', p. 1 (Q7).

129. Stevenage Survey, RS1/305, 'John Collins' [anon.], p. 1 (Q7).

130. Stevenage Survey, RS1/302, 'Mr & Mrs Ince', p. 1. Also RS1/306, 'Dennis Black', where husband and wife disagree (he says no), and RS1/303, 'Mrs Braitwaite', p. 1, who insists 'there is a snob distinction based on "we've got more than you"'.

131. Stevenage Survey, RS1/302, 'Mr & Mrs Ince', p. 2.

132. Stevenage Survey, RS1/305, 'Beryl Watts', p. 1 (Q7).

133. Claire Langhamer, 'The meanings of home in postwar Britain', *Journal of Contemporary History*, 40 (2005), 341–62.

134. Peter Willmott, *The Evolution of a Community: A Study of Dagenham After Forty years* (Routledge, London, 1963), 99–100.

135. Stevenage Survey, RS1/302, 'Linda Jones', p. 1 (Q7).

136. Stevenage Survey, RS1/304, 'Mary Pearce', pp. 1–2 (Q7, Q46).

137. Stevenage Survey, RS1/304, 'Mrs Tufnell', p. 1 (Q7); also RS1/306, 'Continuation of interview in Stevenage with X', p. 6.
138. Stevenage Survey, RS1/303, 'Mr & Mrs Bridge', p. 1.
139. Stevenage Survey, RS1/306, 'Margaret Richardson', p. 1 (Q7), and 'Kevin Burnaby', p. 1 (Q7).
140. Stevenage Survey, RS1/305, 'Valerie Warren', p. 1 (Q7).
141. Stevenage Survey, RS1/305, 'Mrs Tungate', p. 1 (Q7).
142. Stevenage Survey, RS1/303, 'Mrs Burns', p. 1 (Q7); and RS1/304, 'Iris Fry', p. 1 (Q7).
143. Stevenage Survey, RS1/306, 'Lionel Barratt', p. 1 (Q7).
144. See Stuart Hall, 'A Sense of Classlessness', *Universities & Left Review*, 5 (Autumn, 1958), 26–31, though see E. P. Thompson's sceptical, materialist response, 'Commitment in politics', *Universities & Left Review*, 6 (Spring, 1959), 50–5. On the wider context of these debates, see Lawrence Black, *The Political Culture of the Left in Affluent Britain, 1951–1964: Old Labour, New Britain?* (Palgrave, Basingstoke, 2003); Davis, 'Arguing Affluence'; Middleton, '"Affluence" and the Left'.
145. Willmott, *Evolution of a Community*, 99–100.
146. M. J. Daunton (ed.), *Councillors and Tenants: Local Authority Housing in English Cities, 1919–1939* (Leicester University Press, Leicester, 1984), 2–33.
147. See Jevons and Madge, *Housing Estates*, 18–19, 24–6, 64–70; Peter Malpass, *Reshaping Housing Policy: Subsidies, Rents and Residualisation* (Routledge, London, 1990), 42–6 and 49–50, 91–3; Barry, 'Town Development Act', 11, 32–4, 142; Ben Rogaly and Becky Taylor, *Moving Histories of Class and Community: Identity, Place and Belonging in Contemporary England* (Palgrave Macmillan, Basingstoke, 2009).
148. Jon Lawrence, 'Paternalism, class and the British path to modernity', in Simon Gunn and James Vernon (eds), *The Peculiarities of Liberal Modernity in Imperial Britain* (University of California Press, Berkeley and Los Angeles, 2011), 163–80.
149. Daniel Miller, *The Comfort of Things* (Polity, Cambridge, 2008).
150. Thanks to Guy Ortolano for highlighting this point when kindly reading through an earlier version of this chapter.

Chapter 4

1. Peter Scott, *Triumph of the South: A Regional Economic History of Early Twentieth-Century Britain* (Ashgate, Aldershot, 2007), 203–27, at 204.
2. J. B. Cullingworth, *Environmental Planning, 1939–1969*, iii. *New Towns Policy* (HMSO, London, 1979), 5.
3. James Dyer and John G. Dony, *The Story of Luton* (3rd edn, White Crescent, Luton, 1975), 178–9, 187–8; Len Holden, *Vauxhall Motors and the Luton Economy, 1900–2002* (Bedfordshire Historical Records Society/Boydell Press, Woodbridge, 2003), 155. The principal exception to this unplanned growth was the village of Houghton Regis, on the town's northern outskirts, where the LCC built a large 'overspill' estate in the 1950s and 1960s.
4. The questionnaires from the two studies have been archived in Goldthorpe and Lockwood, SN: 6512. From Cambridge, 130 files have been digitized as UK Data Archive, Essex, J. Lawrence (2016), *Affluent Worker Study 1962–1964: Questionnaire Files*, [data collection], ReShare 10.5255/UKDA-SN-852166.
5. John H. Goldthorpe et al., *The Affluent Worker in the Class Structure*, 3 vols (Cambridge University Press, Cambridge, 1968–9). From Luton thirty shop-floor interviews have been transcribed as UK Data Archive, Essex, S. Todd (2009), *Affluent Worker in the Class*

Structure: A Digitised Sample of the Luton Study, 1961–1962 [data collection], UK Data Service, SN: 4871 (http://dx.doi.org/10.5255/UKDA-SN-4871-1). In addition 159 manual home interviews and all 54 non-manual interviews have been digitized in J. Lawrence (2016), *Affluent Worker Study 1962–1964: Questionnaire Files*.

6. Michael Young and Peter Willmott, *Family and Kinship in East London* (Routledge & Kegan Paul, London, 1957), 117.

7. Stuart Middleton, '"Affluence" and the Left in Britain, c.1958–1974', *English Historical Review*, 129 (2014), 107–38; John H. Goldthorpe and David Lockwood, 'Affluence and the British class structure', *Sociological Review*, 11/2 (1963), 133–63.

8. Jon Lawrence, 'Social-science encounters and the negotiation of difference in early 1960s England', *History Workshop Journal*, 77 (2014), 215–39.

9. Ann Mische, 'Projects and possibilities: Researching futures in action', *Sociological Forum*, 24/3 (2009), 694–704; Joanne Bryant and Jeanne Ellard, 'Hope as a form of agency in the future thinking of disenfranchised young people', *Journal of Youth Studies*, 18/4 (2015), 485–99; Giulia Carabelli and Dawn Lyon, 'Young people's orientations to the future: Navigating the present and imagining the future', *Journal of Youth Studies*, 19/8 (2016), 1110–27.

10. Hartmut Rosa and William E. Scheuerman (eds), *High-Speed Society: Social Acceleration, Power and Modernity* (Penn State University, University Park, PA, 2008); Hartmut Rosa, *Social Acceleration: A New Theory of Modernity*, trans. Jonathan Trejo-Mathys (Columbia University Press, New York, 2013).

11. Emily Robinson, '"Different and better times?" History, progress and inequality', in Pedro Ramos Pinto and Bertrand Taithe (eds), *The Impact of History: Histories at the Beginning of the 21st Century* (Routledge, Abingdon, 2015), 110–22.

12. LHI, 187, p. 44 (12 Nov. 1963).

13. Although when asked directly, only 8 per cent said they felt their own job to be either 'fairly' or 'very' insecure: Goldthorpe et al., *Affluent Worker*, iii. 37–8; see also Holden, *Vauxhall Motors*, 196.

14. LHI, 128, p. 44 (10 Sept. 1963). Strangely, workers were not asked their age, but we can use information about recalled vote and age of children to identify their approximate age group. All men were aged between 21 and 46.

15. Eight out of eleven people raising 'security' as their main hope had been born before 1924 (the oldest identifiable cohort consisting of men aged between 40 and 46). The researchers noted that they deliberately excluded men over 46 'to eliminate men with earlier experience of unemployment during the inter-war years'; Goldthorpe et al., *Affluent Worker*, iii. 38.

16. LHI, 206, p. 44 (6 Dec. 1963).

17. Alan Sillitoe, *Saturday Night and Sunday Morning* (1958; Pan, London, 1960), 21, 32, 120, 176.

18. LHI, 209, p. 44.

19. LHI, 222, p. 44; though see LHI, 092, p. 44, where a Vauxhall worker's wife stresses that she wants to see her children settled *and* happy.

20. LHI, 164, p. 44.

21. LHI, 102, p. 44.

22. LHI, 101, p. 44; LHI, 117 (Doyle), p. 44 (original ellipses).

23. Selina Todd, *The People: The Rise and Fall of the Working Class, 1910–2010* (John Murray, London, 2014), 260–1.

24. LHI, 170 (Lewis), pp. 44–5 (M1); LHI, 159, 160, 161, and 211 (all p. 44). The pools involved correctly predicting the scores of Saturday afternoon's League football matches,

particularly those matches that would end in draws. Their central place in popular culture has been replaced by the National Lottery.

25. LHI, 088, p. 44.
26. Vivian Nicholson and Stephen Smith, *Spend, Spend, Spend* (London, Jonathan Cape, 1977); Jonathon Green, 'She had it all and spent it all', *The Guardian*, 9 Oct. 1999; Todd, *The People*, interludes. See LHI, 141, 157, 204 (all p. 44), though having talked about buying a business one Skefko worker's wife conceded they would probably 'just spend it and enjoy ourselves', LHI, 163, p. 20.
27. e.g. LHI, 130, 141, 150, 184, 199, 204, and 217 (all p. 44). See Jon Lawrence, 'Workers' testimony and the sociological reification of manual/non-manual distinctions in 1960s Britain', *Sozial.Geschichte online/Social History online*, 20 (2017) (accessed 12 July 2017).
28. LHI, 064, pp. 1, 20, 45 (F2 and M4).
29. LHI, 086. On the place of betting in working-class life, see Ross McKibbin, 'Working-class gambling in Britain, 1880–1939', *Past & Present*, 82 (1979), 147–78, and Andrew Davies, 'The police and the people: Gambling in Salford, 1900–1939', *Historical Journal*, 34 (1991), 87–115.
30. LNMHI, 508, p. 37.
31. Goldthorpe et al., *Affluent Worker*, i. 132. For a fuller discussion of the significance of these aspirations in workers' lives , see Lawrence, 'Workers' testimony'.
32. LHI, 127, p. 44; see also LHI, 218 and 543 (both p. 44).
33. LHI, 077, p. 44.
34. LHI, 108, 113, 143, 156, and 160 (all p. 44).
35. LHI, 121, pp. 44–5.
36. LHI, 102, 123, 165, and 191 (all p. 44); Todd, *The People*, 260–1.
37. Goldthorpe et al., *Affluent Worker*, iii. 39 (in the digitized sample of 159 manual workers the figure is 56 per cent owner-occupiers, 39 per cent council tenants). On the town's rapid expansion in the 1950s , see Stephen Bunker, Robin Holgate, and Marian Nichols, *The Changing Face of Luton: An Illustrated History* (Book Castle, Dunstable, 1993), 81. See also Graham Turner, *The Car Makers* (Eyre & Spottiswoode, London, 1963), 107–8, who claimed to have met only one Vauxhall worker content to continue living in a council house.
38. On Vauxhall's policy of recruiting in depressed areas , see Margaret Grieco, *Keeping It in the Family: Social Networks and Employment Chance* (Tavistock, London, 1987), esp. 125–34.
39. LHI, 128, p. 44.
40. Selina Todd has written extensively on the importance of this intergenerational dynamic in working-class family life; see esp. *Young Women, Work and Family in England, 1918–1950* (Oxford University Press, Oxford, 2005), and Selina Todd and Hilary Young, 'Baby-boomers to "Beanstalkers": Making the modern teenager in post-war Britain', *Cultural and Social History*, 9/3 (2012), 451–67.
41. Goldthorpe et al., *Affluent Worker*, iii. 116–18.
42. LHI, 182 (Harrison), pp. 2, 44.
43. LHI, 143 (Barnes), pp. 2, 6, 44; also LHI, 120, a Labour-voting Lutonian in his forties, who expressed the same fear about neighbours. On council letting policies, see Leo Kuper, 'Blueprint for living together', in his *Living in Towns: Selected Papers in Urban Sociology* (Cresset Press, London, 1953), 152; Hilda Jennings, *Societies in the Making: A Study of Development and Redevelopment within a County Borough* (Routledge, London, 1962), 125–46; Becky Taylor and Ben Rogaly, '"Mrs Fairly is a dirty, lazy type": Unsatisfactory households and the problem of problem families in Norwich, 1942–1963', *Twentieth-Century British*

History, 18/4 (2007), 429–52; Ben Jones, *The Working-Class in Mid Twentieth-Century England: Community, Identity and Social Memory* (Manchester University Press, Manchester, 2012), 82–110.

44. LNMHI, 538, pp. 1, 54; LHI, 201, p. 45 (M1).

45. LNMHI, 533, p. 45.

46. LHI, 040, p. 2; LHI, 087, p. 2.

47. LHI, 139, p. 1v.

48. LHI, 185, pp. 1 and 2; LHI, 201, p. 2.

49. LHI, 190, p. 20.

50. LNMHI, 540, p. 54. e.g. Mark W. Hodges and Cyril S. Smith, 'The Sheffield estate', in University of Liverpool, *Neighbourhood and Community*, 101–3.

51. Ben Rogaly and Becky Taylor, *Moving Histories of Class and Community: Identity, Place and Belonging in Contemporary England* (Palgrave Macmillan, Basingstoke, 2009), esp. 39–50. See also Jones, *Working-Class in Mid Twentieth-century*, 99–110, and Selina Todd, 'Affluence, class and Crown Street: Reinvestigating the post-war working class', *Contemporary British History*, 22/4 (2008), 501–18, at 510–11.

52. LHI, 135 (Davidson), pp. 1–2.

53. Goldthorpe et al., *Affluent Worker*, iii. 38; in the digitized sub-sample used for this study 32 per cent of men had grown up in the town.

54. LHI, 214, p. 1; LHI, 161, p. 2.

55. LHI, 197, p. 1; LHI, 200, p. 1; and LHI, 216, p. 1 (Todmorden); Grieco, *Keeping it in the Family*, 118, 124, 127–8.

56. LHI, 157, p. 1.

57. LHI, 136, p. 1.

58. LHI, 220 (Houghton), pp. 1–2; a charge also made by LHI, 218, p. 1 (another Londoner), while a Skefko worker from Lancashire complained that local people weren't 'open with each other', LHI, 216, p. 1.

59. LHI, 220 (Houghton), pp. 5v and 45 (M5).

60. Rogaly and Taylor, *Moving Histories*, 6–7; David Feldman, 'Global movements, internal migration and the importance of institutions', *International Review of Social History*, 52/1 (2007), 105–9.

61. LNMHI, 500, p. 10.

62. General Register Office, Census Report England and Wales 1961, County Report Bedfordshire (HMSO, 1963), table 8, 'Birthplaces and Nationalities', p. 11.

63. Lockwood interview with Paul Thompson, 2002: UKDA, P. Thompson, ESDS Qualidata (2014), *Pioneers of Social Research, 1996–2012* [data collection], 2nd edn, UK Data Service, SN: 6226, pp. 33–4.

64. In a sample of 159 digitized questionnaires twenty shop-floor workers had been born in Ireland (the two born in Northern Ireland would probably have been British nationals). In addition three English-born workers had Irish-born wives.

65. Colin Grant, *Bageye at the Wheel: A 1970s Childhood in Suburbia* (Vintage Books, London, 2012), 209–10. Also LHI, 197, p. 2.

66. Based on the 213 scanned questionnaires in Lawrence, *Affluent Worker Study: Questionnaire Files*. Case L047 in Todd, *Affluent Worker: Digitised Sample*, is described as from an 'Anglo-Indian' background, and came to England aged 13. It is difficult to be certain, but from his answers he appears to have been born to an ethnically English family living in pre-Independence India.

67. Satnam Virdee, *Racism, Class and the Racialized Outsider* (Palgrave Macmillan, Basingstoke, 2014), 1–7; on the gradual erosion of these barriers, see Jack Saunders, 'The British Motor Industry, 1945–1977: How Workplace Cultures Shaped Labour Militancy' (University College London, PhD Thesis, 2015), 162–4.

68. LHI, 210 (Banerjee), pp. 1, 20, 43–4.

69. Mike Savage, 'Sociology, class and male manual work cultures', in John McIlroy, Nina Fisher, and Alan Campbell (eds.), *British Trade Unions and Industrial Politics*, ii. *The High Tide of Trade Unionism, 1964–1979* (Ashgate, Aldershot, 1999); Mike Savage, 'Working-class identities in the 1960s: Revisiting the affluent worker study', *Sociology*, 39 (2005), 929–46.

70. LHI, 210 (Banerjee), pp. 2, 9–11, 33, 44, 45, and Q64, pp. 1–3; Virdee, *Racism*.

71. LHI, 222 (Jefferies), pp. 1–2, 7, 10, 44. Mark Abrams found considerable hostility to immigration in Luton when he conducted polling in the town ahead of the 1963 by-election, Labour History Archive, Manchester, NEC Campaigns Committee Minutes, 1963, p. 1 (LP/NEC/Box 88), Mark Abrams, 'Luton after Scarborough'.

72. Chris Phillipson et al., *The Family and Community Life of Older People: Social Networks and Social Support in Three Urban Areas* (Routledge, London, 2001); Nickie Charles and Charlotte Aull Davies, 'Studying the particular, illuminating the general: Community studies and community in Wales', *Sociological Review*, 53/4 (2005), 672–90.

73. LHI, 093 (Hargreaves), pp. 2, 4, 7, 11.

74. LHI, 180, p. 2; LHI, 187 (Ward), p. 2. Chris Waters, '"Dark strangers" in our midst: Discourses of race and nation in Britain, 1947–1963', *Journal of British Studies*, 36/2 (1997), 207–38.

75. LHI, 155, p. 1; LHI, 125, pp. 1, 1v, and 2.

76. LHI, 190 (Miller), pp. 2, 6, 45.

77. General Register Office, *Census Report 1961 England and Wales: Occupation, Industry and Socio-Economic Groups, Cambridgeshire Report* (HMSO, London, 1966), table 3, pp. 8–10, and *Bedfordshire Report* (HMSO, London, 1965), table 3, pp. 8–10.

78. CPI, 070, Q28, pp. 3, 5.

79. CPI, 018, Q28, pp. 1, 4.

80. CPI, 081 (Barnes), Q28, p. 1.

81. Sallie Purkis, 'Over the Bridge: Another Cambridge Between Two Wars: Communal Responses to Political, Economic and Social Changes, 1919–1938' (University of Essex, MA Thesis, 1982), 37–56; Allan Brigham, 'A community in transition: Romsey Town Cambridge, 1966–2006', chs 1–2, at http://www.colc.co.uk/cambridge/tours/article3.htm (last accessed 20 May 2016); Richard Johnson and Ashley Walsh, *Camaraderie: One Hundred Years of the Cambridge Labour Party, 1912–2012* (Cambridge Labour Party, Cambridge, 2012), 25, 33–7; William Ingram, *Romsey Town Labour Club: Mill Road History Project Building Report* (2015), at http://www.capturingcambridge.org/wp-content/uploads/2014/05/Romsey_Labour_Club_2nd_edn-rev.pdf (accessed 12 July 2017).

82. CPI, 081 (Barnes), Q28, p. 1. The Earl of Derby is actually at the foot of Hills Road bridge; the pub at the foot of Mill Road bridge is named after a different Tory prime minister, the Earl of Beaconsfield (Disraeli), and is more likely to be the pub he had in mind. As it happens, it used to be my local in the late 1980s.

83. CPI, 081 (Barnes), Q28, p. 1. The interviewer assumed Barnes meant the Granada TV soap begun the previous year, hence the inverted commas. In fact this was also the name of an impoverished street in the central Newtown district of Cambridge which the council had long planned to clear. It was a mistake that said much about town–gown relations in early 1960s Cambridge.

84. Mike Savage, *Identities and Social Change in Britain Since 1940: The Politics of Method* (Oxford University Press, Oxford, 2010), esp. ch. 9; also Mike Savage, 'Changing social class identities in post-war Britain: Perspectives from Mass-observation', *Sociological Research Online*, 12/3 (2007), #6, http://www.socresonline.org.uk/12/3/6.html.

85. CPI, 081, Q28 (Barnes), p. 4.

86. CPI, 263 (Reynolds), Q28, pp. 5–6; Richard Sennett and Jonathan Cobb, *The Hidden Injuries of Class* (Vintage, New York, 1973).

87. CPI, 220, Q28, pp. 7, 11 and 15—the final comment was his wife's, though he assented. Unusually, his comments about college types were not recorded verbatim.

88. CPI, 079, Q28, pp. 2, 4, and 6.

89. CPI, 002 (Field), Q28, p. 1.

90. CPI, 197 (Smith), Q28, p. 1.

91. Nancy Mitford, 'The English Aristocracy', *Encounter*, 24 (Sept. 1955), 5–11; Nancy Mitford (ed.), *Noblesse Oblige: An Inquiry into the Identifiable Characteristics of the English Aristocracy* (Hamish Hamilton, London, 1956).

92. CPI, 197 (Smith), Q28, pp. 1–3.

93. CPI, 065, Q28, p. 2.

94. CPI, 057 (Chapman), Q28, pp. 1, 3.

95. CPI, 022 (Bates), Q28, p. 5.

96. Figures calculated from digitized manual worker sample of 159 cases.

97. Goldthorpe et al., *Affluent Worker*, iii. 43–4.

98. LHI, 150, pp. 1–2. Also Graham Turner, *The Car Makers* (Eyre & Spottiswoode, London, 1963), 104, 107.

99. Goldthorpe et al., *Affluent Worker*, i. 4n.

100. See Jon Lawrence, 'Workers' testimony and the sociological reification of manual/non-manual distinctions in 1960s Britain', *Sozial.Geschichte online/Social History online*, 20 (2017).

101. Goldthorpe et al., *Affluent Worker*, iii. 191–5.

102. Ferdynand Zweig, *The Worker in an Affluent Society: Family Life and Industry* (Heinemann, London, 1961), 236. See also Turner, *Car Makers*, 103, which also suggests approximately 40 per cent of Vauxhall workers commuted daily from towns across the region.

103. Stevenage Survey, RS1/304, 'Stuart Simpson' (37), and RS1/305, husband of 'Beryl Watts' (23) and 'Frederick Moran' (30).

104. In the digitized sample of twenty-nine cases, five lived outside.

105. R. E. Pahl, *Urbs in Rure: The Metropolitan Fringe in Hertfordshire* (LSE, London, 1965), 35–6 and 42. On historic precedents for working-class commuting, see Trevor Griffiths, *The Lancashire Working Classes, c.1880–1930* (Clarendon Press, Oxford, 2001), 123–4.

106. LHI, 105 (Carr), pp. 3, 12, 17, 32, 42–45 (interviewer M6).

107. LHI, 105 (Carr), pp. 1–2, 7.

108. Mike Savage, Gaynor Bagnall, and Brian Longhurst, 'Ordinary, ambivalent and defensive: Class identities in the northwest of England', *Sociology*, 35/4 (2001), 875–92; Mike Savage, Gaynor Bagnall, and Brian Longhurst, *Globalization and Belonging* (Sage, London, 2005), esp. ch. 3; Chris Phillipson, 'The "elected" and the "excluded": Sociological perspectives on the experience of place and community in old age', *Ageing and Society*, 27/3 (2007), 321–42.

109. LHI, 105 (Carr), pp. 6, 10, and Q64, p. 6.

110. LHI, 040, p. 2 (Eaton Bray) and LHI, 073, p. 2 (Toddington).

111. LHI, 208, pp. 1–2, 6, 45 (M5).

112. LHI, 104 (Hodge), p. 1.
113. LHI, 212 (Green), pp. 1, 1v, 10, 44.
114. LHI, 213 (Ransom), pp. 1, 1v, 7, 8, 10–11, 43–4, 45.
115. John Rule, 'Time, affluence and private leisure: The British working class in the 1950s and 1960s', *Labour History Review*, 66/2 (2001), 223–42; Goldthorpe et al., *Affluent Worker*, iii. 60–1, 97–8; Todd, *The People*, 255–66.
116. Turner, *Car Workers*, 112; more generally, 104–8.
117. Zweig, *Worker in an Affluent Society*, 104–11, 205–12; Goldthorpe et al., *Affluent Worker*, iii. 96–108.
118. Bakke, *Unemployed Man*, 153–6; Kuper, 'Blueprint', 42–82; Geoffrey Gorer, *Exploring English Character* (Cresset Press, London, 1955), 52–63; McKibbin, *Classes and Cultures*, 181–3.
119. LHI, 094, p. 2; LHI, 226, p. 11.
120. Goldthorpe et al., *Affluent Worker*, iii. 98.
121. LHI, 194 (Newlands), pp. 1, 1v, 6, 9.
122. Zweig, *Worker in an Affluent Society*, 116 (one-third claimed to be on visiting terms compared with approximately one-fifth elsewhere).
123. Hoggart, *Uses of Literacy*, 35. For a contemporary discussion of diverse patterns of domestic visiting and entertaining by house type, see Dennis Chapman, *The Home and Social Status* (Routledge, London, 1955), 68–74.
124. Based on a reanalysis of all fifty-four non-manual questionnaires, and the manual workers' digital sample of 159 cases. The affluent worker study did not report exactly comparable data, but in both cases these figures appear to be higher than suggested by their data. Goldthorpe et al., *Affluent Worker*, iii. 92, reports that 42 per cent of manual workers who entertained (and 22 per cent of non-manual workers) invited *only* kin into their homes; this compares with figures of 27 per cent and 16 per cent respectively from the reanalysis. Either they used more selective criteria in determining what counted as 'entertaining' or, more likely, their reported figures are actually for the *whole* population, rather than just those who entertained.
125. Excluding those who never entertained, manual workers averaged 1.67 evenings per month compared with 1.6 for non-manual workers. Again Goldthorpe et al., *Affluent Worker*, iii. 92 n., suggests lower figures, probably for the same reason.
126. This includes a few cases where people appear to use 'tea' to mean an evening meal, rather than just a warm drink.
127. Todd, *Affluent Worker: Digitised Sample*, case L037. The interviewer, M7, was male. On the 'good table', see Hoggart, *Uses of Literacy*, 35 and 37.
128. All figures are percentages of those entertaining rather than of the whole sample.
129. Excluding those who never entertained, 22 per cent of manual workers and 20 per cent of non-manual mentioned either watching TV or going to the pub/club. For gendered activities the split was 7 per cent versus 10 per cent. For the original study's somewhat different picture, see Goldthorpe et al., *Affluent Worker*, iii. 93 n.
130. LHI, 223, p. 11; also LHI 158, 159, 201, and 203 (all p. 11).
131. Grace Lees-Maffel, 'Dressing the part(y): 1950s domestic advice books and the studied performance of informal domesticity in the UK and the US', in Fiona Fisher et al. (eds), *Performance, Fashion and the Modern Interior: From the Victorians to Today* (Berg, Oxford, 2011), 183–96.
132. They reported that 34 per cent of workers with no 'white-collar affiliations' entertained at least once a month and invited non-kin compared with 36 per cent of those with *either*

a job *or* a family affiliation to the middle class, and 44 per cent of those with both: Goldthorpe et al., *Affluent Worker*, iii. 95–6.

133. Averaging 6.8 hours overtime per week compared with 7.8 hours for those who did not entertain non-kin. In households that entertained, only one-quarter of wives had paid employment (24.5 per cent), compared with just over one-third for those that did not (34.4 per cent).

134. For later work questioning the privatization thesis and insisting instead on the need to study changing patterns of sociability, see Ian Prosser, 'The privatisation of working-class life: A dissenting view', *British Journal of Sociology*, 41/2 (1990), 157–80 (1980s Coventry); Fiona Devine, *Affluent Workers Revisited: Privatism and the Working Class* (Edinburgh University Press, Edinburgh, 1992) (1980s Luton); and the historical account of post-war Beverley (East Yorkshire): Stefan Ramsden, 'Remaking working-class community: Sociability, belonging and "affluence" in a small town, 1930–1980', *Contemporary British History*, 29/1 (2015), 1–26.

135. Goldthorpe et al., *Affluent Worker*, iii. 88–91.

136. The most extended discussion of the varied cultures of neighbouring remains Martin Bulmer (ed.), *Neighbours: The Work of Philip Abrams* (Cambridge University Press, Cambridge 1986), esp. pt 1. See also Melanie Tebbutt, *Women's Work? A Social History of "Gossip" in Working-Class Neighbourhoods, 1880–1960* (Scolar, Aldershot, 1995).

137. Deborah Cohen, *Family Secrets: Living with Shame from the Victorians to the Present Day* (Viking, London, 2013); David Vincent, *Privacy: A Short History* (Polity, Cambridge, 2016); Helen Smith, *Masculinity, Class and Same-Sex Desire in Industrial England, 1895–1957* (Palgrave Macmillan, Basingstoke, 2015).

138. Cohen, *Family Secrets*, pp. xvi, 241–53.

139. James Hinton, *Nine Wartime Lives: Mass-Observation and the Making of the Modern Self* (Oxford University Press, Oxford, 2010), 111–35.

140. Anne Hughes and Karen Hunt, 'A Culture Transformed? Women's Lives in Wythenshawe in the 1930s', in Andrew Davies and Steven Fielding (eds), *Workers' Worlds: Culture and Communities in Manchester and Salford, 1880–1939* (Manchester University Press, Manchester 1992), 74–101, at 88–91; Tebbutt, *Women's Talk*, 148–51, 163–8; Helen Smith, 'Love, sex and friendship: Northern, working-class men and sexuality in the first half of the twentieth century', in Alana Harris and Timothy Willem Jones (eds), *Love and Romance in Britain, 1918–1970* (Palgrave Macmillan, Basingstoke, 2015), 61–8.

141. Stefan Ramsden, 'Remaking working-class community: Sociability, belonging and "affluence" in a small town, 1930–1980', *Contemporary British History*, 29/1 (2015), 1–26 at 16.

142. Joanna Bourke, *Working-Class Cultures in Britain, 1890–1960: Gender, Class and Ethnicity* (Routledge, London, 1994), 81–94, and more generally Langhamer, 'Meanings of home'.

143. LHI, 108, 150, and 152 (all p. 45); also LHI, 078, 185, and 218 (all p. 45), and Todd, *Affluent Worker: Digitised Sample*, case L068.

144. LHI, 124, 140, 187, 199.

145. Mass-Observation, *An Enquiry into People's Homes* (John Murray, London, 1943), 99–109; Mark Swenarton, *Homes Fit for Heroes: The Politics and Architecture of Early State Housing in Britain* (Heinemann, London, 1981), 21–2; Judy Giles, *The Parlour and the Suburb: Domestic Identities, Class, Femininity and Modernity* (Berg, Oxford, 2004); Hoggart, *Uses of Literacy*, 34–5.

146. Hoggart, *Uses of Literacy*, 34–5; George Orwell, *Keep the Aspidistra Flying* (1936; Penguin, London, 1987). Chapman, *The Home and Social Status*, ch. 4, emphasizes the strong

attachment to maintaining a best room or 'parlour' in older working-class homes, as well as the more 'rational' use of space often found on council estates.

147. LHI, 078, 093, 118, and 216 (all p. 45); also Todd, *Affluent Worker: Digitised Sample*, case L043. Interviewer M6 welcomed the contrast of visiting a Laporte process worker's council house and conducting the interview in 'a comfortable room which obviously was the one most used', as opposed to 'the cheerless front rooms one usually interviews in', LHI, 094, p. 45.

148. e.g. LHI, 152, p. 45 and LNMHI, 503, p. 54.

149. Mike Leigh, *Abigail's Party* (stage and TV play, 1977).

Chapter 5

The author acknowledges Professor R. K. Brown and Qualidata for making the material discussed in this chapter available to the public, and thanks Peter Brannen and Jim Cousins for their generous help. Those who carried out the original work and analysis bear no responsibility for the reanalysis offered here.

1. Sting, *Broken Music: A Memoir* (Simon & Schuster, London, 2003), 18–26.

2. Shipbuilding Workers, Boxes 1 to 15. See Box 1, File 18, 'Additional and Informal Interviews' [Sunderland Tack Welder], p. 14; File 5, 'Observation notes on Prefabrication Shed', p. 19; File 3, 'Observation notes on blacksmiths', pp. 33 and 54.

3. See https://segedunumromanfort.org.uk/ (accessed 15 May 2017), and W. B. Griffiths, *Segedunum: Roman Fort, Baths and Museum* (rev. edn, Tyne & Wear Archives, Newcastle, 2008).

4. Computer expertise was provided by Mike Samphier. Publications were (from the pilot study): Richard Brown and Peter Brannen, 'Social relations and social perspectives amongst shipbuilding workers—a preliminary statement', pts 1 and 2, *Sociology*, 4 (1970), 71–84 and 197–211; and from the main study: R. K. Brown et al., 'The contours of solidarity: Social stratification and industrial relations in shipbuilding', *British Journal of Industrial Relations*, 10 (1972), 12–41; Jim Cousins and Richard Brown, 'Patterns of paradox: Shipbuilding workers' images of society', in Martin Bulmer (ed.), *Working-Class Images of Society* (Routledge, London, 1975), 55–82; Richard Brown et al. 'Leisure in work: The "occupational culture" of shipbuilding workers', in Michael Smith, Stanley Parker, and Cyril Smith (eds), *Leisure and Society in Britain* (Allen Lane, London, 1973), 97–110.

5. Background information about the study was kindly provided by Peter Brannen, 13 Oct. 2014 (London) and Jim Cousins, 3 Dec. 2014 (Newcastle).

6. Shipbuilding Workers, Box 1, File 3, 'Observation notes on blacksmiths', pp. 63 and 86.

7. These materials are also discussed in Selina Todd, *The People: The Rise and Fall of the Working Class, 1910–2010* (John Murray, London, 2014), 73, 293–4, and Florence Sutcliffe-Braithwaite, 'Class, Community and Individualism in English Politics and Society, 1969–2000' (University of Cambridge, PhD Thesis, 2013), ch. 3.

8. For contemporaneous models of 'traditional' working-class communities, see Josephine Klein, *Samples from English Cultures*, vol. i (Routledge, London, 1965), ch. 4; Ronald Frankenberg, *Communities in Britain: Social Life in Town and Country* (Penguin, London, 1966), ch. 7; and John H. Goldthorpe et al., *The Affluent Worker*, 3 vols (Cambridge University Press, Cambridge, 1968–9).

9. Brown and Brannen, 'Social relations', pt 1, pp. 71–2, 80–1, and pt 2, pp. 208–9; Brown et al., Leisure in work', 98–102; Cousins and Brown, 'Patterns of paradox'.

10. All names are pseudonyms in order to preserve anonymity.

11. Shipbuilding Workers, Box 1, File 6, 'Observation notes on plumbers', pp. 68 and 69. This is reminiscent of an exchange with an American plumber which Richard Sennett uses to argue that 'trust was finally established' when workers felt able to challenge 'people like us': Richard Sennett and Jonathan Cobb, *The Hidden Injuries of Class* (Vintage Books, New York, 1973), 38.
12. Shipbuilding Workers, Box 1, File 8, 'Observation notes on Joiners (shop and ship)', p. 25.
13. Shipbuilding Workers, Box, 1, File 7, 'Observation notes on plumbers' shop', p. 2.
14. David Lockwood, 'Sources of variation in working-class images of society', *Sociological Review*, 14 (1966), 149–67, and Bulmer (ed.), *Working-Class Images of Society*.
15. *Coalface to Car Park Collection*, Focus Group 1 [Ally], p. 13.
16. Firth Papers, 3/1/13 [File 2], Evans–Sexton Genealogy [1948], p. 2.
17. Shipbuilding Workers, Box 1, File 3, 'Observation notes on blacksmiths', pp. 34 and 107.
18. Shipbuilding Workers, Box 1, File 6, 'Observation notes on plumbers', p. 61; File 8, 'Observation notes on Joiners (shop and ship)', p. 36.
19. Shipbuilding Workers, Box 1, File 6, 'Observation notes on plumbers', p. 41.
20. Shipbuilding Workers, Box 1, File 6, 'Observation notes on plumbers', p. 13.
21. See Shipbuilding Workers, Box 1, File 3, 'Observation notes on blacksmiths', p. 33; File 6, 'Observation notes on plumbers', p. 69.
22. Shipbuilding Workers, Box 1, File 3, 'Observation notes on blacksmiths', pp. 105–7.
23. Shipbuilding Workers, Box 4, FM20, 'Informal interview with foreman piece clerk', p. 4.
24. Shipbuilding Workers, Box 1, File 18, 'Additional and Informal Interviews' [Sunderland Tack Welder], pp. 2–3.
25. See Shipbuilding Workers, Box 1, File 3, 'Observation notes on blacksmiths', p. 85.
26. For ill feeling, see Shipbuilding Workers, Box 1, File 14, 'Miscellaneous Observational Notes', p. 5; File 17, 'Accounts of Yard Disputes', p. 1. For improved relations, see Shipbuilding Workers, Box 1, File 5, 'Observation notes on Prefabrication Shed', p. 36, where a marker-off's mate says that before the war different trades 'wouldn't speak to each other, they were at each other's throats. Now relationships are good.'
27. Analysis of database created by Selina Todd, *Digitisation of R. Brown, 'Orientation to Work and Industrial Behaviour of Shipbuilding Workers' Manual Workers' Questionnaires, 1968–1969*, SN: 6586, UKDA, Essex (question 146); the database contains 223 questionnaires.
28. See Shipbuilding Workers, Box 1, File 3, 'Observation notes on blacksmiths', p. 86.
29. Todd, *Digitisation of R. Brown*, SN: 6586, UKDA, Essex (questions 35 and 36).
30. Shipbuilding Workers, Box 1, File 3, 'Observation notes on blacksmiths', pp. 97–8, 104.
31. Shipbuilding Workers, Box 1, File 3, 'Observation notes on blacksmiths', pp. 57 and 96; see also File 5, 'Observation notes on Prefabrication Shed', p. 9. For a discussion of masculinity in dangerous heavy industries, including shipbuilding, see Ronnie Johnston and Arthur McIvor, 'Dangerous bodies, hard men and broken bodies: Masculinity in the Clydeside heavy industries, c.1930-1970s', *Labour History Review*, 69/2 (2004), 135–51.
32. Shipbuilding Workers, Box 1, File 6, 'Observation notes on plumbers', 5 and 7.
33. Shipbuilding Workers, Box 1, File 3, 'Observation notes on blacksmiths,' pp. 25, 70, 85.
34. Shipbuilding Workers, Box 1, File 3, 'Observation notes on blacksmiths', p. 61.
35. Brown et al., 'Leisure in work', p. 107.
36. Helen Smith, *Masculinity, Class and Same-Sex Desire in Industrial England, 1895–1957* (Palgrave Macmillan, Basingstoke, 2015), and 'Love sex and friendship: Northern, working-class men and sexuality in the first half of the twentieth century', in Alana Harris and Timothy Willem Jones (eds), *Love and Romance in Britain, 1918–1970* (Palgrave Macmillan, Basingstoke, 2015), 61–80.

37. Shipbuilding Workers, Box 1, File 3, 'Observation notes on blacksmiths', pp. 105–7.

38. Shipbuilding Workers, Box 1, File 3, 'Observation notes on blacksmiths', p. 85; File 6, 'Observation notes on plumbers', pp. 8 and 10.

39. Shipbuilding Workers, Box 1, File 6, 'Observation notes on plumbers', p. 84.

40. Shipbuilding Workers, Box 1, File 6, 'Observation notes on plumbers', p. 7; File 15, 'Reports on a launch' [the Nacella], 1–2.

41. Shipbuilding Workers, Box 1, File 3, 'Observation notes on blacksmiths', p. 11; File 8, 'Observation notes on Joiners (shop and ship)', p. 22. The joiners were also expected to do 'swag' jobs for management on company time—a pigeon hamper [basket] was said to have taken six man-hours because they didn't have the right tools (File 8, p. 47).

42. See Shipbuilding Workers, Box 1, File 5, 'Observation notes on Prefabrication Shed', p. 6, cited in Brown and Brannen, 'Social relations, Part Two', p. 204.

43. Todd, *Digitisation of R. Brown*, SN: 6586, UKDA, Essex (question 24).

44. Shipbuilding Workers, Box 1, File 8, 'Observation notes on Joiners (shop and ship)', p. 36.

45. Shipbuilding Workers, Box 4, FM08, 'Informal interview with foreman joiners' [assembly shop], p. 1.

46. Shipbuilding Workers, Box 4, FM08, 'Informal interview with foreman joiners' [timber store], p. 1.

47. See Anna Clark, *The Struggle for the Breeches: Gender and the Making of the British Working Class* (University of California Press, Berkeley and Los Angeles, 1995), and Catherine Hall, Keith McClelland, and Jane Rendall, *Defining the Victorian Nation: Class, Race, Gender and the British Reform Act of 1867* (Cambridge University Press, Cambridge, 2000).

48. Shipbuilding Workers, Box 1, File 8, 'Observation notes on Joiners (shop and ship)', p. 19.

49. M. E. Loane, *The Queen's Poor: Life as They Find It in Town and Country* (Edward Arnold, London, 1905), ch. 1; also Maud Pember Reeves, *Round about a Pound a Week* (1913; Virago, London, 1979), 9–10, 6. See Julie-Marie Strange, *Fatherhood and the British Working-Class, 1865–1914* (Cambridge University Press, Cambridge, 2015), and Laura King, *Family Men: Fatherhood and Masculinity in Britain, 1914–1960* (Oxford Uuniversity Press, Oxford, 2015).

50. Robert Moore, *Pit-men, Preachers and Politics: The Effects of Methodism in a Durham Mining Community* (Cambridge University Press, Cambridge, 1974); Huw Beynon and Terry Austrin, *Masters and Servants: Class and Patronage in the Making of a Labour Organisation: The Durham Miners and the English Political Tradition* (Rivers Oram, London, 1994). See also Mark Benney, *Charity Main: A Coalfield Chronicle* (George Allen, London, 1948).

51. Phil Wickham, *The Likely Lads* (BFI/Palgrave, London, 2008), offers a useful introduction.

52. Shipbuilding Workers, Box 4, FM08, 'Informal interview with foreman joiners' [assembly shop], p. 3.

53. Shipbuilding Workers, Box 1, File 6, 'Observation notes on plumbers', pp. 17, 21.

54. Sting, *Unbroken Music*, 86–8.

55. Shipbuilding Workers, Box 1, File 3, 'Observation notes on blacksmiths', p. 53.

56. Shipbuilding Workers, Box 4, FM15, 'Informal interview with foreman shipwrights', p. 1.

57. Todd, *Digitisation of R. Brown*, SN: 6586, UKDA, Essex (questions 165, 168, and 169)—23 of 223 said they preferred the company of fellow shipworkers; Shipbuilding Workers, Box 4, FM15, 'Informal interview with foreman shipwrights', p. 4.

58. Brown et al., 'Leisure in work', 99–102.

59. Analysis based on Todd, *Digitisation of R. Brown*, SN: 6586, UKDA, Essex (question 174). For the growth of working-class home entertaining in a northern town, see Stefan Ramsden, 'Remaking working-class community: Sociability, belonging and "affluence" in a small town, 1930–1980', *Contemporary British History*, 29/1 (2015), 1–26 at 16, 18–19.

60. Shipbuilding Workers, Box 1, File 3, 'Observation notes on blacksmiths', p. 93.
61. Shipbuilding Workers, Box 1, File 3, 'Observation notes on blacksmiths', p. 40 [thanks to Florence Sutcliffe-Braithwaite for this reference].
62. Shipbuilding Workers, Box 1, File 6, 'Observation notes on plumbers', pp. 69, 74, 76–7.
63. For the national picture, see King, *Family Men*, and Pat Ayers, 'Work, culture and gender: The making of post-war masculinities in post-war Liverpool', *Labour History Review*, 69/2 (2004), 154–67, where more home-centred forms of masculinity are associated with the new industries drawn to Merseyside after the war.
64. Shipbuilding Workers, Box 1, File 3, 'Observation notes on blacksmiths', pp. 86, 98; File 6, 'Observation notes on plumbers', p. 72.
65. Shipbuilding Workers, Box 1, File 3, 'Observation notes on blacksmiths', p. 98.
66. For an example of doing just this, see Miriam Glucksmann (aka Ruth Cavendish), *Women on the Line* (1982; Abingdon, Routledge, new edn, 2009).
67. Shipbuilding Workers, Box 1, File 3, 'Observation notes on blacksmiths', p. 107.
68. Shipbuilding Workers, Box 1, File 7, 'Observation notes on plumbers' shop', p. 4; see also File 6, 'Observation notes on plumbers', p. 47, where the apprentice butcher declares it's no good blaming the upper class. I'm just less intelligent than you lot.'
69. Shipbuilding Workers, Box 1, File 6, 'Observation notes on plumbers', p. 66.
70. Shipbuilding Workers, Box 1, File 7, 'Observation notes on plumbers' shop', p. 8.
71. Michael Young, *The Rise of the Meritocracy, 1870–2033: An Essay on Education and Equality* (Thames & Hudson, London, 1958).
72. e.g. Shipbuilding Workers, Box 1, File 4, 'Observation notes on labourers', p. 12; File 6, 'Observation notes on plumbers', p. 47; File 8, 'Observation notes on Joiners (shop and ship)', pp. 12, 30.
73. Shipbuilding Workers, Box 4, FM12, 'Informal interview with foreman platers', p. 1.
74. Shipbuilding Workers, Box 1, File 3, 'Observation notes on blacksmiths', p. 33.
75. Todd, *Digitisation of R. Brown*, SN: 6586, UKDA, Essex (question 94).
76. Shipbuilding Workers, Box 4, FM11, 'Informal interview with foreman painters', p. 1.
77. Shipbuilding Workers, Box 1, File 3, 'Observation notes on blacksmiths', p. 57. As here, the term 'the men' was always used to denote only the manual employees; the origins were probably military, but it also suggested an alternative hierarchy of masculinity.
78. Shipbuilding Workers, Box 1, File 18, 'Additional and Informal Interviews' [Sunderland Tack Welder], p. 12.
79. Shipbuilding Workers, Box 1, File 3, 'Observation notes on blacksmiths', p. 107.
80. Shipbuilding Workers, Box 1, File 3, 'Observation notes on blacksmiths', p. 63.
81. The blacksmiths told the raciest stories at their foremen's expense: Shipbuilding Workers, Box 1, File 3, 'Observation notes on blacksmiths', p. 54; see also FM18, 'Informal interview with foreman transport', p. 1; and FM20, Informal interview with foreman piece clerk', p. 5.
82. Shipbuilding Workers, Box 1, File 3, 'Observation notes on blacksmiths', p. 54.
83. Shipbuilding Workers, Box 1, File 3, 'Observation notes on blacksmiths', p. 54.
84. Shipbuilding Workers, Box 1, File 6, 'Observation notes on plumbers', pp. 30, 39— though overall nearly half the men thought that the consortium would make things better (47 per cent), Todd, *Digitisation of R. Brown*, SN: 6586, UKDA, Essex (question 102).
85. See Shipbuilding Workers, Box 1, File 5, 'Observation notes on Prefabrication Shed', p. 38. The words are from Walter Scott's narrative poem 'The Lay of the Last Minstrel' (1805), from the famous sixth canto, 'Breathes there the man'.

86. Contrary to the picture of decline painted in Jonathan Rose, *The Intellectual History of the British Working Classes* (Yale University Press, New Haven, 2001), 11, 463–4.

87. Shipbuilding Workers, Box 1, File 11, 'Shop Stewards Outing notes'; interestingly this shop steward had voted Tory since 1964 but wanted it kept a secret.

88. Shipbuilding Workers, Box 4, FM08, 'Informal interview with foreman joiners', p. 2.

89. Shipbuilding Workers, Box 1, File 6, 'Observation notes on plumbers', p. 53.

90. Shipbuilding Workers, Box 1, File 6, 'Observation notes on plumbers', pp. 53 and 56.

91. Shipbuilding Workers, Box 1, File 8, 'Observation notes on Joiners (shop and ship)', p. 43 (17 Apr. 1969).

92. Shipbuilding Workers, Box 1, File 6, 'Observation notes on plumbers', p. 53; see also File 3, 'Observation notes on blacksmiths', p. 25, for a denunciation of 'parasites' at Ascot.

93. Gareth Stedman Jones, 'Rethinking Chartism', in his *Languages of Class: Studies in English Working-Class History, 1832–1982* (Cambridge University Press, Cambridge, 1984), 90–178.

94. Shipbuilding Workers, Box 4, FM20, 'Informal interview with foreman piece clerk', p. 5.

95. Shipbuilding Workers, Box 1, File 6, 'Observation notes on plumbers', p. 92.

96. For a reconstruction of this culture among young working-class males, including in the North East, see Celia Hughes, 'Young socialist men in 1960s Britain: Subjectivity and sociability', *History Workshop Journal*, 73 (Spring 2012), 170–92.

97. Shipbuilding Workers, Box 1, File 6, 'Observation notes on plumbers', p. 57.

98. Richard Hoggart, *The Uses of Literacy: Aspects of Working-Class Life* (Chatto & Windus, London, 1957), 73.

99. Shipbuilding Workers, Box 1, File 6, 'Observation notes on plumbers', p. 79.

100. Shipbuilding Workers, Box 1, File 6, 'Observation notes on plumbers', p. 84.

101. Shipbuilding Workers, Box 1, File 6, 'Observation notes on plumbers', p. 41.

102. Shipbuilding Workers, Box 1, File 6, 'Observation notes on plumbers', p. 8; File 7, 'Observation notes on plumbers' shop', p. 2.

103. Amy C. Whipple, 'Revisiting the "rivers of blood" controversy: Letters to Enoch Powell', *Journal of British Studies*, 48/3 (2009), 717–35; Andrew Crines, Tim Heppell, and Michael Hill, 'Enoch Powell's "rivers of blood" speech: A rhetorical political analysis', *British Politics*, 11/1 (2016), 72–94.

104. Laura Tabili, *Global Migrants, Local Culture: Natives and Newcomers in Provincial England, 1841–1939* (Palgrave Macmillan, Basingstoke, 2011); also Robert Colls, 'When we lived in communities: Working-class culture and its critics', in Robert Colls and Richard Rodger (eds), *Cities of Ideas: Civil Society and Urban Governance in Britain, 1800–2000: Essays in Honour of David Reeder* (Ashgate, Aldershot, 2005), 286.

105. Shipbuilding Workers, Box 1, File 3, 'Observation notes on blacksmiths', p. 54, also p. 11; and File 6, 'Observation notes on plumbers', p. 2.

106. Shipbuilding Workers, Box 1, File 4, 'Observation notes on labourers, Part II', p. 9.

107. Shipbuilding Workers, Box 1, File 3, 'Observation notes on blacksmiths', p. 23.

108. Raphael Samuel and Paul Thompson (eds), *The Myths We Live by* (Routledge, London, 1990).

109. Shipbuilding Workers, Box 1, File 6, 'Observation notes on plumbers', p. 41.

110. Shipbuilding Workers, Box 1, File 6, 'Observation notes on plumbers', p. 47.

111. Jon Lawrence, 'Why the working class was never "white"', *New Left Project*, 26 Dec. 2014; for the opposing view, see Alastair Bonnett, 'How the British working class became white: The symbolic (re)formation of racialized capitalism', *Journal of Historical Sociology*, 11/2 (1998), 316–40, and Satnam Virdee, *Racism, Class and the Racialized Other* (Palgrave

Macmillan, Basingstoke, 2014). Alastair Bonnett, 'Anti-racism in "White" areas: The example of Tyneside', *Antipode*, 24/1 (1992), 1–15, explores the efforts of educational professionals to combat 'white' working-class racism from outside.

112. BBC2 *White* series, 2008; Michael Collins, *The Likes of Us: A Biography of the White Working Class* (Granta, London, 2004).

113. See Kjartan Páll Sveinsson (ed.), *Who Cares About the White Working Class?* (Runnymede Trust, London, 2009), and Omar Khan and Faiza Shaheen (eds), *Minority Report: Race and Class in Post-Brexit Britain* (Runnymede Trust, London, 2017).

114. Susie L. Steinbach, *Understanding the Victorians: Politics, Culture, and Society in Nineteenth-Century Britain*, (Routledge, New York, 2012), 108.

115. Lawrence Black and Hugh Pemberton, *An Affluent Society?: Britain's Post-War 'Golden Age'* (Ashgate, Aldershot, 2004); Lawrence Black, *The Political Culture of the Left in Affluent Britain, 1951–1964: Old Labour, New Britain* (Palgrave, Basingstoke, 2003); Stuart Middleton, '"Affluence" and the left in Britain, c.1958–1974', *English Historical Review*, 129 (2014), 107–38.

116. Shipbuilding Workers, Box 1, File 3, 'Observation notes on blacksmiths', p. 25.

117. Shipbuilding Workers, Box 1, File 3, 'Observation notes on blacksmiths', p. 34.

118. Shipbuilding Workers, Box 1, File 6, 'Observation notes on plumbers', p. 74.

119. Shipbuilding Workers, Box 1, File 6, 'Observation notes on plumbers', p. 69.

120. Shipbuilding Workers, Box 1, File 11, 'Miscellaneous notes and reports concerning shop stewards', p. 11; in consequence he now only brought his lunch and cigarette money to work with him.

121. Shipbuilding Workers, Box 1, File 6, 'Observation notes on plumbers', p. 8.

122. Todd, *Digitisation of R. Brown*, SN: 6586, UKDA, Essex (question 191).

123. Shipbuilding Workers, Box 1, File 6, 'Observation notes on plumbers', p. 81.

124. Todd, *The People, passim*.

125. Shipbuilding Workers, Box 1, File 8, 'Observation notes on Joiners (shop and ship)', p. 41; FM03, 'Informal interview with foreman craneman', p. 1; File 13, 'Observational Notes on Cranemen and Stagers', p. 2; File 3, 'Observation notes on blacksmiths', p. 61.

126. Shipbuilding Workers, Box 1, File 3, 'Observation notes on blacksmiths', p. 62.

127. Shipbuilding Workers, Box 4, FM23, 'Informal interview with foreman welder', p. 3.

128. Shipbuilding Workers, Box 1, File 6, 'Observation notes on plumbers', p. 74; it seems likely Morris delivered his monologue direct to tape given he had evidently sought out the researcher.

129. Carol Gilligan et al., 'On the listening guide: a voice-centered relational method', in Sharlene Nagy Hesse-Biber and Patricia Leavy (eds), *Emergent Methods in Social Research*, at http://dx.doi.org/10.4135/9781412984034.n12.

130. Todd, *Digitisation of R. Brown*, SN: 6586, UKDA, Essex (question 150); slightly fewer, 32 per cent, said they would move down south if offered a job there with more money (question 153).

131. Shipbuilding Workers, Box 1, File 3, 'Observation notes on blacksmiths', p. 99.

132. Shipbuilding Workers, Box 1, File 6, 'Observation notes on plumbers', p. 39.

133. Shipbuilding Workers, Box 1, File 8, 'Observation notes on Joiners (shop and ship)', 34, 51.

134. Shipbuilding Workers, Box 1, File 17, 'Accounts of Yard Disputes', p. 1.

135. Shipbuilding Workers, Box 1, File 3, 'Observation notes on blacksmiths', p. 45.

136. See Shipbuilding Workers, Box 1, File 5, 'Observation notes on Prefabrication Shed', p. 4; see also File 8, 'Observation notes on Joiners (shop and ship)', p. 51.

137. Shipbuilding Workers, Box 1, File 6, 'Observation notes on plumbers', pp. 22, 47.
138. Shipbuilding Workers, Box 1, File 8, 'Observation notes on Joiners (shop and ship)', pp. 23–4, 30, 41.
139. Shipbuilding Workers, Box 1, File 8, 'Observation notes on Joiners (shop and ship)', p. 27.
140. Todd, *Digitisation of R. Brown*, SN: 6586, UKDA, Essex (questions 109 and 111).
141. Todd, *Digitisation of R. Brown*, SN: 6586, UKDA, Essex (question 108).
142. Shipbuilding Workers, Box 1, File 15, 'Reports on a Launch (Nacella)', 2nd report, p. 2; File 11, 'Miscellaneous notes and reports concerning shop stewards', 13–14; File 18. 'Additional and informal interviews' [2nd welder], p. 3.
143. Shipbuilding Workers, Box 1, File 18, 'Additional and informal interviews' [welder], p. 3.
144. Todd, *Digitisation of R. Brown*, SN: 6586, UKDA, Essex (question 27); slightly fewer, 30 per cent, fancied becoming a manager, nearly half of whom said that they did not want to be a foreman (question 29).
145. Shipbuilding Workers, Box 4, FM23, 'Informal interview with foreman welder', p. 1.
146. Shipbuilding Workers, Box 4, FM06, 'Informal interview with foreman fitters', tool shop foreman, p. 1.
147. Shipbuilding Workers, Box 4, FM08, 'Informal interview with foreman joiners', p. 1; FM10, 'Informal interview with foreman mould loft', p. 1.
148. Shipbuilding Workers, Box 1, File 3, 'Observation notes on blacksmiths', p. 54.
149. Shipbuilding Workers, Box 1, File 6, 'Observation notes on plumbers', p. 76.
150. Shipbuilding Workers, Box 1, File 3, 'Observation notes on blacksmiths', p. 93.
151. Todd, *Digitisation of R. Brown*, SN: 6586, UKDA, Essex (question 176).
152. Bo Särlvik and Ivor Crewe, *Decade of Dealignment: The Conservative Victory of 1979 and electoral trends in the 1970s* (Cambridge University Press, Cambridge, 1983); Richard Rose and Ian McAllister, *Voters Begin to Choose: From Closed-Class to Open Elections in Britain* (SAGE, London, 1986).

Chapter 6

1. R. E. Pahl, *Divisions of Labour* (Oxford, 1984), 165–77.
2. Pahl, *Divisions of Labour*, 165–6; R. E. Pahl and C. D. Wallace, 'Neither angels in marble nor rebels in red: privatization and working-class consciousness', in David Rose (ed.), *Social Stratification and Economic Change* (London, 1988), 127–49.
3. J. I. Gershuny and R. E. Pahl, 'Work outside employment', *New Universities Quarterly*, 34/1 (1979), 120–35; R. E. Pahl, 'Employment, work and the domestic division of Labour', *International Journal of Urban and Regional Research*, 4/1 (1980), 1–20; R. E. Pahl, 'Family, Community and Unemployment', *New Society*, 21 Jan. 1982, pp. 91–3; and for his auto-critique, Pahl, *Divisions of Labour*, 339–41.
4. Pahl, *Divisions of Labour*, 167–8.
5. Pahl, *Divisions of Labour*, 9–13.
6. Pahl, *Divisions of Labour*, ch. 6, quoted matter at p. 195; also Graham Crow and Jaimie Ellis (eds), *Revisiting Divisions of Labour: The Impacts and Legacies of a Sociological Classic* (Manchester University Press, Manchester, 2017), esp. ch. 1: Tim Strangleman, 'Portrait of a deindustrialising island', 55–68.
7. On the economic difficulties of the 1970s and their consequences, see Lawrence Black, Hugh Pemberton, and Pat Thane (eds.), *Reassessing 1970s Britain* (Manchester University

Press, Manchester, 2013); Richard Coopey and Nicholas Woodward (eds), *Britain in the 1970s: The Troubled Decade* (UCL Press, London, 1996).

8. South East Joint Planning Team, *Strategic Plan for the South East, Studies*, ii. *Social and Environmental Aspects* (HMSO, London, 1971), 14–29; discussed more fully in R. E. Pahl, 'Patterns of urban life in the next fifteen years', *New Universities Quarterly*, 30 (1976), 402–19, and Pahl, *Divisions of Labour*, 6–7.

9. Natalie Thomlinson (University of Reading) is currently engaged in a large-scale exploration of feminism in popular culture from the 1970s; see Emily Robinson et al., 'Telling stories about post-war Britain: Popular individualism and the "crisis" of the 1970s', *Twentieth Century British History*, 28/2 (2017), 268–304, at 289–96.

10. Sheppey Collection, Box 6, HWS-24.391a (Tape), Mrs X ['Pat Clark'], at 45 min. 18 sec. Unlike earlier studies, with the Sheppey Collection we often have access to the original interview recordings, most of which have now been digitally preserved.

11. Claire Langhamer, *The English in Love: The Intimate Story of an Emotional Revolution* (Oxford University Press, Oxford, 2013); on the growing salience of languages of self-realization across the 1970s, see Robinson et al., 'Telling stories'. Dawn Lyon and Graham Crow, 'The challenges and opportunities of re-studying community on Sheppey: Young people's imagined futures', *Sociological Review*, 60 (2012), 498–517, demonstrates the strongly gendered nature of local adolescents' imagined futures in 1978 and their convergence by 2010.

12. Sheppey Collection, Box 6, HWS-28.039a (Tape), 'Baileys', at 6 min. 10 sec. Also Box 10, HWS-27.889, Case 27, 'Archer', Summary Report (a retired couple). On changing ideas about fathering as a yardstick of broader social change, see Laura King, '"Now you see a great many men pushing their pram proudly": Family-orientated masculinity represented and experienced in mid-twentieth-century Britain', *Cultural and Social History*, 10/4 (2013), 599–617.

13. Sheppey Collection, UKDA transcription, HWS-26.084a, Mrs Z ['Spillett'], 36–8.

14. Mike Savage, 'Sociology, class and male manual work cultures', in John McIlroy, Nina Fisher, and Alan Campbell (eds), *British Trade Unions and Industrial Politics*, ii. *the High Tide of Trade Unionism, 1964–1979* (Ashgate, Aldershot, 1999), discusses the 'rugged individualism' of male workplace culture.

15. David Buckley, *Strange Fascination: David Bowie the Definitive Story* (Virgin Publishing, London, 1999); Pete Dale, *Anyone Can Do It: Empowerment, Tradition and the Punk Underground* (Ashgate, Farnham, 2012).

16. Helen McCarthy, 'Women, marriage and paid work in Post-war Britain', *Women's History Review*, 26/1 (2017), 46–61.

17. Helen McCarthy, 'Social science and married women's employment in post-war Britain', *Past & Present*, 233 (Nov. 2016), 269–305. Also Dolly Smith Wilson, 'A new look at the affluent worker: The good working mother in post-war Britain', *Twentieth-Century British History*, 17/2 (2006), 206–29.

18. Ann Oakley, *The Sociology of Housework* (Robertson, London, 1974); Elizabeth Wilson, *Only Half-Way to Paradise: Women in Postwar Britain, 1945–1968* (Tavistock, London, 1980).

19. Pahl, *Divisions of Labour*, 270–6, quoted matter at 275.

20. See Miriam Glucksmann, *Cotton and Casuals: The Gendered Organisation of Labour in Time and Space* (Sociology Press, Durham, 2000), for a detailed exploration of these issues.

21. Pahl, *Divisions of Labour*, 274.

22. Sheppey Collection, UKDA transcription, HWS-26.084a, Mrs Z ['Spillett'], pp. 13, 15, 19–21.

23. Sheppey Collection, UKDA transcription, HWS-26.084a, Mrs Z ['Spillett'], pp. 5, 11, 66–7.

24. Sheppey Collection, UKDA transcription, HWS-29.699a, Mr and Mrs 'Chittenden', pp. 7–14, quoted matter at p. 13.

25. Sheppey Collection, UKDA transcription, HWS-29.699a, Mr and Mrs 'Chittenden', pp. 39–41.

26. On changing conceptions of selfhood in this period, especially among women, see Lynn Abrams, 'Liberating the female self: Epiphanies, conflict and coherence in the life stories of post-war British women', *Social History*, 39/1 (2014), 14–35, and Robinson et al., 'Telling stories'.

27. Sheppey Collection, Box 6, HWS-24.391b (Tape), Mrs X ['Pat Clark'], at 4 min. 32 sec.

28. Sheppey Collection, Box 6, HWS-24.391b (Tape), Mrs X ['Pat Clark'], at 7 min. 50 sec.

29. Sheppey Collection, Box 5, HWS-24.391, Mrs X ['Pat Clark'], Summary Report.

30. Sheppey Collection, Box 6, HWS-24.391a (Tape), Mrs X ['Pat Clark'], at 23 min. 30 sec.

31. Sarah E. Igo, *The Averaged American: Surveys, Citizens, and the Making of a Mass Public* (Harvard University Press, Cambridge, MA, 2007).

32. Sheppey Collection, Box 6, HWS-24.391a (Tape), Mrs X ['Pat Clark'], at 24 min 0 sec.

33. Sheppey Collection, Box 6, HWS-24.391b (Tape), Mrs X ['Pat Clark'], at 3 min. 35 sec.

34. Sheppey Collection, Box 6, HWS-24.391a (Tape), Mrs X ['Pat Clark'], at 5 min. 40 sec.

35. Sheppey Collection, Box 6, HWS-24.391a (Tape), Mrs X ['Pat Clark'], at 21 min. 20 sec.; Box 5, HWS-24.391, Mrs X ['Pat Clark'], Summary Report.

36. Sheppey Collection, Box 6, HWS-23.210a (Tape), 'Wood family', quoted matter at 14 min. 10 sec. and 14 min. 49 sec.

37. Sheppey Collection, Box 6, HWS-HWS-26-084a (Tape), Mrs Z ('Spillett'), at 10 min. 30 sec.

38. Pahl, *Divisions of Labour*, 272–3; Sheppey Collection, Box 10, HWS2.850, 'Mr Birch', Summary Report; HWS6.417 'Fallaci' Summary Report; HWS7.466, 'Godfrey' Summary Report.

39. Sheppey Collection, Box 6, HWS-5.413-1a (Tape), 'Ellis', at 18 min. 30 sec. (speaker's emphasis).

40. Quoted matter at Sheppey Collection, Box 6, HWS-5.413-1a (Tape), 'Ellis', at 3 min. 39 sec., 7 min. 48 sec., and 11 min. 45 sec.

41. Pahl, *Divisions of Labour*, 9–10.

42. Sheppey Collection, Box 10, HWS 30.432, 1982 Report, p. 2. He was keeping sheep himself at this point on a small pasture he and a neighbour had recently reclaimed and fenced: Sheppey Collection, Box 6, HWS-30-432b (Tape), 'Dunkley', at 7 min. 05 sec.

43. Sheppey Collection, Box 10, HWS 30.432, 1982 Report, pp. 2–3.

44. Sheppey Collection, Box 6, HWS-30-432a (Tape), 'Dunkley', at 23 min. 25 sec.

45. Sheppey Collection, Box 6, HWS-30-432a (Tape), 'Dunkley', at 24 min. 52 sec.

46. Sheppey Collection, Box 6, HWS-30-432a (Tape), 'Dunkley', at 35 min. 10 sec.

47. Sheppey Collection, Box 6, HWS-30-432a (Tape), 'Dunkley', at 35 min. 28 sec.

48. Sheppey Collection, Box 6, HWS-30-432a (Tape), 'Dunkley', at 36 min. 49 sec.; Box 10, HWS 30.432, 1982 Report, p. 5.

49. Sheppey Collection, Box 10, HWS 30.432, 1982 Report, p. 6.

50. Sheppey Collection, Box 7, HWS83 Case 29, The Urban Peasant ('Stan Cummings'), Interview Transcript, pp. 7, 8–9.

51. Sheppey Collection, Box 7, HWS83 Case 29, The Urban Peasant ('Stan Cummings'), Interview Transcript, pp. 5, 8, 9.

52. Sheppey Collection, Box 7, HWS83 Case 29, The Urban Peasant ('Stan Cummings'), Interview Transcript, p. 10 ('evenings' in original).
53. Sheppey Collection, Box 7, HWS83 Case 29, The Urban Peasant ('Stan Cummings'), Interview Transcript, p. 1.
54. Sheppey Collection, Box 7, HWS83 Case 29, The Urban Peasant ('Stan Cummings'), Interview Transcript, p. 1.
55. Sheppey Collection, Box 7, HWS83 Case 29, The Urban Peasant ('Stan Cummings'), Interview Transcript, p. 2.
56. Sheppey Collection, UKDA transcription, HWS-26-084a, Mrs Z ['Spillett'], pp. 36, 38–9; see Dawn Lyon, 'Time and place in memory and imagination on the Isle of Sheppey', in Crow and Ellis (eds), *Revisiting Divisions of Labour*, 149–68.
57. Sheppey Collection, UKDA transcription, HWS-2-850a, 'Mr Birch', p. 6.
58. Sheppey Collection, UKDA transcription, HWS-29.699, Mr & Mrs 'Chittenden', p. 49.
59. Sheppey Collection, Box 6, HWS PIL 9, 'Quayle', pp. 6, 11. Mrs Jebb, a local teacher, made a similar claim, arguing that 'there's no snobbery on Sheppey. It doesn't make any difference whether you meet your dustman or the Mayor . . . in fact the dustman could be the Mayor', Sheppey Collection, UKDA transcription, HWS-10.620, 'Jebb', pp. 33–4.
60. Sheppey Collection, Box 6, HWS PIL 9, 'Quayle', p. 12.
61. Sheppey Collection, Box 6, HWS-6-417a (Tape), 'Fallaci', from 15 min. 15 sec. to 16 min. 56 sec.
62. Sheppey Collection, Box 6, HWS-6-417a (Tape), 'Fallaci', at 22 min. 40 sec.
63. Sheppey Collection, Box 10, HWS 6.417, 'Fallaci', Summary and Report, pp. 1, 4.
64. Pahl, *Divisions of Labour*, p. ii.
65. Sheppey Collection, Box 6, HWS-15.473a (Tape), 'Ogden', at 34 min. 44 sec.
66. Sheppey Collection, Box 6, HWS-15.473a (Tape), 'Ogden', at 19 min. 22 sec.
67. Sheppey Collection, Box 6, HWS-8.328b (Tape), 'Harris', from 4 min. 45 sec. to 6 min. 50 sec. Contrary to the argument in Margaret Grieco, *Keeping It in the Family: Social Networks and Employment Chance* (Tavistock, London, 1987), reminding us, again, of the danger of sweeping generalizations about working-class culture.
68. Sheppey Collection, Box 6, HWS-8.328b (Tape), 'Harris', at 18 min. 40 sec.; Box 10, HWS 8.328, 'Harris', Report, p. 1 (punctuation added).
69. R. E. Pahl and C. D. Wallace, 'Forms of work and privatisation on the Isle of Sheppey', in Bryan Roberts, Ruth Finnegan, and Duncan Gallie (eds), *New Approaches to Economic Life: Economic Restructuring: Unemployment and the Social Division of Labour* (Manchester University Press, Manchester, 1985).
70. Sheppey Collection, Box 6, HWS-8.328a (Tape), at 43 min. 50 sec.; and HWS-8.328b (Tape), from 12 min. 9 sec. to 15 min. 55 sec., 16 min. 38 sec. to 19 min. 31 sec., and 27 min. 50 sec. to 29 min. 45 sec.
71. Mike Savage et al., *Globalization and Belonging* (Sage, London, 2005), chs 2 and 3.
72. Sheppey Collection, Box 6, HWS-22.054a (Tape), 'Iles', at 12 min. 49 sec. (original emphasis).
73. Sheppey Collection, Box 6, HWS-22.054a (Tape), 'Iles', from 22 min. 07 sec. to 22 min. 33 sec.
74. Sheppey Collection, Box 10, HWS22.54, 'Iles', Report, p. 1.
75. Sheppey Collection, Box 6, HWS-22.054a (Tape), 'Iles', at 33 min. 14 sec.
76. Sheppey Collection, Box 10, HWS22.054, 'Iles', Summary.
77. Sheppey Collection, Box 6, HWS-22.054a (Tape), 'Iles', at 32 min. 25 sec.

78. Sheppey Collection, Box 5, File: 'Sheppey Work by Claire and Jane Dennett', esp. the paper by Claire Wallace, 'Sub-Community Studies' (Oct. 1982); also Box 7, 'Household Work Strategies 1983: HWS83 Transcripts 1', which includes extracts about neighbours' relationships from twenty-nine interviews.

79. Philip Abrams, *Neighbourhood Care and Social Policy; A Research Perspective* (Volunteer Centre: Berkhampsted, 1978); Philip Abrams et al., *Action for Care: A Review of Good Neighbour Schemes in England* (Volunteer Centre: Berkhampsted, 1981); and the posthumously published Martin Bulmer (ed.), *Neighbours: the Work of Philip Abrams* (Cambridge University Press, Cambridge, 1986).

80. Sheppey Collection, Box 7, Wallace, 'Sub-Community Studies', pp. 24, 36, 42, 47.

81. In contrast to Mark W. Hodges and Cyril S. Smith, 'The Sheffield estate', in University of Liverpool, *Neighbourhood and Community: An Enquiry into Social Relationships on Housing Estates in Liverpool and Sheffield* (Liverpool, 1954), 87–9, 101–3, 106.

82. Sheppey Collection, Box 7, Wallace, 'Sub-Community Studies', p. 7.

83. Sheppey Collection, Box 7, Wallace, 'Sub-Community Studies', p. 47.

84. Sheppey Collection, Box 7, Wallace, 'Sub-Community Studies', app. I, p. i.

85. Sheppey Collection, Box 7, Wallace, 'Sub-Community Studies', pp. 35, 36, 39, 42; and app. I, pp. v–vi, viii.

86. Sheppey Collection, Box 7, Wallace, 'Sub-Community Studies', app. I, p. ii.

87. Sheppey Collection, Box 7, Wallace, 'Sub-Community Studies', app. I, p. x.

88. Leo Kuper (ed.), *Living in Towns: Selected Research Papers in Urban Sociology* (Cresset Press, London, 1953); J. M. Mogey, *Family and Neighbourhood: Two Studies in Oxford* (Oxford University Press, Oxford, 1956); H. E. Bracey, *Neighbours: On New Estates and Subdivisions in England and the USA* (Routledge, London, 1964); R. N. Morris and John Mogey, *The Sociology of Housing: Studies at Berinsfield* (Routledge, London, 1965); Bulmer (ed.), *Neighbours*.

89. B. Jane Elliott, 'Demographic trends in domestic life, 1945–1987' in David Clark (ed.), *Marriage, Domestic Life and Social Change: Writings for Jacqueline Burgoyne (1944–88)* (Routledge, London, 1991), 91–6.

90. Sheppey Collection, Box 7, Wallace, 'Sub-Community Studies', app. I, p. xiv.

91. Sheppey Collection, Box 7, Wallace, 'Sub-Community Studies', pp. 39, 42–3, 45; and app. I, pp. iv and xiv–xvi. See also Bulmer (ed.), *Neighbours*, 54 and 57, where a divorced woman is said to be ostracized on a small council estate because 'they think I'm poison to their husbands'.

92. Sheppey Collection, Box 7, Wallace, 'Sub-Community Studies', p. 47.

93. Sheppey Collection, Box 7, HWS83, Case 29 [Cummings], p. 2 (original emphasis).

94. Sheppey Collection, Box 7, HWS83, Case 29 [Cummings], p. 2.

95. Sheppey Collection, Box 7, HWS83, Case 1 (Mrs Beerling), paras 1.5 and 1.8.

96. Sheppey Collection, Box 7, HWS83, Case 29, p. 2.

97. See Bulmer (ed.), *Neighbours*, 27–31, 96–9.

98. Sheppey Collection, Box 6, HWS-27.889a (Tape), 'Archer', at 25 min. 25 sec.

99. Sheppey Collection, UKDA transcription, HWS-11.631, 'Chopra', pp. 35–7.

100. Sheppey Collection, UKDA transcription, HWS-11.631, 'Chopra', p. 34 (her intonation suggests she meant that Mr Chopra would pop round to the neighbours with flowers, Sheppey Collection, Box 6, HWS11.631b (Tape), at 7 min. 5 sec.).

101. Sheppey Collection, Box 7, Wallace, 'Sub-Community Studies', p. 2; in contrast to Bulmer (ed.), *Neighbours*, 50–1, or Young and Willmott's comment in *Family and Kinship in East London* ((Routledge & Kegan Paul, London, 1957), p. xix.

102. Bulmer (ed.), *Neighbours*, 30–1, 48–9, 53, 86.

103. Bulmer (ed.), *Neighbours*, p. 49; Sheppey Collection, UKDA transcription, HWS-10.620, 'Jebb', p. 23; Box 10, HWS 10.620, Interview Summary, p. 1.

104. Sheppey Collection, UKDA transcription, HWS-10.620, 'Jebb', p. 23.

105. Bulmer (ed.), *Neighbours*, 66–7.

106. Pahl, 'Employment, Work and the Domestic Division of Labour', 10–14; Pahl, *Divisions of Labour*, 339–41.

107. Sheppey Collection, Box 5, HWS PIL6b, 'Simpson', pp. 12–13, and on the general mutualism between neighbours, pp. 4, 5, 8.

108. Sheppey Collection, Box 5, HWS PIL6b, 'Simpson', p. 12.

109. Sheppey Collection, Box 7, HWS83, Case 7, 'Stacey Smith', paras 7.8–7.10.

110. Sheppey Collection, Box 7, HWS83, Case 7, 'Stacey Smith', paras 7.18 and 7.19.

111. Sheppey Collection, Box 7, HWS83, Case 7, 'Stacey Smith', para 7.2.

112. Pahl, *Divisions of Labour*, 169–77; Claire Wallace, *For Richer, For Poorer: Growing Up In and Out of Work* (Tavistock, London, 1987), 18–27 (this book grew out of the PhD which Wallace undertook in parallel to her work for the project that led to Pahl's *Divisions of Labour*).

113. Wallace, *For Richer, For Poorer*, 71–2; Pahl, 'Family, community and unemployment', 91–3.

114. Pahl, *Divisions of Labour*, ch. 11 ('Polarization of workers' lives: Jim and Linda; Beryl and George').

115. See Jane Elliott and Jon Lawrence, 'Narrative, time and intimacy in social research: Linda and Jim revisited', in Crow and Ellis (eds), *Revisiting Divisions of Labour*, 189–204.

116. Pahl, *Divisions of Labour*, p. 309.

117. Pahl, *Divisions of Labour*, p. 309.

118. Sheppey Collection, UKDA transcription, HWS-22.054, 'Mrs Iles', pp. 29–30; HWS-23.210, 'Mrs Wood', pp. 32–3; HWS-26.048, 'Mrs Z', pp. 58–9.

119. Sheppey Collection, Box 7, HWS83, Case 29, The Urban Peasant ('Stan Cummings'), Interview Transcript, p. 7.

120. Sheppey Collection, UKDA transcription, HWS-3.358, 'Cartlidge', pp. 40–1.

121. Sheppey Collection, UKDA transcription, HWS-2.850, 'Birch', p. 8.

122. Sheppey Collection, Box 5, Folder 3 ('Linda and Jim Transcripts'), Interview 7, pp. 7 and 28.

123. Pahl, *Divisions of Labour*, 308. Unfortunately researchers subsequently recorded a follow-up interview with HWS.4 over one side of the interview with Beryl and George (HWS.13) but the first half of the interview survives along with a short summary: Sheppey Collection, Box 10, HWS 13.934, Interview Summary.

124. Pahl, *Divisions of Labour*, 308; Sheppey Collection, UKDA transcription, HWS-13.934b, 'Beryl and George', pp. 10–11; and Box 6, HWS-13.934b (Tape), from 10 min. 1 sec. to 12 min. 3 sec.

125. Sheppey Collection, Box 6, HWS83, Case 1, 'Mrs Beerling', (Tape) at 89 min. 43 sec.; Box 7, HWS83, Case 1, para 1.8.

126. Sheppey Collection, UKDA transcription, HWS-5.413/2a, 'Ellis', p. 25.

127. Sheppey Collection, UKDA transcription, HWS-1.789, 'Brakefield', pp. 33–4.

128. Sheppey Collection, UKDA transcription, HWS-1.789, 'Brakefield', pp. 40–2, 54.

129. Sheppey Collection, UKDA transcription, HWS-3.358, 'Cartlidge', pp. 32–3, 37, 52.

130. See Jane Elliott and Jon Lawrence, 'The emotional economy of unemployment: A re-analysis of testimony from a Sheppey family, 1978–1983', UKDA Special Edition 'Digital representations: Opportunities for re-using and publishing digital qualitative data', *Sage Open* (Dec. 2016) at http://journals.sagepub.com/doi/full/10.1177/2158244016669517.

131. Sheppey Collection, Box 5, Folder 3 ('Linda and Jim Transcripts'), Interview 3, p. 17.

132. Sheppey Collection, Box 5, Folder 3 ('Linda and Jim Transcripts'), Interview 5, p. 6; Interview 6, pp. 1 and 13.

133. Sheppey Collection, Box 5, Folder 3 ('Linda and Jim Transcripts'), Interview 5, p. 5; Interview 6, p. 1.

134. Sheppey Collection, Box 5, Folder 3 ('Linda and Jim Transcripts'), Interview 6, p. 1.

135. Sheppey Collection, Box 5, Folder 3 ('Linda and Jim Transcripts'), Interview 7, pp. 25–6.

136. Sheppey Collection, Box 5, Folder 3 ('Linda and Jim Transcripts'), Interview 7, pp. 26–7 (emphasis added).

137. Sheppey Collection, Box 5, Folder 3 ('Linda and Jim Transcripts), Interview 7, p. 25 (emphasis added).

138. Elliott and Lawrence, 'Emotional economy', 8–9.

139. Office of National Statistics, *Self-Employed Workers in the UK, 2014* (HMSO, London, 2014), 2.

140. Sheppey Collection, Box 6, HWS-24-391a (Tape), 'Mrs X' ['Pat Clark'], at 2 min. 20 sec.

141. Sheppey Collection, UKDA transcription, HWS-23.210, p. 33.

142. This reinforces recent arguments about the need to decentre Thatcher and Thatcherite ideology in historical accounts of the 1980s; see Stephen Brooke, 'Living in "New Times": Historicizing 1980s Britain', *History Compass*, 12/1 (2014), 20–32, and Matthew Hilton et al., '*New Times* revisited: Britain in the 1980s', *Contemporary British History*, 31/2 (2017), 145–65.

143. Sheppey Collection, UKDA transcription, HWS-3.358, 'Cartlidge', pp. 51–2.

144. Sheppey Collection, UKDA transcription, HWS-15.473, 'Ogden', pp. 30–1.

145. Sheppey Collection, UKDA transcription, HWS-15.473, 'Ogden', pp. 31–2, 36.

146. Sheppey Collection, Box 10, HWS-15.473, 'Ogden', Summary Report, pp. 1–2.

147. Sheppey Collection, Box 7, Wallace, 'Sub-Community Studies', p. 47.

148. Sheppey Collection, Box 7, HWS83, Case 5, 'Cathy Taylor', paras 5.2 and 5.9

149. Sheppey Collection, UKDA transcription, HWS-2.850a, pp. 11–12; 'Mr Birch'; Box 10, HWS2.850, 'Mr Birch', Summary Report, pp. 5–6, 8, 10.

150. Sheppey Collection, Box 7, HWS83, Case 2, 'Mr Beerling', para 2.5.

151. Sheppey Collection, Box 6, HWS83, Case 1, 'Mrs Beerling' (Tape), from 85 min. 20 sec. to 86 min. 40 sec.

152. Sheppey Collection, Box 6, HWS83, Case 1, 'Mrs Beerling' (Tape), at 24 min. 30 sec.; Box 7, HWS83, Case 1, 'Mrs Beerling', para. 1.2.

153. Sheppey Collection, Box 6, HWS83, Case 1, 'Mrs Beerling' (Tape), at 87 min. 10 sec. and 29 min. 0 sec.

154. Sheppey Collection, Box 6, HWS83, Case 1, 'Mrs Beerling' (Tape), at 85 min. 20 sec. See Claire Langhamer, 'The meanings of home in postwar Britain', *Journal of Contemporary History*, 40 (2005), 341–62.

155. Sheppey Collection, Box 5, HWS PIL10, 'Lawrenson', 2nd Interview (Nov. 1980), p. 2. If this was a version of Steedman's 'Tidy House' myth entrapping young girls it wasn't learned at mother's knee, Carolyn Steedman, *The Tidy House: Little Girls Writing* (Virago, London, 1982).

156. Sheppey Collection, UKDA transcription, HWS-12.385, 'Mr Lewry', pp. 5–6.

157. Sheppey Collection, UKDA transcription, HWS-8.328, 'Mr Harris', p. 11.

158. Sheppey Collection, UKDA transcription, HWS-8.328, 'Mr Harris', pp. 17–18.

159. Martin J. Daunton, 'Miners' houses: South Wales and the Great Northern Coal Field, 1880–1914', *International Review of Social History*, 25/2 (1980), 143–75; Steven Thompson,

'"Conservative bloom on socialism's compost heap": Working-class home ownership in South Wales, c.1890–1939', in Robert Rees Davies and Geraint H. Jenkins (eds), *From Medieval to Modern Wales: Historical Essays in Honour of Kenneth O. Morgan and Ralph A. Griffiths* (University of Wales Press, Cardiff, 2004), 246–63.

160. Sheppey Collection, Box 5, HWS PIL9, 'Quayle', pp. 4 and 7–8.
161. Sheppey Collection, Box 5, HWS PIL9, 'Quayle', pp. 12, 13.

Chapter 7

1. Nicholas Comfort, *The Slow Death of British Industry: A 60-Year Suicide, 1952–2012* (Biteback, London, 2012), 1–2, 8.
2. Len Holden, *Vauxhall Motors and the Luton Economy, 1900–2002* (Boydell, Woodbridge, 2003), 199; *Bedfordshire on Sunday*, 6 March 2017.
3. General Register Office, *Sample Census 1966 England and Wales, Workplace and Transport Tables Part I* (HMSO, London, 1968), 296–7 (table 5, Tyneside Conurbation).
4. Yvette Taylor, *Fitting into Place? Class and Gender Geographies and Temporalities* (Ashgate, Farnham, 2012).
5. Goldthorpe and Lockwood's Cambridge and Luton studies and Brown's work on Tyneside shipbuilding workers had also been based on place of work/occupation, although in the former case a residence criterion was also used.
6. Joe Moran, *On Roads: A Hidden History* (Profile Books, London, 2009), 26–9.
7. Hartley Dean with Margaret Melrose, *Poverty, Riches and Social Citizenship* (Macmillan, Basingstoke, 1999). Calculations based on data from *Dean and Melrose Study*. Most of those earning between £10,000 and £20,000 also lived in Luton, so that the average distance travelled by these workers was 2.2 miles. In all we have sufficient information to estimate travel to work distances for twenty-four of the twenty-eight workers interviewed in Luton.
8. Taylor, *Fitting into Place?*, esp. 1–20.
9. Employment data from OECD Employment and Labour Market Statistics at http://www.oecd-ilibrary.org (accessed 16 June 2017): Full-time, Part-time Employment—National Definition: Incidence; Incidence of Involuntary Part-time Workers; Incidence of Permanent Employment. Also Guy Weir, 'Self-employment in the UK labour market', *Labour Market Trends*, 111/9 (2003), 441–51; Office of National Statistics, *Trends in Self-Employment in the UK: 2001 to 2015* (HMSO, London, 2016), 5–6.
10. Guy Standing, *The Precariat: The New Dangerous Class* (rev. edn, Bloomsbury, London, 2014), 52–83.
11. John Urry, *Mobilities* (Polity, Cambridge, 2007); Zygmunt Bauman, *Liquid Modernity* (Polity, Cambridge, 2000); Hartmut Rosa, *Social Acceleration: A New Theory of Modernity*, trans. Jonathan Trejo-Mathys (Columbia University Press, New York, 2013).
12. Rosa, *Social Acceleration*, 231–50, 259–76.
13. In 1981 Margaret Thatcher concluded a long interview with *Sunday Times* journalist Ronald Butt by declaring: 'you really are after the heart and soul of the nation. Economics are the method; the object is to change the heart and soul', MTF, 3 May 1981, at http://www.margaretthatcher.org/document/104475 (accessed 15 June 2017).
14. Michael Young and Peter Willmott, *Family and Kinship in East London* (Routledge, London, 1957), 66–7, 90, 111–13; Raymond Firth (ed.), *Two Studies of Kinship in London* (Athlone Press, London, 1956), 60–1, noted the same pattern but stressed that distant kinship ties could be sustained when they were of mutual benefit. See also Firth Papers, 3/1/14, 'Two

Kinship Studies in London—Comments and Subsidiary Notes': notes on 'Kinship Groups'.

15. Dean with Melrose, *Poverty, Riches and Social Citizenship*, iii, 173–7.

16. Fiona Devine, *Affluent Workers Revisited: Privatism and the Working Class* (Edinburgh University Press, Edinburgh, 1992), 32–4.

17. Devine, *Affluent Workers*, 4, 24–5, 32–3, building on the arguments of Margaret Grieco, *Keeping it in the Family: Social Networks and Employment Chance* (Tavistock Publications, London, 1987), 125–34.

18. Devine, *Affluent Workers*, 10.

19. Devine, *Affluent Workers*, 192–4, 198–9.

20. Matthew Hilton, Chris Moores, and Florence Sutcliffe-Braithwaite, '*New Times* revisited: Britain in the 1980s', *Contemporary British History*, 31/2 (2017), 145–65.

21. Devine, *Affluent Workers*, 10.

22. Devine, *Affluent Workers*, 33; the survey questions assume that respondents are living in Luton, see Devine, *Affluent Workers*, 212–13 (app.).

23. Dean with Melrose, *Poverty, Riches and Social Citizenship*, 173. The sample included seventy-six individuals, including twenty-eight workers based in Luton and nineteen based in London. The remainder were scattered across southern England with the exception of three workers based in Sheffield.

24. Excluding five cases where no place of residence is recorded. Data compiled from interview transcripts by the author.

25. Michelle Littlefield and Andrew Nash, *Commuting Patterns as at the 2001 Census, and their Relationship with Modes of Transport and Types of Occupation* (Office for National Statistics, London, 2008), 1–2, 19–22; also Colin G. Pooley, 'Mobility in the twentieth century: Substituting commuting for migration?', in David Gilbert, David Matless, and Brian Short (eds), *Geographies of British Modernity: Space and Society in the Twentieth Century* (Oxford, Blackwell, 2003), 80–96.

26. Moran, *On Roads*, 209–10.

27. *Dean and Melrose Study*, Case R19, pp. 1, 13.

28. *Dean and Melrose Study*, Case R38, pp. 1, 8–9.

29. *Dean and Melrose Study*, Case R31, p. 8 (also pp. 11 and 15).

30. *Dean and Melrose Study*, Case R31, p. 16.

31. *Dean and Melrose Study*, Case R31, pp. 16–17.

32. Between the second quarter peak in 1989 and the fourth quarter trough in 1992; calculated from *Nationwide Regional Property Indices (Post '73)*, downloadable from http://www.nationwide.co.uk/about/house-price-index/download-data#tab:Downloaddata (accessed 15 June 2017).

33. *Dean and Melrose Study*, Case R71, pp. 1–2, 8, 20. Pahl's Linda and Jim on the Isle of Sheppey also lost their home in the early 1990s recession and in 1992 they were living in a holiday home where the power was switched off in the winter months (they planned to buy a generator); see Jane Elliott and Jon Lawrence, 'Narrative, time and intimacy in social research: Linda and Jim revisited', in Graham Crow and Jaimie Ellis (eds), *Revisiting Divisions of Labour: The Impacts and Legacies of a Modern Sociological Classic* (Manchester University Press, Manchester, 2017), 189–204.

34. *Dean and Melrose Study*, Case R71, pp. 4, 8, 20.

35. *Dean and Melrose Study*, Case R71, p. 22 (punctuation added).

36. *Dean and Melrose Study*, Case R37, p. 2.

37. *Dean and Melrose Study*, Case R37, p. 1.

38. *Dean and Melrose Study*, Case R37, pp. 2, 3, 11.

39. *Dean and Melrose Study*, Case R41, pp. 1, 13–14.

40. *Dean and Melrose Study*, Case R41, p. 9.

41. *Dean and Melrose Study*, Case R37, p. 15.

42. Beverley Skeggs, *Formations of Class and Gender: Becoming Respectable* (SAGE, London, 1997). See also Mike Savage, Elizabeth Silva, and Alan Warde, 'Dis-identification and class identity', in Elizabeth Silva and Alan Warde (eds), *Cultural Analysis and Bourdieu's Legacy: Settling Accounts and Developing Alternatives* (Routledge, Abingdon, 2010), 60–74.

43. *Dean and Melrose Study*, Case R69, p. 1; Julia Lourie, *The Social Chapter*, House of Commons Research Paper, 97/102 (September 1997), 7–10, 36–9, at http://researchbriefings. parliament.uk/ResearchBriefing/Summary/RP97-102 (accessed 15 June 2017); also Anthony Forster, *Britain and the Maastricht Negotiations* (Macmillan, Basingstoke, 1999), 93–5.

44. *Dean and Melrose Study*, Case R69, pp. 1–2, 11.

45. *Dean and Melrose Study*, Case R52, pp. 11–12; also Cases R53 (female, 51) and R70 (male, mid-thirties).

46. *Dean and Melrose Study*, Case R48, p. 16 (female, 22).

47. *Dean and Melrose Study*, Case R68, p. 19.

48. *Dean and Melrose Study*, Case R68, pp. 8 (punctuation added) and 1.

49. *Dean and Melrose Study*, Case R68, p. 14.

50. *Dean and Melrose Study*, Case R68, p. 5.

51. *Dean and Melrose Study*, Case R68, p. 3.

52. *Dean and Melrose Study*, Case R68, p. 19.

53. *Dean and Melrose Study*, Case R68, 7–8.

54. UK Data Archive, Essex, Y. Taylor (2012), *From the Coalface to the Car Park? The Intersection of Class and Gender in Women's Lives in the North East, 2007–2009* [data collection], UK Data Service. SN: 7053 (http://doi.org/10.5255/UKDA-SN-7053-1), Interview 001, pp. 8–9, 11–12. Names are Taylor's pseudonyms; information about place of residence is taken from Taylor, *Fitting into Place?*, app. 1, pp. 157–70.

55. *Coalface to Car Park Collection*, Interview 007 [Cathy, 37], pp. 4–5; Interview 002 [Angie, 25], p. 7.

56. *Coalface to Car Park Collection*, Interview 013 [Debbie, 51], p. 13; also Focus Group 1 [Nina], p. 8 and Focus Group 2 [Esther, 68], p. 2.

57. *Coalface to Car Park Collection*, Interview 013 [Debbie, 51], p. 14.

58. *Dean and Melrose Study*, constructed composite file of 220,699 words; *Coalface to Car Park Collection*, constructed composite file of 234,246 words; Sheppey Collection, audio and OCR transcriptions by the author totalling 411,351 words.

59. Florence Sutcliffe-Braithwaite, '"Class in the development of British Labour Party ideology, 1983–1997', *Archiv für Sozialgeschichte*, 53 (2013), 327–62.

60. *Coalface to Car Park Collection*, Interview 005 [Carla, 52], pp. 18–19.

61. *Coalface to Car Park Collection*, Focus Group 2, p. 16 [Lynn, 48, and Esther, 68].

62. *Coalface to Car Park Collection*, Interview 004 [Britney, 28], pp. 3, 5.

63. David Goodhart, *The Road to Somewhere: The Populist Revolt and the Future of Politics* (C. Hurst & Co, London, 2017).

64. Ministry of Fuel and Power, *Explosion at Easington Colliery County Durham: Report on the Causes of, and Circumstances Attending, the Explosion which Occurred at Easington Colliery*, Cmd. 8646 (HMSO, London, 1952).

65. *Coalface to Car Park Collection*, Interview 009 [Charlotte, 57], p. 4.

66. *Coalface to Car Park Collection*, pp. 4, 7.

67. *Coalface to Car Park Collection*, p. 4.
68. See Alan Sinfield, 'Boys, Class and Gender: From Billy Casper to Billy Elliot', *History Worksop Journal*, 62 (2004), 166–71; Cora Kaplan, 'The Death of the Working Class Hero', *New Formations*, 52 (2004), 94–110.
69. *Coalface to Car Park Collection*, Interview 009 [Charlotte, 57], pp. 10–12.
70. *Coalface to Car Park Collection*, Interview 009 [Charlotte, 57], pp. 11–12.
71. *Coalface to Car Park Collection*, Interview 016 [Grace, 57], p. 1.
72. *Coalface to Car Park Collection*, Interview 016 [Grace, 57], p. 4.
73. *Coalface to Car Park Collection*, Interview 016 [Grace, 57], p. 2.
74. *Coalface to Car Park Collection*, Interview 016 [Grace, 57], p. 3 ('gone' rather than 'done' in original transcript).
75. *Coalface to Car Park Collection*, Interview 016 [Grace, 57], p. 7.
76. *Coalface to Car Park Collection*, Interview 016 [Grace, 57], p. 7.
77. *Coalface to Car Park Collection*, Interview 012 [Diane, 51], pp. 10 and 12; also Interview 020 [Mena, 66], pp. 1 and 6.
78. *Coalface to Car Park Collection*, Interview 020 [Mena, 66], pp. 2, 5, 6.
79. *Coalface to Car Park Collection*, Interview 012 [Diane, 51], p. 10.
80. *Coalface to Car Park Collection*, Interview 009 [Charlotte, 57], p. 3.
81. *Coalface to Car Park Collection*, Interview 009 [Charlotte, 57], pp. 3, 6.
82. *Coalface to Car Park Collection*, Interview 016 [Grace, 57], p. 9.
83. Sam Jordison and Dan Kieran (eds), *The Idler Book of Crap Towns: The 50 Worst Places to Live in the UK* (Boxtree, London, 2003), and *Crap Towns II: The Nation Decides* (Boxtree, London, 2004).
84. *Coalface to Car Park Collection*, Interview 016 [Grace, 57], pp. 9–10.
85. *Coalface to Car Park Collection*, Interview 016 [Grace, 57], p. 10.
86. *Coalface to Car Park Collection*, Interview 012 [Diane, 51], pp. 11, 14, 26.
87. 'Byker Wall: Newcastle's noble failure of an estate', *The Guardian*, 21 May 2015.
88. *Coalface to Car Park Collection*, Interview 003 [Anna, 26], p. 3.
89. *Coalface to Car Park Collection*, Interview 003 [Anna, 26], pp. 2–4, 7, 13.
90. *Coalface to Car Park Collection*, Interview 003 [Anna, 26], pp. 7, 12.
91. *Coalface to Car Park Collection*, Interview 003 [Anna, 26], pp. 5,–6.
92. Taylor, *Fitting into Place?*, 80–8, 102–33.
93. Newcastle City Council, *Know Newcastle* website, Byker Ward Full Profile, Questions 14 and 16 (Office for National Statistics, 2011 Census data), and Questions 65, 83, and 88 (2015 Residents' Survey), at http://www.knownewcastle.org.uk/ (accessed 21 Mar. 2017).
94. Newcastle City Council, *Know Newcastle* website, Byker Ward Full Profile, Questions 11 (ONS, 2011 Census data) and 91 (2015 Residents' Survey).
95. *Coalface to Car Park Collection*, Interview 002 [Angie, 25], p. 8 (technically it is Polish for 'Good day').
96. The only exception is Ivy, a funding manager in her mid-forties, who had lived in the suburban coastal town of Whitley Bay since the age of 3; *Coalface to Car Park Collection*, Interview 017 [Ivy, 45]. Although Anna came to Byker speaking only French, she had been born in the North East so is not included in these figures.
97. *Coalface to Car Park Collection*, Interview 006 [Ama 51 and Carrie 54].
98. Ama (Interview, 51), who arrived aged 7 having previously lived in Devon and Oxford, and Ivy (Interview 017), who was only 3 when her parents relocated from a Scottish island.

99. *Coalface to Car Park Collection*, Focus Group 4, pp. 2, 4, and 6.

100. *Coalface to Car Park Collection*, Focus Group 4, p. 38.

101. Taylor, *Fitting into Place?*, 107–20; *Coalface to Car Park Collection*, Interview 005 [Carla, 52], pp. 1–3; Interview 006 [Ama, 51, and Carrie, 54], pp. 4, 13–14; Interview 013 [Elisabeth, 48], pp. 2–3.

102. *Coalface to Car Park Collection*, Interview 013 [Elisabeth, 48], pp. 2, 4, 7, 14, 16.

103. *Coalface to Car Park Collection*, Interview 013 [Elisabeth, 48], pp. 2–3, 4, 9.

104. *Coalface to Car Park Collection*, Interview 013 [Elisabeth, 48], pp. 2–3, 4.

105. *Coalface to Car Park Collection*, Interview 013 [Elisabeth, 48], pp. 4, 9.

106. Norbert Elias and John L. Scotson, *The Established and the Outsiders: A Sociological Enquiry into Community Problems*, (1965; 2nd edn., Sage, London, 1994).

107. *Coalface to Car Park Collection*, Focus Group 1, pp. 3–4.

108. *Coalface to Car Park Collection*, Focus Group 1, pp. 4, 6; also Focus Group 2 [Esther, 68], pp. 2–3 and also Interview 001 [Andrea, 54], pp. 1–2, about the different, more distant, attitude to neighbouring of young middle-class couples moving into Heaton.

109. *Coalface to Car Park Collection*, Focus Group 1, pp. 4, 9–10.

110. *Coalface to Car Park Collection*, Interview 010 [Chelsea, 36], pp. 2–3; Interview 011 [Debbie, 51], pp. 11–12; Interview 017 [Ivy, 45], p. 1; Interview 020 [Mena, 66], pp. 4–5.

111. *Coalface to Car Park Collection*, Interview 011 [Debbie, 51], pp. 7–8.

112. *Coalface to Car Park Collection*, Interview 005 [Carla, 52], p. 6.

113. *Coalface to Car Park Collection*, Interview 011 [Debbie, 51], p. 9.

114. On the distinctiveness of the North East, see Robert Colls and Bill Lancaster (eds), *Geordies: Roots of Regionalism* (Edinburgh University Press, Edinburgh, 1992), and Taylor, *Fitting into Place?*, 21–46; *Coalface to Car Park Collection*, Focus Group 1 [Nina], p. 4; Interview 001 [Andrea, 54], pp. 1–2, 6–7; Interview 015 [Gaby, 24], p. 3; on the decline of 'community', see Interview 016 [Grace, 57], p. 9; Interview 019 [Jill, 57], p. 3; Interview 017 [Ivy, 45], p. 1.

115. *Coalface to Car Park Collection*, Interview 003 [Anna, 26], p. 5.

116. *Coalface to Car Park Collection*, Interview 003 [Anna, 26], pp. 4–5.

117. *Coalface to Car Park Collection*, Interview 019 [Jill, 57], pp. 1–2.

118. *Coalface to Car Park Collection*, Interview 019 [Jill, 57], p. 3.

119. *Coalface to Car Park Collection*, Interview 019 [Jill, 57], p. 2.

120. *Coalface to Car Park Collection*, Interview 019 [Jill, 57], 8–9.

121. *Coalface to Car Park Collection*, Interview 008 [Chantelle, 30], p. 6.

122. *Coalface to Car Park Collection*, Interview 019 [Jill, 57], p. 8.

123. *Coalface to Car Park Collection*, Interview 007 [Cathy, 37], p. 3.

124. *Coalface to Car Park Collection*, Interview 010 [Chelsea, 36], pp. 2–3.

125. *Coalface to Car Park Collection*, Interview 010 [Chelsea, 36], pp. 3–4.

126. *Coalface to Car Park Collection*, Interview 010 [Chelsea, 36], p. 2.

127. Liz Spencer and Ray Pahl, *Rethinking Friendship: Hidden Solidarities Today* (Princeton University Press, Princeton, 2006).

128. *Coalface to Car Park Collection*, Focus Group 1 [Nina], p. 10.

129. *Coalface to Car Park Collection*, Interview 001 [Andrea, 44], p. 4.

130. *Coalface to Car Park Collection*, Interview 007 [Cathy, 37], p. 9.

131. *Coalface to Car Park Collection*, Interview 005 [Carla, 52], p. 5.

132. *Coalface to Car Park Collection*, Interview 004 [Britney, 28], p. 2.

133. *Coalface to Car Park Collection*, Interview 002 [Angie, 25], p. 4; also Interview 005 [Carla, 52], 10, 12; and Interview 014 [Fay, 39], p. 10, on the lack of mixing between Catholic

and non-Catholic schoolchildren in Peterlee. See Callum G. Brown, *Religion and Society in Twentieth-Century Britain* (Pearson, Harlow, 2006), 291–314; and Timothy Jenkins, *Religion in English Everyday Life: an Ethnographic Approach* (Berghahn Books, New York, 1999).

134. *Coalface to Car Park Collection*, Interview 015 [Gaby, 24, and Jody, 26], p. 3.
135. *Coalface to Car Park Collection*, Interview 011 [Debbie, 51], p. 22.
136. Lynn Abrams, 'Liberating the female self: Epiphanies, conflict and coherence in the life stories of post-war British women', *Social History*, 39/1 (2014), 14–35; also her essay 'Mothers and daughters: Negotiating the discourse on the "Good Woman" in 1950s and 1960s Britain', in Nancy Christie and Michael Gauvreau (eds), *The Sixties and Beyond: Dechristianization in North America and Western Europe, 1945–2000* (University of Toronto Press, Toronto, 2013), 60–83.
137. *Coalface to Car Park Collection*, Interview 007 [Cathy, 37], pp. 7, 10; also Interview 010 [Chelsea, 36], p. 5, on her shock at coming to the North East and meeting an older generation of women who expected to be dependent on men.
138. *Coalface to Car Park Collection*, Interview 008 [Chantelle, 30], pp. 6–7 (though she goes on to explain that her mother had to give up nursing while she and her siblings were young because her father could earn more at the pit).
139. *Coalface to Car Park Collection*, Interview 008 [Chantelle, 30], p. 7.
140. *Coalface to Car Park Collection*, Interview 008 [Chantelle, 30], pp. 1–2, 15.
141. *Coalface to Car Park Collection*, Interview 008 [Chantelle, 30], p. 2, 5.
142. *Coalface to Car Park Collection*, Interview 008 [Chantelle, 30], p. 7.
143. *Coalface to Car Park Collection*, Interview 008 [Chantelle, 30], p. 15.
144. *Coalface to Car Park Collection*, Interview 004 [Britney, 28], pp. 3, 11; also Interview 008 [Chantelle, 30], pp. 12–13, 17.
145. *Coalface to Car Park Collection*, Interview 004 [Britney, 28], pp. 1–2, 8–9, 13–14, 15.
146. *Coalface to Car Park Collection*, Interview 004 [Britney, 28], pp. 4–5, 6, 7.
147. *Coalface to Car Park Collection*, Interview 004 [Britney, 28], pp. 3, 4, 8.
148. *Coalface to Car Park Collection*, Interview 004 [Britney, 28], pp. 8, 9.
149. *Coalface to Car Park Collection*, Interview 004 [Britney, 28], p. 15. Goodhart, *Road to Somewhere*, esp. ch. 2.
150. *Coalface to Car Park Collection*, Interview 004 [Britney, 28], p. 15 (punctuation added).
151. *Coalface to Car Park Collection*, Interview 004 [Britney, 28], p. 19.
152. Paul Bolton, *Education: Historical Statistics*, House of Commons Standard Note, SN/SG/4252 (27 Nov. 2012), at https://researchbriefings.parliament.uk/ResearchBriefing/Summary/SN04252 (accessed 16 June 2017); Ronald Dearing, *Higher Education in the Learning Society*, Report of the National Committee of Enquiry into Higher Education (HMSO, London, 1997), 102–3.
153. *Coalface to Car Park Collection*, Interview 001 [Andrea, 44], p. 16; Interview 004 [Britney, 28], p. 6: 'it was assumed that you'd buy a house and get on the property ladder, get married and there'd be lots of grand-children and stay in [Spennymoor]'.
154. *Coalface to Car Park Collection*, Interview 002 [Angie, 25], pp. 11–12.
155. Richard Hoggart, *The Uses of Literacy* (1957; Penguin, London, 1981), 291–304; also Jeremy Seabrook, *The Unprivileged: A Hundred Years of Family Life and Tradition in a Working-Class Street* (1967; Penguin, London, 1973), 143–4.
156. *Coalface to Car Park Collection*, Interview 002 [Angie, 25], pp. 15–16, 16–17.

Postscript

1. Barbara Ellen, 'The Black Friday shopping scrums are so shaming', *The Observer*, 30 Nov. 2014; Carole Malone, 'It's a fight Christmas', *Sunday Mirror*, 30 Nov. 2014; Julia Llewellyn Smith, 'Why does sales shopping turn us into barbarians?', *Sunday Telegraph*, 30 Nov. 2014 [Nexis search, 26 Jan. 2018].

2. *Sunday Telegraph*, 28 Dec. 1986, p. 3. *The Telegraph Historical Archive*, http://tinyurl.galegroup. com/tinyurl/5omzu7 (accessed 21 Jan. 2018).

3. Office for National Statistics, *Families and Households: 2017*, section 6, at https://www.ons. gov.uk/peoplepopulationandcommunity/birthsdeathsandmarriages/families/bulletins/ familiesandhouseholds/2017 (accessed 21 Jan. 2018).

4. Editorial, 'Scourge of loneliness: We need a social revolution to deal with the growing problem of isolation', *The Times*, 20 April 2016, p. 29; Anushka Asthana, 'Jo Cox's campaign to tackle loneliness lives on with help of friends', *The Guardian*, 28 Dec. 2016; Stewart Dakers, 'The minister for loneliness will need all the friends she can get', *The Guardian* 23 Jan. 2018 (at https://www.theguardian.com/society/2018/jan/23/tracey- crouch-minister-loneliness-friends-powerful-vested-interests, accessed 25 Jan. 2018).

5. Eurostat, *Statistics Explained: Private Households by Household Composition, 2006–2016*, http://ec.europa.eu/eurostat/statisticsexplained/index.php/Household_composition_statistics (accessed 21 Jan. 2018).

6. J. H. Sheldon, *The Social Medicine of Old Age: Report of an Inquiry in Wolverhampton* (Oxford University Press, Oxford, 1948), 150–6, 195–6; see also Chris Phillipson et al., *The Family and Community Life of Older People: Social Networks and Social Support in Three Urban Areas* (Routledge, London, 2001), ch. 1.

7. Jeremy Seabrook, *The Unprivileged: A Hundred Years of Family Life and Tradition in a Working- Class Street* (1967; Penguin, London, 1973), 157–9.

8. Stefan Ramsden, 'Remaking working-class community: Sociability, belonging and "afflu- ence" in a small town, 1930–1980', *Contemporary British History*, 29/1 (2015), 1–26, and his *Working-Class Community in the Age of Affluence* (Routledge, Abingdon, 2017); Colin Rosser and Christopher Harris, *The Family and Social Change: A Study of Family and Kinship in a South Wales Town* (Routledge & Kegan Paul, London, 1965), 220–4, 234, 292–5. For Stevenage, see Ch. 3; for Houghton Regis near Luton, see Ch. 4.

9. Paul Thompson, Catherine Itzin, and Michele Abendstern, *I Don't Feel Old: The Experience of Later Life* (Oxford University Press, Oxford, 1990), 251, 272; also Phillipson et al., *Family and Community Life*, 118–32.

10. Howard F. Gospel, 'The decline of apprenticeship in Britain', *Industrial Relations Journal*, 26/1 (1995), 32–44. Robert Roberts, *The Classic Slum: Salford Life in the First Quarter of the Century* (Manchester University Press, Manchester, 1971), paints a particularly stark pic- ture of the social divide between skilled and unskilled families in Edwardian Britain.

11. Michael Sanderson, 'Education and the labour market', in Nicholas Crafts, Ian Gazeley, and Andrew Newell (eds), *Work and Pay in 20th Century Britain* (Oxford University Press, Oxford, 2007), 264–300.

12. Jon Lawrence, 'The people's history and the politics of everyday life since 1945', in John Arnold, Matthew Hilton, and Jan Rüger (eds), *History after Hobsbawm: Writing the Past for the Twenty-First Century* (Oxford University Press, Oxford, 2017), 272–91.

13. Liz Spencer and Ray Pahl, *Rethinking Friendship: Hidden Solidarities Today* (Princeton Uni- versity Press, Princeton, 2006).

14. Mike Savage, 'The politics of elective belonging', *Housing, Theory and Society*, 27/2 (2010), 115–35.

15. Jon McGregor, *If Nobody Speaks of Remarkable Things* (Bloomsbury, London, 2002).

16. Philip Abrams et al., *Action for Care: A Review of Good Neighbour Schemes in England* (Volunteer Centre: Berkhampsted, 1981); Martin Bulmer (ed.), *Neighbours: The Work of Philip Abrams* (Cambridge University Press, Cambridge, 1986), esp. 11–14, 122–7, 203-5; Guy Ortolano, *Thatcher's Progress: From Social Democracy to Market Liberalism through an English New Town* (Cambridge University Press, Cambridge, 2019), esp. ch. 4 ('Community').

17. For an argument along these lines, see Catherine Max, 'Finding place and quiet', at http://www.catherinemax.co.uk/finding-place-quiet/ (accessed 10 Mar. 2018).

18. John Kenneth Galbraith, *The Affluent Society* (2nd edn., Penguin, London, 1970), 212.

Appendix

1. The key text here is Gayatri Spivak, 'Can the subaltern speak?', in Cary Nelson and Lawrence Grossberg (eds), *Marxism and the Interpretation of Culture* (Macmillan, London, 1988), 271–313. See also James Vernon, 'Telling the subaltern to speak: Social investigation and the formation of social history in twentieth-century Britain', *Proceedings of the International Congress History under Debate, Santiago de Compostela, July 1999* (University of Santiago de Compostela, Santiago de Compostela, 2000).

2. See Mike Savage, 'Revisiting classic qualitative studies', *Forum: Qualitative Social Research*, 6/1 (2005), article 31, from http://www.qualitative-research.net/index.php/fqs/article/view/502; and, for a more cautious perspective, Martyn Hammersley, 'Qualitative data archiving: Some reflections on its prospects and problems', *Sociology*, 31/1 (1997), 131–42; and Martyn Hammersley, 'Can we re-use qualitative data via secondary analysis? Notes on some terminological and substantive issues', *Sociological Research Online*, 15/1 (2009), from http://www.socresonline.org.uk/15/1/5.html.

3. Jennifer Platt, *Social Research in Bethnal Green: An Evaluation of the Work of the Institute of Community Studies*, New Perspectives in Sociology series (Macmillan, London, 1971).

4. Michael Young and Peter Willmott, 'On the Green', *New Society*, 28 Oct. 1971; cited in Asa Briggs, *Michael Young: Social Entrepreneur*, 145.

5. Department for Digital, Culture, Media and Sport, *Taking Part Survey, England Adult Report, 2016/17*, https://www.gov.uk/government/uploads/system/uploads/attachment_data/file/664933/Adult_stats_release_4.pdf (accessed 23 Jan. 2018).

6. Pearl Jephcott, *Married Women Working* (Allen & Unwin, London, 1962).

BIBLIOGRAPHY

Primary Sources

Unpublished

Bishopsgate Institute, London, Ruskin Papers, RS1/301–6, 'Survey on Social and Political Attitudes in Stevenage and Clapham, 1959–1960'.

Churchill Archive Centre, Cambridge, Michael Young Papers, Acc. 1577, 'Bethnal Green papers' [uncatalogued deposit, 2010], and 'Debden Survey, 1953–1955', YUNG 1/5/1.

Labour History Archive, Manchester, NEC Campaign Committee Minutes.

London School of Economics Library, London, Sir Raymond Firth Papers.

Modern Records Centre, University of Warwick, Shipbuilding Workers on Tyneside: Research Papers of Professor Richard K. Brown, 'Qualidata: Shipbuilding workers' (MSS.371/ shipbuilding workers).

Talking New Towns: Oral Histories of Hatfield, Hemel Hempstead, Stevenage and Welwyn Garden City at http://www.talkingnewtowns.org.uk/.

UK Data Archive, Essex, H. Dean and M. Melrose (1999), *Poverty, Wealth and Citizenship: A Discursive Interview Study and Newspaper Monitoring Exercise, 1996* [computer file], UK Data Service, SN: 3995 (http://dx.doi.org/10.5255/UKDA-SN-3995-1).

UK Data Archive, Essex, C. D. Wallace and R. E. Pahl (2004), *Social and Political Implications of Household Work Strategies, 1978–1983* [data collection], UK Data Service, SN: 4876 (http://doi.org/10.5255/UKDA-SN-4876-1) [Pahl Papers, Isle of Sheppey Collection].

UK Data Archive, Essex, R. E. Pahl (2004), *Changing Sociological Construct of the Family, 1930–1986* [data collection], UK Data Service, SN: 4872 (http://doi.org/10.5255/UKDA-SN-4872-1).

UK Data Archive, Essex, S. Todd (2009), *Affluent Worker in the Class Structure: A Digitised Sample of the Luton Study, 1961–1962* [data collection], UK Data Service, SN: 4871 (http://dx.doi.org/10.5255/UKDA-SN-4871-1).

UK Data Archive, Essex, J. H. Goldthorpe and D. Lockwood (2010), *Affluent Worker in the Class Structure, 1961–1962* [data collection], UK Data Service, SN: 6512 (http://dx.doi.org/10.5255/UKDA-SN-6512-1).

UK Data Archive, Essex, Y. Taylor (2012), *From the Coalface to the Car Park? The Intersection of Class and Gender in Women's Lives in the North East, 2007–2009,* [data collection], UK Data Service, SN: 7053 (http://doi.org/10.5255/UKDA-SN-7053-1).

UK Data Archive, Essex, P. Thompson, ESDS Qualidata (2014), *Pioneers of Social Research, 1996–2012* [data collection], 2nd edn, UK Data Service, SN: 6226 (http://dx.doi.org/10.5255/UKDA-SN-6226-3).

UK Data Archive, Essex, J. Lawrence (2016), *Affluent Worker Study 1962–1964: Questionnaire Files* [data collection], ReShare 10.5255/UKDA-SN-852166.

UK Data Archive, Essex, S. Todd (2019), *Digitisation of R. Brown, 'Orientation to Work and Industrial Behaviour of Shipbuilding Workers', 1968–1969; Manual Workers' Questionnaires,* [data collection] UK Data Service, SN: 6586 (http://doi.org/10.5255/UKDA-SN-6586-2).

Wiltshire and Swindon History Centre, Chippenham, 'Manchester University Research into Overspill, 1958–1962', Swindon Borough Council, Finance, Law and General Purposes Committee Papers, G24/132/1036.

Published

Official Publications and Reference

Board of Trade, *Enquiry into the Cost of Living of the Working Classes*, PP1908 Cd.3864, vol. cvii.

Craig, F. W. S., *British General Election Manifestos, 1900–1974* (Macmillan, London, 1975).

Dearing, Ronald, *Higher Education in the Learning Society*, Report of the National Committee of Enquiry into Higher Education (HMSO, London, 1997).

Department for Digital, Culture, Media and Sport, *Taking Part Survey, England Adult Report, 2016/17*, https://www.gov.uk/government/uploads/system/uploads/attachment_data/file/664933/Adult_stats_release_4.pdf.

Eurostat, *Statistics Explained: Private Households by Household Composition, 2006–2016*, http://ec.europa.eu/eurostat/statisticsexplained/index.php/Household_composition_statistics.

General Register Office, *Census 1961 England and Wales* (HMSO, London, 1963–6).

General Register Office, *Sample Census 1966 England and Wales, Workplace and Transport Tables Part I* (HMSO, London, 1968).

Ministry of Fuel and Power, *Explosion at Easington Colliery County Durham: Report on the Causes of, and Circumstances Attending, the Explosion which Occurred at Easington Colliery*, Cmd. 8646 (HMSO, London, 1952).

Newcastle City Council, *Know Newcastle* website, http://www.knownewcastle.org.uk/ (accessed 21 Mar. 2017).

Office for National Statistics, *Social Trends*, 40/1 (HMSO, London, 2010).

Office for National Statistics, *Self-Employed Workers in the UK, 2014* (HMSO, London, 2014).

Office for National Statistics, *Births by Parents' Characteristics in England and Wales, 2015* (HMSO, London, 2016).

Office for National Statistics, *Trends in Self-Employment in the UK: 2001 to 2015* (HMSO, London, 2016).

Office for National Statistics, *Families and Households: 2017*, https://www.ons.gov.uk/peoplepopulationandcommunity/birthsdeathsandmarriages/families/bulletins/families-andhouseholds/2017.

Population Census, 1911 Household Returns, St George District, Bristol (Gloucestershire).

South East Joint Planning Team, *Strategic Plan for the South East, Studies*, ii. *Social and Environmental Aspects* (HMSO, London, 1971).

Weir, Guy 'Self-employment in the UK labour market', *Labour Market Trends* [Office for National Statistics], 111/9 (2003), 441–51.

Contemporary Studies and Memoirs

Abrams, Philip, *Neighbourhood Care and Social Policy: A Research Perspective* (Volunteer Centre: Berkhampsted, 1978).

Abrams, Philip, Shiela Abrams, Robin Humphrey, and Ray Snaith, *Action for Care: a Review of Good Neighbour Schemes in England* (Volunteer Centre: Berkhampsted, 1981).

Anon. [Michael Young], 'London under bombing', *Planning* (PEP Broadsheet), 169, 17 Feb. 1941.

Anon., *Building a Community: Construction Workers in Stevenage, 1950–1970* (University of Westminster, London, 2011).

Ashby, Margaret (ed.), *Stevenage Voices: Recollections of Local People* (Tempus, Stroud, 1999).

Bakke, E. Wight, *The Unemployed Man: A Social Study* (Nisbet & Co., London, 1933).

Bauman, Zygmunt, *Liquid Modernity* (Polity, Cambridge, 2000).

Benney, Mark, *Charity Main: A Coalfield Chronicle* (George Allen, London, 1948).

Bott, Elizabeth, *Family and Social Network: Roles, Norms and External Relationships in Ordinary Urban Families* (Tavistock Publications, London, 1957).

Bowlby, John, *Maternal Care and Mental Health* (World Health Organization, Geneva, 1951).

Bracey, H. E., *Neighbours: On New Estates and Subdivisions in England and the USA* (Routledge, London, 1964).

Brown, Richard, and Peter Brannen, 'Social relations and social perspectives amongst ship-building workers—a preliminary statement', pts 1 and 2, *Sociology*, 4 (1970), 71–84 and 197–211.

Brown, R. K., P. Brannen, J. M. Cousins, and M. L. Samphier, 'The contours of solidarity: Social stratification and industrial relations in shipbuilding', *British Journal of Industrial Relations*, 10 (1972), 12–41.

Brown, Richard, Peter Brannen, Jim Cousins, and Michael Samphier, 'Leisure in work: The "occupational culture" of shipbuilding workers', in Michael Smith, Stanley Parker, and Cyril Smith (eds.), *Leisure and Society in Britain* (Allen Lane, London, 1973), 97–110.

Bulmer, Martin (ed.), *Neighbours: The Work of Philip Abrams* (Cambridge University Press, Cambridge, 1986).

Carter, Terry, *Post-War Loughton, 1945–1970: How We Were and How Loughton Changed* (Loughton and District Historical Society, Loughton, 2006).

Chapman, Dennis, *The Home and Social Status* (Routledge, London, 1955).

Common, Jack, *Jack Common's Revolt Against an 'Age of Plenty'* (Strongwords, Newcastle, 1980).

Cousins, Jim, and Richard Brown, 'Patterns of paradox: Shipbuilding workers' images of society', in Martin Bulmer (ed.), *Working-Class Images of Society* (Routledge, London, 1975), 55–82.

Cruddas, Jon, (ed.), *One Nation Labour: Debating the Future* (LabourList ebook, London, 2013).

Cullingworth, J. B., 'Social implications of overspill: The Worsley Social Survey', *Sociological Review*, NS 8/1 (1960), 77–96.

Cullingworth, J. B., 'The Swindon Social Survey: A second report on the social implications of overspill,' *Sociological Review*, NS 9/2 (1961), 151–66.

Dean, Hartley, with Margaret Melrose, *Poverty, Riches and Social Citizenship* (Macmillan, Basingstoke, 1999).

Dench, Geoff, Kate Gavron, and Michael Young, *The New East End: Kinship, Race and Conflict* (Profile, London, 2006).

Devine, Fiona, *Affluent Workers Revisited: Privatism and the Working Class* (Edinburgh University Press, Edinburgh, 1992).

Duff, Alan, *Britain's New Towns* (Pall Mall Press, London, 1961).

Firth, Raymond (ed.), *Two Studies of Kinship in London* (Athlone Press, London, 1956).

Frankenberg, Ronald, *Communities in Britain: Social Life in Town and Country* (Penguin, London, 1966).

Gershuny, J. I., and R. E. Pahl, 'Work outside employment', *New Universities Quarterly*, 34/1 (1979), 120–35.

Glasman, Maurice, Jonathan Rutherford, Marc Stears, and Stuart White (eds), *The Labour Tradition and the Politics of Paradox* (Soundings eBooks, London, 2011).

Glass, Ruth, and Maureen Frenkel, *A Profile of Bethnal Green* (Association for Planning and Regional Reconstruction, Report No. 39, London, Feb. 1946).

Glass, Ruth, and Maureen Frenkel 'How they live at Bethnal Green', *Contact* 3 (1946), 'Britain Between East and West' (eds A. G. Weidenfeld and H. de Hastings), 36–43.

Glucksmann, Miriam, *Cotton and Casuals: The Gendered Organisation of Labour in Time and Space* (Sociology Press, Durham, 2000).

Glucksmann, Miriam (aka Ruth Cavendish), *Women on the Line* (1982; Abingdon, Routledge, 2009).

Goldthorpe, John H., and David Lockwood, 'Affluence and the British class structure', *Sociological Review*, 11/2 (1963), 133–63.

Goldthorpe, John H., David Lockwood, Frank Bechhofer, and Jennifer Platt, *The Affluent Worker in the Class Structure*, 3 vols. (Cambridge University Press, Cambridge, 1968–9).

Gorer, Geoffrey, *Exploring English Character* (Cresset Press, London, 1955).

Grant, Colin, *Bageye at the Wheel: A 1970s Childhood in Suburbia* (Vintage Books, London, 2012).

Grieco, Margaret, *Keeping It in the Family: Social Networks and Employment Chance* (Tavistock, London, 1987).

Hall, Stuart, 'A sense of classlessness', *Universities & Left Review*, 5 (Autumn, 1958), 26–31.

Hanley, Lynsey, *Estates: An Intimate History* (Granta, London, 2007).

Henderson, Nigel, *Photographs of Bethnal Green, 1949–1952* (Newstead Publishing, Nottingham, 1978).

Heraud, Brian, 'Social class and the new towns', *Urban Studies*, 5/1 (1968), 33–58.

Hodges, Mark W., and Cyril S. Smith, 'The Sheffield estate', in University of Liverpool, *Neighbourhood and Community: An Enquiry into Social Relationships on Housing Estates in Liverpool and Sheffield* (University of Liverpool Press, Liverpool, 1954).

Hoggart, Richard, *The Uses of Literacy: Aspects of Working-Class Life* (1957; Penguin edn, London, 1981).

Hoggart, Richard, *Everyday Language and Everyday Life* (Transaction, Brunswick, NJ, 2003).

Hutchinson, Bertram, *Willesden and the New Towns* (The Social Survey/Ministry of Town and Country Planning, London, 1947).

Jennings, Hilda, *Brynmawr: A Study of a Distressed Area* (Allenson & Co., London, 1934).

Jennings, Hilda, *Societies in the Making: A Study of Development and Redevelopment within a County Borough* (Routledge, London, 1962).

Jephcott, Pearl, *Married Women Working* (Allen & Unwin, London, 1962).

Jevons, Rosamond, and John Madge, *Housing Estates: A Study of Bristol Corporation Policy and Practice between the Wars* (University of Bristol, Bristol, 1946).

Jordison, Sam, and Dan Kieran (eds), *The Idler Book of Crap Towns: The 50 Worst Places to Live in the UK* (Boxtree, London, 2003).

Jordison, Sam, and Dan Kieran (eds), *Crap Towns II: The Nation Decides* (Boxtree, London, 2004).

Karn, Valerie Ann, *Stevenage Housing Survey: A Study of Housing in a New Town*, University of Birmingham Centre for Urban and Regional Studies, Occasional Paper no. 10 (University of Birmingham, Birmingham, 1970).

Klein, Josephine, *Samples from English Cultures*, i (Routledge, London, 1965).

Kuper, Leo, 'Blueprint for living together', in Leo Kuper (ed.), *Living in Towns: Selected Papers in Urban Sociology* (Cresset Press, London, 1953), 1–202.

Little, Kenneth, *Negroes in Britain: A Study of Racial Relations in English Society* (Kegan Paul, London, 1947).

Littlefield, Michelle, and Andrew Nash, *Commuting Patterns as at the 2001 Census, and Their Relationship with Modes of Transport and Types of Occupation* (Office for National Statistics, London, 2008).

Loane, M. E., *The Queen's Poor: Life as They Find It in Town and Country* (Edward Arnold, London, 1905).

Lockwood, David, 'Sources of variation in working-class images of society', *Sociological Review*, 14 (1966), 149–67.

Lowe, Bert, *Anchorman: Autobiography of Bert Lowe, Socialist, Trade Unionist and Stevenage Pioneer* (Bert Lowe, Stevenage, 1996).

Lynd, Robert S., and Helen Merrell Lynd, *Middletown: A Study in American Culture* (Harcourt Brace, New York, 1929).

Lynd, Robert S., and Helen Merrell Lynd, *Middletown in Transition: A Study in Cultural Conflicts* (Harcourt Brace, New York, 1937).

MacInnes, Colin, *Absolute Beginners* (1959; Allison & Busby, London, 1980).

McGregor, Jon, *If Nobody Speaks of Remarkable Things* (Bloomsbury, London, 2002).

Mckenzie, Lisa, *Getting By: Estates, Class and Culture in Austerity Britain* (Policy, Bristol, 2014).

Mass-Observation [Anon.], *An Enquiry into People's Homes: A Report Prepared by Mass-Observation for the Advertising Service Guild, the fourth of the 'CHANGE' Wartime Surveys* (John Murray, London, 1943).

Mitford, Nancy, 'The English aristocracy', *Encounter*, 24 (Sept. 1955), 5–11.

Mitford, Nancy (ed.), *Noblesse Oblige: An Inquiry into the Identifiable Characteristics of the English Aristocracy* (Hamish Hamilton, London, 1956).

Mogey, J. M., *Family and Neighbourhood: Two Studies in Oxford* (Oxford University Press, Oxford, 1956).

Morris, R. N., and John Mogey, *The Sociology of Housing: Studies at Berinsfield* (Routledge, London, 1965).

Morris, William, *Hopes and Fears for Art: Five Lectures Delivered in Birmingham, London and Nottingham, 1878–1881* (Ellis & White, London, 1882).

Nicholson, Vivian, and Stephen Smith, *Spend, Spend, Spend* (Jonathan Cape, London, 1977).

Oakley, Ann, *The Sociology of Housework* (Robertson, London, 1974).

Orlans, Harold, *Stevenage: A Sociological Study of a New Town* (Routledge & Kegan Paul, London, 1952).

Orwell, George, *Keep the Aspidistra Flying* (1936; Penguin, London, 1987).

Pahl, R. E., *Urbs in Rure: The Metropolitan Fringe in Hertfordshire* (LSE, London, 1965).

Pahl, R. E., 'Patterns of urban life in the next fifteen years', *New Universities Quarterly*, 30 (1976), 402–19.

Pahl, R. E., 'Employment, work and the domestic division of Labour', *International Journal of Urban and Regional Research*, 4/1 (1980), 1–20.

Pahl, R. E., 'Family, community and unemployment', *New Society*, 21 Jan. 1982, 91–3.

Pahl, R. E., *Divisions of Labour* (Blackwell, Oxford, 1984).

Pahl, Ray, 'Are all communities communities in the mind?', *Sociological Review*, 53/4 (2005), 621–40.

Pahl, R. E. and C. D. Wallace, 'Forms of work and privatisation on the Isle of Sheppey', in Bryan Roberts, Ruth Finnegan, and Duncan Gallie (eds), *New Approaches to Economic Life: Economic Restructuring: Unemployment and the Social Division of Labour* (Manchester University Press, Manchester, 1985).

Pahl, R. E., and C. D. Wallace, 'Neither angels in marble nor rebels in red: Privatization and working-class consciousness', in David Rose (ed.), *Social Stratification and Economic Change* (Hutchinson, London, 1988), 127–49.

Perry, Grayson, *The Vanity of Small Differences* (Hayward Publishing, London, 2013).

Prosser, Ian, 'The privatisation of working-class life: A dissenting view', *British Journal of Sociology*, 41/2 (1990), 157–80.

Putnam, Robert, *Bowling Alone: The Collapse and Revival of American Community* (Simon & Schuster, New York, 2000).

Reeves, Maud Pember, *Round about a Pound a Week* (1913; Virago, London, 1979).

Rice, Margery Spring, *Working-Class Wives: Their Health and Conditions* (Pelican, London, 1939).

Roberts, Robert, *The Classic Slum: Salford Life in the First Quarter of the Century* (Manchester University Press, Manchester, 1971).

Rosser, Colin, and Christopher Harris, *The Family and Social Change: A Study of Family and Kinship in a South Wales Town* (Routledge & Kegan Paul, London, 1965).

Sage, Lorna, *Bad Blood* (Fourth Estate, London, 2000).

Samuel, Ralph, 'The deference voter: A study of the working class Tory', *New Left Review*, 1 (Jan.–Feb. 1960), 9–13.

Saturday Night and Sunday Morning (Woodfall Film Productions, London, 1960), dir. Karel Reisz, screenplay Alan Sillitoe.

Seabrook, Jeremy, *The Unprivileged: A Hundred Years of Family Life and Tradition in a Working-Class Street* (1967; Penguin, London, 1973).

Self, P. J. O., 'Voluntary organizations in Bethnal Green', in A. F. C. Bourdillon (ed.), *Voluntary Social Services: Their Place in the Modern State*, Nuffield College Social Reconstruction Survey series (Methuen, London, 1945), 235–62.

Sennett, Richard, and Jonathan Cobb, *The Hidden Injuries of Class* (Vintage Books, New York, 1973).

Sheldon, J. H., *The Social Medicine of Old Age: Report of an Inquiry in Wolverhampton* (Oxford University Press, Oxford, 1948).

Sillitoe, Alan, *Saturday Night and Sunday Morning* (1958; Pan, London, 1960).

Spencer, Liz, and Ray Pahl, *Rethinking Friendship: Hidden Solidarities Today* (Princeton University Press, Princeton, 2006).

Stevenage Development Corporation, *The New Town of Stevenage* (Stevenage Development Corporation, Stevenage, 1949).

Stockwood, Mervyn, *Chanctonbury Ring: an Autobiography* (Hodder & Stoughton, London, 1982).

Taylor, Yvette, *Fitting into Place? Class and Gender Geographies and Temporalities* (Ashgate, Farnham, 2012).

Thompson, E. P., 'Commitment in politics', *Universities & Left Review*, 6 (Spring, 1959), 50–5.

Townsend, Peter, *The Family Life of Old People* (1957; Pelican, London, 1963).

Turner, Graham, *The Car Makers* (Eyre & Spottiswoode, London, 1963).

University of Liverpool, *Neighbourhood and Community: An Enquiry into Social Relationships on Housing Estates in Liverpool and Sheffield* (University of Liverpool Press, Liverpool, 1954).

Vale, George F., *Bethnal Green's Ordeal* (Bethnal Green Council, London, n.d. [1945]).

Wallace, Claire, *For Richer, For Poorer: Growing Up In and Out of Work* (Tavistock, London, 1987).

Williams, Raymond, *Culture and Society, 1780–1950* (1958; Penguin edn, London, 1963).

Williams, Raymond, *The Long Revolution* (1961; Penguin edn, London, 1965).

Willmott, Peter, 'Housing density and town design in a new town: A pilot study at Stevenage', *Town Planning Review*, 33/2 (1962), 115–27.

Willmott, Peter, *The Evolution of a Community: A Study of Dagenham After Forty Years* (Routledge, London, 1963).

Willmott, Peter, 'East Kilbride and Stevenage: Some social characteristics of a Scottish and an English new town', *Town Planning Review*, 34/4 (1964), 307–16.

Willmott, Phyllis, *Bethnal Green Journal, 1954–1955* (Institute of Community Studies, London, 2001).

Wilson, Elizabeth, *Only Half-Way to Paradise: Women in Postwar Britain, 1945–1968* (Tavistock, London, 1980).

Winterson, Jeanette, *Oranges Are Not the Only Fruit* (Pandora, London, 1985).

Young, Michael, *The Rise of the Meritocracy, 1870–2033: An Essay on Education and Equality* (Thames & Hudson, London, 1958).

Young, Michael, 'Reflections on researching family and kinship in East London: Michael Young interviewed by Paul Thompson', *International Journal of Social Research Methodology*, 7/1 (2004), 35–44.

Young, Michael, and Peter Willmott, 'Social grading by manual workers', *British Journal of Sociology*, 7/4 (1956), 337–45.

Young, Michael, and Peter Willmott, *Family and Kinship in East London* (Routledge & Kegan Paul, London, 1957).

Zweig, Ferdynand, *The Worker in an Affluent Society: Family Life and Industry* (Heinemann, London, 1961).

Secondary Sources

Published

Abrams, Lynn, 'Mothers and daughters: Negotiating the discourse on the "Good Woman" in 1950s and 1960s Britain', in Nancy Christie and Michael Gauvreau (eds), *The Sixties and Beyond: Dechristianization in North America and Western Europe, 1945–2000* (University of Toronto Press, Toronto, 2013), 60–83.

Abrams, Lynn, 'Liberating the female self: Epiphanies, conflict and coherence in the life stories of post-war British women', *Social History*, 39/1 (2014), 14–35.

Abrams, Lynn, Barry Hazley, Valerie Wright, and Ade Kearns, 'Aspiration, agency and the production of new selves in a Scottish new town, c.1955–c.1985', *Twentieth-Century British History*, 29 (2018), 576–604.

Alexander, Anthony, *Britain's New Towns: Garden Cities to Sustainable Communities* (Routledge, London, 2009).

Anon., 'Appreciations of Sir Raymond Firth', *Anthropology Today*, 18/5 (Oct. 2002), 20–3.

Anon., *Thetford Historic Environment Assessment, Part 1* (Breckland Council, Thetford, 2009).

Antonucci, Lorenza, Laszlo Horvath, Yordan Kutiyski, and André Krouwel, 'The malaise of the squeezed middle: Challenging the narrative of the "left behind" Brexiter', *Competition & Change*, 21/3 (2017), 211–29.

Armstrong, W. A., 'The uses of information about occupation', pt 1, app. A, in E. A. Wrigley (ed.), *Nineteenth-Century Society: Essays in the Use of Quantitative Methods for the Study of Social Data* (Cambridge University Press, Cambridge, 1972), 215–23.

Ayers, Pat, 'Work, culture and gender: The making of post-war masculinities in post-war Liverpool', *Labour History Review*, 69/2 (2004), 154–67.

Bailey, Peter, 'Will the real Bill Banks please stand up? Towards a role analysis of mid-Victorian working-class respectability', *Journal of Social History*, 12 (1979), 336–53.

Baines, Dudley E., and Paul A. Johnson, 'In search of the "traditional" working class: Social mobility and occupational continuity in interwar London', *Economic History Review*, 2nd ser., 52/4 (1999), 692–713.

Balchin, Jack, *The First New Town: An Autobiography of the Stevenage Development Corporation, 1946–1980* (Stevenage Development Corporation, Stevenage, 1980).

Bell, Colin, and Howard Newby, *Community Studies: An Introduction to the Sociology of the Local Community* (George Allen & Unwin, London, 1971).

Benson, Richard, *The Valley: A Hundred Years in the Life of a Yorkshire Family* (Bloomsbury, London, 2014).

Beynon, Huw, and Terry Austrin, *Masters and Servants: Class and Patronage in the Making of a Labour Organisation: The Durham Miners and the English Political Tradition* (Rivers Oram, London, 1994).

Black, Lawrence, *The Political Culture of the Left in Affluent Britain, 1951–1964: Old Labour, New Britain* (Palgrave, Basingstoke, 2003).

Black, Lawrence, and Hugh Pemberton, *An Affluent Society?: Britain's Post-war 'Golden Age'* (Ashgate, Aldershot, 2004).

Black, Lawrence, Hugh Pemberton, and Pat Thane (eds), *Reassessing 1970s Britain* (Manchester University Press, Manchester, 2013).

Bolton, Paul, *Education: Historical Statistics*, House of Commons Standard Note, SN/SG/4252 (27 Nov. 2012), at https://researchbriefings.parliament.uk/ResearchBriefing/Summary/SN04252.

Bonnett, Alastair, 'Anti-racism in "White" areas: The example of Tyneside', *Antipode*, 24/1 (1992), 1–15.

Bonnett, Alastair, 'How the British working class became white: The symbolic (re)formation of racialized capitalism', *Journal of Historical Sociology*, 11/2 (1998), 316–40.

Bourke, Joanna, *Working-Class Cultures in Britain, 1890–1960: Gender, Class and Ethnicity* (Routledge, London, 1994).

Briggs, Asa, *Michael Young: Social Entrepreneur* (Palgrave Macmillan, Basingstoke, 2001).

Brigham, Allan, 'A community in transition: Romsey Town Cambridge, 1966–2006', http://www.colc.co.uk/cambridge/tours/article3.htm.

Brooke, Stephen, 'Living in "New Times": Historicizing 1980s Britain', *History Compass*, 12/1 (2014), 20–32.

Brown, Callum G., *Religion and Society in Twentieth-Century Britain* (Pearson, Harlow, 2006).

Bryant, Joanne, and Jeanne Ellard, 'Hope as a form of agency in the future thinking of disenfranchised young people', *Journal of Youth Studies*, 18/4 (2015), 485–99.

Buckley, David, *Strange Fascination: David Bowie, the Definitive Story* (Virgin Publishing, London, 1999).

Bullock, Alan, *The Life and Times of Ernest Bevin*, i. *Trade Union Leader, 1881–1940* (Heinemann, London, 1960).

Bulmer, Martin (ed.), *Working-Class Images of Society* (Routledge, London, 1975).

Bulmer, Martin (ed.), *Neighbours: The Work of Philip Abrams* (Cambridge University Press, Cambridge, 1986).

Bunker, Stephen, Robin Holgate, and Marian Nichols, *The Changing Face of Luton: An Illustrated History* (Book Castle, Dunstable, 1993).

Butler, Lise, 'Michael Young, the Institute of Community Studies and the politics of kinship', *Twentieth-Century British History*, 26 (2015), 203–24.

Calder, Angus, *The Myth of the Blitz* (Jonathan Cape, London, 1991).

Calhoun, Craig, 'Community without propinquity revisited: Communications technology and the transformation of the urban public sphere', *Sociological Inquiry*, 68/3 (1998), 373–97.

Campsie, Alex, 'Mass-Observation, left intellectuals and the politics of everyday life', *English Historical Review*, 131 (Feb. 2016), 92–121.

Carabelli, Giulia, and Dawn Lyon, 'Young people's orientations to the future: Navigating the present and imagining the future', *Journal of Youth Studies*, 19/8 (2016), 1110–27.

Charles, Nickie, and Charlotte Aull Davies, 'Studying the particular, illuminating the general: Community studies and community in Wales', *Sociological Review*, 53/4 (2005), 672–90.

Clapson, Mark, *Invincible Green Suburbs, Brave New Towns: Social Change and Urban Dispersal in Postwar England* (Manchester University Press, Manchester, 1998).

Clapson, Mark, 'Working-class women's experiences of moving to new housing estates in England since 1919', *Twentieth-Century British History*, 10/3 (1999), 345–65.

Clapson, Mark, 'The suburban aspiration in England since 1919', *Contemporary British History*, 14/1 (2000), 151–73.

Clark, Anna, *The Struggle for the Breeches: Gender and the Making of the British Working Class* (University of California Press, Berkeley and Los Angeles, 1995).

Cohen, Anthony P., *The Symbolic Construction of Community* (Ellis Horwood, Chichester, 1985).

Cohen, Deborah, *Family Secrets: Living with Shame from the Victorians to the Present Day* (Viking, London, 2013).

Collins, Michael, *The Likes of Us: A Biography of the White Working Class* (Granta, London, 2004).

Colls, Robert, 'When we lived in communities: Working-class culture and its critics', in Robert Colls and Richard Rodger (eds), *Cities of Ideas: Civil Society and Urban Governance in Britain, 1800–2000: Essays in Honour of David Reeder* (Ashgate, Aldershot, 2005), 283–307.

Colls, Robert, and Bill Lancaster (eds), *Geordies: Roots of Regionalism* (Edinburgh University Press, Edinburgh, 1992).

Comfort, Nicholas, *The Slow Death of British Industry: A 60-Year Suicide, 1952–2012* (Biteback, London, 2012).

Coopey, Richard, and Nicholas Woodward (eds), *Britain in the 1970s: The Troubled Decade* (UCL Press, London, 1996).

Crines, Andrew, Tim Heppell, and Michael Hill, 'Enoch Powell's "rivers of blood" speech: A rhetorical political analysis', *British Politics*, 11/1 (2016), 72–94.

Crow, Graham, and Graham Allan, *Community Life: An Introduction to Local Social Relations* (Harvester Wheatsheaf, Hemel Hempstead, 1994).

Crow, Graham, and Jaimie Ellis (eds), *Divisions of Labour Revisited: The Impacts and Legacies of a Sociological Classic* (Manchester, 2017).

Cruddas, Jon, Nick Pecorelli, and Jonathan Rutherford, *Labour's Future: Why Labour Lost in 2015 and How It Can Win Again* (One Nation Register, London, 2016).

Cullingworth, J. B., *Environmental Planning, 1939–1969*, iii. *New Towns Policy* (HMSO, London, 1979).

Dale, Pete, *Anyone Can Do It: Empowerment, Tradition and the Punk Underground* (Ashgate, Farnham, 2012).

Daunton, Martin J., 'Miners' houses: South Wales and the Great Northern Coal Field, 1880–1914', *International Review of Social History*, 25/2 (1980), 143–75.

Daunton, Martin J., *House and Home in the Victorian City: Working-Class Housing, 1850–1914* (Edward Elgar, London, 1983).

Daunton, M. J. (ed.), *Councillors and Tenants: Local Authority Housing in English Cities, 1919–1939* (Leicester University Press, Leicester, 1984).

Daunton, M. J., *A Property-Owning Democracy? Housing in Britain* (Faber & Faber, London, 1987).

Daunton, M. J., *Progress and Poverty: An Economic and Social History of Britain, 1700–1850* (Oxford University Press, Oxford, 1995).

Davies, Andrew, 'The police and the people: Gambling in Salford, 1900–1939', *Historical Journal*, 34 (1991), 87–115.

Davis, Madeleine, 'Arguing affluence: New Left contributions to the Socialist debate, 1957–1963', *Twentieth-Century British History*, 23/4 (2012), 496–528.

Davis, Rowenna, *Tangled Up in Blue: Blue Labour and the Struggle for Labour's Soul* (Ruskin, London, 2011).

De-la-Noy, Michael, *Mervyn Stockwood: A Lonely Life* (Mowbray, London, 1996).

Delanty, Gerard, *Community*, Key Ideas series (Routledge, London, 2003).

Dicks, Henry V., *Fifty Years of the Tavistock Clinic* (Routledge, London, 1970).

Dresser, Madge, 'Housing policy in Bristol, 1919–1930', in M. J. Daunton (ed.), *Councillors and Tenants: Local Authority Housing in English Cities, 1919–1939* (Leicester University Press, Leicester, 1984).

Dyer, James, and John G. Dony, *The Story of Luton* (3rd edn, White Crescent, Luton, 1975).

Elias, Norbert, and John L. Scotson, *The Established and the Outsiders: A Sociological Enquiry into Community Problems* (1965; Sage, London, 2nd edn, 1994).

Elliott, B. Jane, 'Demographic trends in domestic life, 1945–1987', in David Clark (ed.), *Marriage, Domestic Life and Social Change: Writings for Jacqueline Burgoyne (1944–1988)* (Routledge, London, 1991), 85–108.

Elliott, Jane, *Using Narrative in Social Research: Qualitative and Quantitative Approaches* (Sage, London, 2005).

Elliott, Jane, and Jon Lawrence, 'The emotional economy of unemployment: A re-analysis of testimony from a Sheppey family, 1978–1983', UK Data Archive Special Edition 'Digital Representations: Re-Using and Publishing Digital Qualitative Data', *Sage Open* (Dec. 2016) at http://journals.sagepub.com/doi/full/10.1177/2158244016669517.

Elliott, Jane, and Jon Lawrence, 'Narrative, time and intimacy in social research: Linda and Jim revisited', in Graham Crow and Jaimie Ellis (eds), *Revisiting Divisions of Labour: The Impacts and Legacies of a Modern Sociological Classic* (Manchester University Press, Manchester, 2017), 189–204.

Evans, Geoffrey, and James Tilley, *The New Politics of Class: The Political Exclusion of the British Working Class* (Oxford University Press, Oxford, 2017).

Evans, Tanya, 'Secrets and lies: The radical potential of family history', *History Workshop Journal*, 71/1 (2011), 49–73.

Feldman, David, 'Global movements, internal migration and the importance of institutions', *International Review of Social History*, 52/1 (2007), 105–9.

Field, Geoffrey, *Blood, Sweat and Toil: Remaking the British Working Class, 1939–1945* (Oxford University Press, Oxford, 2011).

Forster, Anthony, *Britain and the Maastricht Negotiations* (Macmillan, Basingstoke, 1999).

Galbraith, John Kenneth, *The Affluent Society* (2nd edn, Penguin, London, 1970).

Giles, Judy, *The Parlour and the Suburb: Domestic Identities, Class, Femininity and Modernity* (Berg, Oxford, 2004).

Gilligan, Carol, et al, 'On the listening guide: A voice-centered relational method', in Sharlene Nagy Hesse-Biber and Patricia Leavy (eds), *Emergent Methods in Social Research*, http://dx.doi.org/10.4135/9781412984034.n12.

Goodhart, David, *The British Dream: Successes and Failures of Post-War Immigration* (Atlantic Books, London, 2013).

Goodhart, David, *The Road to Somewhere: The Populist Revolt and the Future of Politics* (C. Hurst & Co, London, 2017).

Goodwin, Matthew J., and Oliver Heath, 'The 2016 Referendum, Brexit and the left behind: An aggregate-level analysis of the result', *Political Quarterly*, 87/3 (2016), 323–32.

Gospel, Howard F., 'The decline of apprenticeship in Britain', *Industrial Relations Journal*, 26/1 (1995), 32–44.

Gray, Robert Q., *The Labour Aristocracy in Victorian Edinburgh* (Clarendon, Oxford, 1976).

Greenhalgh, Charlotte, *Aging in Twentieth-Century Britain* (University of California Press, Berkeley and Los Angeles, 2018).

Griffiths, Trevor, *The Lancashire Working Classes, c.1880–1930* (Clarendon Press, Oxford, 2001).

Griffiths, W. B., *Segedunum: Roman Fort, Baths and Museum* (rev. edn, Tyne & Wear Archives, Newcastle, 2008).

Hall, Catherine, Keith McClelland, and Jane Rendall, *Defining the Victorian Nation: Class, Race, Gender and the British Reform Act of 1867* (Cambridge University Press, Cambridge, 2000).

Hall, David, *Work Town: The Astonishing Story of the 1930s Project that Launches Mass-Observation* (Weidenfeld & Nicolson, London, 2015).

Hammersley, Martyn, 'Qualitative data archiving: Some reflections on its prospects and problems', *Sociology*, 31/1 (1997), 131–42.

Hammersley, Martyn, 'Can we re-use qualitative data via secondary analysis? Notes on some terminological and substantive issues', *Sociological Research Online* (2009), 15/1 http://www.socresonline.org.uk/15/1/5.html.

Harloe, Michael, *Swindon: A Town in Transition. A Study in Urban Development and Overspill Policy* (Heinemann, London, 1975).

Hennock, E. P., 'The measurement of urban poverty: From the metropolis to the nation, 1880–1920', *Economic History Review*, 40 (1987), 208–27.

Hill, C. N., *A Vertical Empire: The History of the UK Rocket and Space Programme, 1950–1971* (Imperial College Press, London, 2001).

Hilton, Matthew, Chris Moores, and Florence Sutcliffe-Braithwaite, 'New Times revisited: Britain in the 1980s', *Contemporary British History*, 31/2 (2017), 145–65.

Hinton, James, *Nine Wartime Lives: Mass-Observation and the Making of the Modern Self* (Oxford University Press, Oxford, 2010).

Hinton, James, *The Mass Observers: A History, 1937–1949* (Oxford University Press, Oxford, 2013).

Hinton, James, *Seven Lives from Mass Observation: Britain in the Late Twentieth Century* (Oxford University Press, Oxford, 2016).

Hobsbawm, Eric, *Worlds of Labour: Further Studies in the History of Labour* (Weidenfeld & Nicolson, London, 1984).

Holden, Len, *Vauxhall Motors and the Luton Economy, 1900–2002* (Bedfordshire Historical Records Society/Boydell Press, Woodbridge, 2003).

Homer, Andrew, 'Planned communities: The social objectives of the British new towns, 1946–1965', in Lawrence Black (ed.), *Consensus or Coercion? The State, the People and Social Cohesion in Post-War Britain* (New Clarion, Cheltenham, 2001), 125–35.

Houlbrook, Matt, '"A pin to see the peepshow": Culture, fiction and selfhood in Edith Thompson's letters, 1921–1922', *Past & Present*, 207 (May 2010), 215–49.

Hughes, Anne, and Karen Hunt, 'A culture transformed? Women's lives in Wythenshawe in the 1930s', in Andrew Davies and Steven Fielding (eds), *Workers' Worlds: Culture and Communities in Manchester and Salford, 1880–1939* (Manchester University Press, Manchester 1992), 74–101.

Hughes, Celia, 'Young socialist men in 1960s Britain: Subjectivity and sociability', *History Workshop Journal*, 73 (Spring 2012), 170–92.

Igo, Sarah E., *The Averaged American: Surveys, Citizens, and the Making of a Mass Public* (Harvard University Press, Cambridge, MA, 2007).

Ingram, William, *Romsey Town Labour Club: Mill Road History Project Building Report* (2015) at https://capturingcambridge.org/wp-content/uploads/2014/05/Romsey_Labour_Club_2nd_edn-rev.pdf.

Jackson, Alan A., *Semi-Detached London: Suburban Development, Life and Transport, 1900–1939* (Allen & Unwin, London, 1973).

Jeffery, Bob '"I probably would never move, but ideally I'd love to move this week": Class and residential experience, beyond elective belonging', *Sociology*, 52/2 (2018), 245–61.

Jenkins, Timothy, *Religion in English Everyday Life: An Ethnographic Approach* (Berghahn Books, New York, 1999).

Johnson, Richard, and Ashley Walsh, *Camaraderie: One Hundred Years of the Cambridge Labour Party, 1912–2012* (Cambridge Labour Party, Cambridge, 2012).

Johnston, Ronnie, and Arthur McIvor, 'Dangerous bodies, hard men and broken bodies: Masculinity in the Clydeside heavy industries, c.1930–1970s', *Labour History Review*, 69/2 (2004), 135–51.

Jones, Ben, *The Working-Class in Mid Twentieth-Century England: Community, Identity and Social Memory* (Manchester University Press, Manchester, 2012).

Jones, Gareth Stedman, 'Rethinking Chartism', in his *Languages of Class: Studies in English Working-Class History, 1832–1982* (Cambridge University Press, Cambridge, 1984), 90–178.

Jones, Gareth Stedman, 'The "cockney" and the nation, 1780–1988', in David Feldman and Gareth Stedman Jones (eds), *Metropolis—London: Histories and Representations Since 1800* (Routledge, London, 1989), 272–324.

Kaplan, Cora, 'The death of the working class hero', *New Formations*, 52 (2004), 94–110.

Khan, Omar, and Faiza Shaheen (eds), *Minority Report: Race and Class in Post-Brexit Britain* (Runnymede Trust, London, 2017).

King, Laura, '"Now you see a great many men pushing their pram proudly": Family-orientated masculinity represented and experienced in mid-twentieth-century Britain', *Cultural and Social History*, 10/4 (2013), 599–617.

King, Laura, *Family Men: Fatherhood and Masculinity in Britain, 1914–1960* (Oxford University Press, Oxford, 2015).

Koven, Seth, *Slumming: Sexual and Social Politics in Victorian London* (Princeton University Press, Princeton, 2004).

Kuper, Adam, *Anthropology and Anthropologists: The Modern British School* (3rd edn, Routledge, London, 1996).

Langhamer, Claire, 'The meanings of home in postwar Britain', *Journal of Contemporary History*, 40 (2005), 341–62.

Langhamer, Claire, *The English in Love: The Intimate Story of an Emotional Revolution* (Oxford University Press, Oxford, 2013).

Lawrence, Jon, 'The British sense of class', *Journal of Contemporary History*, 35/2 (2000), 307–18.

Lawrence, Jon, *Electing Our Masters: The Hustings in British Politics from Hogarth to Blair* (Oxford University Press, Oxford, 2009).

Lawrence, Jon, 'Paternalism, class and the British path to modernity', in Simon Gunn and James Vernon (eds), *The Peculiarities of Liberal Modernity in Imperial Britain* (University of California Press, Berkeley and Los Angeles, 2011), 163–80.

Lawrence, Jon, 'Class, "affluence" and the study of everyday life in Britain, c.1930–1964', *Cultural and Social History*, 10/2 (2013), 273–99.

Lawrence, Jon, 'Social-science encounters and the negotiation of difference in early 1960s England', *History Workshop Journal*, 77 (2014), 215–39.

Lawrence, Jon, 'Why the working class was never "white"', *New Left Project*, 26 Dec. 2014.

Lawrence, Jon, 'The voice of the People? Re-reading the field-notes of classic post-war social science studies', in Mark Hailwood, Laura Sangha, Brodie Waddell, and Jonathan Willis (eds), *The Voices of the People: An Online Symposium* (2015), at https://manyheadedmonster. wordpress.com/voices-of-the-people/.

Lawrence, Jon, 'Inventing the "traditional working class": A re-analysis of interview notes from Young and Willmott's *Family and Kinship in East London*', *Historical Journal*, 59/2 (2016), 567–93.

Lawrence, Jon, 'Languages of place and belonging: Competing conceptions of "community" in mid-twentieth century Bermondsey, London', in Stefan Couperus and Harm Kaal (eds), *(Re) Constructing Communities in Europe, 1918–1968: Senses of Belonging Below, Beyond and Within the Nation-State* (Routledge, London, 2016), 19–44.

Lawrence, Jon, 'Individualism and community in historical perspective', in Shana Cohen, Christina Fuhr, and Jan-Jonathan Bock (eds), *Austerity, Community Action, and the Future of Citizenship in Europe* (Policy Press, Bristol, 2017), 239–54.

Lawrence, Jon, 'The People's history and the politics of everyday life since 1945', in John Arnold, Matthew Hilton, and Jan Rüger (eds), *History After Hobsbawm: Writing the Past for the Twenty-First Century* (Oxford University Press, Oxford, 2017), 272–91.

Lawrence, Jon 'Workers' testimony and the sociological reification of manual/non-manual distinctions in 1960s Britain', *Sozial.Geschichte online/Social History online*, 20 (2017), at https:// duepublico.uni-duisburg-essen.de/servlets/DerivateServlet/Derivate-43274/03_Lawrence_Work ers_Testimony.pdf.

Lees-Maffei, Grace, 'Dressing the part(y): 1950s domestic advice books and the studied performance of informal domesticity in the UK and the US', in Fiona Fisher, Patricia Lara-Betancourt, Trevor Keeble, and Brenda Martin (eds), *Performance, Fashion and the Modern Interior: From the Victorians to Today* (Berg, Oxford, 2011), 183–96.

Leff, V., and C. H. Blunden, *Riverside Story: The Story of Bermondsey and Its People* (Bermondsey Borough Council, London, 1965).

LeMahieu, D. L., *A Culture for Democracy: Mass Communications and the Cultivated Mind in Britain Between the Wars* (Clarendon Press, Oxford, 1988).

Lieberson, Stanley, *A Matter of Taste: How Names, Fashion and Culture Change* (Yale University Press, New Haven, 2000).

Lieberson, Stanley, and Eleanor O. Bell, 'Children's first names: An empirical study of social taste', *American Journal of Sociology*, 98 (1992), 511–54.

Light, Alison, *Common People: The History of an English Family* (Fig Tree, London, 2014).

Lourie, Julia, *The Social Chapter*, House of Commons Research Paper, 97/102 (September 1997) at https://researchbriefings.parliament.uk/ResearchBriefing/Summary/RP96-76.

McCarthy, Helen, 'Social science and married women's employment in post-war Britain', *Past & Present*, 233 (Nov. 2016), 269–305.

McCarthy, Helen, 'Women, marriage and paid work in post-war Britain', *Women's History Review*, 26/1 (2017), 46–61.

McKenzie, Robert T., and Allan Silver, *Angels in Marble: Working-Class Conservatism in Urban England* (Heinemann, London, 1968).

McKibbin, Ross, 'Working-class gambling in Britain, 1880–1939', *Past & Present*, 82 (1979), 147–78.

McKibbin, Ross, *Classes and Cultures, England 1918–1951* (Oxford University Press, Oxford, 1998).

Malpass, Peter, *Reshaping Housing Policy: Subsidies, Rents and Residualisation* (Routledge, London, 1990).

Malpass, Peter, *Housing, Philanthropy and the State: A History of the Guinness Trust* (Faculty of the Built Environment Occasional Papers, no. 2, University of the West of England, Bristol, n.d. [2000]).

Max, Catherine, 'Finding place and quiet', at http://www.catherinemax.co.uk/finding-place-quiet/ (accessed 10 Mar. 2018).

Meacham, Standish, *Regaining Paradise: Englishness and the Early Garden City Movement* (Yale University Press, New Haven, 1998).

Méndez, María-Luisa, 'Elective belonging, moral ownership claims and authenticity of place', *Housing, Theory and Society*, 27/2 (2010), 151–3.

Middleton, Stuart, '"Affluence" and the Left in Britain, *c*.1958–1974', *English Historical Review*, 129 (2014), 107–38.

Middleton, Stuart, 'Raymond William's "structure of feeling" and the problem of democratic values in Britain, 1938–1961', *Modern Intellectual History*, advance access, Feb. 2019.

Miller, Daniel, *The Comfort of Things* (Polity, Cambridge, 2008).

Mische, Ann, 'Projects and possibilities: Researching futures in action', *Sociological Forum*, 24/3 (2009), 694–704.

Moore, Robert, *Pit-men, Preachers and Politics: The Effects of Methodism in a Durham Mining Community* (Cambridge University Press, Cambridge, 1974).

Nordlinger, Eric A., *The Working-Class Tories: Authority, Deference and Stable Democracy* (MacGibbon & Kee, London, 1967).

Oakley, Ann, *Father and Daughter: Patriarchy, Gender and Social Science* (Policy Press, Bristol, 2014).

O'Carroll, Annette, 'Tenements to bungalows: Class and the growth of home ownership before World War II', *Urban History*, 24/2 (1997), 221–41.

Ortolano, Guy, *Thatcher's Progress: From Social Democracy to Market Liberalism through an English New Town* (Cambridge University Press, Cambridge, 2019).

Pedersen, Susan, 'Gender, welfare and citizenship in Britain during the Great War', *American Historical Review*, 95 (1990), 983–1006.

Peel, Mark, *Miss Cutler and the Case of the Resurrected Horse: Social Work and the Story of Poverty in America, Australia and Britain* (University of Chicago Press, Chicago, 2012).

Phillipson, Chris, 'The "elected" and the "excluded": Sociological perspectives on the experience of place and community in old age', *Ageing and Society*, 27/3 (2007), 321–42.

Phillipson, Chris, Miriam Bernard, Judith Phillips, and Jim Ogg, *The Family and Community Life of Older People: Social Networks and Social Support in Three Urban Areas* (Routledge, London, 2001).

Phoenix, Cassandra, and Andrew C. Sparkes, 'Being Fred: Big stories, small stories and the accomplishment of a positive ageing identity', *Qualitative Research*, 9/2 (2009), 219–36.

Platt, Jennifer, *Social Research in Bethnal Green: An Evaluation of the Work of the Institute of Community Studies*, New Perspectives in Sociology series (Macmillan, London, 1971).

Pooley, Colin G., 'Mobility in the twentieth century: Substituting commuting for migration?', in David Gilbert, David Matless, and Brian Short (eds), *Geographies of British Modernity: Space and Society in the Twentieth Century* (Oxford, 2003), 80–96.

Ramsden, Stefan, 'Remaking working-class community: Sociability, belonging and "affluence" in a small town, 1930–1980', *Contemporary British History*, 29/1 (2015), 1–26.

Ramsden, Stefan, *Working-Class Community in the Age of Affluence* (Routledge, Abingdon, 2017).

Reddy, William M., *The Navigation of Feeling: A Framework for the History of Emotions* (Cambridge University Press, Cambridge, 2001).

Reid, Alastair, 'Intelligent artisans and aristocrats of labour: The essays of Thomas Wright', in J. M. Winter (ed.), *The Working Class in Modern British History: Essays in Honour of Henry Pelling* (Cambridge University Press, Cambridge, 1983), 171–96.

Robinson, Emily, '"Different and better times?" History, progress and inequality', in Pedro Ramos Pinto and Bertrand Taithe (eds), *The Impact of History: Histories at the Beginning of the 21st Century* (Routledge, Abingdon, 2015), 110–22.

Robinson, Emily, Camilla Schofield, Florence Sutcliffe-Braithwaite, and Natalie Thomlinson, 'Telling stories about post-war Britain: Popular individualism and the "crisis" of the 1970s', *Twentieth Century British History*, 28/2 (2017), 268–304.

Rogaly, Ben, and Becky Taylor, *Moving Histories of Class and Community: Identity, Place and Belonging in Contemporary England* (Palgrave Macmillan, Basingstoke, 2009).

Roodhouse, Mark, *Black Market Britain, 1939–1955* (Oxford University Press, Oxford, 2013).

Rosa, Hartmut, *Social Acceleration: A New Theory of Modernity*, trans. Jonathan Trejo-Mathys (Columbia University Press, New York, 2013).

Rosa, Hartmut, and William E. Scheuerman (eds), *High-Speed Society: Social Acceleration, Power and Modernity* (Penn State University, University Park, PA, 2008).

Rose, Jonathan, *The Intellectual History of the British Working Classes* (Yale University Press, New Haven, 2001).

Rose Richard, and Ian McAllister, *Voters Begin to Choose: From Closed-Class to Open Elections in Britain* (SAGE, London, 1986).

Rule, John, 'Time, affluence and private leisure: The British working class in the 1950s and 1960s', *Labour History Review*, 66/2 (2001), 223–42.

Runciman, David, 'A win for proper people? Brexit as a rejection of the networked world', *IPPR Juncture*, 23/1 (Summer 2016).

Saler, Michael, *As If: Modern Enchantment and the Literary Prehistory of Virtual Reality* (Oxford University Press, Oxford, 2012).

Sanderson, Michael, 'Education and the labour market', in Nicholas Crafts, Ian Gazeley, and Andrew Newell (eds), *Work and Pay in 20th Century Britain* (Oxford University Press, Oxford, 2007), 264–300.

Särlvik Bo and Ivor Crewe, *Decade of Dealignment: The Conservative Victory of 1979 and Electoral Trends in the 1970s* (Cambridge University Press, Cambridge, 1983).

Saunders, Peter, *A Nation of Home-Owners* (Unwin Hyman, London, 1990).

Savage, Mike, 'Sociology, class and male manual work cultures', in John McIlroy, Nina Fisher, and Alan Campbell (eds), *British Trade Unions and Industrial Politics*, ii. *The High Tide of Trade Unionism, 1964–1979* (Ashgate, Aldershot, 1999).

Savage, Mike, 'Revisiting classic qualitative studies', *Forum: Qualitative Social Research*, 6/1 (2005), article 31, http://www.qualitative-research.net/index.php/fqs/article/view/502.

Savage, Mike, 'Working-class identities in the 1960s: Revisiting the affluent worker study', *Sociology*, 39 (2005), 929–46.

Savage, Mike, 'Changing social class identities in post-war Britain: Perspectives from Mass-observation', *Sociological Research Online*, 12/3 (2007), #6, http://www.socresonline.org.uk/12/3/6.html.

Savage, Mike, 'Elizabeth Bott and the formation of modern British sociology', *Sociological Review*, 4/56 (2008), 579–605.

Savage, Mike, *Identities and Social Change in Britain Since 1940: The Politics of Method* (Oxford University Press, Oxford, 2010).

Savage, Mike, 'The politics of elective belonging', *Housing, Theory and Society*, 27/2 (2010), 115–35.

Savage, Mike, Gaynor Bagnall, and Brian Longhurst, 'Ordinary, ambivalent and defensive: Class identities in the northwest of England', *Sociology*, 35/4 (2001), 875–92.

Savage, Mike, Gaynor Bagnall, and Brian Longhurst, *Globalization and Belonging* (Sage, London, 2005).

Savage, Mike, Elizabeth Silva, and Alan Warde, 'Dis-identification and class identity', in Elizabeth Silva and Alan Warde (eds), *Cultural Analysis and Bourdieu's Legacy: Settling Accounts and Developing Alternatives* (Routledge, Abingdon, 2010), 60–74.

Scott, Peter, *Triumph of the South: A Regional Economic History of Early Twentieth-Century Britain* (Ashgate, Aldershot, 2007).

Scott, Peter, 'Did owner-occupation lead to smaller families for interwar working-class households?', *Economic History Review*, 61/1 (2008), 99–124.

Scott, Peter, *The Making of the Modern British Home: The Suburban Semi and Family Life between the Wars* (Oxford University Press, Oxford, 2013).

Seeley, Ivor H., *Planned Expansion of Country Towns* (Geo. Godwin, London, 1968).

Sennett, Richard, and Jonathan Cobb, *The Hidden Injuries of Class* (Vintage, New York, 1973).

Sinfield, Alan, 'Boys, Class and Gender: From Billy Casper to Billy Elliot', *History Worksop Journal*, 62 (2004), 166–71.

Skeggs, Beverley, *Formations of Class and Gender: Becoming Respectable* (SAGE, London, 1997).

Smith, Helen, 'Love, sex and friendship: Northern, working-class men and sexuality in the first half of the twentieth century', in Alana Harris and Timothy Willem Jones (eds), *Love and Romance in Britain, 1918–1970* (Palgrave Macmillan, Basingstoke, 2015), 61–80.

Smith, Helen, *Masculinity, Class and Same-Sex Desire in Industrial England, 1895–1957* (Palgrave Macmillan, Basingstoke, 2015).

Southerton, Dale 'Boundaries of "Us" and "Them": Class, mobility and identification in a new town', *Sociology*, 36/1 (2002), 171–93.

Spivak, Gayatri, 'Can the subaltern speak?', in Cary Nelson and Lawrence Grossberg (eds), *Marxism and the Interpretation of Culture* (Macmillan, London, 1988), 271–313.

Stacey, Margaret, 'The myth of community studies', *British Journal of Sociology*, 20/2 (1969), 134–47.

Standing, Guy, *The Precariat: The New Dangerous Class* (rev. edn, Bloomsbury, London, 2014).

Starkey, Pat, *Families and Social Workers: The Work of Family Service Units, 1940–1985* (Liverpool University Press, Liverpool, 2000).

Steedman, Carolyn, *The Tidy House: Little Girls Writing* (Virago, London, 1982).

Steedman, Carolyn, *Landscape for a Good Woman: A Story of Two Lives* (Virago, London, 1986).

Steedman, Carolyn, 'State-sponsored autobiography', in Becky Conekin, Frank Mort, and Chris Waters (eds), *Moments of Modernity: Reconstructing Britain, 1945–1964* (River Oram Press, London, 1999), 41–54.

Steinbach, Susie L., *Understanding the Victorians: Politics, Culture, and Society in Nineteenth-Century Britain* (Routledge, New York, 2012).

Stewart, James D., *Bermondsey in War, 1939–1945* (Bermondsey & Rotherhithe Society, London, n.d. [1981?]).

Sting [Gordon Sumner], *Broken Music: A Memoir* (Simon & Schuster, London, 2003).

Strange, Julie-Marie, *Fatherhood and the British Working-Class, 1865–1914* (Cambridge University Press, Cambridge, 2015).

Strangleman, Tim, 'Portrait of a deindustrialising island', in Graham Crow and Jaimie Ellis (eds), *Revisiting Divisions of Labour: The Impacts and Legacies of a Sociological Classic* (Manchester University Press, Manchester, 2017), 55–68.

Sutcliffe-Braithwaite, Florence, 'Class in the development of British Labour Party ideology, 1983–1997', *Archiv für Sozialgeschichte*, 53 (2013), 327–62.

Sutcliffe-Braithwaite, Florence, *Class, Politics, and the Decline of Deference in England, 1968–2000* (Oxford University Press, Oxford, 2018).

Sveinsson, Kjartan Páll (ed.), *Who Cares About the White Working Class?* (Runnymede Trust, London, 2009).

310

Swenarton, Mark, *Homes Fit for Heroes: The Politics and Architecture of Early State Housing in Britain* (Heinemann, London, 1981).

Tabili, Laura, *Global Migrants, Local Culture: Natives and Newcomers in Provincial England, 1841–1939* (Palgrave Macmillan, Basingstoke, 2011).

Taylor, Andrew, 'Speaking to democracy: The Conservative Party and mass opinion from the 1920s to the 1950s', in Stuart Ball and Ian Holliday (eds), *Mass Conservatism: The Conservatives and the Public Since the 1880s* (Frank Cass, London, 2002), 78–99.

Taylor, Becky, and Ben Rogaly, '"Mrs Fairly is a dirty, lazy type": Unsatisfactory households and the problem of problem families in Norwich, 1942–1963', *Twentieth-Century British History*, 18/4 (2007), 429–52.

Tebbutt, Melanie, *Women's Work? A Social History of 'Gossip' in Working-class Neighbourhoods, 1880–1960* (Scolar, Aldershot, 1995).

Tebbutt, Melanie, 'Imagined families and vanished communities: Memories of a working-class life in Northampton', *History Workshop Journal*, 73/1 (2012), 144–69.

Thane, Pat, *Old Age in English History: Past Experiences, Present Issues* (Oxford University Press, Oxford, 2000).

Thompson, Paul, Catherine Itzin, and Michele Abendstern, *I Don't Feel Old: The Experience of Later Life* (Oxford University Press, Oxford, 1990).

Thompson, Steven, '"Conservative bloom on socialism's compost heap": Working-class home ownership in South Wales, c.1890–1939', in Robert Rees Davies and Geraint H. Jenkins (eds), *From Medieval to Modern Wales: Historical Essays in Honour of Kenneth O. Morgan and Ralph A. Griffiths* (University of Wales Press, Cardiff, 2004), 246–63.

Thompson, Steven, *Unemployment, Poverty and Health in Interwar South Wales* (University of Wales Press, Cardiff, 2006).

Tiratsoo, Nick, and Mark Clapson, 'The Ford Foundation and social planning in Britain: The case of the Institute of Community Studies and *Family and Kinship in East London*', in Giuliana Gemelli (ed.), *American Foundations and Large-scale Research* (CLUEB, Bologna, 2001), 201–17.

Todd, Selina, *Young Women, Work and Family in England, 1918–1950* (Oxford University Press, Oxford, 2005).

Todd, Selina, 'Affluence, class and Crown Street: Reinvestigating the post-war working class', *Contemporary British History*, 22/4 (2008), 501–18.

Todd, Selina, *The People: The Rise and Fall of the Working Class, 1910–2010* (John Murray, London, 2014).

Todd, Selina, 'Phoenix rising: Working-class life and urban reconstruction, c.1945–1967', *Journal of British Studies*, 54/3 (2015), 679–702.

Todd, Selina, and Hilary Young, 'Baby-boomers to "Beanstalkers": Making the modern teenager in post-war Britain', *Cultural and Social History*, 9/3 (2012), 451–67.

Topalov, Christian, '"Traditional working-class neighborhoods": An inquiry into the emergence of a sociological model in the 1950s and 1960s', *Osiris*, 18 (2003), 212–33.

Urry, John, *Mobilities* (Polity, Cambridge, 2007).

Vernon, James, 'Telling the subaltern to speak: Social investigation and the formation of social history in twentieth-century Britain', *Proceedings of the International Congress History under Debate, Santiago de Compostela, July 1999* (University of Santiago de Compostela, Santiago de Compostela, 2000).

Vincent, David, *Privacy: A Short History* (Polity, Cambridge, 2016).

Virdee, Satnam, *Racism, Class and the Racialized Other* (Palgrave Macmillan, Basingstoke, 2014).

Waters, Chris, '"Dark strangers" in our midst: Discourses of race and nation in Britain, 1947–1963', *Journal of British Studies*, 36/2 (1997), 207–38.

Waters, Chris, 'Autobiography, nostalgia and the changing practices of working-class self-hood', in George K. Behlmer and Fred M. Leventhal (eds.), *Singular Continuities: Tradition, Nostalgia, and Identity in Modern British Culture* (Stanford University Press, Stanford, CA, 2000), 178–95.

Weeks, Jeffrey, *The World We Have Won: The Remaking of Erotic and Intimate Life* (Routledge, Abingdon, 2007).

Welshman, John, 'In search of the "problem family": Public health and social work in England and Wales, 1940–1970', *Social History of Medicine*, 9 (1996), 447–65.

Whipple, Amy C., 'Revisiting the "rivers of blood" controversy: Letters to Enoch Powell', *Journal of British Studies*, 48/3 (2009), 717–35.

Whitehand, J. W. R., and Christine M. H. Carr, 'England's interwar suburban landscapes: Myth and reality', *Journal of Historical Geography*, 25/4 (1999), 483–501.

Wickham, Phil, *The Likely Lads* (BFI/Palgrave, London, 2008).

Williams, Chris, *Capitalism, Community and Conflict: The South Wales Coalfield, 1898–1947* (University of Wales Press, Cardiff, 1998).

Wilson, Dolly Smith, 'A new look at the affluent worker: The good working mother in post-war Britain', *Twentieth-Century British History*, 17/2 (2006), 206–29.

Wilson, Elizabeth, *Only Halfway to Paradise: Women in Post-war Britain, 1945–1968* (London, 1980).

Zweiniger-Bargielowska, Ina, *Austerity in Britain: Rationing, Controls and Consumption, 1939–1955* (Oxford University Press, Oxford, 2000).

Unpublished

Barry, John, 'Overspill and the Impact of the Town Development Act, 1945–1982' (University of Cambridge, PhD Thesis, 2015).

Purkis, Sallie, 'Over the Bridge: Another Cambridge Between Two Wars: Communal Responses to Political, Economic and Social Changes, 1919–1938' (University of Essex, MA Thesis, 1982).

Saunders, Jack, 'The British Motor Industry, 1945–1977: How Workplace Cultures Shaped Labour Militancy' (University College London, PhD Thesis, 2015).

Scott-Brown, Sophie, 'The Art of the Organiser: Raphael Samuel and the Making of History' (Australian National University, Canberra, PhD Thesis, 2015).

Sutcliffe-Braithwaite, Florence, 'Class, Community and Individualism in English Politics and Society, 1969–2000' (University of Cambridge, PhD Thesis, 2013).

Young, Michael, 'A Study of the Extended Family in East London' (London University, PhD Thesis [LSE Library], 1955).

INDEX

Abbot, Paul 218
Abertillery (Monmouthshire) 21
Abrams, Lynn 184, 225
affluence 11, 14, 29, 75, 106, 110–11, 114, 127,
    133, 203, 241 *see also* food *and* possessions
air quality 79–80
air raids/the Blitz 35, 40–1, 61
amenities 84, 95
Andy Capp (character) 138, 146–7
anonymity 218, 237
anti-materialism 98
anti-Semitism 63–4
Archer, Jeffrey 20
Arctic Monkeys 18, 248n.53
Armstrong Vickers 206
Army, the 25
Arthur Seaton (character) 12–13, 18, 108, 248n.53
Asia 217
    people of//from 115–17, 154
aspirations 38, 75, 90, 101–2, 107–11, 156, 159,
    168–9, 197, 203, 208, 227, 229, 233, 266n.9
    see also culture, aspirational
Atomic Energy Authority 87
attitudes 38, 43, 106, 226, 238
    class 122
    cultural 10
    social 10, 198, 213, 238–9
    working-class 137, 151–2
Auf Wiedersehen, Pet (television programme) 159
Australia 159, 210
authoritarianism 16
authority 148 *see also* workers, and management
automobile, the *see* cars
autonomy 14, 18, 68, 110, 128, 132, 134, 158, 197,
    236 *see also* self, the, sovereignty of

Bakke, E. Wight 52
Basildon (Essex) 72
Bauman, Zygmunt 2, 197
Beatles, the 107, 118
    Sergeant Pepper's Lonely Hearts Club Band 140
Bedford 115
Bedfordshire 104, 125, 129, 179
behaviour 13, 44, 57–8, 157–8, 163, 181, 184, 231
    of workers *see* workers, behaviour of
belonging 31–40, 54–5, 176, 179, 196, 200, 206,
    210, 214, 227, 229, 234–5

'elective' 14, 16, 38, 125, 179, 217, 234
    not 98, 101, 235 *see also* community spirit, lack
        of *and* place, being out of
    'prescribed' 251n.35
    sense of 31–40, 54–5, 74, 112, 179, 211–12,
        220, 234–5 *see also* place, sense of
    shared 220, 234–6
    types of 36
Berkshire 200
Bermondsey 3, 8, 24, 41–5, 47, 54, 56, 62–5, 67,
    69, 72, 73, 76, 97, 106, 128–9, 132, 139,
    229, 239, 243, 254n.74
    Guiness Buildings, the 42, 44–6, 48, 50–1, 54–6,
        62–3, 239
    Guiness Social Club 56
    people of 5, 48, 51–60, 62, 64–8, 70–1, 107
    Rotherhithe 65, 67–8, 254n.74
    Snowsfields 44–5, 54, 56, 59, 64–5
        Arthur's Mission 54
        Social Club 62, 239
Bethnal Green 8–9, 24, 41, 43–4, 46, 51, 54,
    56–7, 60–1, 63–4, 74–80, 82–3, 97,
    106, 112–13, 128–9, 132, 184, 229,
    237–8, 240
    Chisenhale Road 49
    Institute of Community Studies (ICS) 42–3, 49,
        73, 238
    moving back to 83
    moving from 72, 75, 78–80
    people of 47, 49–56, 58–61, 69, 72, 107,
        115, 237
    Victoria Park 49–50, 83
Bevin, Ernest (Ernie) 31–2
Bewes, Rodney (actor) 144–5
Beynon, Huw and Terry Austrin
    Masters and Servants 144
Billy Elliot (film) 210–11, 213
biography 263n.88
Birmingham 57, 129, 132, 153, 160, 223
    Perry Barr 223
    School of Architecture 258n.5
    Sutton Coldfield 223
Black and Decker 210
Black Friday 230–1
Blair, Tony 208
Bletchley 83
Bob Ferris (character) 140, 144–5, 147

313

competitive 16
disavowals of 17–18, 199
economic 12
ideas about 2, 6, 16
liberal 16–17
popular 17
rise of 75
'rugged' 18, 53, 168, 193
selfish 17–18, 229–30
traditions of 15
individuality 24, 134, 137–8, 162, 228
expressions of *see* self-expression
individuals 2, 138, 194, 216, 236
interconnection of lives 18, 236
Institute of Community Studies *see also* Young
    Foundation 9–10, 42–3, 49–50, 73, 105,
    238, 240
internet, the 1, 200
Iraq 21
Ireland 11, 63, 65–6, 268n.64 *see also* Northern
    Ireland
  people of/from 108–10, 115–16, 118, 154,
    262n.74 *see also* people, Irish
Isle of Sheppey 8–10, 17, 164–7, 169, 174, 176–80,
    184–6, 188, 191–5, 199, 208, 234, 237, 242–3
  Leysdown 164
  people of 168, 170–94, 287n.33
  Sheerness 164–6, 179, 184, 192
Isle of Wight 160
isolation 43, 69–70, 76–7, 101, 172, 185, 203, 216,
    229–32 *see also* loneliness *and* self-isolation
Italy 262n.74

Jarrow 160
Jephcott, Pearl 239
Job Centres 178, 188–9
jobs 30–1, 84–5, 105, 108, 126, 199–205, 234
    see also employment *and* work
  giving up 82
  high status 207
  insecure 161, 196, 201–4, 208–9, 266n.13
  loss of 160–2, 166–7, 201–2, 207–12 *see also*
    unemployment
    to overseas 208–210
  manual 88, 105, 167, 207, 209, 234
    semi-skilled 34, 46, 106, 160
    skilled 34, 105, 121, 207
    unskilled 34
  manufacturing 209
  non-manual 34, 160, 178, 234
  office 106, 171
  professional and managerial 88, 167, 209
  secure 108
  skilled 94, 121, 207

'keeping up with the Joneses' 98–100, 127, 159, 181
Kent 8, 55, 93, 118, 164, 166, 174, 203
Kent, Benjamin 20

Kent, Mary Ann 20, 29
Keynsham (Somerset) 29–30
kin 3, 45, 53, 57–60, 69–70, 75, 80, 114, 130,
    271n.124, 272n.133 *see also* family *and* kinship
kinship 5, 9, 42, 57–61, 69–70, 80–1, 128, 198,
    224, 232, 249n.17, 271n.124, 272n.133,
    see also family *and* kin

labour *see* work *and* workers
Labour Party, the 15–17, 41–2, 45, 67, 73, 84–5,
    98, 135, 137, 151 *see also* Government,
    the, Labour
  'Blue' 16
  support for 25, 90, 111, 113, 120, 124, 131, 143,
    162, 267n.43 *see also under* voters
Labour Research Department, the 42
labour theory of value, the 151
Lancashire 114, 196, 199–200
land use 94
landlords 117, 212
language 14, 122, 152, 197, 208, 229, 233
Laporte 109–10, 113, 125–6, 241
Lawrence, Adrian 29, 39
Lawrence (neé Lewis), Doreen 19, 23, 28–31, 33,
    35–40
Lawrence, Emily (née Strawbridge) 31–2
Lawrence, Emma 20
Lawrence, Joseph 20–1, 31
  Lewis, Patricia 23
Lawrence, Ronald (Ron) 19, 23, 25–8, 30–1, 33–5,
    38–9, 44
Lawerences, the 20–1, 23, 36–7
Lebanon 212
left-wing, the 16, 73, 86, 99–101, 155
Leigh, Mike
    Abigail's Party 134
leisure 3, 144, 157–8, 234
LeMahieu, Daniel 6
Letchworth Garden City 90
Lewis, Desmond 39
Lewis, Florence 24, 31–2
Lewis, George 21, 24, 31
Lewis, George Henry 21–2
Lewis, Lizzie 21
Lewis, Patricia 23
Lewises, the 21–2, 24, 36–7
liberalism 154–5, 201, 233
libertarianism 16
life
  chances in 79, 206–7
  hopes for a better *see* aspirations
  outlook on 180, 196, 206
  pace of 197
  private 75, 111, 132, 236
  quality of 74, 77–80, 99, 101, 108–10, 196, 201,
    203, 208, 236
  search for a better 46, 75, 101–2, 159, 193–4,
    197, 227

Wiltshire and Swindon History Centre, Chippenham: Manchester University Research into Overspill, 1959–1962, Swindon Borough Council, Finance, Law, and General Purposes Committee Papers, G24/133/1026.

Published

Official Publications and Reference

Board of Trade, *Enquiry into the Cost of Living of the Working Classes*, PP1908, c.3864, vol. cvii.

Craig, F. W. S., *British General Election Manifestos, 1900–1974* (Macmillan, London, 1975).

Dearing, Ronald, *Higher Education in the Learning Society: Report of the National Committee of Inquiry into Higher Education* (HMSO, London, 1997).

Department for Digital, Culture, Media, and Sport, *Taking Part Survey: England Adult Report, 2016/17*, https://www.gov.uk/government/uploads/system/uploads/attachment_data/file/644933/Adult_stats_release_4.pdf.

Eurostat, *Statistics Explained: Private Households by Household Composition, 2006–2016*, http://ec.europa.eu/eurostat/statistics-explained/index.php/Household_composition_statistics.

General Register Office, *Census 1961 England and Wales* (HMSO, London, 1963–6).

General Register Office, *Sample Census 1966 England and Wales Workplace and Transport Tables Part I* (HMSO, London, 1968).

Ministry of Fuel and Power, *Explosion at Easington Colliery, County Durham: Report on the Causes of, and Circumstances Attending, the Explosion which Occurred at Easington Colliery*, Cmd.8646 (HMSO, London, 1952).

Newcastle City Council, *Knowyournewcastle* website, http://www.knowyournewcastle.org.uk/ (accessed 21 Mar. 2017).

Office for National Statistics, *Social Trends 40*, (HMSO, London, 2010).

Office for National Statistics, *Self-Employed Workers in the UK, 2014* (HMSO, London, 2014).

Office for National Statistics, *Living Longer: Changes in Household Composition, England and Wales, 2015* (HMSO, London, 2016).

Office for National Statistics *Trends in Self-Employment in the UK, 2001 to 2015* (HMSO, London, 2016).

Office for National Statistics, *Families and Households, 2017*, https://www.ons.gov.uk/peoplepopulationandcommunity/birthsdeathsandmarriages/families/bulletins/families-and-households/2017.

Population Census 1971, Household Returns, St George Distrect Bristol (Gloucestershire).

South East Joint Planning Team, *Strategic Plan for the South East: Studies, II, Social and Environmental Aspects* (HMSO, London, 1971).

Weir, Stuart 'Self-employment in the UK labour market', *Labour Market Trends* (Office for National Statistics, 111.9 (2003)).

Contemporary Studies and Memoirs

Abrams, Philip, *Neighbourhood Care and Social Policy: A Research Perspective* (Volunteer Centre, Berkhamsted, 1978).

Abrams, Philip, Sheila Abrams, Robin Humphrey, and Ray Snaith, *Action for Care: a Review of Good Neighbour Schemes in England* (Volunteer Centre, Berkhamsted, 1981).

Anon [Michael Young], *Sudden under bombing, Planning* (PEP broadsheet), 164, 17 Feb. 1941.

Anon., *Building a Community: Construction Workers at Sea-croft, 1963–1979* (University of Adult Minster, London, 1971).

Ashby, Margaret (ed.) *Statistics: Voices Recollected of Local Trade* (Tempus, Stroud, 1969).

Bakke, E. Wight, *The Unemployed Man*, (Nisbet Publishers & Co, London, 1933).